The Writer's Handbook

Second Edition

John McKernan
Marshall University

Harcourt Brace Jovanovich College Publishers
Fort Worth   Philadelphia   San Diego
New York   Orlando   Austin   San Antonio
Toronto   Montreal   London   Sydney   Tokyo

Publisher   Ted Buchholz
Acquisition Editor   Michael Rosenberg
Developmental Editor   Stacy Schoolfield
Production Manager   Kenneth A. Dunaway
Art and Design Supervisor   John Ritland
Text Design   Impressions Publishing Services
Cover Design   Pat Sloan
Cover Quilt by Ann Trusty

Printed in the United States of America

    2   3   4   039   9   8   7   6   5   4   3

McKernan, John, 1942–
      The writer's handbook / John McKernan,--2nd ed.
         p.   cm.
      Includes index.
ISBN 0-03-053453-4
      1. English language--Rhetoric.   I. Title.
PE1408.M32987   1991   90–48078
808'.042--dc20   CIP

PREFACE TO THE SECOND EDITION

I do not have the space to repeat my acknowledgments to all those who helped me enormously as I prepared the first edition of this text. Their help has taught me the meaning of the phrase "community of scholars" (how valuable that community is!), and it has taught me both persistence and humility. Things graven on the heart need not be elaborated in public. You have my grateful thanks, all of you.

My greatest enjoyment has been finding out that the handbook actually works—that students can easily find things in it, use it to solve their minor writing problems, and improve all aspects of their writing. It was with some trepidation that, while proctoring an in-class essay for another teacher, I watched a student stop writing, pick up a copy of this handbook, and begin thumbing through it. She wanted something from the book. She turned to the Index, and that was not much help. She turned to the table of contents and then leafed through the book. After a few seconds, she found the section she had been searching for and then read for several minutes. I held my breath during the entire exercise, and when she finished reading she gently set the book on the floor and went back to her writing. "It works," I told myself as I breathed normally again. Since then, I have rigorously scrutinized my students and my colleagues as they used my book in and out of class. Generally they have commented favorably on the book, but they have drawn my attention to certain areas that I have strengthened in this revision.

The Index has been completely revised. Students should have a much easier time finding material in the book because of the expanded Index as well as the handbook's clear, easily accessible format.

The Glossary of Grammatical and Rhetorical Terms has been improved so that students can refer to it for definitions of key terms used in and out of the writing classroom.

The Glossary of Usage is now the most comprehensive one available on the market. Students who read through and study the entries over a period of one or two semesters should be able to benefit from this equivalent of a course in clarity, spelling, style, and usage.

A new section on writing descriptive prose has been added to the already strong treatment of specific details in Section 3.1. This new section focuses on the creation and use of static details, kinetic details, dominant impressions, and figures of speech to create evocative and powerful descriptive prose.

Two new and highly effective sections on the use of active and passive voice (Section 21.5) and on the use of effective alternatives for *to be* verbs (Section 21.24) should enable students to improve sentence meaning considerably.

New, interesting, and highly effective Thinking Exercises have been added to various sections. A notable one is found in Section 21.7 on Connotation and Denotation. It clearly gives students an important lesson about the nature of language. This exercise, with all the other Thinking Exercises in the text, allows the student writer to enter into a process of development and to begin to think like a writer. Its goal is to demonstrate the difference between the private meaning a writer attaches to a word and the meaning that a reader beyond the writer may attach to the same word.

The section on parenthetical documentation has been made into a separate chapter so that questions of format are separate from those of research strategies and writing techniques. Coupled with the abundant material on paraphrasing and plagiarism (Chapter 11), and summarizing and précis writing (Chapter 10), the library and research segments of this handbook offer a more thorough coverage than any other handbook can provide.

The section on argumentation has been improved by the addition of material on varieties of evidence in the construction of effective argumentative strategies. Together with the section on logic (Chapter 6) with its clear treatment of deduction and induction and its discussion of logical fallacies, the chapters on argumentation and persuasion allow teachers to emphasize thinking skills as students construct their essays.

The chapter on letters has been completely redesigned, and a reader will find effective examples of different styles of letter writing, including a full discussion of job applications and résumés.

In addition to these new elements, the book contains material that has already helped thousands of students: a unique chapter on introductions and conclusions; a full discussion of thesis statements in essays and in research papers; and an extended discussion and analysis of the value and use of topic sentences in paragraphs, all presented in a friendly tone modulated by the intelligent comments from dozens of college students on all stages of the writing process.

The strong, informative text discusses more fully than any other handbook the following subjects:

- The writing process
- Logic and logical fallacies
- Effective sentence writing and sentence revision
- Journals and journal writing
- Proofreading
- Paragraphing (evidence, arrangement, unity, cohesion)
- Copious and varied Thinking Exercises and Writing Assignments

Acknowledgments

A large debt of gratitude most go to those patient and dedicated reviewers of the first edition who read the pages of my manuscript in all of its numerous stages and versions. Without their incisive and helpful comments, this book would be impoverished. Those readers include A. D. Barnes, Louisiana State University; Saundra L. Barringer, Community College of Allegheny County; Conrad Bayley, Glendale Community College; Samuel Bellman, California State Polytechnic University–Pomona; Paul Beran, North Harris County College; John Caserta, Ferris State College; Peggy Cole, Arapahoe Community College; Beth Daniell, University of Texas–Austin; Alice T. Duxbury, Palm Beach Junior College; Claude Gibson, Texas A&M University; Lynn M. Grow, Broward Community College; Gertrude Hopkins, Hartford Community College; Robert Jackson, Bowling Green State University; Linda Julian, Furman University; Richard Lane, University of Nebraska–Omaha; Rosemary Lanshe, Broward Community College; Ruth Laux, Arkansas Tech University; Nancy Martin, National University; Thomas Martinez, Villanova University; Lyle Morgan, Pittsburg State University; Kirsten Nelson, University of California–Berkeley; Mary Catherine Park, Brevard Community College; Michael J. Rossi, Merrimack College; Robert Ryan, Clark College; Susan Sharpe, Northern Virginia Community College; Beverly Slaughter, Brevard Community College; Elliot Smith, Ferris State College; Joanna Stewart, Drexel University; Thomas Whissen, Wright State University; and Peter Zoller, Wichita State University.

The reviewers for the second edition have been James M. Nutter, Liberty University; Patrice Coleman, Ellsworth Community College; Lex Williford, Auburn University; Kitty Chen Dean, Nassau Community College; Anita Howard, Austin Community College; Elizabeth Byleen, The University of Kansas–Lawrence; Barbara Carr, Stephen F. Austin State University; Margot Soven, La Salle University; Cecile Cary, Wright State University; H. W. Gleason, Shippensburg University. Their keen comments have proved most helpful.

TO THE STUDENT

Even after teaching from this book every semester for the past three years, I still believe what I have written here, but I have two things to add. First, this handbook can help you, but you must believe in yourself and trust that your thoughts and feelings are valuable and worthwhile. Your teachers in elementary and secondary school taught you many things, and I hope they taught you to trust your memory; to trust your capacity for logical thought; to trust the power of a controlled imagination; and to trust that your honest thoughts and feelings have intrinsic value and interest to other people. These lessons are just as important as any basics in writing. Second, as soon as possible, become proficient in using a computer to do word processing, and use it to write and revise. Nothing, not even this book with all its good ideas and advice, can help you deal with the hard work and drudgery of writing as much as a good word processing program and printer can. The sooner you take advantage of the computers at your school or acquire one of your own, the better off you will be as a writer.

In one of Robert Lowell's poems, he tells about a rare book that his father used to prop up a lamp on a table. I hope this book will be a light for the student and not a prop for the table lamp. I believe that composition is one of the most important courses anyone can take because it both enlightens and empowers. Books about writing are rare books because they enable people to acquire skills that give them substantial power in the world. Any student who expresses clearly in words his or her thoughts and emotions so that readers take the writer seriously has real power.

I see this book being used in all classes in college where writing is important. I see it being used by beginning writers who are struggling to express their thoughts clearly and by advanced writers who are continuing the struggle to discover both what they want to say and how they want to say it. I cannot stress too strongly the value of effective instruction in this writing and thinking process. Those two strategies go together and nourish each other to bring about any effective act of communication. Writers think about what they want to write, and the act of writing helps them to think more clearly.

This book studiously avoids complicated theories of rhetoric and grammar. My goal is not to have you learn a mass of grammatical and rhetorical terms you will never use again nor to develop highly analytical skills that are divorced from the process of writing itself. My primary goal has been to present strategies and techniques that illuminate the steps in this process and that enable you to better control, manipulate, and express the material that presents itself to you when you sit down to write.

You will increase the value of this book if you discover the many ways you can employ it to help you develop as a writer. Five different uses come quickly to mind.

1.   Use this book to discover the strategies of effective writers. There are some good rules for effective writing: (a) Have or find something to say. (b) Be clear. (c) Be honest. Say what you really mean. (d) Be interesting. (e) Write for a real reader. This book emphasizes the practical experience, critical comments, and valuable suggestions of other good writers, especially student writers. I include

this material because it is interesting and to the point, and I believe that excellent advice is to be found in the comments of actual writers.

2.   Use this book to help you understand some of the various kinds of writing assigned by your teachers in college. These different types include journal writing, personal essays, in-class essays, expository themes, persuasive papers, argumentative essays, definition papers, letters, and research papers. The book gives the characteristics of these forms, practical advice on how to write in these different forms, and plenty of examples of these different kinds of writing.

3.   Use it when you are planning a writing assignment. Reread the sections in Chapter 1 and study the section dealing with the kind of writing you have been assigned.

4.   Use it while revising. After you have written a rough draft and put it aside for a while, you will have time to read pertinent sections in the book and think about the main point of your essay and whether or not your writing is effective for your intended audience. Because any writing assignment involves a series of steps that are often repeated in different ways and at different times, you will find that the book is divided into separate sections that focus on different concerns in revising. Important sections deal with assignments, topic selection, main idea, statement of purpose, organization, audience, drafting, and revision. Other sections that may help in revising are those dealing with word choice (Chapter 21), paragraphing (Chapters 2–5), and proofreading (1.10).

5.   Use it as a reference guide in matters relating to spelling, punctuation, grammar, diction, and usage. You will find that this handbook contains more information on these topics than any comparable textbook. Let me make

one suggestion. Develop the habit of proofreading your writing *after* you have written it, not *while* you are writing it. You can become a more efficient and effective writer if you divide your writing and your correcting into two distinct activities.

Even though scholars claim that everyone who speaks and listens has a knowledge of grammar, students often worry about grammar and grammatical correctness. This is understandable, and although the relationship between grammatical knowledge and writing skill is difficult to understand completely, many student writers *feel* more comfortable writing their drafts when they believe they have a good knowledge of grammar. If you feel that way, you might want to study thoroughly Parts 6–8 on your own.

All of the material in this book, important in itself, will become valuable to you if you make a commitment as a person and a writer to intellectual honesty, hard work, and clear thinking. These alone lead to good writing and can transform you into an educated person able to express powerfully your thoughts and feelings. I believe that there is nothing more worthwhile to a society than a tradition of effective, honest writing and innumerable good, honest writers. They alone can keep freedom and justice alive and make humane values triumphant.

TABLE OF CONTENTS

PART I

Writing: Some Processes

Stages in the Writing Process

Preliminary Comments

You can teach yourself to become an effective or more effective writer, and your writing instructor and your classmates can help you in the process. You alone, however, must commit yourself to the goal of becoming a proficient writer. To help you achieve that goal, this chapter presents a view of writing as a process, and it asks you to imagine writing as a series of ten different steps involving a number of activities. Although the ten steps overlap and finally result in a single finished product, you can study them independently for the sake of instruction. You may be already familiar with some of the stages of the writing process. If that is the case, then you need to build on that foundation and develop those skills that can help you improve your writing ability. Neither this chapter nor this book offers any magic formula for instant success as a writer. The book does present, however, a coherent and learnable way to think clearly about writing. This way of thinking about writing can help you learn to write and can even make the act of writing a rewarding experience. The information in this first section can help you the most if you think of it not as a set of absolute rules but as useful advice.

The following pages develop a number of ideas about goals and choices in writing. These ideas will be most valuable to you if you keep several things in mind. First, make all your writing assignments a personal challenge to do your best. Second, use this book in connection with actual writing tasks so you can discover the stages in your writing process. Though you will search in vain here for any magic formulas for writing, you should be able to discover a number of tried and effective strategies for writing well. The following pages break down the complex task of writing into a series of ten understandable and manageable steps to be consulted for both instruction and reference.

1.1 Understanding writing assignments

✍ Student Comments on Writing

I am a slow writer. I can do most other things quickly, but writing takes time and concentrated effort. I use the list of steps just the way a cook would use a recipe, one step at a time. My roommate works much quicker, but we're different. I could scarcely write a good sentence when I came to college, but now I'm passing. Writing used to be a mystery to me. Now I know how writers do their work and this helps me do mine one step at a time. I'm not Stephen King or Flannery O'Connor, but I can do my assignments.

D. Schmitz

I have discovered that writing is hard work and that students (from accounting to zoology) have to write constantly in many college courses. The emphasis on writing in school surprises me. I'm an accounting major, but no one ever told me that accountants need good writing skills.

Susan Reilly

a. Understand the aims of writing

Understanding the general aims of writing will help you begin any writing task, in or out of school. In the next few months, your writing assignments will be designed by an instructor or by you. Before beginning a writing task, you can clarify matters by asking yourself, "What is my general purpose for this writing?" Your general purpose will involve one of the following goals: self-expression, information, persuasion, or literary creation.

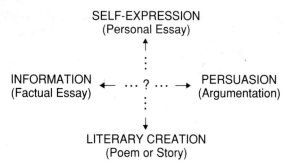

Having a sense of general purpose for a particular writing assignment should give you a sense of direction and help clarify your thinking. With a clear goal in mind, you should be able to create a challenging assignment and master a subject rather than be mastered by it.

b. Understand the value of a challenge

Create an assignment that will lead to effective writing. You will need to do two things: first, have enough interest and learn enough about your subject so that you want to share your interest and discoveries with a reader; second, find some practical value for yourself in the reading and thinking that you will be doing. For the first, choose a subject that will excite you intellectually and emotionally. For the second, you will need to think of writing as more than a repetition of facts for an instructor who already knows them. Find a good reason for writing that goes beyond the answers to a test in school. The following reasons might help you create a challenging writing assignment:

Write for publication. Take yourself seriously, and think of your writing task as something that will lead to publication as an article, editorial, or letter to the editor. Become aware of the multitude of possibilities for general or specialized newspapers or newsletters. Think of publishing your writing in a specialized publication devoted to a subject you want to write on.

Write for an increase in knowledge. Writing an essay about your summer vacation or about washing your car will not generally lead to an increase in your knowledge. However, writing about an academic subject or exploring a topic outside of your personal experience often leads to a growth in your knowledge. You might think of writing about different careers and occupations in answer to questions such as the following: What does a coal miner actually do three miles underground? What does a parole officer have to worry about? What problems do women lawyers encounter working in large law offices?

Write for pleasure. If you have a special feeling for a subject, whether astronomy, old people, or zoos, follow your interest, explore your material, and discover interesting information.

Write for personal growth. People grow and change constantly throughout their lives. This process of growth and discovery can lead to effective writing as people confront problems and solve them or discover and clarify important values. This kind of writing uses personal experience for illustration, but it goes beyond mere biographical details to explore and discover meaning, values, and goals. Many diaries and journals are records of this form of growth.

Write for practice. Practice the kinds of writing required for your courses in college and the kinds of writing expected in your career. Think of writing practice the way athletes and musicians think of their practice: it is an opportunity to maintain and develop skills.

c. Understand clearly the required form

Writing exists in various forms such as personal letters, case studies, recommendations, problem analyses, business letters, paragraphs, five-paragraph themes, editorials, essay examinations, summary reports, and research papers. Each form has its distinctive features. Much of the writing you will be doing in a composition course may involve the student essay. The essay form varies in length and style from class to class and from school to school. Whatever form is required, good writing has something to say and uses a main idea and adequate supporting material to present that idea clearly. Ask your instructor for clear guidelines concerning required forms.

d. Understand the required length and deadlines

Knowing the required length and deadlines will give you some idea of the time you have to complete your writing task. In terms of length, does the instructor want a paragraph, several paragraphs, a long or short paper? What is the minimum and maximum length? In terms of deadlines, when is the rough draft due? The final draft? Has your instructor specified any other deadlines for items such as topic approval, conferences, or peer editing? Understanding deadline dates can help you begin your work and do the various writing tasks before the deadline. Also, many writers discover that an impending deadline becomes a powerful incentive for completing a writing assignment.

e. Understand effective writing conditions

Some writers have efficient and effective methods for producing good work, but others have inefficient and ineffective ones. Most writers are able to improve their work by becoming more reflective and more thoughtful as they go through the stages in the writing process. The following list of questions should provide some insight into the way beginning writers go about doing their work:

- What helps you the most in writing the rough draft?
- What helps you in revising your writing?
- What do you worry about most while writing?
- What part of the writing process is most difficult for you?
- What do you feel you need to become a better writer?

The answers to these questions should reveal your major difficulties in the stages of the writing process. To solve these problems, ask your teacher and your classmates for advice on overcoming writing blocks. Many anxious writers speak favorably about freewriting. (See 1.3e.)

Thinking Exercises

1. What is the most important thing anyone has ever told you about writing?

2. The following assignment was given to A. B. in the first week as a freshman in college: "Write a well-organized, informative four-page essay on a family member or relative who did something you consider important. Have

one main purpose and focus on one important event in that person's life.'' What preliminary ideas do you have about completing a similar assignment?

3. Think of an important thing that happened to you recently. Make a list of at least ten details about the event. How could you use that material to make four different kinds of writing that would be (a) informative, (b) persuasive, (c) self-expressive, and (d) literary?

4. Examine the following topics: (a) a great fear of yours, (b) two important accomplishments in your life, (c) three important black politicians, (d) four things about a park, (e) five instances of Castro's abuse of artists and writers, (f) six instances of Einstein's eccentricity. Which of these topics would be easiest for you to write an informative paper on? Give three or four reasons explaining why. Which of these would interest you the most? Why?

5. How would you explain, in words, the meaning of the following subjects to an alien: (a) tomato, (b) pizza, (c) happiness, (d) needlepoint, (e) tattoo?

Writing Assignments

1. Write a paper on the earliest memory you have. Trust your remembrance and your imagination.

2. Write a paragraph of 150–300 words about an unpleasant experience at a store or at a school. Focus on one unpleasant scene. Compile a list of at least ten details surrounding the event. Think of the writing as a letter of complaint to the manager, principal, or appropriate administrator. Or think of the writing as a warning letter to some people.

3. Write a narrative about a time when you had to be quiet. Choose a time when you wanted to say something but could not. Let the reader know what you wanted to say. Let the reader know the circumstances forcing your silence.

4. Make lists to answer the following questions:
   ✎ What kinds of writing do you want to do?
   ✎ What ten subjects do you really want to write on?
   ✎ What helps you the most to get started writing?
   ✎ What kinds of comments help you?

1.2 Finding and limiting the subject

✍ Student Comments on Writing

In high school I learned that writing was having an idea about a subject. At first I didn't see the difference between the subject and my idea about the subject. My teacher kept pointing it out to me. Now I know!

Fred Shorey

a. Make the subject meaningful to you

If you are allowed to choose the subject, select something interesting that you want to explore. If the instructor assigns the subject, find a way to approach the topic so that it interests you. Without a lively interest, you will probably create boring papers for your classmates and instructor. Good writing occurs when you have something you want to say about the subject. Although you may have your own strategies to select interesting subjects, the following ideas may help you latch onto an attractive subject.

Use writing to satisfy your curiosity. Follow your curiosity to find a subject or to help you focus on one part of the subject. Develop a question to reflect your interest. The following student comment shows how curiosity can point to a good topic:

> I have always been curious about butterflies because I think they're beautiful. When I learned they migrated I was astounded. It was simple to write the question, "How do butterflies migrate?"
>
> *Finola Fogarty*

Use writing to help you learn. Teachers regularly use writing on tests to find out what students have learned, but students can also use writing to develop thinking skills and increase comprehension. The following examples show how some students have approached writing in this manner:

> I want to write on the kinds of mistakes made in using English to help me understand the idea of Standard Written English.
>
> *Cy Neligh*

> When the history teacher gave the topic of writing on an important event happening to a relative, I thought first of my uncle who fought in Vietnam but I knew most of that story. Because I wanted to learn something new about my family, I decided on my grandfather.
>
> *A. B.*

If you have already chosen a major, you have a definite angle from which to approach your writing assignments. You can use your goals in life to help you build your writing assignments. For example, if you plan to teach English in high school, you probably would be interested in a question such as, "What are three different kinds of novels?" If you plan on becoming a geologist, you might choose to write on volcanic lava formation.

Use writing to present your personal experience. A college writing course is not a seminar in self-analysis or a course in autobiography. Although your instructor may occasionally assign personal papers, college writing involves primarily papers on nonpersonal subjects. Because you can't escape your unique personal history and because it can often help develop the main idea, you should learn to use this material. The storehouse of your personal experience is your memory, which contains sufficient material for a number of personal essays and can deepen and enrich your writing assignments. The following journal selections show how some students used personal experience to develop their writing assignments:

> The paper I wrote about conditions at Moundsville was not about me but about the prison. In the introduction, I used my experience of being in the prison as an observer once for three hours to give the reader a sense of what it felt like there.
>
> *B. Akers*

> The paper I wrote on high school football focused on what a team will do to win. I couldn't have written the paper unless I had played ball in high school, but the paper is not about my experience. It relies on my memory of those days.
>
> *Jess Abel*

In your writing, trust your feelings, and develop your ideas according to your real feelings, not what you believe you should feel. Though it is unwise to substitute emotion for thought, it is also unwise to ignore deep feelings.

Use writing to explore and solve problems. Because problems abound in the world, the exploration of a problem, personal or public, provides a good basis for a writing assignment. One strategy in creating this kind of writing assignment involves a three-step process: identifying the problem by providing background information; asking a leading question; and developing the rest of the paper as an answer to the question. The following comment shows how one student used problem solving as the basis for a writing assignment:

> My paper is going to be about my brother and how disruptive he was in school as a third-grader. I am going to tell a few horror stories and then explain what my parents and the teacher did to change the situation.
>
> *Jill Larsen*

b. Avoid certain kinds of topics

Some kinds of topics seem promising at first but soon become frustrating or impossible. If you find that you are going nowhere with a topic, have the courage and the good sense to put the material aside and choose another topic. Above all, avoid writing on a subject in which you have no interest. The following guidelines describe the kinds of topics that present particular problems for many writers.

Avoid an intimidating subject. There is a fine line between being challenged and becoming overwhelmed. Avoid a subject that is too esoteric or complex. An average student who chooses the subject of molecular structure in hydrogen molecules at limitless temperatures is inviting trouble, as is the student who chooses to write on abortion, nuclear war, or gun control. Think of the word "doable" when contemplating any writing assignment. If the subject proves too difficult, change your mind and find one you can handle. A reasonable challenge presents an opportunity for growth. An impossible challenge provides a recipe for failure and discouragement.

Avoid too simple a subject. The most common forms of writing in elementary school involve narrative, and a common task in high school involves listing and summarizing material from a book. Your writing assignments in college will surely involve narrative and summary, but college instructors will assign topics requiring other skills. The differences in these kinds of writing are significant. For example, a writer in grade school might be challenged by writing a narrative on a bee sting. A high school student might be challenged by an assignment asking for a summary of an article on bee stings. A college student might be challenged by an assignment such as "How a bee sting can cause death" or "The differences between a bee sting and a snake bite." As you can see, the college assignments, although they might involve narrative and summary, require thought to explain, contrast, and analyze.

Avoid excessively emotional subjects. Some subjects are just too painful, confusing, or distracting to write about. Topics such as war and peace, life and death, religion and theology, or personal emotional difficulties may simply tie the mind in knots and prevent calm thought and rational presentation. Writers should feel free to discuss all topics, but they should avoid emotional outpouring in place of careful discussion. If your topic creates only emotion instead of thought, select a less emotional subject.

Avoid vast subjects. Some subjects are too vast to write on. Students generally encounter great difficulty writing papers on vast topics, such as America, love, or socialism. Even when broken down, some topics are still too vast for small writing assignments. To help you understand the problem of vastness in subjects, consider the differences between the following topics:

Cosmic	Toys	Family member
Vast	Puzzles	My grandfather
Still Vast	Jigsaw puzzles	His heroism
Still Vast	Small jigsaw puzzles	During retirement
Narrowed	Creating jigsaw puzzles	During the flood

Avoid subjects without unity. (See 1.4 and 2.6.) Limiting a subject makes writing easier. Focusing on one particular aspect of a subject makes for easier writing. Focus on a single thing or aspect of a thing. Consider the comments from the following journal selection

> I have always loved the Cincinnati Reds, but there's enough there for a book—ten books. So I decided to write about the equipment helpers and what they do.
> *Neal Boyer*

c. Use writing to think about and limit the subject

Although the work of limiting a subject is usually planned, it may occasionally be spontaneous. Whether planned or spontaneous, the time required and the methods used for limitation vary widely from writer to writer. The following student comments illustrate some of this variety:

> I chose "Dangers." I was going to write "Home," "Work," and "Play," but when I wrote the words "at home" I knew I wanted to write on electricity be-

cause of the story I heard about the woman who lost an eye when she put a fork in her toaster to pry out a piece of toast.

Margo Bruffy

I chose San Franciso under "Vacations" because I went there last year and loved it. I needed to limit it and I wrote out a long list and chose food because I had more details for it. That was still too vast and I ended up writing on "An Unknown Chinese Restaurant."

Abby North

Once you have decided on an interesting topic, answering the following questions can help you focus and understand the assignment better:

- How do you feel about writing on this subject?
- What part of the subject interests you the most? Why?
- What general purpose do you have in mind?
- What do you need to learn to do a good job?
- Why do you want to write about the subject?
- What is easy about this assignment? What is hard?

Thinking Exercises

1. Which of the following topics means the most to you? Why? Which means the least? Why? (a) white rats, (b) a classroom, (c) punishment, (d) sports, (e) magazines, (f) a poster. How could you make the least meaningful topic interesting to you?

2. Which of the following topics do you know the most about? (a) athletics, (b) poverty, (c) religion, (d)

unfair parents or teachers, (e) work, (f) horror movies, (g) fear, (h) sleep, (i) three ways to fail a course. List the most important information that you know about one. Where could you find more information?

3. Choose the most interesting of the following items and make appropriate lists: (a) a list of current-event subjects that make you angry or fearful, (b) a list of current issues in America that you are opposed to, (c) a list of games, sports, or machines that puzzle you, (d) a list of musicians you actively dislike.

Writing Assignments

1. Write a letter to persuade a parent or a relative to do something for you. Make your desires clear, and present a strong case with three or four good reasons. Use specific language to support your main point.

2. Write some paragraphs describing a person, place, or thing that did not live up to your expectations. First present the expectations; then, present the actuality.

1.3 Thinking about the subject

✍ Student Comments on Writing

My mind wanders when I start a paper. I have two very helpful note cards. One reads: What is your real subject? How can you make a question out of your subject? The other reads: What do you want to say about that subject? What information about that subject has the greatest value and interest? When I

have answered those questions, I have a fairly clear
idea of my paper's content.

Rex Franklin

Think about the subject by asking the following questions:
How can you focus on your subject? How can you find your
main idea? Although the main idea on a subject is always
a general statement, that idea sometimes lacks clarity at
the beginning of a writing assignment. As a result, writers
often have the sense that they need something to help
them draw ideas and material out of hiding in the brain.
This section deals with various kinds of thinking strategies
or discovery techniques that generally help writers discover ideas and generate material. These include observation, clustering, questions, rhetorical patterns, and
freewriting.

a. Observation

In a number of ways, you can improve your skill as an
observer and at the same time gather valuable material for
a writing assignment. Use any or all of the following directions to observe something carefully. First, look at the
object at different times and from a number of different
perspectives: top, bottom, side, front, back, and inside.
Second, use sketching to improve your powers of observation. Make various sketches at different times and from
different perspectives. Don't worry about the artwork. The
goal is not artistic merit but increased skill in observation.
Third, use comparison to observe closely. Compare a
sketch or a photo with the thing you are observing. List
the points of resemblance and points of difference. Fourth,
observe relationships. Connect the parts to the whole in
terms of place, function, and purpose. If possible, write a

paragraph for each of these four kinds of observing activities: perspectives, sketching, comparing, and relating.

In addition to the preceding, a number of other questions can help you improve your powers of observation. You may even obtain enough information for an entire paper by focusing on one object and answering some or all of the following questions:

- ✎ What does the object make you think of?
- ✎ What are the most noticeable features?
- ✎ What can the object be compared to?
- ✎ What are the important parts?
- ✎ How are the parts related?
- ✎ What is the object connected to?
- ✎ What is the object used for?
- ✎ What pleasure or pain is associated with the object?
- ✎ What advantage/disadvantage does it have for you?
- ✎ Does the object have any value? A moral value?

b. Clustering

Clustering is a device to generate ideas and show connections. Clustering is easy. You simply focus on a single word and write down associated ideas as they come to you. Clustering is a quick and valuable exercise with three easy steps: first, in the center of the paper write down a word you want to explore; second, ask yourself, "What do I think of when I see that word?"; third, write down the words that come to mind and circle each. While you are writing and circling your responses, a certain pattern may occur to you. At that time, continue clustering for a while, then write out a single sentence expressing the pattern you have seen and your idea about the content. Continue writing after clustering if you feel like it. Follow your train of thought, and write until you feel the writing makes sense as a whole. The following example shows how one person clustered and then wrote a very rough draft, using the ideas gathered from clustering.

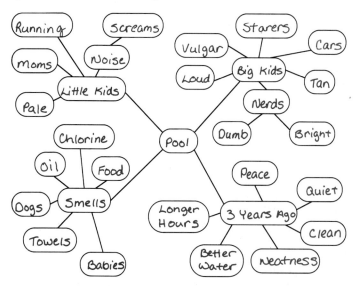

Sometimes a place that seems so good in the mind or in memory just doesn't work out. Harper Pool is a place where young kids in town have been hanging out for years. It has become a noisy and pestery place. People who go there find little privacy. They have to endure hordes of little kids running around making any peace and quiet only a dream. The worst thing has to be the starers, the gawky teenage boys who think it's okay to stare holes in other people's bodies.

This was simple to do and write. As soon as I wrote down the word *pool*, I began thinking of how unpleasant Harper Pool has become. I used to enjoy it so.

Pippy Davies

c. Questions

Use the words *who, what, when, where, why,* and *how.* Journalists use them to discover information on particular events. Besides providing content, these questions can help stimulate thinking. For example, in brainstorming on the topic of "Cats," a class discovered possibilities for a number of different kinds of writing assignments, each with a clear focus.

WHO?   Who trains the wild animals for circuses? [This might lead to a paper discussing an animal trainer, some circus acts, or methods of training big cats.]

WHAT?   What kinds of foods do house cats prefer? [This could lead to a discussion of the favorite foods of cats: mice, birds, insects, rats, table scraps, and cat food.]

WHEN?   When do lions become most dangerous? [This could lead to a discussion of three situations when a lion becomes dangerous. The newspaper had an article last week about a lion in India that mauled some villagers.]

WHERE?   Where in Africa do lions live, breed, hunt? [This could lead to a discussion of lions in the wild.]

WHY?   Why do people keep cats as house pets? [This could lead to a discussion of three reasons why people keep cats as pets or three valuable lessons small children learn by having a cat as a pet.]

HOW?   How do people capture wild animals such as lions or panthers? [This could lead to a paper on a hunting party's capturing and bringing back alive one of the big cats, or to a discussion of lawless hunters in Africa, Asia, or South America.]

Such questions can also help you discover topics and material for a paper with a problem-solving format. Some writing assignments lead naturally to problem-solving activities. Such a method asks several questions: What is the problem and what is the most important background information? What are some ideas that suggest possible solutions? The following list of questions resulted from classroom discussion on the subject of "College coaches":

✎ Who creates the biggest problems for a college coach?

✎ What problems does an unsuccessful coach create?

✎ When should a coach bend the rules for discipline?

✎ Where do coaches go to get help with their problems?

✎ Why do coaches' salaries create problems in a university?

✎ How do most coaches respond to problem athletes?

d. Rhetorical patterns

Some writers plan their writing assignments in terms of the four basic types of writing: narration, description, exposition, and argumentation. If you have used these terms and find them helpful, continue to use them. You may gather new insights and ideas by thinking in new ways. The following questions arose from classroom discussion on the subject of "Cowardice" and "Cowards."

Analysis

Analysis divides a subject into parts or characteristics.

What are the main parts of the plot in *Lord Jim?* In *The Red Badge of Courage?* What emotional and intellectual characteristics does a coward display?

Cause-Effect

To examine cause or effect, a writer asks, "What caused something to happen?" or "What results followed?"

How does cowardly behavior change a person? How does it affect others? List some negative effects and, if you can find them, some positive effects of cowardice. What internal and external forces cause a person to become a coward? Give some facts to explain the behavior of a coward in life or literature. How might a coward defend his or her behavior?

Comparison

A comparison shows similarities and partial resemblances between two selected items. One kind of comparison presents an analogy between two things not normally thought of as similar (animals and cowards). Another compares two things in the same general category (a character in life and a character in a book).

What animal does a coward most resemble? Do you know someone who resembles a coward in a movie or a book? What are the most important points of resemblance?

Contrast

A contrast points out differences or presents opposites.

What is the opposite of a coward? Give some examples of some cowards and heroes from your experience, from some movies, from some comic books. Does the fact of a person's cowardice make any difference or not? Think of some situations when cowardice may be wise. Think of some other situations when bravery seems essential.

Classification

A classification divides a subject into various kinds according to one single standard.

Are there different kinds of cowards? What are they? Give some examples of one kind. What principle of grouping did you use to create the classification?

Definition

A formal definition presents a word's dictionary meaning. An extended definition uses a variety of methods to explain the meaning of a word.

How does a dictionary define the word *coward?* Has any famous writer defined the word in an important way? What are the word's origin and original meaning? What examples from experience or reading would help define the word?

Description

Description presents the physical appearance of something through concrete detail (sight, taste, touch, smell, hearing) in light of one dominant impression.

Have you ever seen a person perform a cowardly act? What did that person look like? Was there any change in the person's appearance either before, during, or

after the experience? What do you think a coward
might look like? How have painters, photographers,
or cartoonists presented cowards?

Example

An example gives a specific instance. It narrates an
action or event in concrete details to illustrate a point.

> What cowardly things have you or your friends done?
> List examples of cowardice from movies, TV, books.

Narration

A narrative tells a story with a beginning, a middle,
and an end.

> Using material that you have either read about,
> viewed, or experienced, tell a story about a coward.

Process analysis

When you analyze a process, you can have one of two
different aims—either information explaining how something occurs, or directions instructing a reader in a correct
method.

> How does a person become a coward? What are the
> stages in the process? What method might one use
> to teach a coward to become brave?

e. Freewriting

Freewriting is unstructured writing for a fixed period of
time. Most students who try freewriting report a "flow" of
ideas and material concerning the subject. Such an exercise allows students to discover what they know and feel
about a subject. If successful, freewriting can provide material and ideas for paragraphs or papers. The best argument for freewriting comes from the experience of

students. They find that freewriting helps them think on paper and helps them overcome hostility or anxiety toward writing. The following comments give one student's response to freewriting as an invention strategy.

> I can still remember the day when Professor Blue told me, "If you cannot do the work or do not want to, then drop the course. Before you do, however, I want you to look through a book called *Writing Without Teachers*. It might help you." I turned to one page, and on that page someone had inked in and underlined the words: "Thank God for this book!" I have no idea why that made me believe in the book, but it did. When the book told me to scribble and doodle if no ideas came into my head, I just scribbled and circled and doodled until ideas and material began slowly to form in my head and then appear, surprisingly, on the page. I would have a feeling about something that had excited me or hurt me and the details, plenty of them, would appear on the page. I wrote for two hours the first time without stopping. I learned that I had things to say and write about. I couldn't believe it. Most of the writing was not great, but it was the first time I had ever written anything when I did not hate the entire experience.
>
> *Curtiss Nunley*

Thinking Exercises

1. Look very closely at a painting or a postcard. Make lists of the following: (a) colors, (b) objects or details, (c) textures, and (d) spatial relationships (background, foreground, right, left, and so forth). What are the most important relationships?

2. What kinds of stories, descriptions, examples, or comparisons could someone write about you to support the following claims: (a) that you are lazy/industrious, (b) that you are serious/not serious about school, (c) that you are moody/good-natured, (d) that you like/dislike a certain musician or musical group?

3. Do a clustering exercise on one of the following subjects: (a) country music, (b) classical music, (c) rock 'n' roll, (d) gospel music, or (e) jazz. After you have written out a sentence expressing the pattern you see in your cluster, answer as many of the following questions as you can that relate to your subject: who, what, when, where, why, and how.

4. Look at the different outlines in 1.7b prepared by A. B. What thinking strategies do you find in those outlines?

Writing Assignments

1. Observe one thing very closely and answer the questions who, what, when, where, why, and how. Write at least two paragraphs to show the object from two different perspectives or at two different times. Make your reader see the object. Use many concrete details and specific language.

2. Find accounts of the same event in two different sources. Examine the rhetorical patterns in the two accounts. Compose a sentence such as "The two writings on X show some interesting differences in rhetorical approach." Write a short paper pointing out the most important differences.

1.4 Focusing on the main idea

✍ Student Comments on Writing

Sometimes my writing confuses me. My ideas keep changing. I need a clear main idea to tie my thoughts together. I work best when I create a numbering sentence such as, "Dorm living beats living at home for three reasons."

Pat Traynor

I plan to write about Christmas. I found out that researching the first historical Christmas took too much work. I decided to write on Christmas in my childhood. My instructor and classmates warned me about being simple and sentimental. I started a list. I was asking the question, "What things have changed or disappeared?" I now have a clear statement of purpose: In thinking back on earlier Christmases, I can see clearly now that several things have vanished forever from my life.

Huey Achinga-Fox

a. State your main idea in a single sentence

By asking questions, you should be able to create a single sentence with a clear main idea to guide your writing:

- ✎ What are you going to write about? Why?
- ✎ What do you want the paper to say on the subject?
- ✎ What are your best ideas about the topic?
- ✎ What material will help get your ideas across?

A clear statement of purpose in the form of a thesis statement can help both writer and reader. Such a sentence helps the writer to focus on the main idea, organize the writing, develop the paper, and ignore irrelevant details.

It also helps the reader to see the main point, follow the idea, and understand the meaning in the writing.

b. A thesis can have different forms

Depending on the situation, writers use different strategies to present their main ideas. The following examples give some ideas of different controlling sentences. Each form can be seen as the answer to the question, "What is the main point this writing will discuss?"

Thesis Statement

POSITIVE   In America, welfare helps families by providing food, clothing, and medical assistance.

NEGATIVE   In America, welfare hurts families by discouraging initiative, separating spouses, and creating the "culture of poverty."

Numbering Thesis

POSITIVE   Welfare works in three ways to benefit needy families.

NEGATIVE   Welfare works in three ways to damage family structure.

Problem Thesis

POSITIVE   Welfare solves certain problems that some families have, namely, hunger, malnutrition, and poor housing.

NEGATIVE   Welfare creates serious problems for many families, such as parental desertion, lack of initiative, and "welfare syndrome."

NOTE: **Avoid an evasive thesis such as the following, which have a subject but take no position:** *Some people support gun control. The question of abortion is highly controversial.* **An effective thesis always presents a main point, which can be argued for or against.**

c. A thesis statement has several parts

A thesis statement clearly states the main idea and performs as many as five different functions:

General Statement. A thesis statement makes a *general statement* that the writer must develop with plenty of relevant, convincing, and specific material. General—but not too general—statements require support in the form of facts, statistics, examples, descriptions, and quotations.

TOPIC   Education

THESIS   Parental support exerts a powerful influence
STATEMENT on a child's achievement in school.

Unity. A thesis statement displays *unity*. It deals with *one* subject, *one* aspect of a subject, or *one* main point about the subject. All the subpoints relate to the main point in some way.

TOPIC   John Kennedy

THESIS   President Kennedy's domestic policy support-
STATEMENT ed economic development in three important
             ways.

Attitude. A thesis statement indicates the author's *attitude* toward the subject matter, either positive or negative. It also sets forth the writer's point of view, which ranges from the personal to the impersonal.

TOPIC My dorm

THESIS
STATEMENT The behavior of the residents at Jackson Hall makes study nearly impossible.

Limitation. A thesis statement *limits* the subject in some important way. It indicates that the author has chosen one particular focus.

TOPIC Part-time jobs

THESIS
STATEMENT Work in outside sales is the best part-time job experience for most college students.

General purpose. A thesis statement makes clear or implies the writer's *general purpose*—that is, self-expressive, informative, persuasive, or literary.

TOPIC Different eating places

THESIS
STATEMENT Students looking for good food, pleasant surroundings, and quick service will always prefer old-fashioned cafes to modern fast-food factories.

These five elements go together to create the "idea" the author will explore, develop, and support in the rest of the writing assignment. A clear controlling statement helps a writer throughout the entire writing assignment.

d. Thesis statements work in different ways

As an exercise, students wrote in their journals on some different kinds of thesis statements. Although the comments are lengthy, they show how much can be seen in a single main idea sentence.

THESIS
STATEMENT
Pornographic movies and publications should be taxed, like tobacco and alcohol, and perhaps as high as 400 percent.

This is an unusual idea. It seems to have interest. It is a general statement that the author will have to develop with some good arguments to make the point. In terms of subject, it will focus on a certain kind of movie, the X-rated film. It is pretty clear that the author has a negative attitude toward the movies. Maybe she is a feminist. But if they tax those films that high then they would cost something like $30. I think this sentence is a good clear statement of the writer's goal—not that I agree with it. It gives clear direction to the paper.

Hector Cruz

NUMBERING
SENTENCE
Students benefit in four important ways from doing research projects on their ethnic backgrounds.

This is a good idea. I like it. My only problem is that the writer does not specify which students. Does he mean grade school, high school, college? My thinking is that high school kids would be the ones to benefit the most. Okay: Does the sentence have the four things we are supposed to find in a good statement of purpose? It has a subject. It will focus, I guess, on some benefits of doing research into one's racial background. Yes, it is a general statement that will need to be developed by specific examples to explain what he or she means by "benefits." And yes, the writer does have a stance. It is favorable. This looks like it will lead to neat paragraphs. The writer has a logical mind.

Gloria Dundee

STATEMENT
> Welfare might have solved certain problems fifty years ago during the Depression, but for some welfare families, the system creates unbelievable problems.

> I grew up in a part of Appalachia where whole white families have never worked so much as a day in the past forty years. The system seems to create a pattern of parasitism and dependency. My paper will explore this problem in terms of these people's lives and behavior.

> *Deems Parr*

e. A thesis statement should be narrowed

Some students prepare very broad thesis statements. Instead of leading to a brief 400-word paper, these broad statements could lead to a research paper, a monograph, or even a book. Consider the following sentences and decide which would make the better thesis statement for a 400-word paper.

- ✎ The history of rock 'n' roll music is very interesting.
- ✎ There are three common kinds of MTV videos.

Writers use a number of different methods to limit a vast thesis statement. One helpful way involves the principle of unity. This involves limiting the broad thesis statement in terms of one person, place, thing, event, activity, or point of view. (See 2.6.) The following example shows some different ways to narrow a main idea.

VAGUE   New York City is a whole new world.

NARROWED Walt Whitman's poem, "Crossing Brooklyn Ferry," gives a glimpse of New York in the nineteenth century.

NARROWED New York City contains three important ethnic groups.

NARROWED A leisurely stroll through Greenwich Village can show several problems that damage the quality of urban life.

Thinking Exercises

1. Transform each of the following statements into (a) a thesis statement, (b) a numbering thesis, or (c) a problem thesis.

    a. The defense budget needs more/less money.
    b. High school should require more/less writing.
    c. I have too much/too little leisure time.
    d. Abuses in college sports should be eliminated/ignored.

2. Revise the following thesis statements in terms of unity:

    a. This year I am planning a trip to the beach and working hard in school.
    b. Poetry has great sound but it also appeals to the mind.
    c. Cancer is caused by cigarette smoking, but many people enjoy smoking and it is a shame to deny people a little pleasure.

3. Write controlling statements (thesis, numbering, or problem) for the following purposes: (a) to persuade voters to build an animal shelter, (b) to express your feelings about having pets, (c) to show that some pets are extremely dangerous, and (d) to show that animals make good companions for elderly people.

Writing Assignments

1. Write a paper on some *different* reasons why students go to college. Interview a few students for their ideas. Try to give your reader some different reasons for going to college. Include a concise thesis statement. Make sure your supporting material is specific, relevant, and convincing.

2. Choose a person you consider a role model, and write a paper on some important things that person has done. In your prewriting, make a list of important facts and examples. Make sure your controlling statement reflects your attitude. Write your drafts using plenty of details about that person's life. Be objective, clear, and concise.

1.5 Considering the audience

✍ Student Comments on Writing

My last paper was about the pitiful dorm food. I wrote it as a letter to the student paper. In my first draft, my tone was so arrogant and so flippant that no one would have taken it seriously. In my revision I took out all the pointless and juvenile

emotionalism. The student paper published my
letter, and the food has improved noticeably.
Finn Willey

a. Understand the four common audiences

Understanding your audience will help you in many important ways. Because different readers have different expectations, some knowledge of the intended audience is essential. An understanding of the audience influences the selection of subject, content, tone, style, length, and intellectual level. You can improve your writing by understanding the four most common audiences for writing.

Are you writing for yourself? Quite often, people write only for themselves, as in a grocery list. Some people keep a commonplace book to copy things they have read or heard. Others keep journals to record their experiences and thoughts. People who write entirely for themselves have absolute freedom. They are their own audience, and they can, without censorship, write anything they want.

Are you writing for someone in business or government? Many people express surprise upon discovering that business and government workers do most of the writing in America. The most common forms for such writing are letters, memoranda, and reports. The topics range from the sexual life of ants to the management of zoos. This kind of writing generally has a specific audience, subject, and purpose. Aimed at effective communication, business writing values clarity, accuracy, and readability.

Are you writing for a public audience? A public audience is as broad as all those who read a letter in *Time* or as narrow as the members in a small club. The public is a large or small group of people outside the writer. For example, two different public audiences at your school are the members of your writing class and the group of all first-year students. Some common examples of public writing are interviews, reviews, editorials, and letters in newspapers.

Are you writing for an academic audience? The many different kinds of writing required in college include book reviews, reports, research papers, definitions, identifications, essay examinations, and freshman themes. Because different teachers make different kinds of assignments, it is wise to know the instructor's requirements before you begin a writing assignment. Remember that college teachers display more skepticism and require more evidence than most other readers.

b. Different audiences look for different things in writing

A careful consideration will show how strongly an audience influences a writer's work. To illustrate the importance of audience, all the following student writing samples have a similar subject, depression, but each has a completely different audience.

> *Self:* This writing takes up about five pages in my journal. I could have made it much longer. I intended to discuss the symptoms and the pain of my depression and to show the dramatic kind of effect a certain kind of therapy had upon my life. I consider this very personal. I would never hand it in. I keep it in my journal.
>
> *Lily Mercer*
>
> *Business:* I wrote this as a memo to the plant manager. I had learned about depression because I had helped

my brother through his struggles with it. I knew quite well the symptoms and the patterns of behavior it causes. I wrote this memo about several co-workers who seemed very depressed on the job. My supervisor is a decent woman. She had to be very tactful as she helped my co-workers get some help.

Chloe Bynes

Public: After taking a course in nutrition, I became convinced that diet plays an important and generally unrecognized role in depression. I wrote this article for my journalism class, and the school newspaper published it as a lead feature article with three columns and a large headline. I wanted to help people because I think college depresses people enough.

Jed Walker

School: I wrote a 1,000-word research paper for Psychology 201. I presented several of the standard, outdated Freudian theories on depression. Essentially, I summarized and paraphrased the data from three books and one journal. I documented everything carefully and prepared a bibliography. It is a clear, concise report.

Gordon Roach

c. Audience analysis improves writing

Knowing the audience can help improve writing. For example, students write differently to parents than to teachers or classmates. The writer who does not know the intended reader will have to guess who he or she will be. An audience of Girl Scouts will differ greatly from an audience of retired people in Florida. The following guidelines provide some ideas to help a writer think about the importance of audience.

✎ Identify a person or group who will learn something from or be persuaded or entertained by your writing.

✎ Identify relevant characteristics. To understand an audience, you need some of the following information about it: (a) experience, (b) intelligence, (c) social class, (d) gender, (e) age, (f) ethnic background, (g) education, (h) occupation, (i) residence, (j) values, and (k) goals.

✎ Identify significant attitudes: (a) presence or absence of prejudice, (b) extent of knowledge, (c) opinions, (d) emotions, (e) open-mindedness, (f) interests.

✎ Identify a role, or pattern of behavior, for your reader. In what role do you imagine your reader? Because of various roles, a writer has to think differently of the same person at different times. For example, a student in the role of athlete differs greatly from the same student in the role of library user. Some further examples of roles include those of dormitory resident, parent, child, part-time employee, or soap opera viewer.

Some students are confused about the audience for their writing. Although they understand that they write letters to relatives, journals for themselves, and essays for their teachers, they have a difficult time adjusting to other situations. The safest advice is that, when confused, students should request and follow the directions of the instructor.

d. Use the analogy of the letter

Thinking of writing a letter can help you in two significant ways. First, because the letter writer actually thinks of the intended reader, it can help you focus. Second, letter writers avoid certain things. They don't waste time on trivial material, but make their points specific and develop them with relevant and interesting material. Think of that kind of relationship for your writing assignments and a sense of audience will develop and improve your writing.

Thinking Exercises

1.   List at least four ways your writing would differ, depending on whether you wrote for an instructor or for a relative. In spite of the following comments from A. B.'s writing journal, what differences are there between writing for relatives and writing for a teacher?

> Choosing my grandfather as my topic made the assignment serious and meaningful. That subject gave me a sense of my audience. I could imagine my family and my history teacher reading the paper. That kept me on my toes. I had never before had any sense of my readers. Having an audience made my work clear to me.
>
> *A. B.*

2.   What kinds of writing would the following people want to read on the subject of fish? (a) a cook (b) a fisher in Ohio (c) a fisher in Hawaii (d) a biologist (e) a scuba diver (f) a pet shop owner (g) you

Writing Assignments

1. Assume the people you are writing to will grant your request. Write two letters asking two persons (one a parent or guardian, the other a financial aid officer) to pay all the expenses for a trip anywhere in America during spring break. In each, present good but different reasons why the trip would benefit you. Be specific.

2. Choose a campus or community topic about which two factions disagree strongly. Write at least one paragraph of factual background information on the topic as if you were writing for the general audience in a newspaper. Then write at least one paragraph to a leader of the faction you are opposed to and present three criticisms of that faction's point of view. Finally, write at least one paragraph in the form of a letter of support to the leader of the faction you agree with.

1.6 Gathering effective material

✍ Student Comments on Writing

Many of my best ideas come while I am busy writing. They pop out of the blue into my mind. I jot them down before they vanish. At first this confused me, but then I discovered that many writers experience this. To find that writing makes me creative surprised me. I thought it was the other way around.

Toni Capezio

a. Gather the best material for your paper

Once you have written a draft of your thesis statement, clarify your main idea by asking, "What material will help me the most to prove, clarify, develop, or support this main idea for my particular audience?" Your memory, intuition, knowledge, and intelligence will help you gather the words and phrases that will develop that idea most effectively.

Students often ask, "What kind of material gives the best support?" Generally, plain facts presented in clear language are the best, because no one has ever found anything more eloquent or more powerful than the truth. Generally, a few well-chosen facts are enough to make each point believable and to convince most readers. The individual facts may be humble and plain, but together they have a force whose momentum overcomes indifferent and skeptical readers and gives them the sense of the main idea.

The rule for gathering material is simple. If the material develops and supports the main idea, include it. If the material has interest but no relevance to the main idea, discard it. Several questions might help you.

- What four points of information does a reader need to know about the topic and the main idea?
- What are the four most interesting things you have discovered about your topic?
- What misunderstandings might a reader have about the topic and the main idea?
- Where is there any additional supporting information?

b. Gather material from many sources

Many writers use only one kind of material. Some always use material from books, whereas others rely on personal experience and their imaginations. Although both approaches can lead to good writing, variety in gathering can help both writer and reader. Using different sources can keep the writer interested in the process and can lead to greater reader interest in the final paper. The following section lists a number of common sources for gathering material on a particular subject.

Memory. Use your memory. It provides a rich storehouse of material that can energize and inform your writing. Include, when appropriate, relevant examples from your own experience as well as intriguing and accurate material other people may have told you.

Observation. Use your powers of observation to gather information from the world around you that will help you develop the main idea. Sketches and diagrams may help you understand unfamiliar or complicated material. If you feel comfortable with drawing and find it helps you to gather new material, use sketching to help you observe. Make diagrams or sketches not to win art awards but to energize and organize your powers of observation.

Reading. Your reading can provide information, new ideas, and direction for your writing. While reading about the subject, gather plenty of information, and use this material to help develop the main idea of the paper. Reading can provide ideas, insights, ways of thinking, examples, specific details, statistics, and quotations.

Discussion. Use discussion to learn. Ask questions. Listen. Every time you talk to another person, you have the chance to learn something about that person or from that person's knowledge. If he or she is bright and energetic or an authority on some subject, these discussions may provide abundant information. You might learn a lot without opening a book. Discussion occurs in and out of class and can furnish valuable material. An idea and material for a paper may come to you while you listen to someone in class or in the student union.

Lists. Making lists can help in all stages of writing. Some lists are short; others are long. Some resemble trees, clusters, maps, or even balloons. A list might contain words, phrases, sentences, points, subpoints, doodles, or pictures. Use any successful method you have for making good lists, or use the following hints:

- ✎ Divide the subject into its most important parts.
- ✎ For each part, list the best information related to the main idea, using plenty of concrete and specific details.

Journal. Read your journal, searching for items related to your topic. Or use the journal as a gathering device by writing in response to the question, "What is the most important thing I want to say about this subject?" Then read the journal and select the best relevant material.

Thinking Exercises

1. Read the following passage by A. B. about finding the material to be used in a paper, and then write a passage about a similar experience in which you discovered some information that totally surprised you or made you feel great pain or great excitement.

> I enjoyed every minute of gathering the material for
> my paper on the flood. I interviewed my grandfather
> and listened. He loves to talk. Sometimes I would
> have to say, "That's enough." I took many notes, but
> I have a good memory. Because I noticed some con-
> tradictions in his accounts, I went to the library and
> read some newspapers. I am now an expert on one
> day of the Great Flood of 1937. Writing the paper
> should not be too difficult.
>
> *A. B.*

2.   What sources would contain information about
your first year in school? Discuss the question with other
people. Make a list of the most important sources. If your
search is fruitful, write a paper.

3.   Make a list of details about someone working in a
house, garden, park, field, or office or at a construction
site. Be specific and detailed in your list.

Writing Assignments

1.   Write at least four separate paragraphs about a job
you had or some work you did. Use memory, observation,
and discussion to help gather material. Explain the work.
Let the reader see what you did and looked like. Say something about your feelings for the job or work. Make sure
the paper has a beginning, middle, and end.

2.   Write a paper reporting to a reader your observations of some person doing some interesting or unusual
work. Show the activity to the reader from several different
perspectives. For example, observe the activity from above,
below, and from one side. Or imagine the activity as seen

by several different observers. Be objective. To help develop your ideas, you might want to make lists or freewrite for a certain period of time.

1.7 Organizing material

✍ Student Comments on Writing

I work best when I can think of a beginning, middle, and end for a paper. When I have a short paper to write, I work with a scratch outline. When I have a longer paper to finish, I write my main idea as a thesis statement and try to find a sentence to guide each paragraph.

Ward Epson

After I have my subject and my main idea, I sit down and write. When I get going, the ideas come to me. I write until I feel I have nothing more to say. Then I go back and rearrange the material until it makes sense.

James Garnados

a. Organize your paper in a logical pattern

For your papers to say what you mean, the writing has to make sense. Good material will make sense to a reader only if you organize it carefully. Most effective writing has a beginning, a middle, and an end, with the parts flowing together smoothly. Understanding the different principles of organization will help you make important decisions while writing, especially while revising.

Because many college writing assignments ask for certain kinds of thought such as comparison, contrast, causal analysis, or classification, a familiarity with these patterns is essential. (See 3.5–3.9.)

Because the most common principles of organization involve space, time, generality, and importance, most informative, expressive, creative, and persuasive writing in college will be organized in either spatial order, chronological order, general order, or order of importance.

Spatial order. Spatial organization works well for describing most things, showing distance, and indicating position. Spatial order generally follows a definite pattern: clockwise, right to left, top to bottom, or occasionally a geometrical form such as a diamond or triangle. Once a writer chooses a pattern, it should be followed consistently. The following example shows the problems one student faced in using a spatial order. (See 2.5b.)

Writing Assignment: Write a description of some person's unusual physical appearance.

Student Comment: My problem in describing Brad's Halloween costume was simple. I didn't know where on earth to begin. I didn't want just a haphazard list. I thought of organizing the material in terms of color, but that didn't seem to work. Walking around him would scarcely have made any sense. Then I saw the way. I could begin at the top and go down to his feet. But then I decided to begin at his feet (he spray-painted his feet black and painted his toenails red!) and after that move up to the top of his head.

Mert Gray

Introduction: I plan to give some background information about the costume party.

B   Detail #1: Feet-shoes
O   Detail #2: Painted slacks
D   Detail #3: Shirt, jacket, tie, jewelry
Y   Detail #4: Face, hair, hat

Conclusion: I plan to end the paper with an unusual comparison.

Chronological order. When people tell stories they generally present the material in chronological order. This refers to time past, present, or future: eight o'clock before nine; January before May; 1980 before 1984. This pattern helps tell a story, give instructions, or explain a process. In narrative, the writer sets the scene, presents the characters, and tells the story. As the King of Hearts in *Alice in Wonderland* says, "Begin at the beginning, and go on until you come to the end: then stop." In regular chronological order, the writer presents the material in the order of occurrence. One common variation involves a flashback to an earlier time. Chronological organization can often help a writer deal with a great number of unconnected facts. The following selection illustrates chronological order. (See 2.5a.)

Writing Assignment: Write a narrative paper from personal experience about a dangerous situation. Give enough specific details so your reader can sense the danger. Write the paper with the idea that the information will help someone who might encounter a similar situation.

Student Comment: A narrative I have always remembered is the story of important events during the day we went white-water rafting on the New River. I just told the story. I didn't plan on us being frightened. I didn't plan the incredible danger. Just telling the story created interest and made the suspense rise. I did not worry about the emotions. There were plenty. I just worried about getting my facts right and in order. All this material makes more sense when I tell it as a story.

Gail Sheehan

Introduction: I plan to present my topic and create interest by asking a few questions.

B   Event #1: Entry into the river
O   Event #2: Problem with the raft
D   Event #3: Effects of problem
Y   Event #4: Quick thinking to solve problem

Conclusion: I plan to summarize the events and warn the readers about a danger in white-water rafting.

General-to-specific order. A general-to-specific order indicates a deductive order of thinking in which the general statement comes before the specific statements. (See 6.2.) To present material in this order, the writer presents a generalization first and then supporting material. One student's comments and a model of the general-to-specific pattern follow.

Writing Assignment: Using a general statement followed by specific related facts, write a paper discussing a social practice or event that occurred in America 100 years ago.

Student Comment: The assignment for this social practice paper came from my sociology class. I recently saw my first circus, and I was struck by the fact that there were circuses in Rome thousands of years ago. That gave me the idea. I would write a paper about a circus coming to a small town in Ohio exactly one hundred years ago. After I read a newspaper editorial from the last century attacking a circus for being "disruptive," I had my topic. I would write on the disruptions caused by a circus coming into a small town in the nineteenth century. My general statement was, "In the nineteenth century, a circus often disrupted the life of a small town for as long as a week." That was my general point, and I then listed the specifics to support and develop my idea. I really enjoyed doing this paper. I think it is hilarious.

Galileo Zimmer

Introduction: I intend to ask some questions and then make my general statement that circuses disrupted life in small American towns in the nineteenth century.

B   Disruption #1: A field is occupied.
O   Disruption #2: The children are excited.
D   Disruption #3: Strangers descend on the town.
Y   Disruption #4: "Low life" activities take place.

Conclusion: I plan to summarize the material and present one final comment about the disruption.

Specific-to-general order. In this pattern, also called inductive order, specific details are presented first and are followed by a general statement. (See 6.1.) This order works well in argumentation and persuasion. A string of examples can be used to lead to a general conclusion that convinces the reader. In the specific-to general order, each bit of evidence contributes something and leads to a definite conclusion. The weight of gathered evidence makes the final inference or generalization probable and believable.

Writing Assignment: Write a paper discussing the effects of a certain kind of music on the listener.

Student Comment: This paper on effects came out of my music appreciation class. I had to write a paper about the effects of a certain kind of music. At first I thought of writing about the effects of all those sick (to my mind) rock 'n' roll lyrics encouraging drug use and goofy sex. When I was doing this, I found that I couldn't support my points. I could only present repulsive examples from the songs. Then for some reason, I began to think of the word *damage* and read something about how rock music makes musicians deaf. Good, I thought—if it's Metallica, Kiss, or Black Sabbath. That was my paper. I would very slowly and carefully present little chunks of information to show that certain kinds of rock made people deaf. I wasn't going to say everything at the beginning. I wanted to build up to my conclusion. That was how I thought about the inductive order for the paper. I could feel my anger give me energy.

Charleen Webb

Introduction: I'm going to give a few words about the effects of some kinds of rock music on the sense of hearing. Some of this will be funny, but I want to lead in to my points slowly.

B   Effect #1: What drums do to the hearing
O   Effect #2: What guitars do to the ear
D   Effect #3: How amplifiers damage the inner ear
Y   Effect #4: How screamers do damage

Conclusion: The final generalization will tell the reader that a rock music concert can damage the ears, and people should avoid the danger or take precautions like using ear plugs.

Order of importance. Writers use this pattern of organization when appropriate. The order of arrangement can move in either direction—from less to more or more to less, as shown in the following figure.

Least Important	Less Important	Important	More Important	Most Important

← — — — — — — — — — — — — — →

For informative and persuasive writing, many writers recommend the order of less important to more important. For narrative writing, a writer usually presents the material in chronological order, paving the way for the climax of the story, which occurs toward the end. In many cases, the writer creates a strong emphasis by waiting until the end to present the most important material.

Sometimes, however, the reverse pattern from most important to least important proves effective. Journalists use this kind of order in their work. The headline boldly attracts the reader's attention; the first few sentences or paragraphs present the most important facts about the story, and the rest of the article goes on to explain the less significant points. The following student example shows how one writer dealt with the problem of ordering in terms of importance of material.

> *Writing Assignment:* Write a letter to a public official commenting on a specific piece of legislation. Present at least three good reasons why the person should vote for or against the legislative bill.
>
> *Student Comment:* I felt that my letter would be most effective if the argument moved from less important to more important material. The most important thing focused on the students' not learning. That was to go last. The order for the other points was somewhat arbitrary.
>
> *Celeste Berne*
>
> Introduction: I will begin by describing a run-down school. This should lead into my main point, arguing for passage of a bond issue to build new schools.

B	1. Good reason:	Overcrowded classrooms
O	2. Better reason:	Half day of school
D	3. Best reason:	Teachers complain
Y	4. Clincher:	Children not learning

Conclusion: I plan to ask the official whether she would have enjoyed going to a school like the one I describe.

NOTE: Be consistent in your ordering. In the overall design of your paper, do not shift from one ordering principle to another.

b. Use outlines and outlining during the entire writing process

A number of different kinds of outlines can help at different stages of the writing process. An outline list can help in the earliest stage. A scratch outline can assist in writing the rough draft, and a formal outline can give a clear idea of the work needed for effective revision. Depending on the style of writing, the directions of the instructor, and the demands of the writing assignment, the following forms of outlining can help most writers, at different times, improve their writing skills.

Outline lists. An outline list contains a random collection of material, all dealing with a single chosen topic. This list might result from observation, clustering, or questioning. The following example comes from A. B.'s writing assignment presented earlier. After interviewing the grandfather for information, A. B. had almost three pages of notes. Reading newspapers from the time of the flood yielded another page. Before beginning the paper, A. B. read through those notes and formed the following list, trying to find some way to order the material. Then A. B. grouped the items in the list into some subgroups. Notice how the items after the word *Actions* begin to assume a narrative shape.

Coal miner
Gramps
Be formal: use
  grandfather
Time: year
  and days
Causes
Move to new
  home
Surprise
Safety: high
  hill
Flood waters
Destruction
Motorboat
Involvement
Neighbors

Floating coffins
Dangers
Garbage in river
Fear
Quickness
Strength
4 reasons for flood
Deputized by sheriff
Heroism
. The grandmother
Blond child on
  door
Drunk on RR trestle

People swimming
Whirlpools
2 boys/stolen boat
Gasoline explosion
Meeting the mayor
Certificate from
  governor
**Actions
Retirement
Moving to new city
Fishing
Waking up
Saving old woman
Saving little kid
Saving JD's
Saving kittens

Scratch outline. Besides being valuable for in-class essay questions, a scratch outline can provide two important kinds of information for a writer. First, it can give a good capsule summary of the material available for the paper. Second, it can help the writer begin to compose the rough draft. To be useful, a scratch outline should contain a statement of the main idea and a list of the most important material to develop that idea. In the process of thinking about the subject, A. B. wrote several scratch outlines, similar to the following.

Main idea: On a single day after the flood in 1937, my grandfather saved four people from great danger.

1. Background information on flood
2. Saving the silent child
3. Saving the elderly woman
4. Saving the young boys
5. Conclusion: Needed but unclear right now. Summary?

Formal outline. Whether the formal outline is composed before the rough draft or after (which is generally the case), it can help a writer in a number of important ways. First, it can help the writer plan a long paper by showing clearly the relationship between the main idea and the supporting material. Second, it can show whether the paper has a logical and sensible pattern of organization. Third, it can help the author identify repetitious or sketchy development and point to areas with little or excessive support. Fourth, occasionally the act of writing an outline can spark new ideas and lead to the discovery of additional supporting material.

Sentence outline. One of the two kinds of formal outlines, the sentence outline uses complete sentences to present the main ideas and all subsequent supporting material. A sentence outline helps a writer to see more easily the relationship between the general statements and the specific support for those generalizations.

> Thesis statement: After moving to Huntington in 1937, H. L. Brothers experienced a vast flood and in the course of a single day saved the lives of various people.
>
>   I. After retiring as a coal miner in 1937, Henry Brothers moved, and his first experience was an encounter with a vast flood of the Ohio River.
>   A. Water rose 38 feet above flood stage.
>   B. The entire river city was flooded.
>   II. Henry began helping people affected by the flood.
>   A. He used his boat to rescue stranded people.
>   B. He used his boat to carry supplies.
>   III. Henry saved the life of a small child.

A. Balanced on a door, the child was floating
      downriver.
   B. The child was in a state of shock.
IV. Henry rescued an old woman.
   A. She was in the attic of an old house.
   B. She had gone without food or water for four
      days.
 V. Henry saved the lives of two young boys.
   A. They had stolen a boat.
   B. They were on a collision course with the
      bridge.

Topic outline. Some writers prefer topic outlines, and
some teachers assign them. A topic outline resembles a
sentence outline; however, it contains precise phrases in
place of sentences.

Thesis statement: After moving to Huntington in
1937, H. L. Brothers experienced a vast flood and in
the course of a single day saved the lives of various
people.
   I. Henry Brother's retirement move and encounter
      with flood
      A. Water 38 feet above flood stage
      B. Entire city flooded
  II. Henry helping people in trouble
      A. Using boat to rescue people
      B. Using boat to carry supplies
 III. Henry saving life of a small child
      A. Child floating on a door
      B. Child in a state of shock
  IV. Henry rescuing an old woman
      A. Trapped in the attic of an old house
      B. Endured four days without food or water
   V. Henry saving the lives of two young boys
      A. Stolen boat
      B. Near collision with bridge

Outline pattern

Thesis statement:
- I. First major idea
  - A. Supporting material
    - 1. Specific example
    - 2. Specific example
      - a. Specific detail
      - b. Specific detail
  - B. Supporting material
- II. Second major idea

Guidelines for formal outlining

1. Link the thesis statement to the paper's main points or major ideas.
2. The paper's major ideas form the outline's major headings.
3. Present the supporting material in a logical order. This means there must be a "II" to go with a "I," a "B" to go with an "A," and so on.
4. Divide the supporting material into logical sections.
5. Use parallel structure when possible. (See 20.7.)
6. Roman numerals indicate main points or major ideas.
7. Capital letters indicate support and development.
8. Arabic numerals, small letters, Arabic numerals in parentheses, and small letters in parentheses mark succeeding subsections.

Thinking Exercises

1. In 1.8, read through the final draft of A. B.'s paper on the left-hand pages and read the outline list in 1.7b. Does A. B. use all the material on the outline list in the draft? What omissions do you notice? Why do you think they were omitted?

2. Examine the following parts from three different outlines. Are the parts logically arranged? Are they parallel? Revise to improve the logic or parallelism.

| (a) | (b) | (c) |

(a)	(b)	(c)
I. *Difficulties*	I. *Goals of Exercise*	I. *Fears*
A. Commuting	A. Weight loss	A. Childhood
II. *Expenses*	B. Hatred of eating	B. My mother's
A. Tuition	C. Better health	C. Adolescent
B. Books	D. Greater strength	D. Adult

3. Make a list of at least ten different forms of transportation and use the list to illustrate each of the following ordering principles: (a) familiar to unfamiliar, (b) expensive to inexpensive, (c) slow to fast, (d) old to new, (e) boring to exciting. Can you think of any other ordering principles?

Writing Assignments

1. Write a paper contrasting two places or persons. Choose one that is neat, well organized, and efficient. Have the other be sloppy, disorganized, and inefficient. In your draft, give enough facts along with specific and concrete details so a reader can see each clearly. Use a formal sentence outline to study the second draft.

2. Write a paper about your favorite park. Answer the following questions: Why do you like the park? What does it contain? How do the parts connect? What physical characteristics stand out: sizes, shapes, colors, textures, and other details? Write the draft using any suitable pattern of organization, such as least enjoyable to most enjoyable or least interesting to most interesting. As part of your strategy, draw a map of the park, not from memory but from the details you have written. Revise accordingly.

3. What is the most disorganized place you have ever seen? If it will help, draw a crude sketch. Label the contents. Write a paper focusing on the disorganization. Try to give your reader a sense of the chaos of the place.

1.8 Writing the rough draft

✍ Student Comments on Writing

In high school I thought every word I wrote had to be perfect. This desire for perfection led to a lot of erasing. I think I spent more time erasing than writing. Now I understand what a rough draft is. One of my friends told me. "Don't get it right at first. Get it written." After learning that rough drafts are imperfect, a great weight fell from my shoulders.

Ginny Metcalf

I can't explain it. Sometimes my second draft bears almost no resemblance to my first draft.

Joan Black

a. The rough draft needs preparation

The rough draft is your first opportunity to write all your ideas down. If you have some practice as a writer, you may have a strategy for the rough draft. If writing rough drafts is unfamiliar to you, some ideas may help:

- ✎ Think of the draft as the beginning, not the end of your work. Accept imperfection at the beginning.

- ✎ Think of the rough draft as an opportunity for learning: a time to clarify your purpose and ideas, to discover your true feelings about the subject, and to gather the parts of your knowledge into a unified whole.

- ✎ Think of the deadline for the final polished draft and allow enough time to do at least one good revision.

✎ Think of the material you need in order to write and have it nearby: a copy of the assignment, your thesis statement, reminders of your audience and purpose, notes, lists, any necessary books.

b. The rough draft requires time

As you begin writing, you should have the sense that you want to get your ideas down on paper quickly. Focus your entire attention on the writing. Avoid distractions. Then begin writing. Most writers pause to gather their thoughts just before writing, but if you discover that you are staring off into space, write yourself a message: "Begin writing now!" Write to answer two questions: What is the main point of this paper? What is the best material to develop that point for your audience?

c. Writers use different strategies

Because different writers have different approaches to work, there isn't one perfect way to do a rough draft. Most writers can improve their writing by trying different strategies and searching for the most helpful approach. The following strategies have all proven effective for different writers.

Write the introduction first. Many writers begin with the introduction. As one student wrote, "The introduction matters most to me. If I don't get it right, nothing else will be right." Another student wrote, "If I can write an introduction that I know will interest a reader in my subject, I know I can write the rest of the paper." The introduction is a good chance to state the main idea, interest the reader, provide background information, and set the pattern for organization. (See 5.1–5.4.)

Write the conclusion first. Some students start with the conclusion and work back to the body and the introduction. One student wrote, "It may sound a little strange to write the conclusion first, but I want to know where I am going to end up." Such a strategy of inductive thinking leads to a pattern of specific material at the beginning, followed by general statements toward the end. (See 5.5–5.7.)

Write the middle or body of the paper first. Many students write the middle paragraphs, or body, first. In such a case, the writer feels that the middle section contains the most important parts. If the introduction and conclusion are clearly subordinate to the body of the paper, this strategy proves quite effective. Some writers need to see the paper's main contents before they can write either the introduction or the conclusion. One student commented, "I need to know what I am saying before I introduce or conclude my material."

Begin with a thesis statement. There are several different forms of thesis statement. (See 1.4.) To begin the draft, some writers use a formulaic numbering sentence, such as "Most players know three ways to cheat at poker." Such a statement indicates and limits the subject. Beginning writers report that such a sentence helps in writing the rough draft.

Begin with freewriting. Freewriting helps writers overcome forms of writing anxiety. Somehow, freewriting helps nervous writers go directly to their main ideas and supporting material. The instructions are simple. Write some questions or comments related to the subject. Begin writing. Write down everything that comes into your mind. Do not stop writing until you can write no more. (See 1.3e.)

Test the power of your imagination. Some students write the entire paper in their heads. Many students are able to compose sentences and paragraphs in their minds, and they make no changes when they write them out. A few students are able to compose longer writings in their minds. One such student ran six miles every day. She would think about her subject and mentally compose whole pages while running. Another case involved a blind student with a strong memory. She would decide on a subject and begin to think. Thinking for her was mental composing, paragraph by paragraph. She created at least one paragraph each for the introduction, body, and conclusion. When she finished, she would recite the paper into a tape recorder and have someone type the final product.

Prepare a scratch outline. A scratch outline contains a few key words or ideas on a topic. (See 1.7b.) This can activate your memory and lead to new ideas. The key ideas will give direction to your paper and help you as you search for supporting material. Don't consider any outline fixed forever. If you think of new ideas, add them. If you want to omit some, do. This kind of list can clarify your main idea and help you find ways to develop it.

Prepare a formal outline. Discover the value of the formal outline. Most writers who have completed lengthy writing assignments attest to the value of a formal outline as a planning device to help write the rough draft. You can use an outline in a number of different ways. Some people use outlines to clarify the relationship between the main and supporting ideas, others to help organize the paper, decide the order of supporting ideas, and see which ideas need revising.

Create rough drafts from different perspectives. For short assignments, you might write different first drafts. To develop the subject, write the draft from different perspectives. For example, one student wrote a paper describing the fireplace at the student union after observing it from six different angles. For the same writing assignment, another student wrote a paper after observing it at six different times. Changing the perspective can yield new ideas and new material. Using different perspectives can help a writer clarify and control the main idea.

Thinking Exercises

1. Which of the following people use rough drafts in their work: house painters, oil painters, sculptors in marble, dentists, musical composers, musical performers, accountants, lawyers, football players, business managers, teachers? For those who do create rough drafts, give an example.

2. How do you know when *you* have finished your rough draft? What tells you? List some reasons why people say their first draft is done. Share these reasons with your classmates. What are some good reasons for saying the writing is finished? What are some poor reasons?

3. Read both drafts by A. B. (pages 66–72). For each, make a list of things you liked. Then make a list of things you disliked. Why did you dislike those things?

4. Which version do you like the best? Make a list of the reasons for your choice.

Writing Assignments

1. Study two drafts of a paper by one of your friends or classmates. Write a brief paper focusing on the three most important changes the author made.

2. Following the same assignment completed by A. B., write a paper (going through all the stages in the writing process) about someone in your family.

3. Find two different reports of the same event. Write a one-paragraph summary of each report. Then write at least one additional paragraph explaining the main differences between the two versions.

Draft of A. B.'s Paper

In January of 1937, the city of Huntington, West Virginia, sank under a flood of water. The Ohio River rose thirty-eight feet above flood stage and covered the roofs of one-story homes and rose to the second-story windows. Even today a person can visit homes in the city and view marks on the walls left by the high waters. Such marks are thirty-five feet above ground level. Today a vast flood wall surrounds the city, and the Corps of Engineers claims the city is safe. What was it like back then when a city of more than 50,000 with an area of more than a hundred square miles lost its connection to the land and became a part of the Ohio River? The past survives in history books and in the voices of those still alive. The stories told by one eyewitness seem worth remembering. That man is my grandfather, Henry Lewis Brothers, known to all as H. L.

After damaging his leg in a Mingo County mining accident in 1936, H. L. retired early and moved with his wife Sarah to Huntington to be near his two daughters and seven grandchildren. Two months after his arrival, the water in the Ohio River began to rise without ceasing for a week.

Continued on page 68

Draft of A. B.'s paper

In January of 1937, my grandfather Hazel L. Brothers, was just-retired no longer a coal miner who had just moved from Mingo County in southern West Virginia to Huntington to be not away from his grandchildren (all seven of them: four boys and three girls) and not distant from his two beloved daughters. It was then that my grandfather was to have the "greatest experience of my life" (his words) when he watched the Ohio River rise slowly from a high hill to flood stage and then keep rising for entire days. The entire city of Huntington, a town extending for many miles and with a large population for West Virginia, was flooded under a great amount of water. There are homes in the city and they can show me the high water mark reached by the flood. The river began rising in the middle of January because of an early thaw. It continued to rise until it reached a crest of 38 feet above flood stage. It stayed at that stage for two days. It gradually began to not rise any more. It settled back into its actual banks six days later.

During this time, we are told many people performed numerous deeds of bravery and heroism and courage. My

Continued on page 69

The flood provided H. L. with "the greatest experience a man could ever have: the opportunity to save someone's life." Not just one person, but several people benefited from that man's bravery and strength. On one single day, H. L. turned his fishing boat into a rescue boat and managed to save four people from danger and pluck a grimy kitten from the top of a submerged tree jutting a few feet out of the water.

The first incident occurred on a Sunday. H. L.'s new home was on high ground on a ridge three miles back from the river and a hundred feet above the flood waters. Rising at dawn, he walked out onto his porch and rubbed his eyes. He rubbed them again. Down the hill and far out on a vast lake of swirling muddy water was a small child. On the water's surface, on its hands and knees, a small blond-headed, blue-eyed child floated almost two hundred yards away from his boat. Shivering and moaning, she was barefoot and wore a thin wet blue dress.

H. L. remembers the scene vividly: "It looked like the child was kneeling, floating slowly past. I couldn't believe my eyes. I thought it was a dream." He leaped down the hillside, started the engine, and raced off. The child was somehow supported by a huge oak door floating level with the water. She was holding on to a wooden towel rack and a glass doorknob. The frightened child could have floated all night. As soon as H. L maneuvered his boat next to the floating door, the whimpering child scrambled into the boat. A week later, the child's parents were found in Pennsylvania and H. L. and his wife drove the little girl, Mabel Dean, back home.

In addition to rescuing an oil-soaked kitten from a tree and saving an old woman from an attic room, H. L. had one other exciting adventure that day. He encountered on the river two young and suicidal Huckleberry Finns. Two young boys, "the Mercen brats ages 9 and 11 from back in the hollow," as H. L. said, had stolen a small rowboat from

Continued on page 70

grandfather was proudly among them. I want to focus on three separate events that all happened on one single day while my grandfather was driving his boat trying to carry needed supplies for disaster relief from one ridge to another hill. On one eventful day, which was the first for him, he managed to save three peoples' lives and rescue a kitten from the top branches of a tree very near the court house.

The first of these four incidences occurred early on a Friday morning. He was just getting ready to step into his boat when he looked out over the water and saw something. He blinked and looked again and it was a small blond-headed blue-eyed child floating about two hundred yards away from his boat. It was floating past him like in a dream. "It looked like the child was kneeling floating slowly past. I couldn't believe my eyes. I thought it was a dream. I sped over there in no time and found the child shivering and kneeling on a huge oak door which was floating just below the surface. The kid maybe had floated downriver all night. I immediately got the child off the door and into my boat. Up to this time the child was silent. It would not even answer a question like, 'What is your name or where is your home or where are your parents? There was no answer.'" This was after Grandfather had just finished filling the boat's motor with gasoline and was putting the gas tank in the boat. This was very dangerous and earlier in the day a terrible accident involving gasoline and a boat had killed four people in the west end of the city. His house was on high ground on a ridge three miles back from the river and the water had not risen anywhere near to his house.

My grandfather has always been a brave man. This reminds me of the time when I was a child and he rescued me from being hung up in a swing in an apple tree at church.

While grandfather was steering the boat around Huntington, grandfather was surprised by a small child saying: "Look! It is my Gramma." The child was pointing to the

Continued on page 71

Reverend Hoagland's now submerged fish pond. Ignorant and unfamiliar with water, the boys were using a crutch and a damaged oar for propulsion.

Their boat squirted out to the center of the three-mile river and began to move in four directions. First, it started to turn around from front to back. Second, it began to rock from side to side. Third, it was moving in a narrowing circle. Fourth, it began to move quickly downstream and seemed headed on a collision course with the huge iron supports on the Sixth Street Bridge. Helpless and facing destruction, the youthful pair grew increasingly bizarre in their behavior.

Both of the boys began screaming, and their voices trailed off like air out of a balloon. As the boat turned, one of the boys lay down in the boat, raised his arms straight up, and began crying. The other child sat to one side, holding on to a short piece of rope. Suddenly the boy lying down stood up in the boat and was immediately thrown into the swirling, cold, brown water. He tried to hold on to the boat, but his hand scraped the side, unable to find any support. Trying to grab the boat only pushed the boat further away.

My grandfather with his tiny cargo sped to the struggling boy and threw him a large life jacket. The boy grabbed on to it and listened to H. L.'s instructions for slipping it on. With the jacket on, the boy was able to float. Then H. L. turned his attention to the boat headed for the bridge. Pulling in back of the runaway boat, H. L. was able to grab the rowboat's rope and secure it to his motorboat. Slowly both boats made their way back across the river away from the Ohio side. Since there was no safe way to pull the swimming boy in the life jacket aboard, H. L. towed him through the swollen, brown, debris-laden river all the way back to safety.

Some days are more full than others. Even though the parents of the small girl never properly thanked H. L. for

Continued on page 72

third story attic window of a huge house. The motor was immediately turned off by Grandfather and it drifted close to the house. Sure enough it was an elderly lady. It was not the child's grandmother but the resemblance was enough to get the child to trust the woman. She came into the boat through a window. She had a large amount of fear on her face. As soon as the woman was in the boat the small child became more relaxed and when the child was spoken to by the woman, the child responded to all the questions. At the end of the boat ride to the shelter point, the child was even smiling.

A final incident in my grandfather's eventful day involved two children. They had stolen a boat somehow and were foolish enough to try to go out on the river. At thirty-five feet above flood stage, Grandfather watched the boat float out to the center of the river and immediately it began to go in circles because of a moving undertow. As the boat turned and turned, one of the boys lay down in the boat. The other one sat up and held on the side. After a few minutes the sitting boy stood and almost immediately, fell. He tried to hold on to the boat but his first grasps were inefficient because of the cold and the slippery water. After those several tries the boat was caught and squirted away from the boy in the river. My grandfather sped to the spot where the boy was struggling and threw him something to save him. The boy grabbed onto it and stayed on the surface. The other boy was still lying on the bottom of the boat and that boat was heading down river at the dead center of the river. It would probably crash several hundred yards ahead. Once more grandfather sped to the rescue. He attach a rope to the boat and began to drag it back to the spot where the other young man was now floating. He slowly instructed him to climb aboard grandfather's boat and the caravan of the three then headed back to the shelter point.

saving their daughter's life, and even though the two young delinquents abused H. L., his wife, and the small child at the first possible opportunity, H. L. Brothers, that brave retired miner, still maintains, "It was one of the most worthwhile and exciting days in my life."

1.9 Revising the draft

✍ **Student Comments on Writing**

I was absolutely astounded by a comment of the world-famous writer James Michener. He wrote, "I have never thought of myself as a good writer. Anyone who wants reassurance of that should read one of my first drafts. But I'm one of the world's greatest rewriters. I write the first draft really to see how it's going to come out. I never write anything important in the first draft."

Glenn Lindsey

The best thing for revising is to use a computer. It saves more time than I could have ever imagined.

T. O.

a. Writers resist revision

Many writers dislike revising. This resistance is perfectly natural and arises from three possible sources. One, a writer might lack commitment or time. Two, a writer may be confused by the demands of a reader. Three, a writer might not know how to revise and instead settle for correction of errors in usage, spelling, mechanics, and punctuation. Resistance to revision is widespread, especially among inexperienced writers, but it can be overcome if the writer focuses on the most important elements of writing: purpose, meaning, and audience.

b. Writers use different revising strategies

The process of revision varies from writer to writer. Each revision will be unique, depending upon the experience of the writer and the audience and the purpose for the writing. The following list presents some strategies that different writers have used to improve their rough drafts.

Learn to use a computer. If there is one simple thing that can make the act of revising easier and more productive, it is word processing. The sooner you use this method, the better off you will be. Take advantage of the services your school offers.

Pause. Before you begin revising, put the paper aside for several hours, a day, a week. This pause will give the draft time to incubate, and when you later sit down with pen and paper to begin the actual revision, you may have new ideas.

Listen to the sound of your paper. Read it aloud to hear how it sounds. Read the paper again out loud, this time to someone else. Ask for comments. Have someone else read it to you. Read the paper into a tape recorder and play it back. Read the paper while listening to your recording. Take notes on strong and weak points.

Write one sentence. Without looking at your paper, briefly tell the contents of your paper to another person, then write one sentence that states the main point of your paper. Examine your draft in light of the sentence.

Example

> This paper lets a reader know what I thought and felt like (plus the circumstances) the time when I broke my knee in a high school football game.

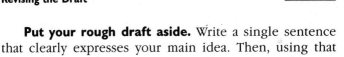
Put your rough draft aside. Write a single sentence that clearly expresses your main idea. Then, using that sentence, write the paper again, trying to capture the most important material and the most interesting details that develop your main idea. Compare the drafts.

Outline your rough draft. Pinpoint your general ideas. Determine what you need to do to develop them more fully for your reader. Make a list of the most important things you need to add to get your ideas across. Is the draft well organized? Rearrange material if necessary.

Read your rough draft critically. Pretend you are somebody else, perhaps your worst enemy. Make a list of the things in your paper that person would pick on. Write a letter to the teacher about your paper with the following first sentence: "I don't think it will help any, but I thought I would bring to your attention a number of weaknesses in this student's writing."

Check your introduction. Will it catch the attention of your intended audience? How? Underline the part that most clearly states your main idea. Is it precise, clear, and interesting? (See 5.2.) Does the introduction convey the general purpose of your paper, whether persuasive, informative, or expressive? Does the introduction need any additional background material? (See 5.1.)

Read the rough draft. Write out answers for each of the following questions:

- How much time do you have to revise the paper?
- What is the main idea you want a reader to get?
- What material helps the most to develop your main idea?
- What other material would help develop the main idea?

❞ What part of your paper needs the most attention? Why?

❞ What more do you need to know about the subject?

Reread the rough draft. Make lists or write sentences to answer the following:

❞ Why do you consider the subject valuable?

❞ What do you like most about the paper?

❞ What other details would make the paper lively?

❞ What five things could you omit from your paper?

❞ What do the sentences sound like when read aloud?

c. Writers use checklists when revising

The following checklists contain material that will help you focus on three different areas: (1) support for the main idea, (2) sensible organization, and (3) effective sentences.

Checklist for main idea and support

❞ Does the paper actually say something?

❞ Place **MI** in the margin beside the first statement of the main idea.

❞ Place a star (*) in the left margin beside each idea or example that develops the main point.

❞ Place an **X** in the right margin beside any unimportant material.

❞ What other material is needed to develop the main idea? Where will it go?

Checklist for organization

❞ Does the paper make sense and seem logical?

❞ Identify the pattern of organization.

✎ Point to those elements in the paper that show the organization.

✎ Mark **B, M,** and **E** in the margins for the beginning, middle, and end.

✎ Mark **SOP** in the margin beside the paper's statement of purpose or its main idea.

Checklist for sentences

✎ Circle pretentious, repetitive words and phrases. (See 21.20–21.21.) Remove or replace them. Revise to remove wordiness.

✎ Underline unnecessary abstract words and any vague general phrases. (See 21.4 and 21.12.) If possible, replace with concrete, specific language. (See 3.1 and 21.12.)

✎ Identify adjective clauses introduced by *who, which,* or *that.* Move each clause as near as possible to the word that it modifies. (See 20.8.)

✎ Mark with **BE** each string of passive verbs and each string of *to be* verbs. If possible, change all verbs to the active voice or to verbs of action. (See 21.5 and 21.24.)

✎ Read the paper out loud. Listen to the sentence structure. Which sentences can you change to improve sentence variety? (See 20.9.)

Thinking Exercises

1. Find a paragraph of very difficult expository prose from a textbook, scholarly journal, or government document. Make a copy of the paragraph. List up to five reasons why you find the passage difficult. Revise one or two sentences to improve readability.

2. After you have finished the rough draft of a paper, put your paper aside for a while before revising. Pick up a book by a serious writer whose work you enjoy, such as Flannery O'Connor or John Updike. Read the book for at least an hour. Begin your process of revision after the reading. Make a list of some ways the reading made you think differently about your writing.

3. Read the two drafts of A. B.'s paper in Section 1.8. List the most important changes. What kinds of changes help the most to improve the paper? What further changes would you suggest to the author?

4. How might the following marks on a draft of A. B.'s paper have helped the writer improve the paper?

22.2
21.21

23.4
20.5d

5P

23.1

In January of 1937 the city of Huntington West Virginia sank under a flood of cold wet water. The Ohio River rose 38 feet above flood stage and covered the roofs of 1 story homes and rose to the second story windows of larger homes. Even today you can visit homes in the city and view marks on the walls left by the high waters. Such marks are 35 feet above ground level. Today a wall surrounds the city, and the Core of Engineers claims the city is safe. What was it like back then when a city of more than 50,000 and with area of more than 100 square miles lost it's **5P** connection to the land and became a part of the Ohio river. The past survives in history books and the in

voices of those still alive. The stories told by one eyewitness seem remembering. That man is my grandfather Henry Lewis Brothers known to all as HL.

5.   The students in A. B.'s class shared papers and
wrote comments on two other students' papers in response
to the following questions: (a) What do you like most
about this writing? (b) What one sentence can you write
to sum up the main idea? (c) What questions do you have
about this paper? (d) What one thing might the writer do
to improve this paper? The following comments were
made on an early draft of A. B.'s paper. Which comments
do you think were the most helpful? Why?

1. I just like the paper because the author has done
   a good job of writing it.
2. I like the scene in the boat with the two delinquents. It is cute, but it might be a bit clearer.
3. The main idea is to tell what the grandfather
   did.
4. The main idea explains how the grandfather act-
   ed in the flood but also a little bit about how
   much the author likes the grandfather.
5. Why don't you improve your spelling and your
   handwriting?
6. What actually did the grandfather do to save the
   two young boys?
7. I think you should focus just on the grandfather.
   You have too many other things in your story.
8. Find a better topic which has more action in it.

6.   The following section from an early draft shows
the kind of revisions A. B. made. What important changes
were made? Refer to the comparable draft paragraphs on
pages 66 and 71.

The boat squirted out to the center of the three mile wide river and began to move all over. It started to turn around from front to back and it began to rock from side to side. Then, it was in motion in a circle. Last it began to move quickly down stream and seemed headed on a collision course with the Bridge. Helpless and facing destruction, the behavior of the youthful pair grew increasingly bizarre. Both of the boys began screaming but no one could hear them. As the boat turned, one of the boys the boat started to cry. The other child sat to one side holding on. Suddenly the boy lying down stood up in the boat and was in the swirling, cold, brown water. He tried to hold on to the boat, but was unable to find any support. Trying to grab the boat only pushed it.

Writing Assignments

1. Write a personal experience paper on the topic "Changing your mind," referring to a specific instance when you changed your mind. Present background information. With a beginning, middle, and end, write a narrative that explains your plans and your actions. Point out any differences between the two.

2. After completing the preceding assignment, revise the material from first to third person on the topic "Changing your mind." Write a short, completely objective essay using the following thesis statement: "X changed his/her mind about Y for one/two/three different reasons."

1.10 Proofreading the paper

✍ Student Comments on Writing

I was surprised to learn that errors are inevitable in rough drafts and that even professors make errors in rough drafts. I used to believe that some writers did everything perfectly from the start. One teacher said he usually had to check the spelling of five or six words on every page. He told us to be sure to proofread twice: after revision and before turning in the final draft, so the paper would not receive a lower grade because of several stupid typos.

Lilly Chann

a. What is proofreading

Because most readers dislike seeing serious errors in spelling, usage, and mechanics, and because some errors in writing make understanding difficult, proofreading is an essential final step. Basically, proofreading is the search for omissions and errors in the sentences of any writing. Because mistakes occur in both rough and final drafts, a writer must read carefully, identify problems, and neatly correct errors before submitting a paper for evaluation.

b. When is the best time to proofread

Several general rules about timing help improve writing efficiency and increase proofreading skill:

✎ First, *wait* until you consider the paper finished to begin proofreading. It makes no sense to proofread parts of a paper that may soon be changed. Proofread both the final handwritten draft and the final typed copy.

✎ Second, *wait* for some time after you have completed the final draft to proofread. Immediately after finishing the draft, you will be so happy that you won't be in the mood to find fault and discover errors. Wait at least two hours after writing the paper to proofread. Ideally, proofread the day after finishing the paper and proofread again the night before the paper is due.

✎ Third, for in-class writing, set aside at least five minutes at the end for careful proofreading. If your teacher allows, proofread again at the beginning of the next class.

c. What proofreading strategies are the most helpful

You should begin to learn a number of different ways to proofread. You may discover that one method helps you discover certain errors whereas another technique helps you find other kinds of mistakes. If you have your own procedure, use it in addition to the following ideas:

✎ Read the paper quickly and silently, then once again slowly. Mark errors or difficulties and correct them. Repeat this process the night before you turn in the paper.

✎ Slowly read the paper out loud from first word to last. Pause briefly at the end of each sentence. Because the presence of another person may make you more attentive, have someone else listen to you while you read your paper. Mark errors or difficulties and correct them.

✎ Have someone read your paper while you listen and look at a copy. Mark any errors. Make corrections later. Or read the paper into a tape recorder and then listen to the recording while looking at a copy. Occasionally, listening attentively to a paper being read without looking at a copy helps some people proofread effectively.

✎ Read only words, and look only for errors: from the last word to the next-to-the-last word on back to the first word of the paper.

✎ Look for your weaknesses. Read slowly, looking for the kinds of mistakes you make frequently. If your problem is spelling, start with the last word and work back to the first. Check each word—and not just difficult words. Pay special attention to words previously misspelled. Consult the list of spelling errors in 21.3.

d. What should a proofreader look for

Read the paper carefully.

✎ Is the handwriting legible?

✎ Does the paper have the correct format?

✎ Are the pages numbered in the right order?

✎ Are the paragraphs in the right order?

✎ Are there any unintentional additions or omissions?

Read each sentence carefully.

✎ Does each sentence make sense?

✎ Does each sentence have a subject and a complete verb?

✎ Does every verb agree with its subject?

✎ Are the verb forms and tenses correct?

✎ Does each pronoun have an antecedent?

✎ Does each personal pronoun have the right case?

✎ Are any sentences fused or spliced together?

✎ Is each modifier close enough to the word it modifies?

Check the spelling of the following:

✎ Problem words you have misspelled

✎ Words ending in *s, es, 's,* and *s'*

✎ Words with apostrophes or words needing them

✎ Homophones such as *to/too/two, their/there/ they're, lead/led, it's/its, who's/whose*

✎ Capitalized first word in each sentence

✎ Capitalized proper nouns and adjectives

✎ Words with unnecessary capital letters

✎ Words with hyphens or needing hyphens

Check for punctuation and mechanics.

✎ Does each sentence have terminal punctuation?

✎ Are any commas needed? Unnecessary?

✎ Are any quotation marks needed? Unnecessary?

✎ Are the forms for numbers and abbreviations correct?

Check for your own most damaging errors.

1.   2.   3.   4.

5.   6.   7.   8.

Thinking Exercises

1.   After 1500, Europeans began printing new editions of ancient books, some more than 2,000 years old. One printer, Aldus Manutius, prepared an edition of Plato, the ancient Greek philosopher. In a preface to the book, he offered a gold coin (probably worth $50 today) to anyone who could find a printing error. Why would anyone make such an offer? Today, why would a publisher or an insurance company pay an employee $40,000 a year to proofread written material?

2.   Proofread and correct the following paper. Which errors are most damaging?

A Case of Mistake Identity

Most students here have been listen to the catchy ads on WHJK for "Bob's Mexican Restaurant over near the Tower." The drums the guitars the castanet and the sultry voice all these—pleasing to the ear. What does not please should be most important—the quality of the food and the service of the employee It is hard for me to tell whether the food or the service worse

A description of what they call "encheereedoe" should send any hungry eater scurrying in another direction. Enchiritos should be warm soft flavorful an delicious. Last week a Bobs they were manufacturin enchiritos that looked like dry oak leaves covered with red salad dressing. The soft corn meal shell probably made out of refried brown paper sacks. The interior contents had probably been remove from some dead parakeet's esophagus and fried in lizard oil. The wrapping on which this concoction was laid and splattered with som drops of catsup resembled a Wendy wrapper. The Coke was great but they only served me a few ounces in a sixteen ounce cup full of chipped ice.

The service was great. There just wasn't any of it. The one worker spent five minutes looking at us banging at the counter bell. He was busy leaning up yesterday's lunch from several tables. He would swing his rag across the top of each counter and try to knock the old contents into the sack. Sometimes he miss and he would walk over the mess. You could hear his tennis shoes kind of crunch on the old tacos and chips.

It wasn't worth it to have him wait on us—finally. I sure did not want the food after looking at it and nibbling just a small amount. Even though the beer is ice cold and the ad music great Bobs Mexican Restauran is no place to spend five minutes—or to spend a penny.

Jeff Hannon

3.   List ten kinds of mistakes in writing that you consider most serious. Make a second list of ten errors that you believe your teacher will penalize most severely. Share your lists with other students in class. Discuss the lists. Ask your teacher which errors will result in lower grades for the writing assignments in your course.

Writing Assignments

1.   Write a cause-effect paper. (See 3.5 and 3.6.) Use one of the following topics: (a) a time you made a mistake, or (b) a time someone gave you wrong information.

2.   What do different people think about the following mistakes in grammar: sentence fragments, subject-verb agreement error, spelling errors such as *to/too*, and fused sentences? With examples of each kind of error, ask some people their opinions on errors in written English. Ask teachers (elementary, secondary, college), businesspeople, and professional workers. Ask them why they feel this way. Record your findings. Write a brief paper summarizing your research.

1.11 Format for final drafts

When preparing the final draft, follow your instructor's directions. If no special guidelines are announced, prepare a neat, legible final draft by observing a conventional format. These conventions make reading easier.

Paper. Use good quality, white bond stock. For typing, select 16- or 20-pound weight, unlined paper, 8½″ × 11″. For handwriting, use the same kind with a line guide slipped under the sheet, or use 8½″ × 11″ lined paper with lines ⅜″ apart. Write on only one side on every other line. Avoid erasable paper, onion skin, sheets ripped from spiral notebooks, colored paper, and papers larger or smaller than 8½″ × 11″.

Margins. Be generous all the way around. Make margins adequate for neatness and for commentary. Except for the first page, leave 1½″ at the top. Maintain a consistent right- and left-hand margin: 1″ or 1½″. Leave 1″ at the bottom.

Typing. Type your paper, if you know how to. Readers always prefer typed material. When typing, use a fresh black ribbon; make sure the keys are clean. Type on only one side and double-space. Single-space between words and after commas, semicolons, and colons. Use two spaces after any punctuation marking the end of a sentence: periods, question marks, exclamation points, and quotation marks. Indent the first line of each paragraph five spaces. If you are using quoted material, use the proper form for poetry, prose, or dialogue. (See 22.7.)

Handwriting. Inquire whether handwritten papers are acceptable. All papers should be legible. Because neatness and legibility do count, your instructor may return a messy or illegible paper for recopying and resubmission. Before turning the final draft in, look it over to make sure that a reader can easily decipher what you have written. Avoid flourishes, swirling letters, and any excessive slant. Make commas distinct from periods. Remember that a dot is not a circle. Dot the *i*'s. Cross the *t*'s. Avoid either tiny or gigantic script. Avoid dividing words at the end of a line. Do not overuse hyphens. As you come to the end of a line, you can sometimes adjust the spacing of the letters to avoid dividing the word.

Word processing. Strive to make the final printout of your paper look as much like regular typed or printed copy as possible. Follow the preceding conventions for typing and margins. Choose a readable font similar to standard typewriter fonts. If a letter-quality printer is unavailable and if your instructor will allow you to submit material prepared on a dot-matrix printer, set the machine to create dense and dark print. Do not, however, turn in papers with large-size print or with boldface. (See Appendix A.)

Title. Have a title. If you have a separate title page, follow the example on page 460. If a separate page is unnecessary, center the title four lines below the identification on the top of the first page as on page 427. Do not underline the title or put quotation marks around it. Capitalize the first word and the last word; any word following a colon; and all other words of the title except articles (*a, an, the*), conjunctions, and short prepositions.

Identification. Know what your teacher requires. If an MLA format is followed, this involves the following information 1″ from the top of the page in the upper left-hand corner: name, instructor, class, date, and any other information your teacher may request. (See page 427.)

Numbering pages. Make sure the pages are in order. Do not number or count the separate title page. If you have an outline, number it using large Roman numerals. Begin numbering on the second page of the body of the paper. Use Arabic numerals and number consecutively. Place your name ½″ from the top in the upper right-hand corner of each page, followed by the correct page number, flush with the margin.

Outline. If your teacher requires an outline, follow the form of one at the end of 16.12.

Copy of paper. Always keep a copy of any paper you submit anywhere. Keep your notes and your rough drafts until after your teacher returns the paper.

Corrections. Correct neatly. To delete something, draw one line through it. To substitute, delete the old material and write in the new immediately above. To insert material, use a caret mark (∧) and add the material immediately above it as in the following example:

The report⟨on the⟩ airplane crash raises⟨three⟩ serious questions.

Avoid turning in a sloppy paper. If a page is littered with more than five additions or corrections, redo the page.

PART 2

Writing Paragraphs

2 Paragraphs as Units of Thought

✍ **Student Comments on Writing**

It helps me to think of paragraphs as miniature compositions with a clear main idea and plenty of material to support and develop that idea. I try to think of a paragraph as the answer to a question or as the support for a main point I'm trying to make.

Joe Napier

When I am reading paragraphs by my classmates, I am happy when I find a topic sentence. I know I am going to get something. Topic sentences are like hooks to hold things together. I like to see them, and I always try to use them. Sometimes, they are unnecessary, but most often they are useful.

R.B. Banks

Your writing can improve if you understand the structure of a paragraph and discover ways to use paragraphs to present your thoughts and feelings. Simply stated, a paragraph is a group of related sentences discussing a certain part of a subject. Each paragraph forms a logical unit of the subject matter, and these units are indicated by indentations.

2.1 Paragraph elements

Paragraphs differ greatly in content, length, style, purpose, and function. Despite the variety, most paragraphs contain a number of key elements that work together to present meaning for a reader. Most clear and effective paragraphs contain the following five elements.

Main idea. This is the point of the paragraph, and it presents the author's thought about a subject. The main idea is either implied by the material in the entire paragraph or stated explicitly in a topic sentence. Not all paragraphs have topic sentences, but they all have a main idea.

Evidence and support. This information develops and explains the main idea. Most often a writer presents relevant facts and specific details about the subject.

Coherence. This involves linking sentences and making them flow together with meaning. Writers use, when needed, coordination, subordination, repetition, and transitional markers.

Order. This refers to the arrangement of ideas and sentences in a clear, logical, and effective pattern.

Unity. This refers to a focusing in the paragraph on one part of the subject. Focusing is essential for effective writing.

You can note these five elements in the following paragraph describing the yeti. Following it is a student journal entry responding to the question, "What key elements of paragraph structure can you find in this paragraph?"

Together, the eyewitness reports construct a detailed description of the yeti. Its body is stocky, apelike in shape, with a distinctly human quality to it, in contrast to that of a bear. It stands five and a half to six feet tall, and is covered with short coarse hair, reddish brown to black in color, sometimes with white patches on the chest. The hair is longest on the shoulders. The face is hairless and rather flat. The jaw is robust, the teeth are quite large, though fangs are not present, and the mouth is wide. The head is conically shaped and comes to a pointed crown. The arms are long, reaching almost to the knees. The shoulders are heavy and hunched. There is no tail.

From "The Yeti" by Edward W. Cronin

You have asked us to write our responses to this paragraph about the Yeti. I think it is amusing to write a whole essay on the abominable snowman as if it really existed. It is hard to see how the author who wrote this for the *Atlantic Monthly* is any different from those who invent such stories for the *National Enquirer*. In terms of support and evidence, the writer claims to have "eyewitness reports," but he does not specify what they are. The main idea of the paragraph is that the writer gives a description of the yeti. What he does is to give a list of details about the body of the yeti. These are pretty good and someone could almost draw a picture from just the details. In terms of coherence, the writer sticks to the main point, but he does not use any transitional devices. It was tricky finding out how the paragraph held together so well. Basically, he uses repetition of sentence structure to hold the sentences together, but this is reinforced by the order of the details. The order is good. He shows the yeti at a distance and then he zooms in on the face and head. He ends with comments about the arms and shoulders. The parts flow together well. In terms of unity, the paragraph is perfect. Nothing is in there that does not belong. Each sentence presents more information about the subject. It would be interesting to see what this paragraph looked like in rough draft. This paragraph does *not* stand alone but is a part of a long essay on the same topic. I guess the author thought the reader needed some visual information to help understanding. Basically this is a good paragraph, even though it is not the most interesting in the world—especially to a college student like me.

Melanie Song

2.2 Paragraph length

Wherever a reader looks—in textbooks, newspapers, business letters, magazine articles, ads, essays, and stories—it is pretty easy to see that paragraphs vary greatly in length. The general guidelines for paragraph length depend on a number of things: the author's purpose; the audience; the function of the writing; and the position within the writing, whether beginning, middle, or end. Although there are no hard-and-fast rules for paragraph length, writers can benefit from an understanding of the different kinds of responses many academic readers might have to paragraph length:

- ✎ At times, short paragraphs are able to attract a reader's attention, emphasize an important point, or provide transition from one paragraph to another.

- ✎ A succession of very short paragraphs, however, each with only one or two sentences, creates the impression of haste and lack of thought.

- ✎ Exceedingly long paragraphs, more than 150 words, create problems for many readers. Often, several minor points can overshadow the major point and effectively conceal important connections between ideas.

- ✎ Readers are able to follow lengthy sentences better if the parts are parallel (see 20.7) and the topic is clearly presented at the beginning.

- ✎ Readers enjoy variety and a balance of long, medium, and short paragraphs.

Thinking Exercises

1. To study paragraph length, read paragraphs from two different places: (a) some writing connected with school, such as a textbook or a scholarly journal, and (b) some popular writing such as *People* or *TV Guide*. Are there any differences in length? What are some reasons to account for the differences?

2. Read the following paragraphs out loud and then make a list of some differences between them. The assignment was to write a paragraph about some object that changed and present a dominant impression of the object, either positive or negative.

> When I came back to school, the ancient tree in front of the dorm shocked me. Last spring, it was huge and its leaves would always shimmer in the sunlight. Now the tree is a runty thirty feet, and the few tiny leaves seem a blighted greenish-yellowy color. Whoever trimmed the tree should have waited until winter.
>
> *Ward Magnuson*

After a summer of endless, boring, and high-paying mindless labor, when I returned to school in the fall, the appearance of the oak tree at the entrance to my dorm was pitiful. In the spring in the time of flowers and robins and new sunlight everywhere, the oak had stretched more than a hundred feet into the blue sky and its leaves shone in the sunlight with a brilliant luster. Now in a September covered with clouds and the threat of rain, the tree extends no more than forty feet and the few pitiful leaves still upon the branches have a dull color. It almost reminds me of a movie about someone dying. What sadness it is I feel when I look at it day after day.

Danielle Adams

Writing Assignments

1.   Write the rough draft of a paragraph in which you imagine what you will be doing on an exceptionally good day about ten years from today. Focus on one interesting thing or activity. Read the rough draft out loud and examine it in light of the elements listed in this section. What does your paragraph need to be improved? Revise accordingly.

2.   Write a paragraph in the form of a letter to the Office of Financial Aid at your school, presenting at least two good reasons why you should be given a scholarship. Give some good examples to illustrate your main point.

3.   Write a paragraph about a dump, a junky place, or a polluted landscape.

2.3 Controlling sentences

Effective writing is purposeful. One of the strongest ways to create purpose in writing is to use a controlling sentence in a paragraph. Not only does the entire paper have a purpose, but each paragraph also has a function. To ensure the effectiveness of the writing, experienced authors create sentences of control that guide the writing and revising. Whether stated explicitly or implicitly, these kinds of sentences help a writer control and develop the paragraph's main idea. A sentence of control, or topic sentence, generally contains two key elements: the *subject* and the *main idea* that limits the subject. Effective writers often strive to use a purposeful statement, such as one of the following, somewhere in each expository paragraph.

Topic sentence

Although a topic sentence may appear anywhere in a paragraph, it generally appears at the beginning and is occasionally the first sentence.

EXAMPLE The automobile exerts great influence on the lives of American teenagers. [The subject is the automobile; the main idea is its great influence.]

Numbering sentence

While presenting the subject, this statement of the main idea lets the reader know how many points the paragraph will develop.

EXAMPLE The automobile exerts three powerful influences on the lives of American teenagers.

Topic sentence after a question

This kind of topic sentence includes the subject and the main idea, but it follows a previous sentence in the form of a question.

EXAMPLE   What influences does the automobile have on the lives of American adolescents? Most observers agree that the automobile has had several important influences.

a. A topic sentence guides the writer and the reader

An explicit topic sentence always states the subject, presents an idea about the subject, and limits the discussion. This kind of controlling sentence should assist both writer and reader. It can help the reader understand the writer's purpose. It can help the author clarify the purpose and find the most important supporting material. Both writer and reader should think of a topic sentence as an *aid*, not as a straitjacket. In that way, such a sentence helps to contribute to the developing meaning in a paragraph. Although effective paragraphs exist without such sentences, many writers design their paragraphs with clear topic sentences.

In the following paragraph, the author presents a topic sentence about the violent nature of a young boy, Radcleve. The paragraph develops the different ways in which the young man expresses his violence using bullets, gunpowder, golf balls, and firecrackers. The author, somewhat humorously in the topic sentence, refers to Radcleve as an "experimental chemist."

<u>Radcleve himself was a violent experimental chemist.</u>
When Radcleve was eight, he threw a whole package
of .22 shells against the sidewalk in front of his house
until one of them went off, driving lead fragments
into his calf, most of them still deep in there where
the surgeons never dared tamper. Radcleve knew
about the sulfur, potassium nitrate, and charcoal mixture for gunpowder when he was ten. He bought
things through the mail when he ran out of ingredients in his chemistry set. When he was an infant,
his father, a quiet man who owned the Chevrolet
agency in town, bought an entire bankrupt sporting-
goods store, and in the middle of their backyard he
built a house, plain-painted and neat, one room and
a heater, where Radcleve's redundant toys forever-
more were kept—all the possible toys he would need
for boyhood. There were things in there that Radcleve
and I were not mature enough for and did not know
the real use of. When we were eleven, we uncrated
the new Dunlop golf balls and went up on a shelf
for the tennis rackets, went out in the middle of his
yard, and served new golf ball after new golf ball with
blasts of the rackets over into the cornfield, out of
sight. When the strings busted we just went in and
got another racket. We were absorbed by how a good
smack would set the heavy little pills on an endless
flight. Then Radcleve's father came down. He simply
dismissed me. He took Radcleve into the house and
covered his whole body with a belt. But within the
week Radcleve had invented the mortar. It was a steel
pipe into which a flashlight battery fit perfectly, like
a bullet into a muzzle. He had drilled a hole for the
fuse of an M-80 firecracker at the base, for the charge.
It was a grand cannon, set up on a stack of bricks at
the back of my dad's property, which was the free

place to play. When it shot, it would back up violently with thick smoke and you could hear the flashlight battery whistling off.

From "Testimony of Pilot" by Barry Hannah

The preceding paragraph uses a single topic sentence at the very beginning of the paragraph. That sentence links together Radcleve, violence, and experimentation. The first sentence in the following paragraph sets a scene, but it does not contain the author's main idea about the pleasantness of the meetings. Sometimes a writer will use an introductory sentence that leads into the topic sentence. The two work as a pair to present the paragraph's main idea. Many writers work hard to design a single sentence that contains the paragraph's main idea.

At the end of each school day, for nearly six months, I would meet with her in the tiny room that served as the school's library but was actually only a storeroom for used textbooks and a vast collection of *National Geographics*. Everything about our sessions pleased me: the smallness of the room; the noise of the janitor's broom hitting the edge of the long hallway outside the door; the green of the sun, lighting the wall; and the old woman's face blurred white with a beard. Most of the time we took turns. I began with my elementary text. Sentences of astonishing simplicity seemed to me lifeless and drab: "The boys ran in the rain. . . . She wanted to sing. . . . The kite rose in the blue." Then the old nun would read from her favorite books, usually biographies of early American presidents. Playfully she ran through complex sentences, calling the words alive with her voice, making it seem that the author somehow was speaking directly to me. I smiled just to listen to her. I sat there and sensed for the very first time some possibility of

fellowship between a reader and a writer, a communication, never *intimate* like that I heard spoken words at home convey, but one nonetheless *personal.*
From The Hunger of Memory
by Richard Rodriguez

In this paragraph, the first sentence states the *topic* of the student's meeting with the teacher. The second sentence *restricts* the topic by emphasizing the pleasantness of the experience. The rest of the paragraph adds specific details to *illustrate* the ongoing activity and the boy's feelings. This pattern of topic, restriction, and illustration is often referred to as the TRI method for paragraph development.

Thinking Exercises

1. Use a specific fact, example, or detail to write at least a single sentence about each of the following: (a) why a photograph or poster pleases you; (b) what you like most about your favorite TV show; (c) when a good friend annoys you with a bad habit; (d) where you find the best place to relax; (e) how you feel on Sundays; (f) what in high school you disliked the most; and (g) three benefits of taking a certain class.

2. Begin a clustering exercise (see 1.3b) on one of the following: secret places, church, gluttony, pride, envy, anger, lust, fear, greed, or sloth. When you feel you have generated enough material for either a paragraph or a paper, write a sentence containing your main idea about the subject.

b. A numbering sentence can help organize a paragraph

A numbering sentence is a wonderful device for inexperienced writers. For example, the sentence "There are three ways to fail freshman composition" can control and direct an entire paragraph. The topic is presented, then limited, and a number is used to indicate how many points the paragraph covers. The following paragraph gives some indication of the clarity of a numbering sentence.

> <u>The two things that seem to occupy Conrad's imagination are loneliness and fear of what is strange.</u> *An Outcast of the Islands* like *The Heart of Darkness* is concerned with fear of what is strange. Both come together in the extraordinarily moving story called "Amy Foster." In this story a Slavic peasant, on his way to America, is the sole survivor of the wreck of his ship, and is cast away in a Kentish village. All the village fears and ill treats him, except Amy Foster, a dull, plain girl who brings him bread when he is starving and finally marries him. But she, too, when, in fever, her husband reverts to his native language, is seized with a fear of his strangeness, snatches up their child and abandons him. He dies alone and hopeless. I have wondered at times how much of this man's loneliness Conrad had felt among the English and had suppressed by a stern effort of will.
>
> *From "Joseph Conrad" by Bertrand Russell*

c. A topic sentence can follow a question

Some writers like to use a question to guide the paragraph into a discussion of the subject. The topic sentence follows soon after the question and indicates the paragraph's main idea. Because the question-answer format provides one of the basic structures of communication, most writers can profit from considering paragraphs in terms of a question seeking an answer. The following paragraph illustrates the linkage of a question with a topic sentence.

> <u>Does laughter have any beneficial effects? The evidence is mounting that it does.</u> Dr. William Fry of Stanford University School of Medicine, who is one of the leading researchers in this field, points to the fact that laughter enhances respiration and stimulates the endocrine system. Drs. Jonathan Levine and Howard Fields of the University of California, San Francisco have done research showing that laughter stimulates endorphin and encephalin activity, thus accounting for the phenomenon frequently observed that hearty belly laughter sometimes sets the stage for pain-free sleep. Meanwhile, there seems to be little doubt that the physical activity induced by laughter is a form of internal jogging that confers benefits of its own.
>
> *From "Laughter" by Norman Cousins*

Thinking Exercises

1. Following the example below, narrow at least one of these general subjects: (a) overeating, (b) things to fear, (c) being bored, (d) physical exercise, (e) work, (f) music.

Subject	Sports	**Where**	Cammack Field
Who	Children	**Why**	Parental interference
What	Baseball	**How**	Objectionable behavior
When	This summer		

ASSIGNMENT I am going to write on the bad examples of sportsmanship shown by some of the parents.

2. Examine the following topic sentences in light of the questions who, what, when, where, why, and how. Then write at least one topic sentence of your own in imitation.

> a. When are children in school able to begin learning to write? Generally they are able to write much earlier than most people think.
> b. As a house pet, a pelican has three undesirable characteristics.
> c. The first day in Mr. Beck's English class surprises most students.
> d. Some chores around the house I dislike, but others I despise.

d. Topic sentences can be improved

A topic sentence looks in two directions. One, it links all sentences back to it and to the purpose of the entire writing assignment. Two, it links together all the sentences in the paragraph as they move forward developing that purpose. Skillful writers work to design effective topic sentences.

A topic sentence has work to do in the paragraph. It presents the subject, states the main idea, expresses an attitude toward the subject, and flows into the rest of the paragraph. To accomplish all these goals, writers constantly revise their topic sentences. Writers can improve most topic sentences by focusing and clarifying. Notice the differences in the following examples. The first sentence illustrates a weak topic sentence. The second shows some improvement, but the third—although not excellent—is a workable topic sentence. The third sentence could lead to a paper on the subject of sound effects in the poem.

GENERAL   Poetry has wonderful sounds.

SPECIFIC   Poe's poem, "The Bells," has interesting sounds.

FOCUSED   Poe's poem, "The Bells," uses many devices to create different sound effects.

One effective way to improve a paragraph is to clarify the topic sentence and develop the other sentences in light of the main idea in the topic sentence. The following suggestions for improving topic sentences can help most writers create workable topic sentences.

Be specific. Focus in some particular manner on a person, place, time, action, or subject.

GENERAL   Many occupations are dangerous.

SPECIFIC   The work of miners is quite dangerous.

FOCUSED   For years underground mining of coal has been one of the most dangerous jobs in America.

The preceding example moves from the vagueness of "occupations" to the limitation of "underground mining of coal."

Use a rhetorical signal. Include in the topic sentence a key word such as *cause, effect, comparison, contrast, description, question, problem, difficulty,* or *example* to indicate the mode of thought and pattern of development.

GENERAL   College life is different.

SPECIFIC   Living in a dorm is a different experience.

FOCUSED   Coping with a new roommate presents three problems for many freshmen.

Effective topic sentences set up a contract with the reader. In this case, the sentence about living in a dormitory might introduce material explaining the causes of new emotions.

Divide the subject. Find the significant parts. Emphasize those elements.

GENERAL   Jobs now require writing skills.

SPECIFIC   Many business jobs today require writing skills.

FOCUSED   Students might not believe it, but many jobs in business require good writing skills, and accounting is one good example.

The improvement in this case results from a limitation to business writing and a further focus on accounting.

Thinking Exercises

1. Revise the following sentences in two ways. First, limit the sentence in some way; then add a sentence of restriction.

ORIGINAL   Dancers are graceful.
LIMITATION   Ballet dancers are graceful.
RESTRICTION   Ballet dancers are graceful. Nijinski's grace, however, surpassed all expectations.

a. Trash is everywhere today.
b. Clouds are fascinating.
c. Sports teach certain values.
d. Pets are fun.
e. Natural disasters cause great damage.
f. People like animals.
g. Schoolchildren can be humorous.
h. College is hard.

2. Revise each of the following in two ways: first, into a numbering sentence and second, into a question.

ORIGINAL   Writing is hard.

NUMBERING SENTENCE   Three things make essay exams difficult.

QUESTION   Why are essay exams so difficult for some students?

a. Children do not think like adults.
b. Some people dislike reading.
c. Some people hate religion.
d. Sports are becoming too violent.
e. Vacations are fun.
f. People are confused about sex.
g. Vacations are no fun.

e. Topic sentences appear in different places

Writers insert topic sentences at different places within their paragraphs. Theoretically, a writer can place a topic sentence, or other controlling sentence, anywhere in a paragraph, and some writers even omit the topic sentence from some paragraphs. Readers appreciate clear topic sentences, and most writers use them. Several suitable locations for such sentences are at the beginning, at the end, or at both the beginning and end.

Topic sentence at beginning

A few examples will show that some emotions and physical problems are symptoms of depression in young people. At the school I visited, the youngest in the group, Kyle, age seven, reported the persistent feeling of deep sadness, saying, "I feel as if the sadness made my body heavier than iron." Mary, who just turned twelve, expressed a self-hatred. In one of her many writings about herself, she said, "If anyone thought I was anything more than garbage, I would be afraid of that person." Thirteen-year-old Nelson discussed his sleep problems by stating, "It takes a year to fall asleep for ten minutes." Jane, the oldest in the group and just sixteen, confided that she didn't think she could ever be thin enough. Having lost more than twenty pounds in several months, she was damaging her health by refusing to eat anything more in a single day than Jell-O and Ritz crackers.

Ward Epson

Topic sentence at end

The streets and sidewalks surrounding the library are continually coated with a thin layer of oozy mud. One hundred parking places have been removed. Students living in Baker Hall have to walk two blocks out of their way because one worker erected a barricade in order to ensure himself a parking place every morning. Female students endure continual harassment by swaggering and vulgar workmen. *The process of constructing the new Science Building has created many problems for students.*

Jolene Henders

Topic sentences at beginning and end

The science of predicting the weather has improved during recent years. This improvement results mainly from the use of satellite photography. From great heights, cameras can photograph vast areas of Earth. By comparing these photographs, scientists chart the paths of large storm systems. Radar has also proven valuable in showing smaller storm systems. In addition to radar and photography, scientists have collected vast amounts of data on the weather. Using this data, meteorologists create computer models to predict changes in weather. *People still complain about the weather, but recent improvements in meteorology enable scientists to accurately predict the weather.*

Javier Miro

Topic sentence omitted but implied

During practice, Larry Bird has been able to connect on more than a hundred free throws in a row. During games, he only connects on 85% of his free throws. Bird can score easily from the perimeter and in some almost magical way manages to thread himself through a thicket of much taller players on his way to a successful reverse spinning lay-up. His pump fake is so effective that he has been able to make opponents lurch and fall to the ground. Because he scores at will, the opposing team will key on him during a fast break, enabling him to make one of his pinpoint last-second passes.

Ted Stanley

NOTE: **Some instructors insist that each paragraph have a directly stated topic sentence.**

f. Topic sentences should be placed carefully

- ✎ Placement of the topic sentence should vary from paragraph to paragraph.
- ✎ The topic sentence at the beginning of the paragraph emphasizes the paragraph's main idea.
- ✎ The topic sentence at the end of the paragraph emphasizes the examples and allows the reader to slowly discover the paragraph's main point.
- ✎ For emphasis, repeat the initial topic sentence at the very end of the paragraph, but do this rarely.
- ✎ To vary the pattern and to create interest in the main idea, present one or two examples before stating the topic sentence in the middle of the paragraph.
- ✎ When the paragraph's main point is clearly obvious from the examples presented, the topic sentence may be omitted. However, some instructors require a direct statement of the topic sentence in each paragraph.

2.4 Evidence and support in paragraphs

Effective writing uses evidence to support the main idea. Good evidence is material, from any available source, that will enable a reader to say, "I see what the writer is saying and it makes sense." The evidence should be clear, relevant, and interesting. Although almost anything can be used as evidence, college instructors expect the writing to be objective and generally impersonal, unless the assignment calls for personal experience. Instructors and other readers look for specific details and specific facts to support the paragraph's main idea. The following sections discuss and illustrate some of the different kinds of material writers use for evidence or support.

a. Observation

The poet Wallace Stevens wrote, "Accuracy of observation is the equivalent of accuracy of thinking." Observation leads to the knowledge of concrete details, and the use of concrete details improves a person's writing. The ability to observe precise details helps a writer create emphatic sentences and avoid clichés. (See 21.6.) The following writing sample would have been impossible to write without accurate observation.

> The entire body of a tarantula, especially its legs, is thickly clothed with hair. Some of it is short and wooly, some long and stiff. Touching this body hair produces one of two distinct reactions. When the spider is hungry, it responds with an immediate and swift attack. At the touch of a cricket's antennae the tarantula seizes the insect so swiftly that a motion picture taken at the rate of 64 frames per second shows only the result and not the process of capture. But when the spider is not hungry, the stimulation of its hairs merely causes it to shake the touched limb. An insect can walk under its hairy belly unharmed.
>
> *From "The Spider and the Wasp"*
> *by Alexander Petrunkevitch*

b. Personal experience

Readers generally show interest in personal experience. They read for information and feel cheated by writing that lacks specific details. A believable report of personal experience can convince a reader of the author's knowledge and experience. The author of the following passage presents details to convey a troubling experience.

> That incident anticipates the shame and sexual inferiority I was to feel in later years because of my dark complexion. I was to grow up an ugly child. Or one who thought himself ugly. (*Feo.*) One night when I was eleven or twelve years old, I locked myself in the bathroom and carefully regarded my reflection in the mirror over the sink. Without any pleasure I studied my skin. I turned on the faucet. (In my mind I heard the swirling voices of aunts, and even my mother's voice, whispering incessantly about lemon juice solutions and dark, *feo* children.) With a bar of soap, I fashioned a thick ball of lather. I began soaping my arms. I took my father's straight razor out of the medicine cabinet. Slowly, with steady deliberateness, I put the blade against my flesh, pressed it as close as I could without cutting, and moved it up and down across my skin to see if I could get out, somehow lessen, the dark. All I succeeded in doing, however, was in shaving my arms bare of their hair. For as I noted with disappointment, the dark would not come out. It remained. Trapped. Deep in the cells of my skin.
> *From* The Hunger of Memory
> *by Richard Rodriguez*

c. Memory

Memory can form the basis for a paragraph. The memory can stand alone as personal experience or it can be used to support a general point. In relating a scene from memory, a writer must always consider the audience. Readers want a clear sense of reality and not a jumble of confused thoughts and feelings. When a writer uses plenty of concrete details to convey a memory, the reader will be able to see the scene and appreciate the writer's main point. The following paragraph presents its main idea in the first sentence and uses plenty of concrete details.

> Unlike the white high school, Lafayette County Training School distinguished itself by having neither lawn, nor hedges, nor tennis court, nor climbing ivy. Its two buildings (main classrooms, the grade school and home economics) were set on a dirt hill with no fence to limit either its boundaries or those of bordering farms. There was a large expanse to the left of the school which was used alternately as a baseball diamond or a basketball court. Rusty hoops on the swaying poles represented the permanent recreational equipment, although its bats and balls could be borrowed from the P.E. teacher if the borrower was qualified and if the diamond wasn't occupied.
>
> *From* I Know Why the Caged Bird Sings
> *by Maya Angelou*

d. Reading

Because experience, observation, and memory have their limits, people gain much of their knowledge from reading. This source can provide information to support and develop a main idea. The following example illustrates how a writer uses material gathered from reading to create an informative paragraph.

> Paris was at a standstill. The crowd had been waiting in the Place de la Révolution since early morning. It was not every day that a queen was executed. There was a nip in the air, but the crowd did not seem to notice as they waited silently for the arrival of the

hated Marie Antoinette. It was almost noon before the queen came into view. She was seated, her hands bound behind her back, in an open cart drawn by two plowhorses. After months of imprisonment her face was ashen; her eyes were bloodshot from weeping and fatigue. She seemed deaf to the crowd, even the taunts of the *tricoteuses*, the old women who were forever knitting on the steps of the church of Saint-Roche. The cart drew up before the scaffold. Marie Antoinette got down unassisted and climbed the steps to the guillotine. It was over quickly. At exactly quarter past twelve her head fell to "the national razor" and the executioner showed it to the crowd amid shouts of "Vive la République! Vive la Liberté!"

From "Terrorism" by Sandra Stencel
Reprinted from The Skeptic

Thinking Exercises

1. Make three lists of details that you might use to develop and explain the following statements:

    a. Music makes people feel in different ways.

    b. Being a teenager is different from being a child.

Have each list come from one different category: your personal experience, your observations, and your reading.

2. What is the relationship between observation, personal experience, and memory in the following paragraph?

In the afternoon of the day when I reached New Bedford, I visited the wharves, to take a view of the shipping. Here I found myself surrounded with the strongest proofs of wealth. Lying at the wharves, and riding in the stream, I saw many ships of the finest model, in the best order, and of the largest size. Upon the right and left, I was walled in by granite warehouses of the widest dimensions, stowed to their utmost capacity with the necessaries and comforts of life. Added to this, almost everybody seemed to be at work, but noiselessly so, compared with what I had been accustomed to in Baltimore. There were no loud songs heard from those engaged in loading and unloading ships. I heard no deep oaths or horrid curses on the laborer. I saw no shipping of men; but all seemed to go smoothly on. Every man appeared to understand his work, and went at it with a sober, yet cheerful earnestness, which betokened the deep interest which he felt in what he was doing, as well as a sense of his own dignity as man. To me this looked exceedingly strange. From the wharves I strolled around and over the town, gazing with wonder and admiration at the splendid churches, beautiful dwellings, and finely-cultivated gardens; evincing an amount of wealth, comfort, taste, and refinement, such as I had never seen in any part of slaveholding Maryland.

From Narrative of the Life of an American Slave
by Frederick Douglass

1.   Write at least one paragraph on one of the following topics:
>   a. The most startling thing you ever read
>   b. The strongest memory from your childhood
>   c. Something you could look at for days
>   d. The job of your dreams at $500 an hour.

2.   Write at least one paragraph imitating one of the paragraphs in chapter 2.

2.5 Arrangement in paragraphs

Writers organize their paragraphs in a number of different ways. There is no one "perfect" way to organize the material in a paragraph. Basically, narrative involves chronological order; description relies on spatial ordering; persuasion uses the order of importance; and informative prose functions with a general-to-specific or specific-to-general order. The organization in each paragraph should be sensible, logical, and clearly apparent. Although certain kinds of paragraphs (question-answer, problem-solution, comparison, contrast) have an organization built into the presentation of the material, most other kinds of writing are organized in one of the following ways.

a. Chronological order

A chronological order places material in a time sequence. Depending upon the purpose of the writing and the effect intended, writers will use time sequences that represent the material first-to-last, last-to-first, or middle-to-end.

Some writers occasionally use a flashback sequence, jumping from the present to the past or vice versa. A chronological order supports most fiction and journalism. The following example displays an order based on time.

> The last hour of her life was typical of its happiness. She came home from a day's work at school, topped off by a hard grind with the copy of the High School Annual, and felt that a ride would refresh her. She climbed into her khakis, chattering to her mother about the work she was doing, and hurried to get her horse and be out on the dirt roads for the country air and radiant green fields of the spring. As she rode through the town on an easy gallop she kept waving at passers-by. She knew everyone in town. For a decade the little figure with the long pigtail and the red hair ribbon has been familiar on the streets of Emporia, and she got in the way of speaking to those who nodded at her. She passed the Kerrs, walking the horse, in front of the Normal Library, and waved at them; passed another friend a few hundred feet further on, and waved at her. The horse was walking and as she turned into North Merchant Street she took off her cowboy hat, and the horse swung into a lope She passed the Tripletts and waved her cowboy hat at them, still moving gaily north on Merchant Street. A Gazette carrier passed—a High School boy friend— and she waved at him, but with her bridle hand; the horse veered quickly; plunged into the parking lot where the low hanging limb faced her, and, while she still looked back waving, the blow came. But she did not fall from the horse; she slipped off, dazed a bit, staggered and fell in a faint. She never quite recovered consciousness.
>
> *From "Mary White" by William Allen White*

b. Spatial order

The material in a paragraph may display a spatial order. Spatial ordering shows the position of items and their relationship, whose pattern forms the basis for paragraph organization. Some common spatial patterns include the arrangements from right to left, top to bottom, inside to outside, farthest to nearest, or vice versa. Occasionally a writer will use a geometrical pattern, such as a circle or triangle, to organize the material.

A spatial order can help the reader clearly visualize the material. To make the ordering clear, writers often use two kinds of common linking devices. One kind includes prepositional phrases, using prepositions such as *above*, *under*, *beside*, and *within*. A second kind includes transitional markers such as *here*, *in the distance*, or *to the right*. Such devices present clear signals to the reader and emphasize the paragraph's spatial ordering.

The following paragraphs show arrangements in a spatial order. In the first paragraph about the nervous young man, the writer wants the reader to know the man's location and position at all times. Notice how verbs and prepositional phrases make clear to the reader the man's motion or stillness. The second example, written by a student, shows the aftermath of a practical joke and relies on prepositional phrases and transitional markers.

> Haze turned and looked at the house he was going into. It was little more than a shack but there was a warm glow in one front window. He went up on the front porch and put his eye to a convenient crack in the shade, and found himself looking directly at a large white knee. After some time he moved away from the crack and tried the front door. It was not locked and he went into a small dark hall with a door

on either side of it. The door to the left was cracked and let out a narrow shaft of light. He moved into the light and looked through the crack.

From Wise Blood *By Flannery O'Connor*

The center of Larry Babendure's dorm room in Baker Hall suggested a tornado, but the weather had been clear for three days. Someone had pulled the old, moldy mattress from the top bunk bed and dragged it to the center of the room. The ruined mattress looked like the carcass of a murdered chicken. On top of the mattress lay a three-foot pile of wet newspapers. Resting on top of the papers was a gigantic white glob resembling whipped cream or shaving foam. Next to this quivering mess lay a fire extinguisher completely empty of spray foam. On the single wall mirror and on both windows, someone using a bar of soap had written, "Too Bad Larry. Happy Halloween."

Scooter Bigsbee

c. Order of importance

Not all the items in a paragraph have equal value or weight. Importance depends on purpose and audience. Some writers arrange the material in a paragraph from least important to most important; however, other writers might reverse that order. Readers of newspapers expect to find the most important material at the beginning of the article. Readers of argumentative essays expect to find the most important material toward the end. When you arrange the items in a paragraph, think of your main idea, and trust your sense of each item's importance. If you have a problem in deciding the order of importance, consider the main point of your paragraph and try to imagine the order that would help your reader the most. The following paragraph by Bertrand Russell presents in a clear three-part order his ideas on the importance of love.

> I have sought love, first, because it brings ecstasy—ecstasy so great that I would often have sacrificed all the rest of life for a few hours of this joy. I have sought it, next, because it relieves loneliness—that terrible loneliness in which one shivering consciousness looks over the rim of the world into the cold unfathomable lifeless abyss. I have sought it, finally, because in the union of love I have seen, in a mystic miniature, the prefiguring vision of the heaven that saints and poets have imagined. This is what I sought, and though it might seem too good for human life, this is what—at last—I have found.
>
> *From* Autobiography *by Bertrand Russell*

d. General-to-specific order

In general-to-specific order, a general statement is at the beginning of the paragraph. Such a topic sentence focuses on the subject and restricts it in some significant way. The rest of the paragraph develops the main idea, supporting it with specific details, facts, and examples. The following paragraph shows this kind of order, and in a detached, impersonal language describes an autistic child.

> *Joey was convinced that machines were better than people.* Once when he bumped into one of the pipes on our jungle gym he kicked it so violently that his teacher had to restrain him to keep him from injuring himself. When she explained that the pipe was much harder than his foot, Joey replied: "That proves it. Machines are better than the body. They don't break; they're much harder and stronger." If he lost or forgot

something, it merely proved that his brain ought to be thrown away and replaced by machinery. If he spilled something, his arm should be broken and twisted off because it did not work properly. When his head or arm failed to work as it should, he tried to punish it by hitting it. Even Joey's feelings were mechanical. Much later in his therapy, when he had formed a timid attachment to another child and had been rebuffed, Joey cried: "He broke my feelings."

From "Joey the Mechanical Boy"
by Bruno Bettelheim

e. Specific-to-general order

When using specific-to-general order, the writer moves from specific details to a general statement. The general statement serves as the natural climax to an accumulation of evidence. In this way the evidence speaks for itself. The following paragraph illustrates this kind of arrangement.

College dictionaries pose problems for students. They are too bulky. They have incredibly small print, and this fact discourages their use. In addition, students with spelling problems find dictionaries difficult and frustrating. Many students have no way of knowing how to tackle a difficult word such as *aphrodisiac* or *psychotic*. Because these dictionaries rely heavily on unexplained symbols and abbreviations, such books lack value for some freshmen seeking help with pronunciation or etymology. To make matters worse, many collegiate dictionaries have abandoned labels for slang or nonstandard usage. *Although college dictionaries contain valuable information, many students have problems using them and need instruction in their use.*

Anna M. Johansen

Thinking Exercises

1. Rearrange the sentences in the following paragraph into a general-to-specific order.

> I noticed eyes that were blurred, faded, opaque, or bloodshot. There were many toothless mouths (I counted seventy-eight). I saw faces that were wrinkled, or bloated, or raw as the surface of a peeled plum. Several of the middle-aged and the old looked healthy and well preserved. There were good faces, particularly among the young. But the damaged and decayed faces were in the majority. Some of the noses were purple and swollen, some broken, some pitted with enlarged pores. *I began evaluating my fellow tramps as human material, and for the first time in my life I became face-conscious.* I was struck by the fact that the old men, even the very old, showed their age mainly in their face.
>
> *Rearranged from* Working
> *by Studs Terkel*

2. Make a list of at least six bits of information about one of the following subjects: (a) a serious social problem, (b) your feelings for someone you have not seen for some time, (c) how advertising controls behavior, (d) the artist as a free spirit. After compiling the list of details, organize the information in at least two of the different ways mentioned in this chapter.

Writing Assignments

1.   Identify some policy or activity at your school or in your community that you would like to see changed or halted. Make a list of the ways that the change might occur. Write the draft of a brief letter to a good friend encouraging that person to join you in changing or halting the policy or activity. After finishing the draft, outline the material, and examine its order. Make sure the final draft has adequate material and consistent order.

2.   Write the draft of a paragraph about a time you were totally confused about someone or something. Explain the situation so a reader can understand what happened and why you were confused. In the revision, focus on creating a smooth narrative flow and clear chronological order.

2.6 Unity in paragraphs

Effective writing has unity both in the whole and in the parts. Imagine trying to sing three different songs at the same time. Skillful writers want to avoid difficulties for their readers. They know that readers want paragraphs to have unity and make sense. Part of a paragraph's basic unity arises from the subject and the main idea. However, writers use other strategies to create unified, meaningful paragraphs. The most common kinds include the unities of place, subject, time, action, and person.

a. Unity of place

A focus on one single place benefits both writer and reader. Unity improves readability and comprehension. A reader can understand a paragraph with four facts about one place more easily than a paragraph with four facts about four different places. The writer of the following paragraph has observed very carefully the activity occurring in one place. The paragraph shows how a limited focus can help a writer produce effective writing.

> One recent evening, we spent an interesting couple of hours observing the fate of a strip of wet concrete that lay unprotected in front of the Food City on Columbus Avenue at Seventieth Street. . . . In the time we spent in front of Food City—which was closed for the night, its dimmed lights giving a lunar glow to a line of honeydew melons in the window—we saw in the behavior of passersby a sort of small drama of conscience. We saw Columbus Avenue strollers succumb to the temptation to write in the concrete; we saw temptation pondered and successfully resisted; and we saw manifestations of outrage at those who had succumbed. As the evening fleets of taxis raced down the avenue toward midtown, we watched a well-groomed man of perhaps sixty, wearing a pinstriped summer-weight suit and carrying a briefcase with gold initials on the side, pause, stare at the concrete, and then, without a hint of self-consciousness, bend down in a dignified swooping motion and scratch two initials with the end of a pen that he produced from his jacket pocket. (We couldn't see if the letters were the same as those on his briefcase.) He studied his handiwork for a second and then walked briskly away. A young man with thinning curly

hair who was wearing a Pac-Man T-shirt stepped in a gingerly fashion into the center of the concrete with his eight- or nine-year-old daughter, who had blond braids and was wearing starched overalls and a battery-powered light-up visor. They began writing their names. "Put a heart around mine, Daddy, please?" said the little girl, hopping up and down.

From "The Talk of the Town"
in The New Yorker

b. Unity of subject

Everyone can understand the unity of subject in a paragraph, but many writers have a tendency to veer away from the subject. Effective writers work hard to ensure that each paragraph sticks to one subject or one aspect of a subject. Unrelated sentences, no matter how interesting, need to be excluded. Although the following paragraph gives a multitude of examples, it sticks to its main subject, the smoke in a nineteenth-century mill town.

The idiosyncrasy of this town is smoke. It rolls sullenly in small folds from the great chimneys of the iron foundries, and settles down in black, slimy pools on the muddy streets. Smoke is on the wharves, on the dingy boats, on the yellow river—clinging in a coating of greasy soot to the house front, the two faded poplars, the faces of the passersby. The long train of mules, dragging masses of pig-iron through the narrow street, have a foul vapor hanging to their reeking sides. Here, inside, is a little broken figure of an angel pointing upward from the mantel shelf; but even its wings are covered with smoke, clotted and black. Smoke is everywhere! A dirty canary chirps desolately in a cage beside me. Its dream of green fields and sunshine is a very old dream—almost worn out, I think.

> *From "Life in the Iron Mills"*
> *by Rebecca Harding Davis*

c. Unity of time

The unity of time in a paragraph might include a minute, an hour, a day, a month, or even a longer period. A paragraph with several related details or examples about a subject, focusing on one particular time, has unity. Readers appreciate the care and attention shown in a paragraph unified in terms of time. A paragraph discussing simultaneously a subject at two different times resembles a double negative in photography. Such a blurring damages clarity and precision. The following paragraph presents a number of clear, specific details. It focuses on a certain time, a few minutes after supper on a summer evening.

> Supper was at six and was over by half past. There was still daylight, shining softly and with a tarnish, like the lining of a shell; and the carbon lamps lifted at the corners were on in the light, and locusts were started, and the fire flies were out, and a few frogs were flopping in the dewy grass, by the time the fathers and the children came out. The children ran out first hell-bent and yelling those names by which they were known; then the fathers sank out leisurely in crossed suspenders, their collars removed and their necks looking tall and shy. The mothers stayed back in the kitchen washing and drying, putting things away, recrossing their traceless footsteps like the lifetime journeys of bees, measuring out the dry

cocoa for breakfast. When they came out they had taken off their aprons and their skirts were dampened and they sat in rockers on their porches quietly.

From A Death in the Family
by James Agee

d. Unity of action

Many paragraphs contain the details of one complete action. If the details fit together and form a unity, then the paragraph will make sense to a reader. If the details do not fit together, the reader will be confused. Unifying the action in a paragraph improves readability. The following paragraph attempts to make the reader see clearly and precisely an unusual event. Notice the rigorous focus and the clarity of perception, both of which help to unify the action.

One night a moth flew into the candle, was caught, burnt dry, and held. I must have been staring at the candle, or maybe I looked up when a shadow crossed my page; at any rate, I saw it all. A golden female moth, a biggish one with a two-inch wingspan, flapped into the fire, dropped her abdomen into the wet wax, stuck, flamed, frazzled and fried in a second. Her moving wings ignited like tissue paper, enlarging the circle of light in the clearing and creating out of the darkness the sudden blue sleeves of my sweater, the green leaves of jewelweed by my side, the ragged red trunk of pine. At once the light contracted again and the moth's wings vanished in a fine, foul smoke. At the same time her six legs clawed, curled, blackened, and ceased, disappearing utterly. And her head jerked in spasms, making a spattering noise; her antennae crisped and burned away and her heaving mouth parts crackled like pistol fire. When it was all over, her head was, so far as I could determine, gone, gone the long way of her wings and legs. Had she been new, or old? Had she mated and laid her eggs, had she done her work? All that was left was the glowing horn shell of her abdomen and thorax—a fraying, partially collapsed gold tube jammed upright in the candle's round pool.

From Holy the Firm
by Annie Dillard

e. Unity of person

Like all the other unities listed earlier, unity of person helps both the writer and reader. It leads to clarity and emphasis. The following section of a paragraph by James Baldwin looks at its subject from a variety of different time frames and different points of view, but it continues from beginning to end to discuss one person, the writer's father.

He was, I think, very handsome. I gather this from photographs and from my own memories of him, dressed in his Sunday best and on his way to preach a sermon somewhere, when I was little. Handsome, proud, and ingrown, "like a toe-nail," somebody said. But he looked to me, as I grew older, like pictures I had seen of African tribal chieftains: he really should have been naked, with war-paint on and barbaric mementos, standing among spears. He could be chilling in the pulpit and indescribably cruel in his personal life and he was certainly the most bitter man I have ever met; yet it must be said that there was something else in him, buried in him, which lent him his tremendous power and, even, a rather crushing charm. It had something to do with his blackness, I think— he was very black—with his blackness and his beauty,

and with the fact that he knew that he was black but
did not know that he was beautiful.

From Notes of a Native Son
by James Baldwin

2.7 Coherence and linkage in paragraphs

The words *coherence* and *linkage* refer to the grammatical
and logical connections between words and phrases. In a
well-written paragraph the individual sentences are linked
together by a number of different devices to form a coherent unit of meaning. Most writers use several direct and
indirect ways to create coherence and linkage in their paragraphs. The most common strategies involve coordination, subordination, repetition, and transitional markers.

a. Coordination

In terms of paragraphing, coordination refers to sentences
that have approximately equal value in the paragraph and
that generally display parallel structure. Coordinate sentences have a kind of equality among themselves with the
same approximate level of abstraction or concreteness.
Quite often coordinate sentences have one idea expressed
in a main clause. The following short student paragraph
contains mostly coordinate sentences. The listing of facts
creates a parallel pattern for the paragraph.

> I began smoking a pack of cigarettes a day. I learned
> how to waste time hanging out at Tiner's Drive-In. I
> discovered how good beer can taste. I encountered
> the pleasures associated with mildly illegal drugs. I
> acquired the ability to pass my courses with a mini-

mum exertion of energy. In short, I developed bad habits and wasted three of the best years of my life in a state of coma.

Jim Ray Harpeth

The linkages between sentences can be diagrammed. The following kind of diagram, developed by Francis Christensen, shows the relationship among sentences. This method of diagramming is especially effective in showing the levels of generality and the levels of specificity of the sentences in a paragraph. Notice how the sentences in the following paragraphs have been numbered. Each sentence receives a number. The first sentence always has number 1. If the next sentence is coordinate, it receives the same number. If, however, the next sentence is either subordinate or at a higher level of generality, it is indented to the right and receives the next higher number.

1. I began smoking a pack of cigarettes a day.
1. I learned how to waste time hanging out at Tiner's Drive-In.
1. I discovered how good beer can taste.
1. I encountered the pleasures associated with mildly illegal drugs.
1. I acquired the skill to pass courses with a minimum exertion of energy.
   2. In short, I developed bad habits and wasted three of the best years of my life in a state of coma.

b. Subordination

Some paragraphs use a pattern of subordination. A subordinate sentence develops an idea contained in a preceding sentence. Some sentences are more general, others more specific. However, a main idea or topic sentence is always more general than the supporting sentences. Supporting sentences are always subordinate. The following paragraph contains a good deal of subordination, and the subsequent diagram clearly shows the subordination, co-ordination, and generality present in the paragraph.

> Most coaches are models of virtue, but some have major weaknesses in character. Fred Granger has coached successfully for ten years at Murphy High. His football teams always have good records. Last year his team won all its games and was ranked fifth in the state. One word best describes Coach Granger, *angry*. He is angry with players and nonathletes, angry on the field and off the field. During one game he became so angry with an official that he was ordered off the field. Stories of mistreated players have become legendary. In addition to his uncontrollable anger, Coach Granger has a love of drinking. On two occasions he was arrested for drunken driving. One time he overturned his sports car in the Byrd Park Rose Garden. A second time he smashed into a light pole and destroyed his Jeep. How he stays alive and how he keeps his job are minor miracles.
>
> *Roseanne Jackson*

1. Most coaches are models of virtue, but some have major weaknesses in character.
   2. Fred Granger has coached successfully for ten years at Murphy High.
      3. His football teams always have good records.
      3. Last year his team won all its games and was ranked fifth in the state.
         4. One word best describes Coach Granger, *angry*.
            5. He is angry with players and nonathletes, angry on the field and off the field.

5. During one game he became so angry with an official that he was ordered off the field.

5. Stories of mistreated players have become legendary.

6. In addition to his uncontrollable anger, Coach Granger has a love of drinking.

7. On two occasions he was arrested for drunken driving.

8. One time, he overturned his sports car in the Byrd Park Rose Garden.

8. A second time, he smashed into a light pole and destroyed his Jeep.

9. How he stays alive and how he keeps his job are minor miracles.

Thinking Exercises

1. Discuss the preceding paragraph and diagram, particularly the relationship in the levels of generality and specificity between number 4 and the number 5s; and between 7 and the 8s.

2. Diagram two paragraphs in 2.5d and 2.5e using the Christensen method.

Writing Assignments

1. Select a brief narrative from your journal and revise it so that the sentences are primarily coordinate.

2. Combine the following sentences to create several longer sentences.

> It was a very proper wedding. The bride was elegantly dressed. The two bridesmaids were duly inferior. Her father gave her away. Her mother stood with salts in her hands, expecting to be agitated. Her aunt tried to cry, and the service was impressively read by Dr. Grant.
>
> *Jane Austen*

c. Repetition

Coherent paragraphs inevitably contain certain kinds of repetition. The structural device of repetition links the thoughts together. In most paragraphs, the common forms of repetition are nouns, pronouns, and synonyms. Effective repetition links sentence to sentence and makes the parts of the paragraph cohere, or stick together.

Repetition of nouns. As the following example shows, the repetition of nouns provides an effective way to link different sentences together.

We walked down the path to the well-house, attracted by the fragrance of the honeysuckle with which it was covered. Some one was drawing water and my teacher placed my hand under the spout. As the cool stream gushed over one hand she spelled into the other the word water first slowly, then rapidly. I stood still, my whole attention fixed upon the motions of her fingers. Suddenly I felt a misty consciousness as of something forgotten—a thrill of returning thought; and somehow the mystery of language was revealed to me. I knew then that "w-a-t-e-r" meant that wonderful cool something that was flowing over my hand. That living word awakened my soul, gave it light, hope, joy, set it free!

From *The Story of My Life* by Helen Keller

Repetition of pronouns. Pronouns function in sentences as noun substitutes. Pronouns form links within sentences, from sentence to sentence, and across sentences.

In the late 1920's my mother ran away from home to marry my father. Marriage, if not running away, was expected of seventeen-year-old girls. By the time she was twenty, she had two children and was pregnant with a third. Five children later, I was born. And this is how I came to know my mother: she seemed a large, soft, loving-eyed woman who was rarely impatient in our home. Her quick, violent temper was on view only a few times a year, when she battled with the white landlord who had the misfortune to suggest to her that her children did not need to go to school.

From *In Search of Our Mother's Gardens* by Alice Walker

Repetition of synonyms. A synonym's meaning is the same or almost the same as the meaning of another word. Writers use synonyms for explanation and for sentence variety. Synonyms link words across sentences. They tie different sentences together to form a tightly structured paragraph. The following paragraph about starving prisoners in a Russian concentration camp includes a number of interesting synonyms.

> In 1949 some friends and I came upon a noteworthy news item in *Nature,* a magazine of the Academy of Sciences. It reported in tiny type that in the course of excavations on the Kolyma River a subterranean ice lens had been discovered which was actually a frozen stream—and in it were found frozen specimens of prehistoric fauna some tens of thousands of years old. Whether fish or salamander these were preserved in so fresh a state, the scientific correspondent reported, that those present immediately broke open the ice encasing the specimens and devoured them with relish on the spot.
>
> *From* The Gulag Archipelago
> *by Aleksandr Solzhenitsyn*

Thinking Exercises

1. Form coherent paragraphs from each of the following collections of sentences by placing the italicized general statement at the beginning of its paragraph and then arranging the sentences to develop the general statement.

a. There is one sort, very coarse, often irregular in thickness, used to form the permanent frame of the web, and another, very even in diameter, by which mistress spider lets herself down and up. There is a thick, often bright or heavily colored silk in which the eggs are encased—a sort of baby blanket for cold nights. It is much too beautiful and too sticky! *Spiders have a silk to meet every need and emergency of their lives.* But for these guests she reserves quite a different kind, on which she would not dream of setting foot. There is a dry cord for the radial lines on which the spider runs out to meet her dinner guests.

Rearranged from "Spider Silk"
by Donald Culross Peattie

b. If you *looked* like you were going to make an error, she'd let you have it with anything handy, fists, an eraser, a ruler. That I do remember her and have written about her speaks for itself. Because of Miss Wooley, I make my eights from the wrong side. *I'd almost forgotten about Miss Wooley, whose name and image now come raging back without hesitation.* I know it's easy to place psychological blame on the past, but the truth of the matter is that Miss Wooley scared me and ruined my capacity to deal effectively with numbers. She taught arithmetic. Miss Wooley was one of those experiences I could not outgrow.

Rearranged from "Roots of Black Awareness"
by John A. Williams

Writing Assignments

1. Write at least one paragraph about some natural process, such as nest building or web weaving, common to a particular, nonhuman, animal species. Base your rough draft on direct observation or inspection of pictures. In revising toward the final copy, examine the draft in terms of careful and effective repetition.

2. Write at least one paragraph about a teacher who praised you or caused you some discomfort. Be as specific as you can in answering questions such as who, what, when, where, why, and how. In revising, avoid needless repetition and try to find effective synonyms.

d. Transitional markers

Writers use transitional markers to signal a change in person, place, action, emphasis, or thought. These markers provide important information for the reader about an upcoming change. Transitional markers function within sentences, between sentences, and between paragraphs.

Transitional markers within sentences. Writers use these words to signal meaning and structure to the reader. Sentence adverbs, coordinating conjunctions, subordinating conjunctions, and prepositions serve a transitional function in sentences. Such function words and phrases show the relationships among the parts in a sentence. The student author of the following argumentative paragraph has used a number of transitional markers indicating time and place to link the sentences into a cohesive paragraph.

Fun Week *here at school* should be renamed "Grief Week" *and then* outlawed. What is "fun" about violence? *Last year*, five students were injured seriously enough in a fight to be hospitalized for days. *The year before*, the fireworks blew out one student's eye and left another student completely deaf. What is "fun" about gluttony *and* drunkenness? What is "fun" about the huge messes created on campus? *This year*, a work crew slaved for several days to clean up the garbage on South Lawn, *and* they have *yet* to repair the broken windows on the north side of the Student Center. *Although* Fun Week collects $5,000 for needy children, this school would be better off *next year* taxing each student twenty-five cents *and* donating that $5,000 to charity.

Miriam Schwartz

Transitional markers between sentences. These function words and phrases can help a writer to arrange material in a paragraph. Some common and useful signals are the words *first*, *second*, and *third*. These markers present an order to the reader and help show relationships between the sentences in a paragraph. Notice the transitional words that signal time in the following paragraph.

The life story of the bee begins with the tiny white egg that the queen lays in a cell of the honeycomb. The egg stands up straight and is glued at one end to the bottom of the cell. After three days a little white grub hatches from it and is continuously fed by worker bees. It grows until it fills almost the entire cell. The bees then cap the cell with a mixture of wax and pollen which is porous enough to allow the air to circulate. Meanwhile the larva lines the cell walls with a fine silken cocoon, within which it changes to pupa. After gnawing through cocoon and cell cap, the full-grown bee emerges.

Stella Center

Transitional markers between paragraphs. Readers expect paragraphs to flow together smoothly. They dislike having to stop at the end of each paragraph and begin again at the start of the next. Awkward transitions can create a jerky effect, resembling the ride in a bumper car at a carnival. Although writers use a wide variety of methods to ensure smooth transitions between paragraphs, two devices seem most effective: the repetition of a word, phrase, or idea, and the brief transitional paragraph. The following paragraphs illustrate the use of careful repetition to link two paragraphs.

> Many years ago a friend of mine took a room in an obscure hotel in the heart of the city. There was a blaze of street lights outside, and a few shadows. He had opened the window and retired, he told me, when something soft and heavy dropped on his feet as he lay stretched out in bed. Though he admittedly was startled, it occurred to him that the creature on his legs might be a friendly tomcat from the fire escape. He tried to estimate the weight of the crouched body from under his blankets and resisted the frightened impulse to spring up. He spoke soothingly into the dark, for he liked cats, and reached for a match at his bedside table.
>
> The match flared, and in that moment a sewer rat as big as a house cat sat up on its haunches and glared into the match flame with pink demoniac eyes. That one match flare, so my friend told me afterward, seemed to last the lifetime of the human race. Then the match went out and he simultaneously hurtled from the bed. From his incoherent account of what happened afterwards, I suspect that both rat and man left by the window but fortunately, perhaps, not at the same instant. That sort of thing, you know, is like getting a personal message from the dark. You are apt to remember it a lifetime.
>
> From *The Night Country* by Loren Eiseley

List of common transitional signals

Addition or amplification. Again, also, and, and then, besides, further, furthermore, in addition, more, moreover, next, too.

Cause or effect. Accordingly, as a result, because, consequently, for this purpose, hence, since, then, therefore, thereupon, thus, to this end, with this object.

Chronological order. After a while, afterward, again, as long as, as quick as, as soon as, at last, at length, at that time, at the same time, before, earlier, final, finally, first (second, third), formerly, from now, immediately, in the meantime, in the past (present, future), lately, later, meanwhile, now, presently, shortly, simultaneously, since, so far, soon, subsequently, then, thereafter, today, tomorrow, until now, when, while, yesterday.

Comparison. Also, as, comparably, in like manner, in the same manner, in the same way, like, likewise, similarly.

Contrast, opposition, conflict. Although, and yet, but, but at the same time, conversely, despite, different, differently, even so, even though, for all that, however, in contrast, in spite of, nevertheless, notwithstanding, on the contrary, on the other hand, otherwise, regardless, still, though, to contrast, unfortunately, whereas, yet.

Emphasis, summary, conclusion. All in all, altogether, as has been noted, finally, in brief, in conclusion, in other words, in particular, in short, in simpler terms, in summary, of course, on the whole, once again, that is, therefore, to be sure, to conclude, to emphasize, to repeat, to state it differently, to summarize, to sum up.

Example. An illustration of, as an example, for example, for instance, indeed, in fact, specifically, that is, to illustrate.

Numerical order. First, second, third, fourth, finally, in the first place, in the second place, in the third place, last, next, to begin with, to start with, finally, also.

Purpose. Intentionally, for this purpose, to this end, with this in mind, with this intent, with this object.

Qualification. Although, but, however, if, I recognize, in this case, it may be that, it seems, naturally, nonetheless, perhaps, possibly, probably, somewhat, to some extent.

Reminder. As stated, as presented earlier, as we have seen, as the next section will show.

Spatial order. Above, adjacent to, at the top (bottom), behind, below, beyond, elsewhere, farther on, here, in back, in front, in the distance, near, nearby, on the opposite side, on the other side, opposite to, there, to the east (west, north, south), to the left (right, center).

2.8 Forming larger units

Although paragraphs resemble miniature compositions, and although paragraphs function as units in final examinations, letters, and newspaper articles, the most common use of the paragraph involves larger units such as essays, reports, or chapters. Most often in college writing, paragraphs are expected to connect to each other and form larger units.

These larger units vary in size. The length of a complete work, whether essay or book, depends on the writer's purpose and audience. A book on Elvis Presley, for example needs pages and chapters of paragraphs to build a large-scale psychological portrait. An essay by a student trying to persuade her mother to visit a doctor requires more than one paragraph listing and developing her reasons. The following selection comes from a lengthy book on Elvis Presley. In that book, which some people consider unfair, the author describes Presley's plane in great detail. The selection from the Elvis book contains an abundance of specific details and witty observations.

In this case a larger meaning depends on a succession of paragraphs: bite-size chunks of thought that a reader can easily grasp and understand. The following selection gives some sense of how paragraphs work in groups to organize and create a larger unit of thought. Careful paragraphing is an effective way to organize ideas and present meaning in larger topics.

Elvis Presley's Plane

Elvis likes to boast that he is the only entertainer ever to own for his personal use a four-engine jet airliner. He acquired the big plane to mark his fortieth birthday, his original intention being to fly about the world in an exact replica of *Air Force One*. When he discovered that the cheapest Boeing 707 on the market was $888,000 and that customizing it to suit his tastes would bring the cost up to a million and a half dollars, he yielded to reality to the extent of purchasing a plane that was fifteen feet shorter: a Convair 880 that had carried ninety-six passengers when it was owned by Delta Airlines. When you run your eye along the great white hull of the royal coach, you're reminded instantly of *Air Force One* because the plane bears the same broad red and blue band from nose to tail. Elvis was chagrined by the fact that he could not have the glittering silver hull of the presidential plane. . . .

What Elvis demanded for his travels was a flying hotel suite. The forward cabin is a very plushy, oddly effeminate club room, furnished with two long curving bench sofas covered with fat cushions of crushed velour, one aquamarine, the other chocolate brown. The plush aqua carpet catches the light from the arch ceiling, which is padded with canary yellow vinyl. Along both sides of the cabin run continuous bands of short drapes, like cafe curtains, made of fabric dyed like bull's-eyes of blue, orange and brown stained glass. The club room contains also some card tables, leather lounge chairs, TV monitors and a fifteen-thousand-dollar quadraphonic sound system.

Behind this room is the dining-conference room, which is furnished with six huge leather spaceman chairs ranged along either side of a surfboard-shaped Danish modern table with a green leather surface and a teak rim. Meals served on this spiffy board are framed with silverware bearing Elvis's personal monogram. The room also boasts a communications center, including a skyphone that can be used to make calls anywhere in the world.

The most important compartment is, of course, the bedroom. . . . The bedroom of the *Lisa Marie* is decorated entirely in shades of restful blue: royal blue for the carpeting, which runs up to the windowsills; pale blue for the huge velvet bedspread; royal blue again for the suede headboard. At one end of the bed is the TV monitor, ready to display the antics of the Monty Python troupe. Just beyond the TV installation is the dressing room, with its large plate-glass mirror bordered with theatrical lightbulbs. Finally, there is the bathroom, which gathers together in a fine flourish the whole *esthétique d'Elvis*.

Picture a plastic bathroom counter in a shade of brilliant lapis lazuli with a canary yellow sink. Atop the sink is an ornately patterned, goldplated nozzle and a faucet fixture, whose handles are real lapis, à la Sherle Wagner. *Voila!* With this assemblage of precious metal, semiprecious stone and cheap plastic, combined ostentatiously but unimaginatively into the sort of private fixture dear to the heart of a Palm Springs matron (or a rich old queen), you have the epitome of the King's taste.

From Elvis *by Albert Goldman*

Writing Assignments

1. Write a series of paragraphs about some building, person, or event that you consider outrageous or preposterous. Have each paragraph focus on one particular aspect of the subject.

2. Write the rough draft of a persuasive letter. Try to persuade a friend to do something or refrain from doing something. (See 7.4.) Think of three good reasons. Write a paragraph for each. Use an introduction and a conclusion so that your paper has at least five paragraphs. (See 5.1–5.7.) Revise your rough draft in terms of the elements of a paragraph: main idea, supporting evidence, clear arrangement, unity, and coherence.

3 Strategies for Paragraph Meaning

I have always liked to write. In high school I wrote mainly journalism, things for the school paper. I had no sense of paragraphing. I would just squirt something down and then indent. It is a challenge to think of the paragraph as a unit of thought or the building block of an argument.

Venn Mehta

It helps to think of a paragraph as a chunk of thought. I tell myself, "Okay, let's think in this way about the subject," and that becomes a paragraph.

Mary Swann

To help illustrate that paragraphs communicate meaning, both alone and all together, this chapter has been divided into nine sections. Each section deals with a common kind of thinking strategy that often appears in paragraphs. These thinking strategies include specific detail, example, description, narrative, effect, cause, comparison, contrast, and classification. These are not the only ways a writer thinks; in fact, writers often combine these kinds of strategies in one paragraph or even one sentence. Remember that this chapter can help you if you think of it not as a set of absolute rules for paragraph construction but as a set of possible alternatives for you to consider as you work to present your main idea to a reader.

When creating paragraphs for a college writing assignment on any subject, keep in mind three questions:

- ✎ What is your main idea about this subject?
- ✎ What three or four things would a reader need to understand your main point?
- ✎ What thinking strategies will help you develop your main idea most effectively?

These questions will help you clarify your subject and develop supporting material. They will also help you choose the most effective thinking strategy to present your ideas to a reader.

3.1 Specific details

Two sentences, one general and another specific, may help a writer understand the concept of specific details.

GENERAL The animal moved there.

SPECIFIC The python coiled itself around the water pump.

The details in the second sentence help a reader see the motion of the python. Just as details improve most sentences, they improve paragraphs as well. Paragraphs filled with concrete details communicate vividly to the reader. At times, generality is needed in writing, but a writer should always know that most general language can quickly be transformed into specific detail, as in the following cases:

GENERAL The animal ate something.

SPECIFIC The small white poodle ate a moldy potato chip.

GENERAL He lost a lot of money.

SPECIFIC My brother Joe lost $15,000 at the race track.

GENERAL Williams was involved in medicine and literature.

SPECIFIC William Carlos Williams was both a baby doctor and an experimental poet.

The following drafts were written in response to a rather elementary paragraph assignment: Write a paragraph presenting three wishes, and use specific details.

Early draft

There are many things I want. First, I would like to get through college without having to go broke after school. I don't like being in debt. Second, I would like better transportation. A used car always has something going wrong with it. Third, I would like to be able to afford a vacation. If I had a choice, I would probably go someplace nice in the South where it is nice and warm.

Later draft

I want many things, but three things come instantly to mind. First, I would like to have enough money to pay my way through Marshall without having to get student loans. I don't like the idea of debt. I hate the thought of having to pay back almost $15,000 after I graduate. Next, I dream of a new car. Used cars generally have mechanical problems. If it is not the radiator, it is the fan belt. Finally, I would enjoy a vacation in the sun in January to escape the miserable cold. If I had a choice, I would prefer Daytona Beach with its beautiful white beaches.

Student comment

In revising the paper I tried to present more information for the reader to see my point. Does it work?
Dana Warner

The following set of sentences was developed into an effective paragraph over a period of five days in response to the following assignment:

Writing Assignment: Observe something in order to make a list of concrete details that appeal to the senses. Include details of sight, sound, smell, taste, touch, and motion. Let the reader see what you have seen. As you write each new sentence, add more information. Have your readers learn something new as they continue to read. Be specific; be concrete.

Early drafts

a. The wagon was in one piece, crumpled all up.

b. We avoided looking at the wagon. It was in the street, all crumpled into a ball.

c. No one looked at or touched the red wagon. It rested against the curb, crushed into a ball. The parts were pressed against each other.

d. People avoided looking at or touching the small child's red wagon. Lying upside down, it looked tiny, almost miniature. It rested against the curb, all crumpled into a ball. Its wheels were pressed against each other and the handle was bent.

e. The adults and children milling about the scene of the accident avoided looking at or touching the small child's red wagon. Lying upside down, it looked tiny, almost miniature, as if it had been shrunk. It rested against the curb, all crumpled into a ball. Its black wheels were pressed against each other and the handle had been driven into the wagon. A few items were still in the wagon.

f. The people milling around the scene of the accident avoided looking at or touching the small child's red wagon. Lying upside down, it looked tiny, almost miniature, as if it had been shrunk. It rested against the curb, all in one piece crushed into a ball. Its black wheels were pressed against each other and the handle had been driven into the wagon. A few items were still in the wagon: a pack of crayons, a coloring book, some M&Ms, and a small handful of gravel. A rain storm, which had stopped an hour ago, began again, and drops plinked against the empty, dented metal of the red wagon.

Student comment

This was not easy to write. This was something I had seen. I don't know what I would have done if I had known the little child who was wiped off the face of the earth here or if I knew his parents. I am glad I didn't. I just put down what I saw. I had to walk home that day because I missed my ride. My friends told me it was powerful stuff. I don't know.

Sam Larson.

Thinking Exercises

1. Make a list of concrete details about an unattractive place on your campus.

2. Make a list of at least ten specific details from the following poem by Llewellyn McKernan. Then, list ten specific details about a person working.

Mother Milking

Turn down the brim of your old felt hat
So all I can see are your rosy lips.

Chew on them absently.
Think thoughts I have no way of hearing.

Step carefully through
the muck of the barn.

Stop to look at the beginning of sun:
beside each brown slat a blue one.

Sigh and rub the ache in the bone
the place over the heart where fullness

has flown like a hen out of the coop. Go
around the black snake that lies in your path,

the eggs inside its belly strung out
like cocoons just before the butterflies

emerge from their safekeeping. Shush the hens
that roost in a row on the cow's back.

Listen to the soft cooing issuing
from their throats, to the ruffling

of their shiny feathers as they rise
to the rafters like powder puffs.

Here where nothing moves but the cow chewing
its cud, its dull stare turning to rock,

make your hands flash in the dark;
make them light up the barn

as they take me back to that moment
in my childhood where nothing belongs but milk

filling the pail inch by inch
with its white froth,

warm and sweet
as the breath of a baby.

3.   Choose two different kinds of the same thing to observe closely, such as two kinds of jeans, plants, or tennis shoes. Make separate lists of specific details about each. Make sketches of both.

4.   Choose a topic from the following general statements. What kind of material would help support that topic? Make a list of at least ten facts to use as supporting evidence: (a) I am/am not a friendly person. (b) The people on this campus are/are not friendly. (c) Being friends with a parent is/is not difficult.

Writing Assignments

1.   Write one or two paragraphs about a summer night, imitating the following paragraphs.

> It was February, the middle of summer. Great green fireflies spattered lights across the air and illumined for seconds, now here, now there, the pale trunks of enormous, solitaire trees. Cicadas ground out their long noise. Beneath us, the brown Napo was rising, in all silence; it coiled up the sandy mud bank and tangled its floating foam in vines that trailed from the forest and roots that looped the shores.

Each breath of night smelled sweet, more moistened and sweet than any kitchen, or cradle, or garden; each star in Orion seemed to tremble and stir with my breath. At once, in the thatch house across the clearings behind us, one of the Jesuit priests, filled with unknown feelings, lifted his alto recorder and played, played a wordless song, lyric, in a minor key, that twined over the village clearing, that caught in the big trees' canopies, muted our talk on the bankside, and wandered over the river, dissolving downstream.

From "Ecuador" by Annie Dillard

2. Use the details you created in Thinking Exercise 2 above. Write at least one paragraph about the work and the worker. In your writing provide plenty of specific details.

3. Write at least one paragraph imitating the paragraph about the red wagon above. Follow the assignment.

3.2 Examples

Examples form one of the bases of all expository writing. The word *example* comes from a Latin word meaning "a selection or sample," and an example is any illustration used to support, prove, or clarify a general statement. A good example will help the reader to see and accept the writer's main point. The following drafts show how two writers used examples to develop ideas in paragraphs.

> *Writing Assignment:* Create a general statement about some activity and use a number of examples to support and develop that generalization. Write a paragraph to show your reader that some activity, such as a hobby or sport, is difficult for you.

Early drafts

a. Though not a pure "klutz," I have difficulty with my hands.

b. I have difficulty with my hands, such as knitting or sewing. Whenever I have to sew something complex, such as a button on a shirt, I end up with the button at least two inches off target.

c. Though I am skillful, I have difficulty doing careful work with my hands. Sewing is a perfect example. Whenever I have to sew something simple, such as a button on a coat, I end up placing the button wrong. I also generally end up with a dozen or so stab wounds.

d. Though I am skillful in many things, I have difficulty doing careful work with my hands. Whenever I need to sew something simple, such as a button on a coat, I end up placing the button at least two inches off. I also generally end up with a dozen or so stab wounds in several fingers. On one unfortunate occasion, it took me more than an hour to sew a single collar button on an old shirt I treasured.

e. Though skillful in some things, I have extreme difficulty doing careful work with my hands. Sewing is a perfect example. When I sew something simple, such as a button on a coat, the button always ends up at least two inches off target. I also generally stab myself at least a dozen times in my fingers. On one unfortunate occasion, I spent more than an hour sewing a single collar button on a beautiful old shirt. When I finished I saw little, moist, rose-colored dots on the white cotton fabric, and I felt like weeping.

Student comment

This paragraph was fun to write because I exaggerated everything. My general idea was that I am clumsy doing things with my hands. Since that is so true, it wasn't hard to find plenty of examples. Sometimes I have to spend most of my time thinking about what I want to say. Here I knew exactly what I had to say, so I could spend my time making the sentences well written.

M. I.

Writing Assignment: Write a paragraph that clearly shows an eccentric person. Use one example to develop your point.

Early draft

Some of the kids are eccentric in their rooms. One has to win the most eccentric award. She spent her first days on campus putting new wallpaper in her room. You won't believe what she did. She went and bought aluminum foil and paste. Then she cut the foil and pasted it everywhere. The only time we saw here for two days was at lunch and dinner. She asked me whether she should do the ceiling and the windows. Her result is now a very eccentric bright, shiny, silvery room. It will surprise anyone who walks in.

Later draft

Some of the students in our dorm have worked hard to make their rooms as eccentric as possible. One student, though, wins the award for most exotic interior decoration. Maria P. spent her first two days on campus putting new wallpaper in her room. It is not ordinary wallpaper such as most people might think of. No, Maria went to the K-Mart and bought huge rolls of wide and thick aluminum foil and the gigantic bucket-size of Elmer's Glue. She worked from morning to night neatly cutting and carefully pasting the foil to all four walls. She joked about covering the ceiling and the windows. The result is a shiny, silvery room that surprises anyone who enters it.

Student comment

My problem in doing the assignment was deciding what to write about. I could have described Maria, who tries to look like Madonna with pink hair. I could have told about her unbelievable behavior at a football game. The room seemed the easiest for a single paragraph. I can put the parts together to make a complete paper.

Mel Grace

Thinking Exercises

1. As if you were presenting evidence in a courtroom, give two-sentence examples using plenty of concrete details for four of the following: caution, boldness, bigotry, excess, fear, cowardice, hope, hatred, pride, self-love, humility, honesty, dishonesty, sloth, gluttony, joy, innocence, generosity, or hard work.

2. Make a brief oral report using information from TV, movies, or reading to illustrate one of the topics in the preceding Thinking Exercise.

Writing Assignments

    1. For you, high school was valuable or not valuable. Write a factual, detailed paragraph presenting one clear example that best expresses your opinion.

    2. Choose an abstract virtue or vice, such as loyalty or treachery. Write a series of paragraphs, and have each paragraph give a clear example of a different person's actions that illustrate the topic.

3.3 Description

By the use of description, a writer can present an idea, express a feeling, argue for a point, or persuade someone to act. A strong description, full of specific details, can actually make a reader see the author's point. The writing samples in this section present some of the different ways to create effective descriptions: through the use of static details, the use of kinetic details, the focus of a dominant impression, and the use of figurative language.

a. Static details may create the effect of a photograph

The following paragraph presents for a reader the images the author saw outside after leaving her house. The author presented a series of specific details in a spatial order, all to the west, the direction she was looking.

> Early the next morning I ran out-of-doors to look about me. I had been told that ours was the only wooden house west of Black Hawk—until you came to the Norwegian settlement, where there were sev-

eral. Our neighbors lived in sod houses and dug-outs—comfortable but not very roomy. Our white frame house, with a story and a half-story above the basement, stood at the east end of what I might call the farm yard, with the windmill close by the kitchen door. From the windmill the ground sloped west-ward, down to the barns and granaries and pig-yards. This slope was trampled hard and bare, and washed out in winding gullies by the rain. Beyond the corn-cribs, at the bottom of the shallow draw, was a muddy little pond, with rusty willow bushes growing about it. The road from the post-office came directly by our door, crossed the farmyard, and curved round this little pond, beyond which it began to climb a gentle swell of unbroken prairie to the west. There, along the western skyline it skirted a great cornfield, much larger than any field I had ever seen. Everywhere, as far as the eye could reach, there was nothing but rough, shaggy, red grass, most of it as tall as I.

From My Antonia *by Willa Cather*

b. Kinetic details may create the effect of a motion picture

Not all descriptions resemble a picture or a still photo-graph. Many things in human society and nature are full of energy and motion. The following paragraph describing Yosemite Falls focuses on "the blinding spray" of water that gathers together to fall like a comet.

At the top of the fall they seem to burst forth in ir-regular spurts from some grand, throbbing mountain heart. Now and then one mighty throb sends forth a mass of solid water into the free air far beyond the others, which rushes alone to the bottom of the fall with long streaming tail, like combed silk, while the others, descending in clusters, gradually mingle and lose their identity. But they all rush past us with amazing velocity and display of power, though apparently drowsy and deliberate in their movements when observed from a distance of a mile or two. The heads of these comet-like masses are composed of nearly solid water, and are dense white in color like pressed snow, from the friction they suffer in rushing through the air, the portion worn off forming the tail, between the white lustrous threads and films of which faint, grayish pencilings appear, while the outer, finer sprays of waterdust, whirling in sunny eddies, are pearly gray throughout.

From "Yosemite Falls" by John Muir

c. A dominant impression improves the effect of a description

You may have noticed that most effective writing has a strong focus and a good sense of unity. A good writer of description can sharpen a focus and use specific details to directly convey a powerful statement with a clear emotional and intellectual meaning. The following paragraph presents an abundance of specific details to show a reader what life was like in part of California in the 1930s.

The living conditions of many of these new immigrants were wretched. One investigator in 1935 reported that he found a two-room cabin in which forty-one persons from southeast Oklahoma lived. Another described a one-room shack in which fifteen men, women, and children were huddled, living in unimaginable filth. On December 3, 1937, the California State Immigration and Housing Commission ordered thirty shanties near Visalia condemned as unfit for human habitation. Most camps had no baths, no showers or plumbing, and workers bathed in and drank from the same water supply found in nearby irrigation ditches. Near Kingsbury eighteen families were found living under a bridge. Other workers lived in cardboard cartons, or in tents improvised from gunny-sacks, with coffee cans serving for chimneys. In such an environment health conditions were appalling. Six thousand cases of influenza were reported in one county during February 1937. Scores of babies died of diarrhea and enteritis. Social worker Tessie Williams in 1937 reported the case of one woman who, upon leaving the county hospital, returned with her baby to live under a tree. A family of seven had reported to have eaten little more than bread and potatoes over a period of several months. Some ate nothing but beans and fried dough and oatmeal; one family of eight lived on dandelions and boiled potatoes. "I'm getting mighty tired of just beans and water," one woman moaned, "but even that may run out any day now."

From The American Nation *by John Garrity*

d. Figurative language can enrich a description

Whether an announcer reports that an injured linebacker "moved like a wounded lobster" or whether a teacher refers to a hyperactive child as "a perpetual backfire on a semi-trailer truck," readers and listeners enjoy figurative language that enables them to see more clearly the author's intended point. This concise sentence by William Faulkner from the story "A Rose for Emily" provides a good description: "Her eyes, lost in the fatty ridges of her face, looked like two small pieces of coal pressed into a lump of dough as they moved from one face to another while the visitors stated their errand." The figurative language of "pieces of coal" and "lumps of dough" is especially memorable. In the following paragraph another author describes an aging, Revolutionary soldier who has dressed up to impress a young woman.

> Braggioni catches her glance solidly as if he had been waiting for it, leans forward, balancing his paunch between his spread knees, and sings with tremendous emphasis, weighing his words. He had, the song relates, no father and no mother, nor even a friend to console him; lonely as a wave of the sea he comes and goes, lonely as a wave. His mouth opens round and yearns sideways, his balloon cheeks grow oily with the labor of the song. He bulges marvellously in his expensive garments. Over his lavender collar, crushed upon a purple necktie, held by a diamond hoop; over his ammunition belt of tooled leather worked in silver, buckled cruelly around his gaping middle; over the tops of his glossy yellow shoes Braggioni swells with ominous ripeness, his mauve silk hose stretched taut, his ankles bound with the stout leather thongs of his shoes.
>
> *From "Flowering Judas" by Katherine Anne Porter*

Thinking Exercises

1. Using the phrase "point of view in description" to mean a physical point from which the observer looks at the scene being described, what are the points of view in the preceding paragraphs by Cather, Muir, Garrity, and Porter? What is the point of view adopted by Annie Dillard in 2.6d?

2. Choose a narrative passage you have written that you would like to revise. Make two lists of specific details:

one list should include at least ten static details and the other at least ten kinetic details. Have the lists be from the point of view of another person in the story at an important moment in the plot. If there is no other person, imagine that the lists could have been compiled by a living or inanimate object present at that moment. Trust your imagination and list or cluster details that might help you develop the narrative.

3. Read the paragraphs by Annie Dillard at the end of 3.1 and make two lists. In the first list, include static details; in the second, include kinetic details. Make two lists of your own with images from a nighttime scene.

Writing Assignments

1. Write at least one descriptive paragraph that will make a reader feel uncomfortable. Use carefully chosen specific details to create a graphic image. What would be the point of using such language to make a reader feel uncomfortable?

2. Looking at a photograph of yourself, create a list of specific details and write a description of yourself. What character trait stands out in the photograph? What details would you use to emphasize that trait?

3. Describe an object of clothing from the point of view of a thief or shoplifter.

4. Use a clustering exercise (see 1.3b) to gather details about the appearance of an extremely angry person. Write a rough draft describing that person. In your revision, try to include numerous sound images. What does the person sound like? What sound images are associated with anger?

3.4 Narrative

Many people believe that one of the strongest skills in effective writing is story telling or narration. Most students are better storytellers than they think they are. Narrative material, whether long or short, can help writers in college. A clear narrative can help a writer present information, persuade someone to act, or express strong feelings. Narrative is a powerful tool. Some people even argue that narrative forms the foundation of all expository writing. They point to the fact that many arguments and analyses contain narrative elements.

The elements of narrative are simple. They involve questions: Who? What? Where? When? Why?

- *Who?* An agent is necessary for a narrative. Some agent, living or nonliving, has to do something.
- *What?* An action or a series of actions is necessary.
- *Where?* Everything that happens on this earth happens somewhere.
- *When?* Everything that occurs happens at a specific time, over a specific period of time, or intermittently at various times; so do the events in a story.
- *Why?* The human mind wants to know why things happen, and readers want writing to have some kind of order and sense. The explanation may be imperfect, but that is better than no explanation at all.

The following sample student narrative gives the reader some idea of the development of the sentences and the direction of a narrative. How a story moves through time and over time can fascinate a reader.

Writing assignment: Write a paragraph about an experience when someone else's words or actions hurt you in some way or another. In revising the paragraph, try to answer the questions *Who? What? When? Where?* and *Why?*.

Early drafts

a. When Bruce came in, Mary looked up. Before he could ask her opinion, she laughed at him.

b. Mary was studying. When Bruce came in with the costume, Mary looked up. Before he could ask her opinion, she laughed and he left.

c. Mary had been studying chemistry. When Bruce came in wearing his costume, Mary looked up. Before he could ask for her opinion, she laughed at him. Her laugh was loud.

d. Mary had been studying for the chemistry final. When Bruce bounced into the room wearing his fisherman costume, Mary looked up from her book. Before he could ask for an opinion, she laughed at him. Her laugh was sharp, loud, and cruel. It reminded Bruce of his childhood and made him tense as aluminum foil.

e. Mary had been studying for the chemistry final all afternoon. When Bruce bounced through the door smiling and wearing his fisherman costume, Mary looked up from her book. Before he could ask for an opinion, she laughed at him. Her laugh was sharp, loud, long, and cruel. It reminded Bruce of all the times when as a child his sister had laughed and ridiculed him. He immediately felt his muscles tighten. He felt as if his hands were crushing a beer can. Without saying one single word, he frowned, turned, and left the room. Walking away rapidly, he heard her voice call out, but he refused to listen to the words.

Student comment

Mainly this is the truth. I'm not as innocent as this paragraph makes me out to be, but the narrative is mainly what happened. It is told from my point of view, of course. I had a little problem making the "tenseness" part right. When I read it again, "aluminum foil" just didn't sound right. Worse, it didn't make any sense. I still don't know if this is right. I like this as a narrative. It still hurts to remember. Especially hard is how her laugh made me feel.

B.H.

Thinking Exercises

1. Explain how a writer might use narrative materials for the following purposes:

   a. To show that a person is brave/cowardly, fair-minded/bigoted

   b. To explain how a person had a problem with a teacher, coach, employer, parent, or friend

   c. To explain how a person behaved differently on two occasions or how two people reacted differently to the same situation

   d. To persuade someone to avoid a person or place.

Writing Assignments

1. Write a narrative account on one of the preceding Thinking Exercises or one of the following topics: (a) an event that changed your life forever; (b) the time you stopped doing something you had been doing for some time; (c) a task you had to do that you never want to do again; (d) something you were eager to do but changed your mind about doing before you finished.

2. Read a story by Ernest Hemingway, Joyce Carol Oates, Flannery O'Connor, or John Updike. Write a narrative, imagining what one character in the story would do during a weekend at your school or in your hometown.

3. Write about a place where people gather to eat, indoors or outdoors. It might be somewhere in this country or another. Recall an experience that took place there. Perhaps something made you happy, embarrassed, surprised, or angry. Imagine you are there again. Using many *details*, write as if you were telling this to a good friend to express your knowledge and feelings. Help your friend feel that experience too. Write a paper long enough to present your material.

3.5 Effects

The word *effect* has many good synonyms: result, consequence, conclusion, or outcome. An effect always follows its cause; however, a cause may have one or more effects. Writers commonly present effects by using narrative material, descriptive material, or examples. The following writing presents a clear picture of an idea developed by, and focused exclusively on, effects.

> *Writing Assignment:* Write one sentence that contains a cause-effect relationship. Make a list of facts and details focusing on the effects. Using your list, write a paragraph full of specific and concrete information.

Early draft

Last summer I learned drought. Temperatures and no rain had disastrous effects. The vegetables in our garden had been growing okay one week and the next week it was all over. They looked sickly for a while. Then they looked dead, very dead like leaves. The lettuce was destroyed, then the zucchini, then the tomatoes, cucumbers, and finally the grass. Pretty soon everything was dusty. The outside was full of dust and the inside of the house also like with a fine powder. One day the neighbor children screamed when I saw our cat kill a scrawny bird trying to get a drink in the little bit of water in the bird bath.

Later draft

Last summer our town learned the meaning of the word *drought* firsthand. The temperatures remained in the high nineties and the skies were clear blue for two months: no rain. The effects of this on our house and garden were disastrous. First to go were the beds of lettuce: one day a lush green and the next day a crinkly brown. After that the zucchini perished. They just lay down one afternoon as if going to sleep. Their huge prickly leaves covered the ground like green sheets of paper. These events occurred before the rationing of water. After the water laws came in, the garden became a quilt of brown and yellow. Tomato vines shriveled. Cucumbers withered. Grass turned into a thick brown carpet. Then fine, faint powdery dust began to appear everywhere: on the dead plants outside, on windows, shelves, sheets, records, even on dishes waiting to be dried after washing. On one occasion, the children in the neighborhood became hysterical when our cat captured and killed a scrawny robin in the mud-coated bird bath.

Student comment

This was simple. How could I forget it? I didn't have to go and make a list. I had the material in my memory. I just had to get it down on paper. I think I could have written a series of paragraphs with the effects on the garden, on the animals (wild, tame), and on the people.

L. R.

Thinking Exercises

1. What difference has *your* going to college made on your life? Make two lists. In one, list the effects on your relatives and friends. In the other, list the effects on your values, attitudes, study habits, and behavior.

2. Analyze some particular human quality, such as physical beauty, athletic ability, high intelligence. Make lists of the positive and negative effects of this condition.

Writing Assignments

1. Choose a situation involving a great change such as moving, illness, failure, or success. List the major effects of the change. Make a list of details about the situation. State the cause in one sentence and use it as the first sentence in a paragraph exploring effects.

2. Choose a book, a movie, or a person that has influenced you significantly. Write two paragraphs: one setting forth the elements in the cause and the second stating facts and concrete details about the effect on you. You are trying to answer the question, "How did this influence me and what effects did it have?"

3. Write three separate paragraphs about something that backfired or failed for either you or someone else. In one paragraph, explain the background. In a second paragraph, explain the effects that were intended. In the third, present the effects that actually happened.

3.6 Causes

When writers ask *why*, they are searching for causes. The word *cause* refers to something that produces some effect or consequence. It also refers to a reason or motive for an action. When thinking about causes, be specific. Be precise in looking for the cause or causes of a single event or situation. Most of us have an intuitive understanding of the concept of causality that needs to be sharpened by careful analysis. The following writing sample shows one way of thinking about a subject, using the concept of causality.

Writing Assignment: Choose something in American culture that is very popular or very unpopular. Write a paragraph or a series of paragraphs exploring the question, "Why is this so popular or unpopular?" To help you gather some ideas on your topic, you might ask some different people for their opinions and explanations.

Early draft

Why do people watch soap operas? First, I like the characters. They interest me a lot. I thought I was strange thinking of them as friends until I talked to someone on my floor who told me that she watched one soap for years and they were just like her neighbors. Second, let's face the truth: people also like sex. The characters are attractive and evil. The programs are filled with sex and sexy characters and romance. Any afternoon you can expect love, romance, first, second, and third marriages; first, second, and third divorces; affairs; rapes; adultery; murders; pregnancies; and abortion.

Later draft

Why do soap operas cause millions of people to ignore their children, postpone their work, give up food, and cut classes? In the first place, the characters on the soaps are interesting. The viewers identify completely with the characters or think of them as friends, family members, or neighbors. One dormitory resident said she had been watching *The Days of Our Lives* since junior high and that the characters were as real to her as the people in her family or her neighbors. Also, let's face the truth: many viewers watch the soaps with a strong, vicarious sexual interest. The characters are attractive even if they are evil as Satan, and the soaps deliver a steady stream of sex and sexy characters with plenty of romance. This steady stream of love and romance includes first, second, and third marriages; first, second, and third divorces; affairs; rapes; adultery; murders; pregnancies; and abortion.

Student comment

As you can see, I am an addict. The first draft has too much of me in it. I revised to have an impersonal paragraph. I think the revision presents more important information for the reader. I worked hard here on the transitional devices.

Joe Davis

Thinking Exercises

1.   Select some of your recent writing that you like. List some things you *did* or *felt* while writing the paper that helped make the writing good. Then select some writing you have recently done that you do not like. Make a list of the reasons why the second writing sample is not as good as the first.

2.   Interview people of different ages and ask them why they think teenagers drink alcoholic beverages.

Writing Assignments

1.   Analyze a personal situation in terms of causality. Write a short paragraph about the time another person hurt you or attempted to hurt you. Explain in one sentence what

happened; then, use precise facts and details to explain the situation *entirely from the other person's point of view.*

2.   Explain one of the following conditions in terms of causality: migraine, headache, hypersexuality, insomnia, allergy, grief, diabetes, joy, prejudice.

3.7 Comparison

Comparison points out similarities. Suppose you had just met an alien, a friendly one, and you took it to a football game or a concert. Would you be able to use comparisons to explain to the alien what was happening in the game or in the musical performance? Probably you would not because when a person uses comparisons to explain the unfamiliar to someone else, a certain amount of knowledge must be shared between them. However, writers do find comparisons helpful. If you examine your ordinary conversations on an average day, you will find that you use comparisons repeatedly to explain something or to make a point. Most writers do the same thing.

Effective comparisons need a clear structure so the reader can easily see the main point and understand the basis of the comparison. Two common ways to organize a comparison are point-by-point structure and block structure. The following paragraphs illustrate these different organizational patterns. (Note how the comparisons are developed with many concrete and specific details.)

a. Comparison using point-by-point organization

Writing Assignment: Develop a comparison between two things to support a general statement. Organize the paragraph by moving from one element of the comparison to another.

Early draft

My roommate is a barbarian. Our dorm room is a barbaric cave. Just as those early homes were cruddy and filthy, our dorm room is garbage. All the early caves were dark, and our room is like a lunar eclipse society: one light: my reading lamp right above my desk. The windows are black; the walls are gray. Our room is full of orange peels, cherry pits, Snickers, Fritos, and other junks.

Later draft

Because my roommate is a barbarian, our room in the dormitory closely resembles a prehistoric cave dwelling. Most inhabited caves were coated with a fine powder of dust, animal hair, and ashes. Our dorm room has several thick layers of debris: an undercoating of dust, a secondary level of shredded paper, and a sort of frosting of cigarette ashes and lost clothing. In addition to the filth, most caves peopled by early humans had little light. Our room has only one light: a reading lamp above my desk. The windows are spray-painted black and the walls a quaint shade of dark gray. Most early caves contained the remains of eating rituals: dried bat wings, stale animal bones, the inedible husks of nuts, fruits, and vegetables. Similarly, our room seems a small museum of orange peels, cherry pits, Snickers wrappers, stale Fritos, and other gourmet delicacies.

Student comment

I had great fun writing this. My choices in making a comparison were prehistoric cave, junkyard, pigsty, or garbage dump. The cave seemed the most appropriate. I think it will help me get out of the dorm. I used the point-by-point pattern: Some of A: Some of A-1, Some of B: Some of B-1, etc. I asked myself, "What are the two things I am comparing?" I made a diagram of the main points of comparison between my room and a cave. Here is what the map of my paper looked like.

Cave A-1: Cover on the floor—dust, hair, ashes
Room A-2: Cover on the floor—paper, ashes

Cave B-1: Darkness
Room B-2: Darkness

Cave C-1: Debris from food and eating.
Room C-2: Debris from food and eating.

I like how the parts fit together. I like to think of it as kind of the steps in a ladder. I wrote this mainly for myself. I am sure that I did not want my roommate to see it. It is bad enough as it is without his knowing I am writing things about him behind his back. I wrote it, though, with my Dad and the composition teacher in mind. I guess I had several audiences. I tried to use some of these transition words: *like, similar, likewise, as, resemble, in a way, similarly, in like manner*, and *compared.*

Art Cyrus

b. Comparison using block organization

Writing Assignment: Write a paper exploring two or three similarities between freshman composition and something else. Make a positive or negative point about them. Organize the paragraph in blocks. Present the information about composition first; then present the material to make the comparison in the same order.

Early draft

1. Uneasy
   Patients suffer pain.
   Patients fear
   possible pain.
2. Outside forces
   Patients
   are motionless.
   Patients do what
   dentist says.
3. Long-range benefits
   Patients have no pain.
   Patients keep teeth.

1. Uneasy
   Students feel nervous/fearful.
   Students fear writing/criticism.
2. Outside forces
   Students are controlled in the
   class.
   Students submit to assignments/
   grading.
3. Long-range benefits
   Students finish the course.
   Students acquire valuable skill.

Later draft

Does freshman composition resemble a visit to a dentist? It seems to in two important ways. First, most patients going to a dentist's office feel uneasy. They often suffer actual pain or they fear possible pain from the dentist's work. Second, these patients see themselves as vulnerable, subject to uncontrolled outside forces. Do patients argue with their dentists? No. Their role is submission. Similarly, many freshman students feel great unease in taking a writing course. Some remember the pain inflicted by earlier English teachers; others feel anxious about the writing they will have to do or the criticism they will inevitably receive. Students feel keenly that the assignments, the grading standards, and the reasons for the course are totally out of their control. All they can do is submit. Needless to say, such a situation might not be favorable for good writing.

Student comment

> I don't think I followed the directions exactly. The block organization is more effective than the point-by-point organization of the first draft. This was hard work.
>
> *S. C. B.*

Thinking Exercises

1. Analyze the pattern of organization in the following paragraph.

> When a child, I feared my Uncle Bill: a big hairy man. I always thought of him as a giant monkey. His low, overhanging forehead with thick blond eyebrows almost hid a pair of tiny blue eyes. A thick, red, bushy, prickly beard sprouted from almost every pore of his face and seemed to flow onto his head. Whenever I looked at him, I was always trying to figure out where his yellow hair ended and his red beard began. When he stood up straight, his shoulders sloped and his long arms reached to the middle of his calves. Incredible as all this may sound, when he moved, he strode from place to place—with a sideways sort of motion, half walking, half jumping. Whenever I heard his loud voice and laughter, I remembered certain sounds from TV or the movies. Can you guess what his favorite fruits were? It never pleased me to see Uncle Bill's forest-green Packard slide into our driveway.
>
> *Andrew Sheets*

2. Choose one of the following pairs to compare. List at least five points of similarity between them.

    a. A friend and an animal or an insect
    b. You and one of your parents
    c. A class and a game, war, or foreign country
    d. Old people and infants or children

3. What kind of a comparison would you write to make the following points? Write at least three sentences for each comparison.

    a. That parents are sometimes unconcerned/angry
    b. That a friend of yours was suspicious/afraid/silly
    c. That a meal was wonderful/terrible
    d. That the room was dirty/spotless

Writing Assignments

1. Think of a character in a movie, book, story, or history who resembles someone you know. Make a list of the points of similarity. Use this comparison to express either a positive or a negative attitude toward that person. Do not, however, write about yourself or your feelings. Use plenty of specific facts and details to write at least one paragraph developing the comparison.

2. Think of a room or a place on your campus that could be improved to make it more attractive or more useful to students. List similarities between that room or place and something unpleasant, such as a dungeon, a prison cell, or a garbage dump. Write at least one paragraph in the form of a letter to your college president developing your comparison with the aim of having the room or place improved in some significant way.

3. Develop one of the comparisons you developed in the preceding Thinking Exercise.

3.8 Contrast

The human mind recognizes differences. Ask yourself how you recognize the difference between the sound of a guitar and that of a violin, or how you know a pine tree is different from an oak tree. The discovery of contrasts can help in learning. The human mind, consciously and unconsciously, recognizes large and small contrasts. Writers use contrast as a device to develop and explain their ideas. A careful contrast can help a reader see the writer's point clearly. Contrast is one of the most important thinking and writing skills a writer can develop. Many writing assignments, in one way or another, involve contrasts.

a. Contrast using point-by-point organization

Writing Assignment: Think of a person who has changed considerably. Make a list of details about the character before the change and a second list about the character after it. Using these lists, write one or two paragraphs contrasting the character "before" and "after," using the point-by-point organization. For an alternate assignment, contrast a place or a thing that has changed.

Early draft

Bert Smith's behavior has begun to puzzle and worry all of his friends. Last semester, Bert was a model student. He studied so diligently that his roommates labelled him "the Rhodes scholar." Now his roommates refer to him as "the king of the road." Before Christmas vacation, Bert spent his evenings in the library and his weekends in the chemistry laboratory. This semester, he has not even bought a book, much less read one. A few months ago, Bert began to read about medicine and talked about going to medical school. This semester, Bert spends his time sleeping or lying around on his bed staring off into space. If he is not playing pool in the afternoon, he is looking for wild parties at night.

Later draft

Bert Smith's behavior puzzles and troubles his friends. Last semester, Bert was a model student. After he earned a 4.0 average, his fraternity brothers called him "the Rhodes scholar." Now Bert is failing 18 hours of classes, and his friends have labelled him "king of the road." Before Christmas, Bert spent his evenings in the library and his weekends in the chemistry laboratory. This semester, he has not even bought a book, much less read one. In fact, he used the book money from his scholarship to buy six cases of beer. A few months ago, Bert read a book about surgeons by Richard Selzer and started talking about medical school. This semester, Bert spends his days sleeping or lying around like a corpse. If he is not playing pool in the afternoon, he is looking for wild parties at night. It may be that his father's sudden death over Christmas brought all this on, but whatever the cause, Bert Smith has certainly changed and for the worse.

Student comment

This was pretty easy to write. I have known Bert Smith for two and a half years. I like him and am worried about him. I could have gone on and on. Some of the stuff might be pretty gross, so I held back. Strangely, I thought of writing something his mother might read, or even Bert in a certain mood so he might see what he was doing to himself—not that I would ever send it. Or would I? I worked to get my reader to learn about Bert and see the change.

B. B.

b. Contrast using block organization

Writing Assignment: Write at least two informative paragraphs for someone who habitually confuses two related but different things, such as hen/rooster, crow/raven, loneliness/solitude, coma/sleep, sea/ocean, love/lust, frog/toad, poetry/verse, sorrow/depression, or another pair. Your goal is to supply enough information so that someone can quickly distinguish between the two. Be sure to use block organization and follow the same order in each part.

Earliest draft

Crows and blackbirds are a lot different even though they are birds, especially in terms of sound, size, weight, food, and colors. I need to know more.

Early draft

Although crows and blackbirds are both birds, they have many differences. They have different sounds. The crow sounds like a frog sometimes with a sore throat. In terms of size the crow is much larger measuring sometimes two feet. Thinking about the crow's diet (which includes anything. I mean anything on the earth no matter how yucky) can make you sick. The biggest difference is the intelligence of the birds:

with the crow being the winner in this department. The blackbird, which is related to the robin and oriole, has a quieter voice sounding more like a chirp than anything else. In addition, the blackbird is a puny eight inches long. They both gather in huge flocks, sometimes as many as 40,000–50,000 at one time. Something like this was in the horror movie *The Birds*. The blackbird will generally prefer dining on grains and berries.

Later draft

A careful inspection of blackbirds and crows shows many differences. Both male and female crows are solid black: with large, thick, black bills; small, black eyes; and black, wiry feet. The crow (with a size of twenty-four inches) builds nests of twigs, wood, and even wire in tall trees and makes a distinctive *caw*. For food, the crow will eat anything, including waste, dead bodies, rotting matter, grass seed, and berries. Some people fear crows and consider them bad omens. Silhouetted against a huge blue sky, a crow looks like a slice of nothing with wings. In contrast the smaller blackbird seems humorous. It is hard to fear an eight-inch bird out on the softball field with its head bobbing up and down searching for crumbs, seeds, and berries. In terms of color, the blackbird exhibits enormous variety. Some blackbirds have red wings; other have yellow heads; a few are rust colored. The most common blackbird is the grackle with its black-purplish feathers and white eyes. All blackbirds have different colors in winter and spring and different colors for male and female. Blackbirds have thin bills, twiggy legs, spindly feet, and small bodies. Their sound varies from chirps, clucks, and whistles going up the scale.

Student comment

Knowing and, more than that, getting the knowledge down on paper make all the difference. Being forced to use the block/block method made me choose what was most important. Really, I might have two separate paragraphs here. This paragraph makes me want to write a longer paper, adding information about the blackbird's nest to complete the contrast.

Joe Kenner

Thinking Exercises

1. How would you use contrast to accomplish the following: (a) to show someone that you are serious/not serious about school; (b) to express a feeling of sadness/happiness; (c) to persuade a friend to cut a class?

2. Choose two different comic strips you like and make a list of significant differences.

3. For your major or career plans, find the names of two important publications. Read several recent issues of each. List some differences between them in terms of size, format, frequency, editors, content, audience, language, style, and readability.

Writing Assignments

1.   Remember a time when you changed your mind about a person, place, or thing. Write at least two paragraphs about that topic: one dealing with before and one dealing with after. Arrange the items of contrast in the same order.

3.9 Classification

Classification is a valuable tool for organizing and interpreting different things. To classify, a writer has to choose a general category and explore the different *kinds* of that thing. Classification can help a writer learn about a subject. For example, a student who explored the different kinds of war in terms of place (naval, land, aerial, submarine) would probably make some startling discoveries about human behavior. The following guidelines can help you prepare a careful, informative classification.

✎   Understand different ways to classify a subject. For example, a writer could classify cats in terms of size (small, medium, large) or origin (Persia, Siam, alley). In light of your purpose, use the most appropriate system for classifying a subject.

✎   Choose a subject that interests you. Make sure that there are some classes of the subject and that it is not one of a kind. For example, you could classify kinds of monuments, but you could not consider the Washington Monument as a general category with classes under it.

✎   Identify the subject and give its definition. For example, the word *star* might refer to a popular personality or to a distant sun. Make your meaning clear and maintain it throughout the entire paper.

✎ Choose a sensible classifying principle. Look for different *types* according to this principle. Avoid a random listing of words. A mere list of desserts, such as Jell-O, ice cream, and yogurt, is not a classification of the word *dessert*. Consider the following different ways to classify the word *dessert*: according to calories, method of preparation, or origin:

Super fattening	Baked	French
Fattening	Frozen	Chinese
Nonfattening	Fresh	Hawaiian
Low calorie		American

✎ Be consistent. Maintain the same classification principle throughout the entire classification. Notice the differences between the following classifications:

Consistent	*Inconsistent*	*Consistent*
Transportation	Trucks	Winter sports
Taxicabs	Large trucks	Ice skating
Buses	Dump trucks	Skiing
Limousines	Small trucks	Sledding

✎ Avoid overlapping classes. Overlap occurs when two classes are presented but there is really only one class. In the list of trucks, "dump trucks" overlaps because it could belong in one of the other classes.

✎ Include all or the most important classes within the category. Make sure the items in the category are representative.

✎ Include at least two elements in each class. Do not present a class with only one element.

✎ Have at least three classes to a category.

✎ When describing the classes, develop at least two characteristics that are common to all but have distinguishing features. For example, a taxicab, a bus, and a limousine differ in *size* and also in the *cost of travel*.

✎ Present the characteristics of each class in the same order.

✎ When describing each class, use lots of concrete details, facts, and examples.

To write an effective classification, you need to answer the following questions:

✎ What is the general category?

✎ What are the three most important kinds?

✎ What features best illustrate each different kind?

✎ What principle have you used to divide the items into classes?

Let's use as an example the word *book*. Classification involves different kinds of the same thing. Let's divide the word *book* into two different categories:

Category 1	*Category 2*
a. ancient Roman books	a. mysteries
b. medieval hand-copied books	b. romances
c. modern hardcovers	c. science fiction
d. modern paperbacks	d. comic books

In Category 1, the classification depends on the physical properties of the books. The word *book* meant something different in ancient Rome, in the medieval period, and after the invention of the printing press. In Category

2, the classification depends on the contents of the different books. When making a classification, check to see that all the terms in that category belong. Avoid including words that are similar but not related enough to be part of that category. The following writing samples illustrate a kind of elementary writing assignment often assigned in college.

> *Writing Assignment:* Write a brief paper classifying students on a particular campus into some different types.

Early draft

> "Hunkies" are everywhere with good looks, bodies, sports clothes, and indifference. They are getting ready to be "Yuppies." "Flunkies" are harder to see. They are off campus: in places you'd never want to be. The "spunkies" are heard before they are seen. They bounce around campus with their huge radios or they cruise the campus with radios. The "wonkies" are nearly invisible. They discover all the silly places on campus: computer labs, libraries, science labs, and lecture halls, and on occasion can be found barely conscious in front of *Star Trek* reruns.

Later draft

> The students on this campus are so unique that new terms must be invented to accurately describe them. On most days, a casual observer can discover "hunkies," "flunkies," "spunkies," and "wonkies." "Hunkies" are "Yuppies" in a larval stage. They are everywhere with their clean good looks, athletic bodies, bright sports clothes, and their air of utter indifference. The "flunkies" keep out of sight. They lurk off campus in bars, opium dens, fields, and police

3.9
¶

stations. You can hear the "spunkies" before you see them. They bounce around campus with their monstrous portable radio transmitters, or they cruise the perimeters of the campus with their sixteen-track stereos blaring Bo Diddley tapes. "Wonkies" are the hard workers, but they are nearly invisible. They have discovered all the boring places on campus: the all-night computer labs, the library reading rooms open until midnight, the science labs open on Saturday mornings, and the large lecture halls where the teacher never takes attendance.

Student comment

I think this paragraph would be much better if I developed it into a long paragraph for each of the different kinds. I don't like it much. My peer editor was critical. He said he couldn't visualize the different kinds clearly. I think they are different enough however. I like some of the sentences more than the whole.

Alexis Denfee

Thinking Exercises

1. From each of the following groups, select the three items that seem to belong most together. What principle did you use to make your selection?

A. College students
   1. Working adults
   2. Men
   3. Women
   4. Teenagers
   5. Retired people
   6. Sophomores

B. Automobiles
   1. Steam cars
   2. Sports cars
   3. Police cars
   4. Limousines
   5. Taxis
   6. Foreign cars

C. Criminals
   1. Assassin
   2. Shoplifter
   3. Rapist
   4. Embezzler
   5. Burglar
   6. Murderer

D. Food
   1. Snack
   2. Banana
   3. Lunch
   4. Pineapple
   5. Mango
   6. Dinner

2. Make a list of three to five different *kinds* of movies. Select a good example of each kind. Then, for each different kind, list at least five characteristics.

Writing Assignments

1. Write a paper on either different kinds of love or different kinds of hate. Use examples from each of the following: (a) personal experience, (b) something you read, (c) something from a movie or television.

2. Write a paper explaining three different kinds of one of the following: (a) fads, (b) taboos, (c) sports cars, (d) cheating, (e) ants, (f) snakes, (g) fruits, (h) music, (i) sculptures, (j) paintings, (k) dances, (l) dives.

4 Revising Paragraphs

At first I thought revising was simply correcting mistakes. Then I discovered that revising meant improving. In high school one of my teachers had us write only paragraphs. I learned a few things writing those. When I revise, I try to see how each paragraph works (or doesn't work) to get my main idea across. I revise first for that main idea.

Debbie Mano

I can see now that some paragraphs stand by themselves (like a letter or essay exam answer), but other paragraphs link together to form a larger unit. When I revise I have to know whether the paragraph is a unit by itself or a part of a larger unit. Then I can revise.

Colin Mayer

4.1 Careful reading

Writers usually change things while they write, and the process of revision occurs throughout the writing of a paper. You should, however, make revision a conscious step in the writing process. After you finish the draft, someone has to read it and make comments. You, of course, will be one of the readers, but a classmate or your instructor may read the draft and comment. The following questions will help you to focus on certain kinds of difficulties:

- What is the best thing about the paragraphing?
- What is the subject of the paper?
- What is the main idea in the paper? Is it clearly stated?
- Would a person learn something from reading your paper? What?
- How do the paragraphs work to develop the main idea?
- How is each paragraph organized?
- Do the paragraphs make sense?
- Do any paragraphs puzzle you?
- What does the paper need most to improve it?

Write out your answers to these questions to help you begin revising. At all times, keep your main point clearly in mind. All your revising should work to clarify and develop that main idea. Sometimes the answers to the preceding questions will prompt you to write new paragraphs. Whatever the case, use the answers to guide your revision.

4.2 Strategies for revising

Think of revision as an ongoing activity and a response to a problem. Don't limit yourself. Practice different strategies for revising. Basically any writer can revise a sentence or a paragraph in one of four different ways: addition, deletion, substitution, and transposition. Notice how the changes in the following sentences illustrate these different ways. Keep these possibilities in mind while revising.

ORIGINAL	Something frightened him.
ADDITION	Dangling from the kitchen ceiling, a large insect frightened my brother.
SUBSTITUTION	Dangling from the kitchen ceiling, a large black spider terrified my father.
DELETION	Dangling from the ceiling, a spider terrified my father.
TRANSPOSITION	A large black spider dangled from the kitchen ceiling and terrified my father.

As these examples show, effective revision involves several different kinds of strategies. When revising paragraphs, think of them as units, as chunks of thought that work to develop the main idea of your writing.

4.3 Revision: Addition

One of the most common ways a writer can improve a paragraph is to add specific details or examples to develop the main idea more fully. An examination of 3.1 and 3.2 will show how the addition of specific details and examples can develop a main idea. Because many paragraphs are incomplete, a writer needs to add material to help the reader get the point. The following example illustrates a common form of revision. In the later draft, a reader can easily spot the addition of a topic sentence and several transitional devices that work to improve clarity.

Early draft with revisions

What can be done? The legislators can pass a few laws.

First,
Keep drunks off the road͜ They' should change the

defining drunkeness as
definition of drunkenness. Instead of/three drinks,

they should deFine it as new deFinition
make it͜one. This will keep people who drink off the

MAIN IDEA ???

road, and it will enable the police to arrest drunk

Two, they should
drivers more easily͜ Pass a law to limit the number

drink in one place. Three, they should
of drinks that a person can͜be served anywhere͜ Set

up drunk driver detection squads and reward police

Finally, the law should be changed
who arrest drunk drivers͜ Judges should impose harsh

keep the judges busy   ing
penalties on drunk drivers. They should revoke li-

ting   ing
censes, set heavy fines, and impose stiff jail sentences,

Later draft

and the drunks will stay off the road.

What can people do to keep drunk drivers off the
road? The legislators can pass new laws dealing with
drunken drivers. One, they should change the definition of drunkenness. Instead of defining drunkenness as the alcohol in the blood after three drinks,
they should define it as the alcohol in the blood after
one drink. This new definition will stop a lot of drinking and enable the police to arrest drunk drivers more
easily. Two, they should pass a law to limit the number of drinks that a person can drink in one place.
Three, they should occasionally set up roadblocks to
detect drunk drivers and reward police who arrest

drunk drivers. Most importantly, they should revise the laws so that judges impose harsh penalties on drunk drivers. Keep the judges busy revoking licenses, setting heavy fines, and handing out stiff jail sentences, and the drunk drivers will stay off the road.

Jenny Adkins

4.4 Revision: Deletion

Two questions can help in revising: What is the paragraph's main point? Does each sentence help to develop the main point? Extra words and phrases creep into most rough drafts, but a careful writer will identify and remove them. The following draft and revision illustrate the deletion of unnecessary sentences, phrases and words. Although it is difficult, writers should develop the habit of critical reading to spot unnecessary words and wordy phrases and sentences. You can gain additional ideas and practice in this art of deletion by studying the material in 19.2, 21.21, and 21.24.

Early draft with revisions

In the folklore of Lincoln County numerous super-

What's my main point? — remove

stitions relate to the arrival of winter weather. [This is

because the people like to tell stories and most of

them have not taken lectures from the extension ser-

vice people at the university.] Some people study corn

My father — beehives?

cobs. They say the thicker the corn cob the colder

He — hive

and longer the winter *will be* [My grandfather was [~Wordy~]

always spending cold winter nights on the farm carv-

ing corn cob pipes and looking out the window at

the snow coming down. He would take out his shiny

knife and begin carving away at the corn cob. He

would cut it in two pieces and then hollow out the

center with his knife. There are many other super-

stitions too] There are ones about roses and how more

of them mean more snow, chipmunks, caterpillars,

and cats. If a cat walks around a well three times in

a row, the water will freeze *over* ~in December like it did~

~at our farm two winters in a row~ completely. If a

hornet should ever sting a chipmunk, ~you had better~

~be on the lookout and plan for snow because~ a bliz-

zard will surely arrive in early September. ~Especially~

~important is the behavior and appearance~ of the *country*

squirrels ~in the country.~ *have great signif—* The thicker the fur and the

darker ~brown~ the color, the colder *the weather.* ~and more severe~

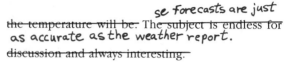

~~the temperature will be.~~ The ~~subject is endless for~~
se forecasts are just
as accurate as the weather report.
~~discussion and always interesting.~~

Later draft

In the folklore of Lincoln County, numerous super-
stitions relate to the arrival of winter weather. My
father studies corn cobs. He says the thicker the cob,
the colder and longer the winter. Others count the
number of roses. The more roses that bloom in October, the more snow will fall in January. Some country people insist that a black cat walking around a
well three times in a row predicts that the well will
freeze over completely. If a hornet should ever sting
a chipmunk, a blizzard will surely arrive in early September. The country squirrels have great significance.
The thicker the fur and the darker the color, the colder the weather. Often these forecasts are as accurate
as those of the meteorologist.

Gina Summars' imitation of a paragraph in
Wandering Through Winter *by Edwin Way Teale*

4.5 Revision: Substitution

Substitution involves removing one word, phrase, clause,
sentence, or paragraph and substituting something else in
its place. The following paragraphs illustrate different
kinds of substitutions. The comment on the revision il-
luminates some reasons for changes. A writer can generally
improve a piece of writing by making the following kinds
of changes: (a) substituting specific language in the place
of vague general language (see 3.1 and 21.12); (b) substituting active verbs for lifeless verbs (see 21.24); and (c)

substituting fresh language for stale clichés and abstract language (see 21.6, 21.18, and 21.19).

Early draft with revisions

~~You and other~~ Most/Many/Some people ~~are of the opinion~~ think ~~that~~ the life of a college football player~~'~~s a life of leisure and ~~is one that is filled with~~ glamor. Although Football ~~is and~~ has been a big part of my ~~college~~ life for the past two years and it is not all ~~that~~ it is cracked up to be. I have no Spare time ~~for any kind of~~ ~~relaxing~~ to relaxing is ~~almost impossible~~ I have to during the season. Practice ~~takes time and I can't skip even once.~~ constantly The constantly ~~Play books keep~~ changing play book. ~~weekly and~~ and ~~must be~~ memorized. I have to do three Weight training ~~takes~~ time, ~~and the~~ a week, and weekends are taken up with boring travel on planes that frighten us and grungy filthy buses that smell like wino's last breath. When we're not trying to figure out what Coach wants ~~(usually for us to be Pros)~~ I'm ~~we're~~ trying to ~~be attending to~~ read ~~our~~ my books and study to prepare assignments ~~that~~ For the next test ~~the teachers lay on us without any mercy.~~

Later draft

> Some people probably think college football players lead lives filled with leisure and excitement. Although football has played a big role in my life for the past two years and although I love the game, I have yet to discover any leisure. I have no spare time to relax during the season. I have to attend practice five days a week and memorize a constantly changing playbook. I have to work out in the weight room three nights a week. I spend my weekends in boring travel on terrifying planes or sometimes on buses reeking of cheap perfumes or some wino's last breath. If I am not trying to figure out what Coach wants, I am trying to read my textbooks and study for the next test.

Student comment

> Generally I know what I want to say, but I say it wrong. In the Writing Center, one of the tutors made a list of things for me to check in all my sentences: *that*, forms of the verb *to be*, and the passive voice. I look for those things and revise if possible. This seems to work. I know the revision generally sounds better.
>
> *M. R.*

4.6 Revision: Transposition

Moving things around in a paragraph is often done for a number of good reasons: (a) to improve emphasis and clarity (see 20.10); (b) to correct errors (see 20.8); (c) to create strong parallel structures (see 20.7); and (d) to improve the organization of material (see 3.5–3.7 and 6.1–6.2). To transpose means to shift something from one place to another. This might be a word, a phrase, a clause, a sentence, sentences, or a paragraph. Consider the following sentences.

ORIGINAL In "Christina's World" Andrew Wyeth painted [in a large field] a woman and several old farm buildings in the background.

REVISION In "Christina's World," Andrew Wyeth painted a woman in a large field and several old farm buildings in the background.

ORIGINAL Timothy Leary *where he* experimented with LSD, *before he* preached the glories of drug use, and [taught at Harvard.]

REVISION Timothy Leary taught at Harvard where he experimented with LSD before he began preaching the glories of drugs.

Most effective paragraphs have a clear ordering of sentences. When that order confuses the reader, understanding becomes difficult. For a discussion of the different kinds of order and ordering principles, see 1.7, 2.5, and 6.1–6.2. The following revisions show how a careful writer can improve the clarity of different paragraphs.

Early draft
Use chronological order—morning, noon, night ③

A park changes personality during the day. In the late afternoon, the high school students near the statues in the rose garden begin to congregate. They are invariably rowdy when drinking beer or sucking on their "reefers," believing such behavior makes them "grown up." ① At dawn, joggers prance around the running track. ④ In the quiet evening beneath the stars and the silent trees, the lonely muggers and occasional policemen supervise acres of frightening shadows. ② At

Rearrange

noon, the mothers descend upon the playground area with their toddlers, strollers, and voluminous diaper bags. Tiny children spin in the dirt, weave themselves through the Jungle Jim, and slide with abandon down the shiny curved slide.

Later draft

A park changes personality during the day. At dawn, joggers prance around the running track. At noon, the mothers descend upon the playground area with their toddlers, strollers, and voluminous diaper bags. Tiny children spin in the dirt, weave themselves through the Jungle Jim, and slide with abandon down the shiny curved slide. In the late afternoon, the high school students began to congregate near the statues in the Rose Garden. They act invariably rowdy when drinking beer or sucking on their "reefers." They believe that such behavior makes them "grown up." In the quiet evening beneath the stars and the silent trees, the lonely muggers and occasional policemen supervise acres of frightening shadows.

C. N. P.

Writing Assignments

1. Revise the following paragraph to improve readability. Use your dictionary and substitute better words or phrases for any unintelligible ones.

The venomous extrusion emitted from the dreaded arachnid, the black widow spider, registers fifteen to twenty times greater lethality than the venom ejected by the common rattlesnake. In spite of this alarming hostility and despite the fact that the solitary insectoid has been vigorously proliferating in every city, town, and countryside in the entire USA, people should not be seriously fearful. This is because it can be stated unequivocally that the black widow spider displays a great degree of shyness. Scientists have demonstrated that the dangerous black spider will scurry back to its abode and place of habitation at the least sensitivity that a force of some kind is disturbing the widow of danger in one way or the other. The black widow demonstrates a great hesitancy to defense. It is completely pacifistic and will engage in aggressive behavior only toward its known ecological prey.

2.   Examine the shifts in time in the following paragraph. Revise by clarifying and improving the time sequence.

Many people will procrastinate when given a writing assignment, and they give ingenious reasons for their delays. My roommate always has delayed any writing with the excuse that he will need energy in the form of an ice cream cone. Other overworked students put off writing assignments in one class and will say they have been assigned to read a mountain of work in another class. An insurance salesman puts off working on a report because he was afraid he won't perform well enough for his boss. Some people have been lazy, and instead of finishing an essay they prefer to go to the movies or the mall. Sometimes teachers will refuse to write comments on a student's paper because they feel the comments will not be helpful. Generally speaking, many people have delayed writing as long as possible.

R. B.

3. Examine the shifts in diction and tone in the following sample. Revise the paragraph to achieve a consistently formal or informal tone and diction.

> A public university is a large and complex organism—a really big deal. Because it is not private, it must be responsive to a variety of different public groups. In the first place, it must offer the students spiffy digs with neat grub and an environment where thought and learning can go on in a big time way. It must also offer to the faculty decent bread and the opportunities to teach and do mind gliding research in one's hang up. Furthermore, it must offer to the public the goodies of knowledge and research. And every spring, it must graduate a group of guys and gals who will go forth into the world with knowledge and dedication committed to making waves with a positive contribution and a difference to society.

4. What specific details might you use to write on the topic of changing your mind about school?

5. Analyze a paragraph assigned by your teacher by responding in the following different ways:

   a. Use the numbering or correction symbols at the front of the book to identify problems or errors.

   b. Write out answers to the following questions for peer evaluation: (1) What do you like the best about this writing? (2) How would you state the main idea of the passage in one sentence? (3) What material might the author add to improve the writing? (4) What might the writer remove or change to improve the main point of the writing? (5) What one question do you have about the passage?

5 Introductions and Conclusions

5.1 Contents of introductions

Make your introduction clear, direct, honest, and helpful. Find ways to help your reader get your meaning. An effective introduction presents the subject, states the main idea, and creates interest; at the same time, it displays a clear sense of the paper's purpose and audience.

The following hints can help you write effective, lively introductions.

- Avoid using a sentence such as "I am going to write . . ." or "My paper will be about. . . ."

- Avoid sweeping claims, especially phrases such as "from the beginning of history" or "throughout time."

- Avoid writing a very general introductory paragraph, the kind you may have written in high school to go with a three-point enumeration essay. Trust your feeling for the subject and find some angle that will spark your readers' interest.

- Focus on one particular part of the subject. Include this focus in the introduction. Include the main idea.

- Don't magnify, minimize, evade, apologize for, complain about, or boast about the subject.

- Spare telling that "Webster says. . . ." Use a definition only if it leads smoothly into the body of your paper.

- Avoid a string of generalizations on the subject.

- Link the introduction to the title and especially to the body of the paper.

- Use the most interesting fact that you have—the newest, the strangest, the most dramatic. Startle your reader if you can.

If you look at a number of successful introductions by different writers, you will find great variety. In terms of content, for example, some writers use quotations, clever word play, interesting figures of speech, or humor; others use relevant personal experiences or statements of strong emotion, such as anger or pity.

5.2 Thesis statements in introductions

A thesis statement expresses the main idea of the writing in one or two sentences. Although it is possible to imply the main idea without a direct statement, a writer can usually benefit from the careful use of a thesis statement in the introductory paragraph. First, it sets up a contract with the reader that a certain idea is going to be presented and developed. Second, it can guide the writer in presenting and developing ideas. Although scholars use different terms to name, analyze, and explain this element in the introduction, some common terms are *thesis statement*, *numbering thesis*, and *thesis response*. Here are some examples:

THESIS STATMENT   A visit to the McDonald's on Wayne Avenue early in the morning yields some curious surprises.

NUMBERING THESIS   An observer who wanders into the McDonald's on Wayne Avenue early in the morning might notice three unusual kinds of people.

THESIS RESPONSE   What does a fast-food employee do on the graveyard shift? A worker often feeds the hungry, ministers to the lonely, and may call the police on criminals.

5.3 Length of introductions

How long is an introduction? Consider your introduction the right length if it (1) presents the subject, (2) states your main idea, (3) interests the reader, and (4) provides necessary background information. Some writing assignments need one sentence for an introduction; others require more. Mainly, the introduction depends on the audience and the purpose. Writers show great variation in their introductions—in style, content, and length.

For college writing assignments, learn to adjust the length of the introduction to the complexity and size of the whole composition: one or two sentences for a paragraph, one short paragraph for a five-paragraph essay, two or three paragraphs for a longer essay or research paper. Keep your reader in mind. Use the introduction to interest and inform your reader. Above all, avoid a string of vague generalities on the topic. Adjust the length accordingly.

5.4 Kinds of introductions

The more you read, the more you will find different kinds of introductions. Keep your eyes open and notice the variety of introductions in letters, textbooks, editorials, newspaper or magazine articles, scholarly essays, and advertisements. The following kinds of introductions are generally appropriate for the different assignments in college.

a. Short narrative

A narrative might contain a brief story or anecdote to interest your readers. It should lead smoothly and directly into the subject in some way. The following narrative introduces an essay exploring the meaning of the word *bravery*.

> When I was twelve, I went camping with our Boy Scout troop from church. Because of the heat, we slept outside around a campfire. One morning I woke up before dawn. When I opened my eyes, I was staring right at a small rattlesnake. It was no more than two feet from my face. I don't know how I thought clearly because I was just a kid, but I very calmly lifted up a stick and pinned the snake to the ground. Then I screamed. The scoutmaster finished off the rattler with a machete, and then I started to shake. I was brave and frightened at the same time. This experience led me to think seriously about the meaning of the word *bravery*.
>
> *Jack Jordan*

b. Clear examples

Writers often use an example or a series of examples to gain the reader's attention and present the main idea of the paper. The examples should be clear, believable, and connected to the main point of the paper. The following introduction contains *several* examples of ingenious ways some students cheat in college. This material introduces a paper in which the author argues for an honor code at her school. Another writer might present a *single* striking example to introduce a theme.

> Recent stories in several national magazines show that cheating in college is a nationwide problem. Solutions to the problem elude most people in authority. Here on this campus, students have exhibited

more ingenuity cheating than they would ever exert in studying in a proper way. They have scribbled answers on walls, floors, arms, shoes, jeans, fingers, desks, and coffee cups. They have scribbled answers on the tops of hats, the bottoms of shoes, inside their clothes, outside the windows, upon the ceiling, below the desks, everywhere known to man and woman except where the answers should be—inside the brain. Here on campus, people are discussing the possibility of an honor code to replace the pitiful pattern of cheating.

Billie Watts

c. Questions

A question or two may provide an excellent way to introduce a subject. Good questions often lead directly to answers in the body of the paper. The questions should relate to the subject, and they should be presented in an orderly fashion. Some writers relate the order of the questions to the order of discussion in the paper. Such careful ordering could lead to a string of paragraphs, each dealing with the answer to a single question. The following paragraph served as an introduction to a research paper on teenage prostitution.

People are understandably puzzled by teenage prostitution anywhere, but especially in New York City. They begin to ask questions. Why would any young girl become a prostitute? How many young people are involved? Where are these children's parents? What can be done to prevent such a problem? Are any people or groups working to liberate these children from this hideous form of life? The answers to these questions give an interesting glimpse into modern life.

Roberta N.

d. Problem

Just as an introduction with questions leads to answers in the paper, an introduction presenting a problem leads to a solution or possible solutions in the body of the paper. This technique works well to introduce papers exploring causes or effects, papers making predictions, and papers arguing for some kind of change. The following introduction shows a lighthearted approach to a problem as perceived by a student.

> It is depressing to think who gets to use the library in the evenings and on the weekends now that the Director of Libraries has decided to cut back the hours. Certainly the mice will be able to enjoy all the new books. Most likely the janitors will find the quiet a good time to catch up on the latest games by the Celtics, Red Sox, Patriots, or Bruins. Sure there are other good libraries in town; and, yes, students can use their time more wisely. However, the problems caused by the cutback in library services can only harm this school.
>
> *W. T.*

e. Overview

An overview gives the reader a broad glimpse of the subject. Such an introduction presents relevant background information: key facts, brief history, or expert opinion. An overview focuses on the subject, creates reader interest, and states the paper's purpose. A paper entitled "A Report on Writing at Several Local High Schools" begins with an introduction presenting a broad overview of the topic.

> Many people nationally are complaining about student writing skills. Employers complain that many high school graduates can barely read and write. Officials of the Armed Services express alarm at the declining language skills of new recruits. College professors become frustrated with entering freshmen who have great difficulty writing acceptable academic papers. Wherever one looks, the complaints resemble each other. An examination of the writing done at several local high schools leads to some interesting conclusions.
>
> *Paula Eiseley*

f. Definition

A formal or informal definition provides an effective way to introduce a difficult or unfamiliar subject. A formal definition can be found in a dictionary (see 9.1b and 21.2). An informal definition might include the following: information about the origin of the word, special meanings for the word, or the author's own personal definition of the word. Caution: Do not begin a paper on a common word, such as *apple* or *school*, by writing, "Webster says. . . ." The following introduction uses a definition of the word *psychoanalysis* to lead into a criticism of Freudian ideas. The succeeding introduction offers two definitions of the word *God*: one is by a great philosopher, and the other is by a child.

> A dictionary gives the following definition of the word *psychoanalysis*: "a method, developed by Freud and others, of treating neuroses and some other disorders of the mind . . . through the use of such tech-

niques as free association and dream analysis." This theory has come under attack recently from three separate groups of thinkers concerned with mental health in America. Feminists, biochemists, and psychologists have begun openly to criticize Freud's theories.

John Hagar

The philosopher Wittgenstein defined God as "the sum total of all possible propositions," but if you ask a child to tell you who or what God is, you might get this response: "God is everything good, like candy." Ideas about God change radically according to whom you ask. Nothing could be more different than people's ideas about God in different religions.

Sharon Desko

5.5 Contents of conclusions

An effective conclusion can become a strong part of the composition. It gives the author one final opportunity to emphasize the paper's main idea, one last chance to affect the reader's thoughts and feelings. An effective conclusion should tie the parts together, emphasize the main idea, and give a sense of closure to the material. Most good conclusions contain the following elements:

- ✎ A sense of finality, not the sense of an abrupt stop
- ✎ A final, emphatic thought or feeling
- ✎ A summary (not repetition) of the most important material
- ✎ A skillful restatement (not merely a repetition) of the central idea
- ✎ A statement of the relationship between the parts of the paper

A statement of the importance of the material presented

Think of the emotions of your reader. What emotion do you want that person to feel at the end of the paper: anger, happiness, sadness, concern, skepticism, or confusion? The emotion your reader feels at your conclusion helps that person accept or reject your main point.

After you have written the conclusion, you might read through it with a critical eye, asking the following questions:

- Do you restate and emphasize the paper's main point?
- Would a reader have a sense of the paper's completeness and importance?
- Do you state the obvious, apologize, hesitate, digress, or repeat verbatim?
- Do you bring in unrelated new ideas and material?
- Do you say anything to weaken your main point?
- Do you use redundant phrases such as "in final summary" and "last but not least," or do you use effective signals of conclusion such as "finally" and "to conclude"?

5.6 Length of conclusions

In doing some research for writing this section, the author examined hundreds of different sorts of conclusions by professional writers. Some were as short as one or two sentences. Some were short or long paragraphs. Other conclusions contained as many as two, three, or even four paragraphs. Most student papers contain a concluding paragraph with anywhere from four to twelve sentences. Keep your concluding paragraphs short and consider them finished when they contain the elements listed in 5.5.

5.7 Kinds of conclusions

Many writers use summary or restatement of main ideas to end a paper. Both strategies work. In certain cases, they are perfect. In other cases, they are boring and obvious. The most effective conclusions emphasize the paper's most important elements and also show relationships among ideas and supporting details. A good conclusion does more than merely summarize or repeat. It wraps things up and ties them together even though it may be omitted in a very short paper.

Experienced writers will use whatever works for the occasion, but some of the most common conclusions involve one or more of the following thinking strategies: effects, general statement, prediction, quotation, rephrasing, importance, summary, exhortation, and analogy.

a. Effects

By listing effects, a writer is able to tie together loose ends of an action or situation. An effective conclusion works to unify the paper. The following conclusion ends a paper exploring problems in the freshman year.

> These paragraphs described the problems of some students during their first and last semester on this campus. A few notes about their lives after college should have some interest. George still cannot find a job he likes, and he still has a drug problem. Because his parents are wealthy and tolerant, he lives at home. He reports that he "feels empty with a hun-

ger for belief" and he says that he "really would like a job that meant something, even if it was mowing lawns." Mari enrolled in beauty school the day after she dropped out of college. She recently passed her state licensing test and reports that she "reads more now than in college." She works as a stylist in Dayton, her hometown. Roger works for his father as a brick-layer. He is happy and does not miss college one bit. It seems that many young people find a fuller life after leaving college without a degree.

B. Cedric Vane

b. General statement

A concluding generalization can effectively end a certain kind of paper. A general statement can tie together examples in a rigorous, logical manner. For instance, after presenting examples to illustrate the weakness of high school graduates in reading, writing, and mathematics, a writer might end the paper with a concluding generalization. The following conclusion contains two generalizations derived from a number of examples.

These examples of student apathy could be multiplied indefinitely. Everyone has his or her story to tell, one which leaves an observer with two general impressions. First, in America today, public, and even private, high schools are full of students who have little, if any, interest in education. Second, the situation seems to be getting worse every year.

Lydia Gyvens

c. Prediction

Prediction concerns the future. People listen to predictions and are moved by them, so this is a powerful way to end a paper. Plan a strategy for your forecast of future events. Make your prediction clearly positive or negative. Predict advantages or disadvantages. Have the prediction follow from the material in the paper itself. Don't spring a great surprise on your unprepared reader in the final paragraph. The following paragraph illustrates a conclusion predicting some immediate benefits obtained from basic medical research.

> Basic medical research projects, such as those mentioned above, will have enormous benefits for society. In the near future, scientists will discover the mechanism that causes cancer in the human body. In a few years, researchers will soon uncover the chemical or dietary deficiency which causes mental illnesses such as schizophrenia and depression. In only a few years, scientists will understand completely how arthritis causes crippling pain. Such discoveries will come about not because doctors treat patients, but because research scientists have explored important questions in their laboratories far away from pain and suffering.
>
> *James Ladd*

d. Quotation

A quotation can sometimes sum up the main point perfectly. A phrase or one or two sentences can tie together the material and make a final point. Some writers prefer popular or common sources, whereas others prefer literary or scholarly sources. Especially effective can be a quotation from a poem, story, play, or song. Whatever sources are used, a good quotation makes an effective way to emphasize a final point to the reader. The following paragraph illustrates the use of a quotation to end a paper contrasting democratic and Marxist ideas of freedom.

> The differences between these two societies are so vast that the imagination bends under the weight. In a totalitarian society, a small group of people, or maybe one person, like Stalin, controls everything. This is in radical opposition to the democratic principle. In our country, Abraham Lincoln said it best: "Government of the people, by the people, and for the people shall not perish from the earth."
>
> *Rae Ann Barr*

e. Rephrasing

To emphasize a point, an author may simply rephrase sentences presented earlier in the essay. This is the simplest kind of conclusion. It forcefully emphasizes the paper's main ideas but risks boring the reader. To succeed, such a conclusion needs to be short and direct.

> By now we are all familiar with the bad news about drug abuse in our culture. Teenage use of marijuana in America has become an epidemic. Youths who use this drug regularly inflict damage upon their minds, their lungs, and their bodies. The best research indicates that the active components of marijuana are powerful chemicals with toxic effects. To solve this problem will involve a systematic effort not to frighten young people but to educate them with the simple facts.
>
> *Greg Herrera*

NOTE: Rephrasing is monotonous in a short, concise essay, but it may be effective in a speech because of the tone and manner of the speaker.

f. Importance

The following paragraph by the historian Bruce Catton concludes an essay contrasting the Civil War generals, Lee and Grant. In it he makes a final claim of importance.

> Lastly, and perhaps greatest of all, there was the ability, at the end, to turn quickly from war to peace once the fighting was over. Out of the way these two men behaved at Appomattox came the possibility of a peace of reconciliation. . . . No part of either man's life became him more than the part he played in this brief meeting in the McLean house at Appomattox. Their behavior there put all succeeding generations of Americans in their debt. Two great Americans, Grant and Lee—very different, yet under everything very much alike. Their encounter at Appomattox was one of the great moments of American history.

g. Summary

This is the most common kind of conclusion. In this method the writer sums up the main ideas of the paper, often stressing their importance.

> In summary, the present system of intercollegiate athletics in America creates a number of problems in education. The system brings to many campuses young people who have minimal skills in reading, writing, and thinking. These students have no chance whatsoever of graduating from college. It brings to many campuses energetic young people whose study time is consumed by athletic. training. Finally, it brings to many college campuses paid, semi-profes-

sional athletes who would never attend school just for an education.

Phil Omar

h. Exhortation

An exhortation makes a strong or urgent appeal. Such a conclusion tries to persuade the reader to act in some manner. The exhortation can be general or personal. This works fine for persuasive or argumentative writing.

> As the facts above indicate, drunk drivers cause most traffic deaths today. But you might be asking, "What can I do?" You can begin at home. If you have friends who drink, stop them from driving. Do their driving for them. Pay for their taxis. Make them walk. Put them to sleep. If necessary, let the air out of their tires. Next, tell the facts and the gruesome details of drunken driving. Do not be squeamish. What is worse: being mangled in a wreck or being upset by a true story? Finally, get involved in politics. Support laws that severely punish drunk drivers. Get your police involved in detecting drunk drivers.
>
> *Martha Hall*

i. Analogy

Writers use analogy, a form of comparison, to emphasize the main idea. An analogy makes the reader think in a new and positive way about the main idea. Many writers find an analogy a useful device to conclude an argumentative or persuasive paper. In the following paragraph a writer ends a paper on cocaine with an analogy between drug use and Russian roulette.

> Many songs and some glamorous people praise cocaine, but the use of such a drug by junior high school

students resembles the insane game of Russian roulette. Although some teenagers report having great "fun" or "important experiences" while using the drug, the other cylinders are loaded with dangers: the danger of unreal thinking, the danger of paranoia, the danger of overdose, the danger of arrest, and the danger of health problems. Junior high students who experiment with drugs might compare them to an innocent "squirt-out" with toy water pistols, but in reality they are as dangerous as Russian roulette.

Barney Upton

Thinking Exercises

1. Read the final paragraphs of three articles in a recent issue of a weekly news magazine such as *Time* or *Newsweek*. Write a single paragraph briefly stating how the different writers conclude their articles. Judge the effectiveness of each.

2. Examine the introductions to three articles in magazines such as *Harper's, New York, America*, or *Commentary*. How long are the introductions? What kind of strategies do the writers use? Which was most effective in making you want to read the article? Why and how?

3. Identify three important periodicals in your major or intended profession. Read the introduction to an article in each one. What material do the introductions contain? How do they interest the reader? Do any of the introductions present a review of research?

Writing Assignments

1. Write a paper to lead up to one of the following sentences at the end:

   a. In this manner I was able to remove the large shark from my room without causing too much damage.

   b. During the time the match burned down, I was able to see with clarity enough details in that room to etch it forever in my memory.

2. Write an introduction describing a setting where a violent action occurred.

3. Choose a paper that you have written and write two different kinds of introductions to it. Imitate an introduction in this chapter or one in some magazine. Have one introduction consist of a single startling sentence.

PART 3

Writing
Longer Forms

6 Logic and Writing

✍ Student Comments on Writing

Before I learned about induction and deduction, I had a fixed idea that every paper had to follow a certain predetermined structure. I can remember feeling that what I wanted to say did not always fit into that tidy, neat, little, three-part package. Learning about the inductive and deductive orders made it easier for me to organize my ideas clearly.

Seth Walker

I like the principles of logic, but I have always thought of myself as a poetic kind of writer: you know—freewrite and then find something valuable. The idea of an inductive or deductive order for my essays helps me to be true to my own thoughts and feelings and yet it helps my reader who—as I have slowly learned—wants to read my material with the least possible amount of difficulty.

Penny Brisbee

The principles of logic help us reason correctly. They help a reader or writer determine whether the material in a sentence or paragraph is worthy of belief. The principles of logic are all extensions of one fundamental truth: A statement cannot be both true and false in the same way and at the same time and place. If a pencil is entirely blue, you cannot say that it is not entirely blue. Writers have an obligation to strive for honesty and objectivity in their expository writing. Imaginative writing may be as fanciful as one likes, but expository writing is logical and strives for truthfulness. The principles of logic are basic to all written discourse. This chapter will present information on two different forms of reasoning and will explore some of the different kinds of logical problems in writing.

Logic deals with the thinking needed to support general statements and to draw a conclusion from a series of statements. Logicians generally divide traditional logic into two categories of reasoning: induction and deduction. Induction proceeds from the specific to the general, and deduction proceeds from the general to the specific. Induction leads to a generalization that is *probably* true. Deduction leads to a conclusion that is *necessarily* true.

6.1 Induction

Think of induction as a series of facts leading to a valid conclusion. Inductive writing moves from specific instances to a general statement. Consider the following sentences from a student's journal.

MAY 1   After I ate a package of M & Ms today, I began sneezing.

MAY 2   I ate a piece of cherry pie today. It was delicious. I had no kind of allergic reaction.

MAY 4   I greedily devoured an entire Hershey bar with almonds. It was delicious, but I began sneezing again and my eyes watered some.

MAY 7 I drank one cup of hot chocolate for breakfast, began sneezing, and felt a kind of itching rash begin on the back of my hands.

MAY 8 It is safe to conclude that I am allergic to chocolate. I am going to have to change my diet completely to avoid all chocolate. Woe is me.

In induction, the thinking mind moves from fact to knowledge. This process of reasoning can form a solid basis for your thinking, organizing, and writing.

6.2 Deduction

Deductive reasoning moves from the general to the specific. This manner of reasoning may be illustrated by the syllogism. A syllogism is a logical plan containing three parts: (1) major premise, (2) minor premise, and (3) conclusion. The major premise contains the general statement, the minor premise contains a specific example, and the conclusion follows from the logical connection between the major and minor premises:

MAJOR PREMISE All hang-gliders take great risks.

MINOR PREMISE Jane is a hang-glider.

CONCLUSION Jane takes great risks.

The following entry from a student's writing journal gives some idea how deduction can be used to help in the writing process.

It is funny that I should construct the following syllogism: Major: Students who don't study for Professor Green's chemistry tests cannot pass those tests.

Minor: I'll take Green's test tomorrow and haven't studied. Conclusion: I will fail the test. My syllogism about the test follows the rules of logic, but I think it is also true. The syllogism is not an essay, however. My goal is to use this material to write a paper. I am going to turn my disaster in one course into a triumph in another. I can build up my chem. grade by good lab grades and a good final. I have to write this essay now, though. Okay. Here we are. The major premise has to be true. That means I need to show that lazy students don't pass the test. Two things: It is possible in many courses to pass a multiple-guess test. It is impossible to pass one of Green's tests. He expects knowledge and thought. I need to show this for my reader. Now for the minor premise. I need to explain why I have not been able to study for Green's test. That's easy. I will just tell my reader how busy I have been this week—with no partying and no goofing off: work and problems. The conclusion is obvious. I worry that it will sound obvious or feeble-minded.

Dan McCoy

One special form of the syllogism deserves some attention. It is called the enthymeme, which is a syllogism with one of the premises missing but implied. The following sentence is an enthymeme with the major premise missing: *Because the teachers will receive a large pay increase, the cost of tuition will rise.* As a complete syllogism, the reasoning would go like this:

MAJOR PREMISE   A large teacher pay raise will lead to an increase in student tuition.

MINOR PREMISE   The teachers will receive a large raise.

CONCLUSION   The cost of tuition will rise.

Thinking Exercises

1. Construct the syllogisms that would lead to the following conclusions.

EXAMPLE   John is brave.

MAJOR   All the Smith children are brave.

MINOR   John is a Smith.

CONCLUSION John is brave.

>   a. John is a coward.
>   b. Joseph Stalin was a tyrant.
>   c. These crows are pests.
>   d. This book is humorous.
>   e. Walt Whitman wrote an epic poem.

2. Make a list of specific facts, information, and details to support at least one of the following general statements.

>   a. I was brave/cowardly as a child.
>   b. Watching the evening news can be an emotional experience.
>   c. That dog/cat has been behaving strangely.
>   d. County governments should require AIDS testing before issuing marriage licenses.
>   e. Reading modern poetry is difficult.

3. In a publication assigned by your instructor, read an editorial for the day of your birth. Write out one sentence stating the main point of the editorial. Point to examples of deductive and inductive thinking. Overall, how is the editorial organized—inductively or deductively?

4.   If a claim is a proposition or statement that can be affirmed or denied, which of the following sentences are claims?

> a. The armadillo is a very intelligent animal.
> b. Teach this monkey to read and write.
> c. Mother Teresa helps poor people in India.
> d. How could you teach this monkey to read?
> e. This yacht is the fastest sailing vessel in the world.
> f. Americans have grown complacent recently.
> g. Monkeys can be taught to read and write.
> h. Shakespeare did not write plays.

Writing Assignments

1.   Write a brief inductive essay on the topic of *change*. Have the examples precede the general statement at the end. Focus on one specific kind of change. Decide for yourself whether you consider the change good or bad. Present clear ideas of whom or what the change is good or bad for. Develop in your paragraphs a series of specific facts and examples to show your reader the nature of the change. In your conclusion, formulate a general statement about the meaning and importance of the change.

2.   Using the same material that you included in the preceding assignment, write a deductive essay on the topic of change. In your introduction, make a general statement about a particular kind of change. In the following paragraphs, present a series of specific facts and details that illustrate, explain, and support your general statement.

6.3 Logical problems

While working on their papers, most writers encounter problems dealing with logic and evidence. Attentive reading of the rough draft should help eliminate common problems such as the following.

a. Lack of evidence

Have enough evidence to support your general statements. Readers need enough material to make them willing to agree with the paper's general statement. In a word, they ask for evidence. This evidence must be adequate, relevant, and accurate. One of the most common weaknesses in much student writing is the scarcity of evidence in support of the general statements being made.

Lack of evidence

> My uncle Cletis is what some people would call an alcoholic. I believe he is. Whenever our family has a party, Cletis will come with a case of beer in his own cooler. He has the cooler painted fancy with his own name on the side. He is very loud and likes to tell everyone that he needs his beer the way he needs air to breathe. I have seen him drinking beer on the beach at 7:00 in the morning before he has even had any breakfast. He is a good worker and builds houses, but my father said once that Cletis even drinks on the job.

Comment

> The author of this paragraph claims that Cletis is an alcoholic. The paper refers to the uncle drinking in the morning, at work, and at a party. But these facts do not support the claim that he is an alcoholic. A

person could drink at all those places and still not be an alcoholic. An alcoholic is a person who behaves in a certain way. The writer makes a claim but does not actually support the claim with any evidence. No examples are given that would prove that Cletis is an alcoholic. The author needs to clarify the generalization and present specific evidence for support.

Revision

My uncle Cletis is an alcoholic. He drinks every day. He drinks by himself, and he drinks in company. He feels unsure of himself unless he has a drink in his hand. He drinks in the morning, at noon, and in the evening. In an average day, he will consume three six packs of beer. He has told me he "needs" to drink the way he needs air and has confessed to having blackout periods of which he has no memory.

H. O.

b. Emotion in place of evidence

Emotional material can have a powerful effect on a reader. This has been long understood by politicians and others who try to persuade people to behave in certain ways. But emotional arguments do not necessarily lead to truth. Writers should aim at the truth. The basis of academic writing must be a belief in reason and fact as opposed to emotion and human desire. Careful readers appreciate facts and want more than emotional statements about the facts. Use emotion in your writing, but avoid substituting emotion for logic and fact.

Emotional argument

The nationalism and anti-communism of these scum were in direct opposition to our multi-racial unity and our chants for communist revolution to drown all the bosses. We spent our time talking and selling to the city workers who, because of their passivity, have allowed the bosses to pay them to support the city's fascist policies.

From Arrow, *July 1985*

Comment

One sign of emotionalism is the presence of abuse and name calling. The preceding paragraph is from an article criticizing severely the mayor and park director in Gary, Indiana. In 1985, a group of children drowned in an abandoned pool. The article charges the mayor and director with serious crimes, but it offers no evidence or support for the charges and relies instead on vituperation and abuse. Anger is often a moral force against oppression, injustice, and stupidity. But anger is no substitute for thought nor is it to be used in place of evidence in writing.

Revision

In the past few years a number of children have drowned in an abandoned city pool at Fischer Park in Gary, Indiana. Although the pool is surrounded by a fence, it still proves an attractive lure to young children. City officials—including the mayor and the park director—should feel some responsibility for these tragedies. They have probably not done all they could to ensure that the pool is drained and that small children are not enticed into a deadly, yet attractive, trap.

c. Personal attacks

Some people confuse issues and personalities. Personal attacks may be fun to write, but they do not prove anything to a reader. Often, the personal attack is merely a digression from the main point and the issue. Personal attacks prove nothing. One fair and logical way to criticize someone is to show that that person is not qualified to make a judgment in a certain field. A medical doctor is worth trusting for comments about heart disease. A coal miner is the person to trust for comments about underground mining conditions. It is fair and proper to inform the reader that someone is or is not an authority on a topic. It is not fair to attack an idea or a position by attacking a person associated with that idea or position. The two are not at all the same. Logicians classify this form of thinking as the *ad hominem* fallacy; this Latin phrase means "to the man" and refers to an attack on the person presenting a claim rather than use of logic to examine the claim.

Personal attack

> The question of a local income tax comes up before the voters of this city next week. Before you cast your ballot, one way or the other, just remember two important facts. Jack Sanderson, a leading advocate of the new tax, is a convicted criminal. He spent six months in prison as a young man for stealing automobiles and bicycles. Homer Tygart, a local businessman who is worth millions and has been photographed at Hialeah racetrack with known Mafia characters, is another strong supporter of the tax. He has spent close to a thousand dollars in support of the new tax. Why are these criminal types supporting the new tax, and is it wise for you to vote just like Sanderson and Tygart?

Comment

> It is a logical error to criticize an idea by attacking the person who supports that idea. In regard to the

proposed tax, the issue should be debated and decided on the facts and not with any reference to the personality or behavior of any supporter.

d. Assuming the conclusion

One of the most famous arguments in philosophy involves Descartes's attempt to prove that he existed. His words when translated mean, "I think; therefore, I exist." The conclusion of his argument, *I*, is contained in the beginning. Writers occasionally lapse and assume the conclusion instead of supporting or proving it.

Circular reasoning

High schools should require two years of study in a foreign language because each student should learn a foreign language.

Comment

The sentence does not present any evidence in favor of the study of foreign languages. This kind of reasoning is called "arguing in a circle." The author might have mentioned that learning a foreign language leads to personal growth and has great value in the business world.

Circular definition

A miracle is a miraculous happening, such as the healing of the blind man in the New Testament.

Comment

Avoid defining a word by repeating the same or a similar word in a definition. A miracle is an event that is completely out of the ordinary, such as the healing of a blind man in the New Testament.

e. Confusion of fact and opinion

Learn to distinguish fact from opinion. A fact is something that has happened, something that is true, something that is. A fact has a certain objective and nonpersonal quality.

FACT Chicago defeated New England in the 1986 Super Bowl.

FACT Hamlet delivers a monologue on suicide.

FACT The apple on my desk is rotten.

An opinion is a conclusion not based on absolute certainty but is an expression of a personal view or a judgment in the mind about something. An opinion manifests the personal subjective character of the person who has it.

OPINION The Super Bowl game is generally less interesting than most regular-season games.

OPINION Hamlet is a spoiled, ignorant, and whimpering adolescent.

OPINION Apples are the most delicious fruit.

If you use opinions to support your general claims, use informed opinions. Present the opinions of recognized authorities on your topic. The strongest evidence is fact. True statements about things in the world make powerful evidence. Beware of writing a string of personal opinions. Make sure that the factual evidence you present is accurate and relevant.

Confusion

People who say cocaine is a dangerous drug don't know what they are talking about. As anyone who has used it will tell you, cocaine is a nonaddictive drug. It is safe and creates no serious health problems. People who criticize cocaine users are just puritans who want to control other people's lives.

Comment

This is a string of opinions bunched together. They are not presented clearly. Cocaine is or is not dangerous. It is or is not addictive. It does or does not cause health problems. These statements deserve analysis and factual evidence for support or refutation. The factual research evidence is completely ignored by the writer.

Incompleteness

College is a great waste of money.

Comment

For some people, this may be true. It is not true for everyone. The statement needs to be qualified. *For some students, college is a great waste of money.* In either case, the claim needs to be supported by specific examples with concrete details.

Thinking Exercises

1. Look up the following words in your dictionary and write a sentence to provide an example of each: *belief, persuasion, truth, prejudice, deception, lie*, and *view*.

2. Read each of the following sentences and decide whether it is a fact or an opinion.

   a. Excessive sun can cause skin cancer.

   b. Eating apricots can protect people from cancer.

   c. Sigmund Freud believed that human beings are "savage beasts for whom the idea of saving their own kind is completely alien."

   d. The Crusaders destroyed Jerusalem in the 12th century.

   e. The food in the student union is cheap but ghastly.

   f. Athletics is good training for the "real world."

   g. Jean-Paul Sartre was a member of the Resistance to the German occupation of France during the Second World War.

   h. People who take drugs are usually more intelligent than those who are afraid to experiment.

   i. Human beings are savage beasts.

   j. Violent persons—especially sexual abusers of children—should be flogged publicly.

If the sentence is a fact, what material might you use to develop and explain it? How would someone prove the fact was true? If the sentence is an opinion, what material could be used to support or criticize it?

f. Hasty or faulty generalization

One common way of expressing this fallacy is to speak of "leaping to conclusions," "thinking the best," or "thinking the worst." A hasty generalization is the creation of a general statement on the basis of a single example or a limited number of examples. One variety of this kind of logical fallacy is the use of stereotypes. In a stereotype, a writer allows one predetermined and unchanging idea about reality to stand for reality.

A faulty generalization often contains an absolute word. Certain words arouse the suspicion of a careful reader. Some of these words are *all, always, every, everyone, forever, must*, and *never*. These words generally do not allow any exceptions. Use them with great care, or use other words in their place to avoid making absolute and false claims. Learn to use the following important qualifiers: *many, some, few, perhaps, sometimes, often*, and *occasionally*.

QUESTIONABLE All the books for school are boring.

QUALIFIED Many of the books for school are boring.

QUESTIONABLE Football is the most dangerous sport. [Is football more dangerous than hang-gliding, scuba diving, or boxing?]

QUALIFIED Football is perhaps the most dangerous sport.

A hasty generalization follows after too little evidence.

Hasty generalization

I have been sick for the past two weeks. My roommate is thinking about leaving school. We have heard that four students were admitted to the clinic suffering from mononucleosis, and this is the third week of class. College certainly destroys the students' mental and physical health.

Comment

One cannot deny the facts. One can and must say that the generalization about the destructiveness of college is somewhat hasty. After all, college lasts four years, and the United States contains almost 2,400 colleges. The author is indulging in some inaccurate overstatement. Beginning writers should beware of vast generalizations from their own limited and personal experience.

Revision

Many students have serious problems coping with college life.

A stereotype is a fixed idea about reality. A person who thinks in stereotypes refuses to accept facts and denies reality.

Faulty generalization

College athletes do not know how to read, much less how to write.

Comment

This negative statement ignores the fact that most college athletes at many schools take the same courses as nonathletes, receive comparable grades, and have similar graduation rates.

Revision

Some college athletes—just like some other students—cannot read or write very well.

Thinking Exercises

1. Decide which of the following statements is a fact or an opinion.

   a. Poor people always have a stronger sense of morality than rich people.

b. Cézanne is the greatest modern artist.

    c. Some art critics believe that Cézanne is the greatest modern artist.

    d. After tasting this Slurpee, I know 7–11 stores have great food.

    e. Football is, according to some people, over-emphasized in high school.

    f. The Beatles were a famous rock group in the 1960s.

    g. Football is always overemphasized in high school.

    h. Chuck Berry sang the song "Memphis."

    i. *Philosophy* comes from a word that means "the love of wisdom."

    j. Most people fall asleep watching television.

2.   Identify any hasty or faulty generalizations in the preceding exercise and revise those sentences accordingly.

3.   Choose a sentence from the first exercise above and make a list of specific facts and details you might use to develop an essay on that subject.

4.   Substitute an item of your own choice for the *X.* in the five following sentences. Make a list of facts to support one of these general statements. If possible, make another list of facts to oppose the general statement.

    a. X. is cruel.

    b. X. is funny.

    c. X. does not like to read.

    d. X. is afraid of nothing.

    e. X. is a problem student.

g. Either-or thinking

If someone told you, "There are only two good places to go for a vacation: either New York or Chicago," you might say, "Aren't there any other places in the world?" The either-or fallacy ignores alternatives. Many conditions in the world are not either-or situations. Some situations are clear-cut, but not all. To demand that everything be seen in terms of either-or simplifies and distorts reality.

Either-or reasoning

If we do not disarm our nuclear arsenal, the world will be destroyed. [Compare: *We will either disarm or destroy ourselves.*]

Comment

The either-or fallacy presents reality in terms of an absolute equation. It always assumes a sort of complete inevitability. One of the glories of the human mind is its ability to imagine alternatives and possibilities. The either-or fallacy ignores the possibility of other ways of thinking about the subject.

Revision

Because nuclear destruction is a distinct possibility, countries should begin thinking about plans for limiting and dismantling nuclear weapons.

h. Errors in causation

A cause is a reason for something to happen, the person or agent that makes something occur. Some causes are single; others are multiple. Some causes happen instantly; others occur over short or long stretches of time.

CAUSALITY The chalk dust made the students sneeze.

CAUSALITY After a month of rain, the river flooded.

CAUSALITY The quarterback fumbled and the team lost to Oklahoma.

CAUSALITY John sneezed and blew the paper out the window.

CAUSALITY The flood washed away my father's new car.

CAUSALITY After the Oklahoma game, the coach was fired.

As you can see from this second set of sentences, an effect may, in time, cause something else to happen. An effect is something that occurs inevitably after a preceding circumstance. Three conditions must occur for something to be labeled an effect:

- The effect must follow the cause in time.
- The effect must be different from the cause.
- The effect cannot be reversible.

CAUSALITY Sidney threw a handful of chalk dust into the Biology Lab after Michael dared him.

CAUSALITY A change in the jet stream led to massive rainstorms in the East.

CAUSALITY After the quarterback learned that his father was dying of cancer, he couldn't sleep the night before the game with Oklahoma.

Writers often confuse cause and effect, and they also lapse into logical errors using causal analysis. The causal fallacy has many varieties. In one, the writer ignores the real cause. In a second, an effect is confused with a cause. In a third, the writer simplifies matters by ignoring multiple causes in favor of a single cause. In the most common, as the following example shows, the writer errs by using a time sequence to indicate a causal connection.

Time sequence: no causality

A snowfall is bad for people's health. Whenever it snows, people come down with bad colds.

Comment

These sentences confuse a time sequence with a causal sequence. There is no logical or medical connection between snow and people having colds.

Thinking Exercises

1. Identify the causes and effects in the following sentences, whether stated or implied.

a. Mary bothered me three times yesterday.

b. Mary asked the teacher to define the word *ganch*.

c. Mary asked, "What do I have to do to make an A in this course?"

d. Mary asked, "Why did the first few weeks in college excite me?"

e. Mary whistled. That bothered me, and I lost my place in the book.

f. Mary ran away from the barking dog.

g. This course has given Mary a great mass of knowledge about Russia, and it has also given her an ulcer.

h. Mary has a new and positive attitude toward school after talking to Dean Goldsmith.

2. Designate each of the following statements as a cause or an effect. If you designate a statement as a cause, write a few sentences that present three or more possible effects. If you designate a statement as an effect, write a few sentences that present three or more possible causes.

    a. The policeman was carrying a loaded shotgun.

    b. Two dorm students were arrested for brawling in the cafeteria.

    c. Amy stayed awake all night, crying in her room.

    d. We drove four hours to the Springsteen concert.

    e. Evan did not finish his term paper on socialism.

3. Examine the following sentences in terms of the connection between cause and effect. Identify the causes. Identify the effects. Then choose one of the following and write a few sentences answering the question, *why*.

    a. After his brother died, Carlos quit smoking.

    b. The principal will expel any student caught possessing or using drugs.

    c. Mark became indignant when he learned he had to take a course in writing to graduate.

    d. Otto chugged a pint of crème de menthe and we had to take him to the hospital emergency room.

4. Identify causes and effects in the sample sentences at the beginning of 6.3h. What relationships are there between the different sentences?

i. Straw-man argument

Avoid turning the opposition into a straw man—that is, a scarecrow and not a real person. The straw-man argument misstates and distorts the opposition. One variety of this fallacy is claiming that the opponent holds ridiculous or obviously evil opinions, which are easy to attack. In this sense, it is a form of emotional argument and personal attack. Another strategy is to present the weakest element in an opponent's argument as the central element, thereby distorting that person's position.

Straw-man argument

Those who are opposed to censorship of books are in favor of child pornography.

Comment

This blurring of distinctions with an element of meanness often characterizes the straw-man argument. It neglects or refuses to make careful distinctions. This fallacy can be refuted by factual contrary evidence. Many people are opposed to both book censorship *and* child pornography.

j. Non sequitur reasoning

Non sequitur is a Latin phrase meaning "It does not follow." This can refer to a number of situations in which the conclusion does not follow from the main points. This kind of error may result from faulty organization or from the omission of necessary material.

Non sequitur

Because children today are exposed to television at an early age, they are much smarter than their parents. [What proof is there for this questionable assertion?]

Revision

> Because children today are exposed to information on television from an early age, they might know more than their parents.

Non sequitur

> If you take Professor Baker's course Philosophy and Business, you will be ready to get a job with a big corporation. [It is difficult to see the logical link between a course and obtaining a job in the business world.]

Revision

> Some students report that after taking Professor Baker's course they have a clear idea of what a business career involves.

k. Analogy in place of evidence

An analogy is a form of comparison that shows points of resemblance between unlike objects. A comparison may help explain a point, but it never proves a point. An analogy can help a reader understand something in a paragraph or an essay, but an analogy is never evidence for any main point. (See 3.7.)

Analogy

> If you want to know why American products are inferior to Japanese goods, compare the average American worker to the Japanese worker. The Japanese worker is just like a bee working for the benefit of the entire hive. The bee will go out on its own and not waste any time. Then it returns straight to the hive, full of pollen ready to produce honey. The

American worker is just like a mosquito looking for a free lunch at someone else's expense.

Comment

The contrast or comparison between the two workers might be interesting, but the topic concerns products. The author avoids any discussion of the workers or the products in favor of an emotional analogy calculated to anger some readers.

I. Equivocation: Shift in word meaning

Define your words carefully. Do not use the same word in two different senses without alerting your reader. Many words have two or more meanings and these meanings may be changed by emphasis and context. Stick to the meaning of all words being discussed, and avoid shifting meanings in the middle of an essay.

Equivocation

Karl Marx called for a vast revolutionary movement led by the workers which would bring in a new system of common ownership or communism. This idea of communism was founded by the ideas of Jesus, who told his followers to share everything they owned in common.

Comment

The word *communism* is used in two completely different senses there. In one sense, it refers to an organized plan of revolutionary change. In another sense, it refers to the members of a group sharing all things in common. An equivocation is a shift in word meaning with no explanation.

m. Bandwagon effect

Have you ever tried to persuade someone you know by saying, "Everyone else is doing it?" If so, then you have used a logical fallacy known as the *bandwagon effect*—the use of an unqualified statement to suggest that a vast majority of people support or oppose something. It implies that logic, truth, and value are determined by large numbers of people. Such a logical fallacy often makes exaggerated claims using pronouns such as *everyone* or *no one*.

Questionable

> As everyone knows, cocaine is a harmless and pleasurable drug.

Qualified

> A few people believe that cocaine is a harmless and pleasurable drug.

n. Appeal to tradition

One common argument some people use involves an appeal to tradition. The fact that a certain practice has occurred in the past does not give any *logical* support that it should be done that way in the future.

Appeal to tradition

> The school board has to appoint the teacher with the most seniority to the position of superintendent because they have followed that policy in the past. [There is no *logical* connection between any past and present practice.]

Revision

The school board might appoint the teacher with the most seniority to the position of superintendent as they have done in the past.

Thinking Exercises

1. Revise each of the following groups of words. If part of the material is illogical, remove it or revise the wording. Add or delete material if necessary. Make separate sentences if need be.

   a. Seth and his brother like to listen to rock 'n' roll music on the radio; they will certainly grow up to be drug addicts.

   b. Our new neighbors belong to a charismatic Christian church. They probably don't know how to read or write and hate medical doctors.

   c. If you do not own a new or a late-model car, you cannot ever be happy.

   d. Every time you buy something made in a foreign country, you damage America.

   e. Students in high school should not be asked to read any of the writings of Karl Marx. It would create a whole generation of communists.

   f. Pornography is harmless. Who does it hurt?

   g. It is not important to teach children to read. They will pick it up on their own when they are interested.

   h. People talk about drugs as if they were dangerous. Have you noticed that those who are most opposed to drugs are those who love their beer, wine, or mixed drinks?

   i. I would never want to even visit New York City. Everyone in that place is out to rob you.

   j. It is obvious that all these catastrophic illnesses appeared just about the same time that sexual liberation got going strong in this country.

2.   Examine each of the following statements and discuss their possible meanings. Do any have problems in logic? Find some examples to support one statement. Find some other examples to oppose that statement.

   a. "I love justice and hate equality." John Randolph

   b. "Beauty is truth." John Keats.

   c. "Religion is the opiate of the masses." Karl Marx.

   d. "Human beings have no free will. They are machines." La Mettrie

   e. "All men are created equal." Thomas Jefferson

3.   Examine the following sentences. Identify any errors in logic. Revise the weak sentences to avoid any logical problems.

   a. Everyone in my class smokes; how can people say smoking is harmful if everyone smokes?

   b. If you touch a toad on a warm day you will get warts.

   c. If you do something wrong for a good reason, that changes it from wrong to right.

   d. We can't really say that any statement is true or false because everything is relative.

   e. That story was on the news again last night; it has to be the truth.

    f. Mary wore her orange dress again today, and she had another headache just like the last time she wore it.

    g. People in France only seem friendly. I know from my experience.

    h. Barbara would be a great president. Look how hard she campaigned!

    i. Buying a Japanese car is an insult to our veterans.

    j. The average American diet is completely worthless.

4.   Read an editorial in a daily newspaper and summarize in one or two sentences the writer's main idea. Make a list of the supporting material presented in the editorial. Make a second list of material you might use to oppose the point of view presented in the editorial. Does the editorial have any logical weaknesses? Identify them.

5.   Identify the logical errors in the following passages. Underline any general statements.

    a. Jimmy is going to fail this course. He spends too much time studying.

    b. Senator Milton does not deserve to be reelected. Last month, he paid his business taxes only after the fact was printed in the newspaper.

    c. Sarah dislikes Ireland and Irish people. She will never go to a party on St. Patrick's Day.

    d. You cannot ever trust the British. Look at what they did in America and India.

    e. All the intellectuals on this campus are rude. Yesterday at dinner two of them were throwing Jell-O all over the cafeteria.

6.   For at least two of the following statements make lists of specific details that might be used for support or opposition.

a. Movies present negative influences to adolescent viewers.
b. Large corporations have no interest at all in the customers.
c. Nature is vastly overrated as a source of beauty, peace, and quiet.
d. Athletic competition is bad for young people.
e. Hatred is most often self-destructive.

6.4 Checking the logic

In reading your paper over before revising, you will need to pay special attention to its logic and organization. You will need to ask all the questions found on the checklists for revising in 1.9c. But you will also need to read the paper through once, asking whether it makes sense and whether it proves its point. Here are some questions to use when reading through your draft for logic and effectiveness:

✎ Is the paper effective and mature? Does it actually get its points across with pertinent evidence? Would a reader take the argument seriously or ignore the paper?

✎ Does the paper use metaphor, simile, and analogy to try and prove its point? Or does it use those devices to explain, clarify, and emphasize points? Analogy does *not* prove anything—even though it may be especially apt or striking.

✎ Does the paper stick to the facts? Does it attack personalities? Does is appeal to emotion or prejudice? Does it jump to conclusions? Does it contain other fallacies?

- ✎ Is the important material relevant, accurate, intelligent, and precise? If the evidence causes problems, the entire argument is damaged. Change any weak or inaccurate material.

- ✎ What assumptions does the paper make? Are they valid? If the assumptions are incorrect, the entire argument is called into question.

- ✎ Do any words need to be defined? Are the definitions accurate and do they help develop the paper? Are the meanings of the words consistent throughout the paper?

- ✎ Does the paper actually prove or support its point? Would an intelligent person agree with it or disagree?

7 Writing Persuasion

7.1 Achieving purpose in persuasion

Persuasion involves practical writing, and most people,
when they use the word *persuade*, have a practical aim in
mind. They believe that persuasion tries to convince others
to act some way; for example, "I want to persuade Anna

to quit smoking cigarettes." Effective writing that seeks to persuade avoids theory and vague generalities. Instead, it focuses on a subject, knows its audience, and looks to a certain goal. Effective persuasion always has a precise goal. When you decide to write a paper of persuasion, you should have your intention clearly in mind. In fact, you can clarify your entire writing task by completing a sentence, such as "I want A to do B because of C." The following examples illustrate this kind of sentence:

> I want to persuade my parents to buy me a computer for my school work.

> I want to persuade the state legislature to pass a clean water bill for three reasons.

Effective persuasion leads to action. Persuasion appeals to logic, moral principles, personal advantage, and occasionally emotion. Persuasion avoids coercion, bribery, and force. Nagging, pestering, bothering, and complaining form weak substitutes for effective persuasion.

7.2 Considering audience in persuasion

The audience in persuasion is clear and obvious. Consider a persuasive situation: a daughter wants to convince her father to quit smoking after she has read about the damage that cigarettes can cause. Or consider another situation: a mother whose daughter was killed by a drunk driver tries to persuade a state legislature to write stringent and effective laws to deal with drunk drivers. In both cases, the audience is perfectly obvious. Understanding the audience helps the writer in every writing assignment, but in persuasion, the audience is from the very beginning connected with the entire writing process. Because effective persuasion must identify an audience, some teachers require that all writing assignments have a persuasive intention.

Besides knowing the intended audience, you can improve the persuasive effect of your writing by considering how the audience might respond negatively. First, list some practical reasons the audience might give to reject your suggestion. Second, list some possible emotional reasons your audience might give to reject it. Take these practical and emotional elements into account as you write the paper.

7.3 Persuasive assignments

An effective persuasive paper needs a clear subject, a specific audience, a main point, and some good supporting reasons. The following selections from student writing journals show how some students changed the general topics of styles in clothing and overpopulation into writing assignments whose goal was persuasion.

> I want to write a letter to the student newspaper to persuade students in the spring to have a little more style in what they wear. I mean this campus is not yet a nudist colony. I have heard complaints from teachers and students, both male and female. I think a little bit of humor might be called for here.

> I want to write a letter to the general audience of talented and secure young married couples, persuading them to have children. I think that the people

who can best afford to be parents are the ones who are not having children and the people who are least able to afford to be parents are the ones who have many children. I want the reader to see this contrast.

7.4 Strategies in persuasion

To write an effective persuasive paper you need to clarify in your mind the answers to the following questions:

- ✎ What person or group do you want to read this paper?
- ✎ What do you want that reader to do?
- ✎ What are the three best reasons you can present?
- ✎ What reasons will the reader give for *not* acting?
- ✎ What material will help develop your best reasons?

In thinking about a topic, find different kinds of strong reasons. Make them convincing. The reasons should help convince your readers. Use facts and specific details to get your points across. Where necessary, use any of the other thinking strategies available: defining terms, making comparisons and contrasts, presenting examples, analyzing material, and so forth. No one has found one specific way to persuade. Persuading is the goal. The means depend on the circumstances and the audience. Three kinds of thinking turn up frequently in persuasive writing: presentation of advantages, presentation of disadvantages, and a moral or ethical appeal.

Show advantages to the reader. To persuade an audience to do something, show that person or group the benefits of following your advice. Don't let the reader guess the benefits. Give graphic examples with plenty of facts and specific details. Help your reader believe in the value of your advice by making the advantages clear. The following comments show how one student turned an assignment calling for persuasive writing into something valuable.

> Remember my pickup truck from the first paper? Well, it broke down and I wrote a paper on that dilapidated pickup truck. I commute to school and help my father on our ranch. I need the truck to get to school and he needs me at work on time. The truck kept getting more and more expensive. The cost of gas and the cost of this last repair were getting out of sight. I wrote the paper to my father about the costs, my problem, and how it would be cheaper for him if he would get me a new truck. Well, he did not buy a new truck, but he bought me a later model one that is much better and much less expensive to operate. I had complained before but this time I worked to persuade by showing him how it was to his advantage to get a newer model truck.
>
> *Rod H.*

Show disadvantages to your reader. To persuade someone not to do something (e.g., not to use hard drugs), refer to actual disadvantages. Point these out to the reader. Be graphic. Make a strong case. The following comment illustrates how one student writer presented disadvantages to make a point.

> I knew I wanted to write about drugs because two of my friends, one an athlete and the other a brilliant student, had seriously damaged themselves with steroids (the athlete) and cocaine (the good student). I am talking about people coming close to ruining their *lives*. I decided to write the one about cocaine because it is more attractive and people don't really know that it is as dangerous as speed or angel dust.

Besides, how many people want to be great athletes? At this school? What I did was to think of those things that I actually said to my cocaine friend which seemed to make a difference to his behavior. Then I wrote it out with some strong details to make my point. I wanted to show the disadvantages. It was easy to do that.

Strom Harpur

Include a moral or ethical appeal. A moral or ethical appeal is an appeal that asks a reader to examine his or her moral or ethical beliefs and come to some kind of judgment regarding right or wrong. This kind of argument appeals to a person's sense of fair play, decency, or honesty. Some people live their lives by moral codes. Muslims respect the sayings in the Koran. Christians follow the moral ideas in the New Testament. Reminding someone that a moral system involves a certain kind of behavior may have a strong effect. Avoid preaching to your audience. No one wants to be told that he or she is evil or wrong. Make your persuasion by appealing to principle rather than by criticizing behavior.

This was the most difficult thing I have ever had to do in my entire life. I wanted to persuade a friend of mine *not* to have an abortion. It was hard to say anything. In talking we both felt sometimes that our breath had been taken away. Writing helped me talk to her at a distance. I wanted to be as gentle as possible and remind her that I believed a child was living inside of her. I am absolutely convinced the father of the child is a decent person and will marry my friend. I had to, as they say, walk softly.

L. W.

Thinking Exercises

1. Write several paragraphs describing a situation in which you tried to persuade someone to do something that person was reluctant to do. Let the reader know about the situation. What was the person persuaded to do? What were the means of persuasion? What objections were raised? What was most difficult to refute? What was the result?

2. Discuss the strategies used by the authors of the following sets of persuasive writings.

    a. I feel I should be allowed to make up the philosophy test I missed last Thursday because, even though I was well prepared, I was sick in bed with a fever of 104 and I have never missed a single class yet this semester.

    b. I feel you should let me make up the philosophy test I missed last Thursday. I know you have let other students make up tests in other classes, and I try very hard. Plus it's goodbyesville to school if this class goes down the tubes.

    c. It's not fair in any way, shape, or form to keep Pablo off the track team. Why should he be penalized this semester for what he did last year? There are a lot of kids in this school who get away with murder and don't lose any privileges. I guess you just want to tell certain people they can't make it no matter what.

    d. I am writing on behalf of Pablo Miro, who is a student in my third period art class. I believe he should be allowed back on the track team because his attitude has improved 100 percent;

his grades have come up from barely passing to a B+; and his presence on the track team will boost the team's morale and help them place in the state meet.

3.   In the following paragraph by Adrienne Rich, what ethical or moral principle underlies and supports her argument? Who is her audience? What is she trying to persuade her audience to do? Why?

Responsibility to yourself means that you don't fall for shallow and easy solutions—predigested books and ideas, weekend encounters guaranteed to change your life, taking "gut" courses instead of ones you know will challenge you, bluffing at school and life instead of doing solid work, marrying early as an escape from real decisions, getting pregnant as an evasion of already existing problems. It means that you refuse to sell your talents and aspirations short, simply to avoid conflict and confrontation. And this, in turn, means resisting the forces in society which say that women should be nice, play safe, have low professional expectations, drown in love and forget about work, live through others, and stay in the places assigned to us. It means that we insist on a life of meaningful work, insist that work be as meaningful as love and friendship in our lives. It means, therefore, the courage to be "different"; not to be continuously available to others when we need time for ourselves and our work; to be able to demand of others—parents, friends, roommates, teachers, lovers, husbands, children—that they respect our sense of purpose and our integrity as persons. Women everywhere are finding the courage to do this, more and more, and we are finding that courage both in our study of women in the past who possessed it, and in each other as we look to other women for comradeship, community, and challenge. The difference between a life lived actively, and a life of passive drifting and dispersal of energies, is an immense difference. Once we begin to feel committed to our lives, responsible to ourselves, we can never again be satisfied with the old, passive way.

Writing Assignments

1. Think of something that you want: a trip or vacation somewhere, a new car, an *A* in a difficult course, a new roommate, or something else. Identify a person able to grant your wish. Then write a well-developed persuasive paper addressed to that person.

2. Identify a real injustice somewhere in the world, such as planned famine in Africa or Afghanistan or political torture in China or Chile. Gather specific information about the situation. Who would have the power to change the situation? Write a letter to that person. Be clear and objective about the situation. Present good reasons—practical, ethical, and emotional—why the injustice should be stopped. Mail the letter to the person. Or, using the material, write a letter to your student newspaper. Persuade your readers to become involved.

3. Think of a friend with a pattern of behavior that you consider less than responsible. Write a letter to that person presenting a serious case for a change in behavior. Or imagine that you are someone else who is concerned about your life, and write a letter to yourself encouraging a positive change in your behavior.

4. Choose an advertisement from the classified section of a newspaper and write a paragraph explaining how

the writer is trying to persuade you to buy the item mentioned. Choose a full-page advertisement from a national magazine and write at least two paragraphs analyzing the persuasive techniques used to try to sell the item. How does the advertisement use product quality, prestige, glamour, authority, personal testimony, or sex to try to sell the item?

8 Writing Argumentation

Argument is like a debate or a trial. Now I realize how important evidence is with good solid examples and details to back up my points. I have never had to provide evidence in my other classes. Up to now, all I have been asked to do is to parrot information or scratch a score sheet. Argument forces me to see what I really believe.

Sonja Ramirez

I learned the most about argument somewhere else. On the TV show *People's Court* two people come before a judge and argue. Each side has the opportunity to present its case, and then the judge asks important questions to find out the truth. I've seen honest people lose to crooks because they didn't have the evidence. This means specific examples. Now I know the value of strong examples.

Jess Stevens

One clear fact on paper is worth a thousand pictures in my brain.

Wayne Deal

8.1 Achieving purpose in argumentation

In the planning of an argumentative essay, a writer makes a fundamental choice and takes a position toward the subject: either favorable or unfavorable. Argument deals with propositions about which people have different opinions.

AGAINST   Professional athletes are grossly overpaid.

FOR   Professional athletes deserve the salaries they earn.

AGAINST   Weldon Kees is a weak, minor, unimportant poet.

FOR   Weldon Kees is an excellent poet.

This choice creates the purpose and influences the entire paper. The writer of an argument needs a subject, a clear and consistent main idea, and enough material so that an interested reader will understand and possibly agree with the writer's main idea.

Good arguments have clear purposes. The arguer wants other people to agree with the paper's main idea. People who write arguments have made a commitment to reason. They believe certain ideas contain value and that other less valuable ideas may present a danger. Arguers do not have to be angry as they attempt to convince other people to agree with their point of view. People who understand how to write argumentative papers know that language is a powerful tool that can change the way things happen in the world.

The importance of argument cannot be overstressed. Ideas have vast consequences in society. Until the passage of laws and amendments that were argued for strenuously, neither blacks nor women had full legal status in America. Many other legal questions continue to arouse fierce debate. Passionate issues create intense arguments. Your composition teacher may never assign such topics, but you should understand that the skills you learn in argumentation have great value outside the classroom, for on a daily basis men and women raise argumentative issues of vast importance.

Discover your own sense of importance. Writers recognize and choose topics important to them. Topics and their complexity do vary. One person will argue about a candidate for the football Hall of Fame. Another person will argue about the value of busing for racial reasons. As a beginning writer, you need to realize the value of argumentative writing and the different strategies for getting your ideas across to others. Choose interesting topics to argue about. Right now, school issues may concern you: dorm life, library hours, boring lectures, attendance policies, meaningless tests, athletics, advising, expenses, or vacations. Avoid frivolous topics such as colors for shirts or the best way to wash a car.

8.2 Considering audience in argumentation

In a curious way, the audience determines purpose and strategy. In creating an argument, you must take the audience into account. Basically, you will encounter three situations:

- Your audience agrees with your main idea.
- Your audience is neutral toward your main idea.
- Your audience disagrees with your main idea.

Understanding your audience will help you formulate your strategy. Different audiences lead to different strategies. The following kinds of analysis should help you plan your writing.

If the audience agrees with you, avoid boring them. Do not tell them again what they already know. You might present vivid and fresh examples or emphasize in a new way the importance of the position. New evidence and fresh insight will interest an audience that already agrees with you.

If the audience has not made up its mind, be fair-minded and objective. Stress the importance of the subject. Present enough material so that a fair-minded person will read the paper and say, "Yes, that makes sense and seems reasonable. I agree with that." The strongest argument for anything is the truth. Present your information honestly, simply, and strongly. Show clearly the personal advantages of your main idea, or explain fully the personal disadvantages of the opposing point of view.

If the audience has already made up its mind, walk softly. Try to understand the reasons why they hold the position they do. You need to know the strongest factual, logical, and emotional reasons for that opinion. If necessary, you need to undermine that position using facts and logic. Above all, do not criticize the *person* who believes the argument. Criticize the *argument* and its evidence, logic, and assumptions.

You may never know who will pick up your essay and read it. Writers try to have some sense of the average reader. One way to do this is to imagine the average reader of a certain newspaper or magazine. The people who read *Penthouse* differ in many ways from the readers of *Chris-*

tian Science Monitor. The audience for your school's newspaper differs from the audience of *Jack and Jill.* Such imagining can provide some sense of an average reader's intellectual level and general attitude. A knowledge of the reader can help a writer set the proper tone for the essay.

The tone of a paper has an important effect on the audience. Tone is the writer's attitude toward the audience and toward the subject matter. It is important to consider both these attitudes. Avoid negative attitudes and treat both your reader and your subject matter with respect. Try to convey to your reader a sense of knowledge, a pattern of concern, and an objective manner. A negative attitude can destroy any chance of communication. You want your reader to have an open mind to your subject and your ideas.

Some writers adopt a superior attitude and think of the reader as a dunce or a child. Needless to say, a reader will be offended from the very first and stop reading. Other writers create problems for the reader by relying heavily on emotion instead of logic and reason. No reader wants to be emotionally browbeaten. The following set of guidelines for dealing with the reader should help improve the effectiveness and readability of your argument.

- Discuss arguments, not personalities.
- Find out the facts in the case. Present them calmly, forcefully, objectively.
- In the absence of evidence, do not attack or question another person's motives.
- Admit that you do not know everything.
- Criticize policies and ideas—not people.

Ask yourself two important questions as you plan to write your argument: One, what kind of magazine or newspaper might publish your argument? Two, what kind of strategy will create the strongest argument?

8.3 Evidence in argumentation

Every good argument contains a purpose, an audience, and a supply of evidence. To develop that argument, a writer is helped enormously by having a main idea, a real feeling for the subject, and a clear sense of the intended audience. The purpose and the audience, valuable as they are, will not provide the writer with the evidence needed for an effective argument. One of the best ways to explore the many kinds of evidence is to study what effective writers have felt worked for them. The following collection of comments from student journals is not exhaustive in any sense, but it does provide a good sample of some effective strategies for gathering and presenting evidence.

> Facts! Facts! Facts! Facts wedged inside of facts and then some more facts. When someone in class said that there was no real evidence to link smoking and cancer, I nearly exploded. When I came down from the ceiling, I marched over to the library and dug out fact after scientific fact to show the links. After a while, because there was so much evidence against smoking, I had the sense that I could have been beating a dead horse, but the abundance of facts gave me the luxury of picking and choosing the most effective, clearest, and best-written material. I enjoyed digging those facts out of the library.
>
> *Billie Watts*
>
> I need to learn to choose my material more carefully. Above all, I have to learn to make sure that I do not sabotage my own argument. I might have ruined my last paper if I had not shown it to my response group. They criticized it because to them it seemed like I was arguing that poor people and people who are ethnic minorities have no right to have children. That

was not what I intended at all, so my group's negative comments made me see how my supposed "evidence" went against my main point. It is a strange experience to have my paper read in a way I never intended. The criticism helped me revise and improve my paper.

Jenny Adkins

How to write an effective argument? It is easy. Think of someone you dislike and have the person be smart but also have that person be your relentless opponent. Write the paper over again from the opposite (your enemy's) point of view. Ask anyone you can (parents, siblings, peers, friends, enemies) for evidence to support the other position. This second paper will contain the argument that you can then take apart piece by logical piece. If you know how your opponent's mind works, you can create a stronger argument than you would otherwise.

Joe Davis

I love to watch courtroom scenes in movies and on television. When I wrote my argument paper on helmet laws for motorcycle drivers, I imagined in my mind a string of characters arguing before a judge. First I summoned up those in favor of the laws, then I brought up those opposed. I clustered these ideas and developed a sense of what was just emotional and what was logical and factual. I included some of the emotional, but the facts about accidents without helmets made my argument very powerful and effective.

J. Grant

The best evidence is targeted for a specific audience. Who said, "Only a fool would try to muscle a dead weight"? I've found that once I understand who I am writing the paper *to*, then I know what I need to put *in*. Until I have a sense of what might convince my reader, I am confused. Once that light clicks on, it's full speed ahead with facts and information directed to a specific person or group.

Paula Eiseley

What works? Quote or paraphrase your opponent and then pick it apart with logic until there is nothing left of the argument. Then pull out your little cart full of facts and information. Make your point. What fun it is to shred an opponent's argument!

Andrew Sheets

8.4 Strategies in argumentation

The perfect plan for an argument does not exist because writing assignments differ and writers have different work plans. Some things might help beginning writers as they learn how to select, clarify, and develop an argument. The following list can help most writers prepare for the rough draft.

Understand the writing assignment. Know the minimum and maximum lengths. Develop a sense of personal commitment to the work. Avoid a subject with no intellectual or emotional interest for you. Choose a writing assignment where you would like to see something changed and answer the following questions: Why are you interested in this subject? What difference does it make to you? Do you really care?

Make sure you have an argument. Make sure you have more than a subject and that you actually make a claim. A claim is essential to argument. Notice the differences between the subject, the positive claim, and the negative claim in the following:

SUBJECT   Lotteries

FOCUSED SUBJECT The Maryland state lottery

POSITIVE CLAIM   The Maryland state lottery is a good thing for the state and for the people, and it should be expanded.

NEGATIVE CLAIM   The Maryland state lottery has generally negative effects on the state and on the people, and it should be abolished.

Consider your audience. Who will read this argument? Would you read this paper you are planning to write? Who do you want to read this argument? Can you think of writing it for one specific person? Can you think of a particular group with an interest in the topic? In which publication would you like to see this appear?

Understand the importance of the subject. Make a list of the reasons why the subject is important to you and to your audience. Who would consider it most important? Why? List the reasons why it is important. What can you say to your reader to make clear the importance of the subject you have chosen?

List the strongest points in favor of your position.
Find specific material with good details to illustrate each of your major points. After you have gone through your strongest points, ask the following questions: Would including an authority help your argument? What advantages will a reader gain from agreeing with the points you make? What moral or ethical principles might you use to help

support your position? How can you make your reader feel intelligent by agreeing with your position?

Understand the point of view of your opponent. Make a list of reasons why a decent, rational person would hold a point of view contrary to yours. What is your opponent's strongest point? Weakest point? What errors in logic can you point to? What facts or examples would help undermine the opposing point of view?

Present valuable background information. Include this material if it can help your readers see clearly the main ideas you are presenting.

8.5 Structure in argumentation

Greek and Roman writers described a five-part formal pattern for argumentation 2,000 years ago. This provides an effective pattern, but it is not the only method for argument. Writers use other formal patterns for effective argumentation. Some of them follow the format of a courtroom or a debate with a back-and-forth presentation of the evidence. Another pattern developed from the work of Carl Rogers, a psychologist, presents the opposing point of view first and then tries to show areas of agreement between the two sides before it develops the main points to support the affirmative position. In the traditional pattern, a formal argument contains five distinct parts.

1. Introduction

This section presents and limits the subject. It states the importance of the topic and involves the reader in the paper by creating interest. It hopes to influence readers positively, gaining their attention and goodwill. It is generally one or two paragraphs.

2. Proposition

This section presents the author's ideas about the subject. It includes any necessary definitions and background information and usually has one or two paragraphs.

3. Evidence

This section, the longest of the paper, presents valuable information to support and explain the main points of the argument. Evidence often includes answers to questions such as the following:

> What expert opinion provides support?
> What moral or ethical principles provide support?
> What practical advantages provide support?
> What personal testimony might provide support?
> What facts, statistics, specific details, and examples might provide support?

4. Recognition of opposition

This section presents clearly the most serious objections to the argument. Then it refutes or diminishes these objections.

5. Conclusion

This section ends the paper and gives the writer an opportunity to summarize and emphasize the main points. Although this section must not introduce new material, it should do more than merely restate previous material. It might focus on the importance and significance of the argument.

You will discover that many good arguments lack one or more of the five parts. Some present only the main point and the strongest evidence, whereas others skimp on the introduction and conclusion or ignore the opposition. Do not consider the preceding discussion of structure a cookbook. Consider it a tool kit. If you will help your argument by developing all the elements, by all means use them. If a shorter version will be effective, use the shorter model.

Thinking Exercises

1.   Analyze the following essays in light of the five-part formal structure discussed in this chapter, and answer the following questions: What is the essay's main idea? What evidence best supports that idea? What is the weakest point the author makes? What material could strengthen the argument?

In Defense of Hunting

The only opponents of hunting I'll listen to for long are vegetarians. I won't listen for a minute to meat eaters who pay the butcher and supermarket to kill, package and distribute their meals. But even the sophistic arguments of the vegetarians inevitably irritate me. It's funny, but they all think I'm kidding when I ask if plants feel pain. Plants can fill their lives with peace and their stomachs with nourishment; plant life fashions dazzling displays of color and shape and even responds to classical music. But when the gardener approaches with pruning shears, suddenly plants are numb and indifferent.

I am not a theologian who can argue complicated precepts of morality. I am, I hope, a reasonably intelligent and sensitive man who tries to think clearly about what he does. And what I do is hunt, and sometimes kill.

So who doesn't? Does the power that orchestrates affairs in our universe accord a deer more importance than a fly quivering in a strip of sticky tape? Show me where. No sensible person will argue that significance is related to size—but there are few advocates of the small.

The universe shows no less enthusiasm in exterminating life than in creating it. What do all the opponents of hunting think the sweet-singing "feathered glories" are doing, carving graceful arcs in the evening air? They're killing, just as fast as they can. Even doves, man-made symbols of gentleness, pick through the farmer's silage bins down the road, looking for juicy bugs to snip in half and devour. And the jewel-like trout, darting among the mossy rocks— they're busy killing, too. The foxes and bobcats of our forests are predators as well, and it's fortunate for their prey that they are. As wise Theseus points out at the conclusion of Chaucer's "Knight's Tale," death is forever busy "Converting all things back into the source/From which they were derived, to which they course."

> *From "In Defense of Hunting"*
> *by John C. Dunlap*

Killing for Sport

It would not be quite true to say that "some of my best friends are hunters." Nevertheless, I do number among my respected acquaintances some who not only kill for the sake of killing but count it among their keenest pleasures. And I can think of no better illustration of the fact that men may be separated at some point by a fathomless abyss yet share elsewhere much common ground.

To me, it is inconceivable that anyone can think an animal more interesting dead than alive. I can also easily prove, to my own satisfaction, that killing "for sport" is the perfect type of that pure evil for which metaphysicians have sometimes sought.

Most wicked deeds are done because the doer proposes some good for himself. The liar lies to gain some end; the swindler and the thief want things which, if honestly got, might be good in themselves. Even the murderer is usually removing some impediment to normal desires. Though all of these are selfish or unscrupulous, their deeds are not gratuitously evil. But the killer for sport seems to have no such excusable motive. He seems merely to prefer death to life, darkness to light. He seems to get nothing other than the satisfaction of saying: "Something which wanted to live is dead. Because I can bring terror and agony, I assure myself that I have power. Because of me there is that much less vitality, consciousness and perhaps joy in the universe. I am the spirit that denies." When a man wantonly destroys one of the works of man, we call him Vandal. When he wantonly destroys one of the works of God, we call him Sportsman.

The hunter-for-food may be as wicked and as misguided as vegetarians sometimes say, but he does not kill for the sake of killing. The ranchers and farmers who exterminate all living things not immediately profitable to them may sometimes be working against their own best interests; but whether they are or not, they hope to achieve some supposed good by the exterminations. If to do evil not in the hope of gain but for evil's sake involves the deepest guilt by which man can be stained, then killing for killing's sake is a terrifying phenomenon and as strong a proof as we could have of that "reality of evil" with which present-day theologians are again concerned.

From "Reference for Life"
by Joseph Wood Krutch

2.   Read the editorials in a newspaper, such as the *New York Times*, for the day of your birth. Make a copy of an editorial. Does the author use any of the following: examples, statistics, direct quotation, summary, paraphrase, refutation, figures of speech, or specific language? What is most effective about the editorial?

3.   Make a list of ten reasons in favor of something you dislike, such as strenuous physical exercise, television, study, or sports.

4.   Ask a graduate student or faculty member in your major for a controversial topic in that academic discipline. Identify the opposing sides of the argument.

5.   Which of the following are arguable propositions? Choose one arguable proposition and explain how you would go about arguing that point—pro or con.

a. Richard Nixon was a great president.
b. God exists.
c. The legal age for alcohol should be sixteen.
d. Using animals for research is wrong.
e. Some people are allergic to broccoli.
f. Communism leads to tyranny.
g. Columbus was the first European to reach North America.

6.   Martin Luther King's "Letter from Birmingham Jail" is a careful argument in favor of nonviolent civil disobedience to change an unjust law. In the course of his argument, King uses emotional material. What is your emo-

tional response to the following sentences? Why did King include these in his letter?

> Before closing I feel impelled to mention one other point in your statement that has troubled me profoundly. You warmly commended the Birmingham police force for keeping "order" and "preventing violence." I doubt that you would have so warmly commended the police force if you had seen its dogs sinking their teeth into unarmed, nonviolent Negroes. I doubt that you would so quickly commend the policemen if you were to observe their ugly and inhumane treatment of Negroes here in the city jail; if you were to watch them push and curse old Negro women and young Negro girls; if you were to see them slap and kick old Negro men and young boys; if you were to observe them as they did on two occasions, refuse to give us food because we wanted to sing our grace together. I cannot join you in your praise of the Birmingham police department.

Writing Assignments

1. Choose as a topic something at your college or town that offends you. Write a letter to the student newspaper arguing that the practice should be banned or limited. Give as many good reasons as you can for your proposal. Or think of something that your college or town needs and would benefit from. Write a paper developing your idea about that need.

2. Choose as a subject something that you and your parents have disagreed on. Make two lists: the first representing your point of view, the second your parents'

point of view. State the reasons why you believed you were right and why your parents believed they were right. Write a series of connected paragraphs presenting the two points of view as clearly as possible.

3. If you could change one thing at the high school you attended, what would it be? Write a letter to the principal. Identify the situation. Then present at least three or four reasons for the change.

4. Write a paper defending or criticizing the following idea proposed by Gore Vidal:

> It is possible to stop most drug addiction in the United States within a very short time. Simply make all drugs available and sell them at cost. Label each drug with a precise description of what effect—good and bad—the drug will have on the taker. This will require heroic honesty.

9 Writing Definition

I thought every definition was in a dictionary. That was a rather simple idea. Sure, the words are in the dictionary, but the words in the dictionary do not convey enough meaning. Some words, like *fear*, *love*, or *pornography*, deserve more than a dictionary definition.

Tye Welker

The meaning that people attach to certain key words has a tremendous effect on the way people live their lives. For me the word *football* in high school was sacred. It was the greatest thing in the world. Nothing could even come close to that word for its magic and its greatness. The word has a different meaning to me now, but I can still see how important words are in a person's life.

Glen Dean

9.1 Kinds of definition

Essentially, student writers use three kinds of definitions in college writing assignments: synonyms, formal definitions, and extended definitions. These definitions are different in purpose, audience, content, and length.

a. Synonym

Writers use synonyms to help their readers quickly understand the meaning of unfamiliar words. A synonym is a word with the same or nearly the same meaning as another. For example, a synonym for the adjective *magnanimous* is *largehearted*, and a synonym for the word *madrigal* is *song*. Often the dictionary lists several synonyms for the same word, and the writer chooses the word closest in meaning to the one he or she is defining. Consider the following synonyms for the word *insipid*, taken from *Webster's Ninth New Collegiate Dictionary*:

> **in·sip·id** \in-'sip-əd\ *adj* [F & LL; F *insipide*, fr. LL *insipidus*, fr. L *in-* + *sapidus* savory, fr. *sapere* to taste — more at SAGE] (1620) **1 :** lacking taste or savor : TASTELESS **2 :** lacking in qualities that interest, stimulate, or challenge : DULL, FLAT — **in·si·pid·i·ty** \,in(t)-sə-'pid-ət-ē\ *n* — **in·sip·id·ly** \in-'sip-əd-lē\ *adv*
>
> *syn* INSIPID, VAPID, FLAT, JEJUNE, BANAL, INANE mean devoid of qualities that make for spirit and character. INSIPID implies a lack of sufficient taste or savor to please or interest ⟨*insipid* art and dull prose⟩ VAPID suggests a lack of liveliness, force, or spirit ⟨a potentially exciting story given a *vapid* treatment⟩ FLAT applies to things that have lost their sparkle or zest ⟨although well-regarded in its day, this novel now seems *flat*⟩ JEJUNE suggests a lack of rewarding or satisfying substance ⟨on close reading the poem comes across as *jejune*⟩ BANAL stresses the complete absence of freshness, novelty, or immediacy ⟨a *banal* tale of unrequited love⟩ INANE implies a lack of any significant or convincing quality ⟨an *inane* interpretation of the play⟩

In your papers, you will often use synonyms. Some of the many ways to incorporate synonyms in your writing are to (1) use parentheses to enclose the synonym for explanation, (2) use commas to separate the synonym that explains

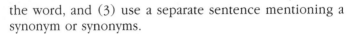
the word, and (3) use a separate sentence mentioning a synonym or synonyms.

SYNONYM   Hoto Tanka constantly refers to *a ganch* (a farm implement for impaling field mice) in his poems and stories.

SYNONYM   Naturally occurring sugars include lactose, found in milk, and fructose and glucose, both common in fruits and vegetables. (From "Sweet Truths about Sugar" by Elizabeth M. Whelan and Frederick Stare)

SYNONYM   Tropical cyclones of the same type as hurricanes are called *typhoons* in the North Pacific, *baguios* in the Philippines, and *cyclones* in the Indian Ocean. (From *Twenty Questions for the Writer* by Jacqueline Berke)

b. Formal definition

A formal definition has three parts: the word defined; the general class to which the word belongs; and one or more *differentiae*, or distinguishing characteristics. For example, the word *cocoon* means "a protective covering made mostly of silk produced by an insect larva in which it passes the pupa stage." This definition contains three parts:

1. **Word defined**	Cocoon
2. **General class**	Protective covering
3. **Differentiae**	a. Made of silk
	b. Spun by an insect larva
	c. Home during pupa stage

The division of a formal definition into three parts can help a writer because such a division resembles a formal outline. A careful outline often can help a writer organize material by listing the main point and the supporting parts. (See 1.7.)

c. Extended definition

An extended definition gives more than a synonym and extends the meaning found in a formal definition. Such a definition might include several sentences, a paragraph, several paragraphs, or an entire essay. In the following essay Susan Sontag attempts to define the term *science fiction film* by dividing the term into its component parts and discussing them.

> The typical science fiction film has a form as predictable as a Western, and is made up of elements which, to a practiced eye, are as classic as the saloon brawl, the blonde school teacher from the East, and the gun duel on the deserted main street.
>
> One model scenario proceeds through five phases.
>
> (1) The arrival of the thing. (Emergence of the monsters, landing of the alien spaceship, etc.) This is usually witnessed or suspected by just one person, a young scientist on a field trip. Nobody, neither his neighbors nor his colleagues, will believe him for some time. The hero is not married, but has a sympathetic though also incredulous girl friend.
>
> (2) Confirmation of the hero's report by a host of witnesses to a great act of destruction. (If the invaders are beings from another planet, a fruitless attempt to parley with them and get them to leave peacefully.) The local police are summoned to deal with the situation and massacred.
>
> (3) In the capital of the country, conferences between scientists and the military take place, with the hero lecturing before a chart, map, or blackboard. A national emergency is declared. Reports of further

destruction. Authorities from other countries arrive in black limousines. All international tensions are suspended in view of the planetary emergency. This state often includes a rapid montage of news broadcasts in various languages, a meeting at the UN, and more conferences between the military and the scientists. Plans are made for destroying the enemy.

(4) Further atrocities. At some point the hero's girl friend is in grave danger. Massive counter-attacks by international forces, with brilliant displays of rocketry, rays, and other advanced weapons, are all unsuccessful. Enormous military casualties, usually by incineration. Cities are destroyed and/or evacuated. There is an obligatory scene here of panicked crowds stampeding along a highway or a big bridge, being waved on by numerous policemen who, if the film is Japanese, are immaculately white-gloved, preternaturally calm, and call out in dubbed English, "Keep moving. There is no need to be alarmed."

(5) More conferences, whose motif is: "They must be vulnerable to something." Throughout the hero has been working in his lab to this end. The final strategy, upon which all hopes depend, is drawn up; the ultimate weapon—often a super-powerful, as yet untested, nuclear device—is mounted. Countdown. Final repulse of the monster or invaders. Mutual congratulations, while the hero and girl friend embrace cheek to cheek and scan the skies sturdily.

From "The Imagination of Disaster"
by Susan Sontag

9.2 Purpose and audience in definition

Generally, writers define words for specific purposes. Quite often, a writer will provide a synonym or a definition for any unfamiliar word in a paper. And in college, students learn to expect questions asking for both short and long definitions on essay examinations. Most important, definitions supply knowledge. They let a writer discover new things. In this way, learning to write a definition provides one of the most important skills a student can acquire because the ability to define and explain words is the sign of an educated person.

Words, however, have meaning and value apart from the classroom. Words are crucially important in people's lives. Certain words, such as *honesty, loyalty, children, marriage*, and *career*, can be found in the dictionary. Such a word seems perfectly clear—at least until a writer starts thinking about the meaning. Then the word carries a greater weight than the dictionary definition. The need for a definition can give writers the opportunity to think seriously and discover meaning or lack of meaning in their lives.

Just as a purpose may vary, so may an audience change. In college, students need one kind of definition to help them read, and their professors ask for other forms of definition, perhaps even extended definition papers. The kind of audience determines the length and complexity of any definition. An explanation of the word *star* for a classmate in composition will differ from an explanation intended for an astronomy professor. In preparing a definition, a writer should keep two things clearly in mind:

> Avoid making the definition overly complex. Use familiar material so your reader can understand

your writing. Avoid highly technical material that the reader might not be able to understand.

Avoid making the definition simplistic. Gear your language and your explanation to your intended audience. Estimate the kind of background information your reader needs to understand the term.

In addition to writing shorter definitions, a writer will occasionally feel challenged and want to explore the meaning of a common or esoteric term. This kind of challenge, this desire to know more about a subject, forms an effective basis for an extended formal definition. One of the best reasons for writing a definition occurs when the writer says, "I want to know more about this topic. What does this really mean?"

9.3 Strategies for definition

A workable strategy for an effective definition involves asking some or all of the following questions:

What are some synonyms?

How can the dictionary help you?

What do the origin and the history of the word reveal?

What examples best illustrate the word?

What characteristics distinguish the word?

What contrasts help show the word's meaning?

a. Consult standard and specialized dictionaries

The dictionary may give you one or more synonyms. If the entry discusses different synonyms, you will be able to examine the shades of meaning for those words. Of primary importance, the formal definition can guide your development of an extended definition. In addition, the etymology, or origin, of the word may give you important insights into its meaning.

The origin of a word may provide a clue to its meaning. For example, the word *television* derives from a Greek word *tele* meaning "distant" and a Latin word *visio* meaning "seeing." The word means literally "seeing things at a distance." In addition to having an origin, words have a history. The history of a word can record the changes in its meanings. An excellent dictionary for studying this changing meaning of a word is the *Oxford English Dictionary*, whose second edition has twenty volumes.

The standard college dictionaries are listed in 21.2. The following specialized dictionaries provide an abundance of information not found in a standard dictionary.

- Bernstein, Theodore. *The Careful Writer: A Modern Guide to English Usage.* 1965.
- Fowler, H. W. *A Dictionary of Modern English Usage.* 2nd ed. 1983.
- Morris, William, and Mary Morris. *Harper Dictionary of Contemporary Usage.* 2nd ed. 1985.
- Onions, C. T. *Oxford Dictionary of English Etymology.* 1966.
- Partridge, Eric, ed. *A Dictionary of Slang and Unconventional English.* 9th ed., 2 vols., 1985.
- *Webster's Collegiate Thesaurus.* 1976.
- Whitford, Harold C., and Robert J. Dixson. *Handbook of American Idioms and Idiomatic Usage.* 1973.

b. Present distinctive characteristics

Though a dictionary cannot explain the importance of a word, it always lists some distinctive characteristics. You may be able to supply additional distinctive characteristics of the word from your own reading or experience. Trust and use your knowledge. Do not attempt the perfect definition of the word. Write what you know and what you learn through reading and thinking. Get away from the idea that you are writing this for the *World Book* or for a Webster's dictionary.

One way of thinking about distinctive features involves the game of taking features away. For example, in defining the word *cat*, what would the cat be like without its fur? Without its claws? Without its particular sound? Such a pattern of thinking may help a writer to focus in a new way on essential characteristics and increase his or her knowledge of a word's meaning.

An accurate description may help convey the word's meaning by letting a reader see the object the word refers to. To do this, you would need to make a lengthy list of sensory details, select the most significant ones, and present those details to a reader in an organized manner.

One form of description is pictorial. Many authors, especially technical writers, use charts and drawings as an aid in defining and explaining. Anyone familiar with a dictionary knows that a picture can help a reader understand the meaning of a word. Close observation can increase knowledge, and the picture might form a part of the final paper. Consider, for example, how *Webster's Ninth New Collegiate Dictionary* uses a visual image to help increase a reader's understanding of a word such as *intaglio.*

in·ta·glio \in-'tal-ˈ-(ˌ)yō, -'täl-; -'tag-lē-,ō,
-'täg-\ *n, pl* **-glios** [It. fr. *intagliare* to en-
grave, cut, fr. ML *intaliare*, fr. L *in-* + LL
taliare to cut — more at TAILOR] (1644) **1**
a : an engraving or incised figure in stone or
other hard material depressed below the
surface of the material so that an impression
from the design yields an image in relief **b**
: the art or process of executing intaglios **c**
: printing (as in die stamping and gravure)
done from a plate in which the image is sunk
below the surface **2** : something (as a gem)
carved in intaglio

intaglio 1a

c. Present clear examples of distinctive characteristics

Examples help any definition. Clear, striking, and distinctive examples are more effective than trite and obvious
ones. Use fresh and lively language to present specific
details. Make the examples interesting, accurate, realistic,
and detailed.

The ideal is one good example for each distinctive
characteristic. Use your knowledge and present material
from a wide range: personal experience, literature, textbooks, history, current affairs, movies, television, and art.
Make the examples clear for your reader. Relate the examples to the general characteristic being discussed.

d. Illustrate contrasts

Make clear contrasts to help your reader understand what
the word is not. For example, a definition of Impressionism
in art might benefit from a contrast with Realism and
Expressionism. Many things and ideas have points in common, but an explanation of the *differences* can help explain meaning. For example, a bicycle, a moped, and a

motorcycle have many things in common; however, the differences count. Clear points of contrast can help a reader understand a word's meaning.

e. Use other strategies

Because the process of defining varies with the subject, occasion, and audience, some approaches work better than others in various situations. The following possibilities may help a writer develop a formal definition:

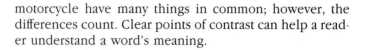 Present some historical information about the word being defined. For example, a definition of the word *marriage* might benefit from a discussion of ancient Roman or Greek marriages.

Explain the word in terms of a process. For example, the word *alcoholism* might be understood clearly if certain biochemical processes are explained.

Use an apt quotation. Occasionally a quotation dealing with a subject may spark reader interest and throw light on the meaning of a term.

9.4 Writing the definition

An effective extended definition includes thinking strategies such as description, narration, contrast, comparison, classification, causal analysis, and illustration. The following ideas may help clarify the thinking involved in writing the first draft.

Identify clearly the term to define. Do not shift the meaning during the definition. Do not begin by defining or explaining the word *music* and end up by defining or explaining the term *rock and roll.* Stick with the same term throughout the entire definition. If a word has several different meanings in various contexts (for example, *bridge* in dentistry and in engineering), identify the precise meaning.

Provide some kind of context for the word. When appropriate, give the reader some important social and historical background. For example, a definition of the word *crusade* might involve some discussion of medieval European politics.

Identify your audience. Involve the reader in the definition. For whom are you defining this term? Show the audience why the word is important. For example, the word *plagiarism* has great importance for freshmen who take writing courses in college.

Present some information about the word's importance. Explain to the reader your interest in the definition and try to make the reader share your interest. Make your point of view clear. If possible, show the reader how an understanding of the word might have a practical benefit in solving a problem or answering a question.

Present a preliminary definition in the introduction. This may be a formal definition adapted from a dictionary or an informal one you have created. Avoid the childish phrase, ''As Webster's says. . . .''

Write "your" definition of the term. Do not follow slavishly someone else's ideas or thought. Put down on the page what you think and feel.

Read the draft carefully. Make sure you have included the most important distinguishing characteristics or criteria for the term. Make sure you have provided an example or a discussion so the reader can understand these characteristics.

9.5 Problems in defining words

The task of creating an effective definition is difficult and can lead to certain problems. The most common difficulties in defining a term include circular reasoning, vague generality, exclusiveness, complexity, and incompleteness.

CIRCULAR   A botanist is a person who studies botany. [This definition does not add any relevant information. Instead it goes in a circle.]

REVISED   A botanist is a scientist who studies plants.

TOO GENERAL   A boulevard is a wide and spacious city area. [This definition is too broad because it includes baseball fields, parks, and parking lots.]

REVISED   A boulevard is a wide, often carefully landscaped, street or highway in a city.

EXCLUSIVE   A book is a bound volume containing a story. [This definition is inadequate because it excludes books such as phone books.]

REVISED   A book is a bound volume containing printing or writing.

TOO COMPLEX   A friend is one who manifests qualities of associativeness and eclectic affinities. [This definition requires a number of further definitions.]

REVISED   A friend is someone known, liked, respected, and esteemed.

INCOMPLETE Pacifism is when you don't want war. [Avoid defining a term by using the form *X is when* . . . or *X is where.* . . . See Section 20.12.]

REVISED   Pacifism is the principled belief that war or violence is wrong in settling disputes.

Thinking Exercises

1. Explain the errors in the following definitions and revise the sentences to improve their meaning.

    a. A human being is a two-legged animal without feathers.

    b. A moccasin is when you have the bottom of the shoe come up and be the sides and connect to the part with leather laces over the toes.

    c. Santa Claus is someone at Christmas.

    d. Beer is a fermented alcoholic drink made out of barley, hops, and pure mountain spring water from Colorado.

    e. An orangutan is a being like a monkey or a gorilla.

    f. A caterpillar is an upholstered worm.

    g. A gymnast is a girl who likes and does gymnastics.

    h. Dyslexia is a cognitive disfunctionality relative to the processing of printed material.

2. What different strategies would a writer use to define the word *tomato* and the word *pride*?

3. What methods do the authors of the following definitions of *the Oxford Method*, *fear*, and *neighbor* use to create their definitions? What are some other ways that might be used to define those words?

The Oxford Method

Nor could anything be more profitable from the pupil's point of view than the way in which this scheme of education was carried on. The student would prepare a paper on some special subject, and go with it, generally alone, and read it to his tutor, who would then discuss it and criticize it at length; or a group of two or three would meet in the tutor's room for a kind of Socratic discussion of some special point. These discussions were carried on much in the spirit of the Socratic dialogues; and the Socratic irony and assumed ignorance of the instructors, their deferential questions, as if the pupil were the teacher and they the learners, was a method which I found it hard at first to understand.

From "The Oxford Method"
by Logan Pearsall Smith

Fear

What is fear? Fear is a basic human emotion and one that is most shared with the lower primates. Although seldom frightened by the *same* dangers as animals, we are frightened by *more* dangers because the psyche is a wider flank to defend than the body.

Fear is the feeling of anxiety caused by the presence or pending presence of danger. The danger can be physical, but the vast majority of the threats we experience are psychological. Interestingly, some people who are virtually fearless in the fact of physical harm are quite skittish when they meet a psychological threat.

Psychological threat attacks the self-concept. This is why what is a threat to one person is appropriately laughed off by another. If part of my self-concept is "I'm an empathetic individual," and one of my students says to me, "I'm surprised at what you said in class today; I would have thought you to be more understanding than that," my psyche would perceive this as a threat, and I would react with fear.

If another student says, "Your diagram on the blackboard was atrocious; you certainly are not an artist," I would not find it a threat or feel any accompanying fear because my self-concept does not include "I'm a good artist."

Some dimensions of self-concept that produce fear when threatened are the concepts that we are intelligent, important, creative, well-meaning, mature, reasonable, honest, sensitive, moral and generous.

Fear is a pervasive emotion and affects us daily. Its value is primarily *positive* because fear can act as a warning signal of impending danger. Unfortunately, most of us define fear as "unpleasant" instead of correctly viewing it as helpful. It is when our fears are denied, exaggerated or misplaced that they pose problems.

From "Fear: Making it Work for Us"
by Michael E. Cavanagh

Parable of the Good Neighbor

A lawyer said to Jesus, "Who is my neighbor?" Jesus replied, "A man was going down from Jerusalem to Jericho, and he fell among robbers, who stripped him and beat him and departed, leaving him half dead.

"Now by chance a priest was going down that road, and when he saw him he passed by on the other side.

So likewise a Levite, when he came to the place and saw him, passed by on the other side. But a Samaritan, as he journeyed, came to where he was; and when he saw him, he had compassion; and went to him and bound up his wounds, pouring on oil and wine; then he set him on his own beast and brought him to an inn and took care of him. And the next day he took out two denarii and gave them to the innkeeper, saying, 'Take care of him; and whatever more you spend, I will repay you when I come back.' Which of these three, do you think, proved neighbor to the man who fell among the robbers?"

The lawyer said, "The one who showed mercy." Then Jesus said to him, "Go and do likewise."

Luke 10:29–37

Writing Assignments

1. Write a paper on a kind of movie or television show following the pattern of Susan Sontag's definition of science fiction films.

2. Discover a passage explaining or defining love from one of the following authors: Plato, Aristotle, St. Paul, Dante, Machiavelli, Shakespeare, Samuel Johnson, de Sade, Shelley, Dickinson, Colette, Freud, Plath, or Skinner. Explain what the person meant and write a paper supporting or criticizing that definition of love.

3. Choose an interesting word or concept from your major. Write a draft explaining the meaning of the term. Then write a passage explaining why the term is important. Combine the two drafts into a definition.

4. Choose something that you believe is damaging to society and write an extended definition of the term

focusing on negative effects. Give fresh, vivid examples, and avoid all clichés. Be specific as you explain the nature of the damage. Some possible terms are *alcohol, working conditions, banks, unions, illegal drugs, corporations, school,* and *television.*

5.   Read the following paper that defines a term using personal experience. Define an abstract term, such as *loss, victory, greed, glory, habit, hero, haste, fear, introvert, religion, pain,* or *poverty,* by referring to personal experience.

Injustice

What is injustice? I understood the meaning of the word before I knew the word itself. From the time I was very young, I understood things I could not verbalize; I saw my parents suffer and sweat each month when the bills came due, heard their quarrels over the small paychecks Dad brought home and the large grocery bills that fed a growing family. Even before I knew the value of a quarter, I knew that money was somehow awful and important and that my parents didn't have enough of it. I didn't understand why. They were good people, I reasoned; they loved God and worked hard; didn't they deserve money? Didn't they deserve to have a car that ran quietly and nice clothes and a life without constant anxiety—like other children's parents? My education in injustice was furthered when, from the age of five until I was nine, I suffered intermittent ear infections. For days at a time the blanket of insufferable pain would descend upon me, leaving me almost incoherent at times; when the pain would recede enough for me to think, I wondered why I should have such torture inflicted upon me. It wasn't fair. I didn't deserve it. Why me, and not someone else who had been bad? I suppose that even then my concept of justice was based on some sort of fundamentalist Protestant notion that good behavior should be rewarded and bad punished. And I suppose that hasn't changed much. Injustice, then, is that—whether through human means or through the careless hand of fate—which rewards and punishes without regard to merit.

Regenia Lucas

PART 4

Writing
Shorter Forms

10 Writing a Précis

When I began to do these précis, I was angry and couldn't see the value of the work. I must confess that it has helped me in my other classes to write essay examinations, and it will certainly help me next semester when I do a research paper. This kind of writing makes me a better reader.

Erika Muller

I had never done précis writing before. I discovered that it helped me "fix" the material in my memory, and it helped me understand the material better. It is hard work, especially writing in the third person, but it's worth it.

Chris J.

10.1 Definition of précis

The word *précis* is French. It is pronounced "pray-see." It means, literally, a trimmed or cut-down statement. It is a summary of some other writing. It is not a translation, nor is it a paraphrase. It is the condensation, in a short space, of the entire meaning of a paragraph, a page, several pages, or even an entire essay. The length of a good précis varies. Though some experts are able to create one-sentence versions, most good writers are able to reduce their versions to a third or fourth of the original. As a rule, the shorter a précis, the better it is—if the meaning is intact.

The précis is entirely objective and written in the third person. A précis writer should avoid judgments, figures of speech, illustrations, direct quotations, most adjectives, and all adjective phrases. The précis focuses on and attempts to reproduce essential meaning. A précis calls for presentation, not interpretation. A précis reproduces the meaning while it reduces the length of the original.

10.2 Guidelines for writing a précis

1. Once you have identified the passage you want to summarize, read it through once. What is the main point? Jot it down. What things in the passage help you to determine the main point? Some writers like to use a scratch outline (see 1.7b) to jot down the main points.

2. Unfamiliar words need to be looked up in a dictionary. The sense of each sentence should be clear.

3. Read the selection again. If the passage puzzles you or seems lacking in sense, perhaps an understanding of the context will help. Why is the author dealing with this subject? If the author is trying to prove something, what is it? How does the author arrive at the conclusion?

4. Identify the key sentence or sentences. What general statement (topic sentence or thesis statement) controls the entire passage? What key words does the author use?

5. You might find it easier to organize the contents once you identify the thinking strategies that the author

used: definition, comparison, contrast, causality, analysis, examples, process, classification, or others. How does the author use the material for support? How is the material organized?

6. After putting the passage aside, you might write a numbering sentence; for example, "This passage discusses three different kinds of depressions." Read the passage through one final time in light of the numbering sentence.

7. Now is the time to write your précis—entirely in the third person. You might do this by imagining an audience listening to you explain the meaning of the passage simply and clearly in your own words. Your précis should contain the meaning and should express it precisely following the structure of the original. A précis is generally one half the length of the passage being condensed, and it is held together with the appropriate transitional devices.

8. What does the précis sound like when you read it out loud? Does it make sense? Is it accurate? Does it present the author's meaning clearly and effectively? Read the passage again. If possible, ask someone to listen to your précis. You want to discover whether you have captured the meaning without omissions or distortions. Your first revision should focus on meaning and the second on sentence clarity.

10.3 Examples of précis writing

Original

It was at Stanford, one day near the end of my senior year, that a friend told me about a summer construction job he knew was available. I was quickly alert. Desire uncoiled within me. My friend said that he knew I had been looking for summer employment. He knew I needed some money. Almost apologetically he explained: It was something I probably wouldn't be interested in, but a friend of his, a contractor, needed someone for the summer to do menial jobs. There would be lots of shoveling and raking and sweeping. Nothing too hard. But nothing more interesting either. Still, the pay would be good. Did I want it? Or did I know someone who did?

From The Hunger of Memory
by Richard Rodriguez

First draft

Before his junior year, I worked as a laborer after someone asked me if I would take a laboring job. He planned to not tell his parents about the job.

Revised draft

At the end of Richard Rodriguez's senior year at Stanford, a friend asked him if he would like a good summer job as a construction worker. His friend told him the job would be full of hard work but it would also pay high wages.

Comment

The first draft is inaccurate, incomplete, and awkward. It mixes first- and third-person pronouns, but a précis should always be in the third person. It errs in saying the job was before the junior year when it should be after the senior year. It omits the author's name, the college, and the time of year. Notice that the revised draft includes the names and the time of year. The first draft seems hasty and careless.

Original

> The oddest feature of the trophy room is the soda fountain that stands in one corner, one of two at Graceland, the other one being downstairs in the poolroom. Soda fountains and jukeboxes are symbolic objects for fifties rock heroes, no more to be wondered at than the old binnacle in the den of a steamship captain or the pair of crossed sabers on the wall of a retired general. What is disconcerting about this domestic altar is its formica meanness. Yet it would be out of character for Elvis to own a handsome old green marble counter with mottled glass lamps and quaint seltzer pulls because Elvis detests everything antique with the heartfelt disgust of a real forward-looking American of his generation. Like so many of his kind, he gloats over the spectacle of the wrecking ball bashing down the walls of historic Memphis. In fact, he likes to get into the driver's seat of a bulldozer and smash down old buildings himself. As he says, "When I wuz growin' up in Tupelo, I lived with enough . . . antiques to do me for a lifetime." That is why everything about the King must be spanking new, from his Louis XV furniture to his late model Seeburg jukebox—so drab compared to a dazzling peacock Wurlitzer.
>
> *From* Elvis *by Albert Goldman*

First draft

> The oddest feature of the Elvis Presley trophy room is a 1950s soda fountain complete with formica top,

stools, and juke boxes. The writer compares this assortment of items to a retired general having a pair of swords in his den, or a ship captain having a compass in his den. This is surprising, though, because Elvis hated antiques because they reminded him of his poor childhood in Tupelo, Mississippi. And everyone knows that city is the bottom of the barrel. In fact, Elvis loved to see old buildings destroyed and had been known to leap into a bulldozer to lay waste to a building being demolished. Everything about the King must be spanking new and not drab.

Revised draft

Albert Goldman has fun describing the formica soda fountain in the trophy room at Graceland, Elvis's home in Memphis. The soda fountain seemed mean and ugly without a marbled top, nice lamps, or handsome accessories. The ugly fountain might very well symbolize Elvis' attitude toward old things and antiques in America. They reminded him of his hated childhood in Tupelo, Mississippi, and he was glad to see them destroyed. Elvis rejoiced when old buildings in downtown Memphis were demolished. In fact, he liked to jump into the driver's seat of a bulldozer and help rip down any old building. This hatred of the old explains why everything he bought for Graceland was brand new—even if it was fake antique furniture, the latest model jukebox, or a brand new and ugly formica soda fountain.

Comment

The first draft adds, in two different places, material taken verbatim from the original without quotation marks. The original material needs to be presented in a concise fashion in the précis writer's own words. In addition, the first draft adds erroneous, irrelevant, and judgmental material about Tupelo completely lacking in the original.

Thinking Exercises

1. How would you characterize the tone of the following writing passages? Tone is the author's attitude toward the subject matter or toward the audience. For each passage, write at least one sentence commenting on the author's attitudes toward the subject and the audience.

> a. When I arrived I was met by the mother, a big startled looking woman, very clean and apologetic who merely said, "Is this the doctor?" and let me in. In the back, she added, "You must excuse us, doctor, we have her in the kitchen where it is warm. It is very damp here sometimes."
>
> *W. C. Williams*

> b. So, now I shall talk every night. To myself. To the moon. I shall walk, as I did tonight, jealous of my loneliness, in the blue-silver of the cold moon, shining brilliantly on the drifts of fresh-fallen snow, with the myriad sparkles.
>
> *Sylvia Plath*

> c. Having more meanings than one is the result of not entering into the full commitment of unequivocal assertion; to use an extralocution, to permit a context to remain extraloquial, is to decline citizenship in that kingdom of single-eyed men to which language (as ordinarily used) aspires.
>
> *Winifred Nowottny*

> d. James McNeill Whistler came from Lowell, Massachusetts. At the age of nine, he was taken to Russia.

where his father was building a railroad. After the boy had lived for a few years like a wealthy aristocrat, he was sent to London for his health.

J. T. Flexner

Writing Assignments

1. Read some brief descriptions of programs found in *TV Guide*. For a movie you have recently seen, write a similar synopsis of important information. Prepare a second synopsis of a recent sporting or cultural event.

2. Study two abstracts from two different periodicals such as *Journal of the American Medical Association, New England Journal of Medicine, Nature, Scientific American*, or *PMLA*. You might choose two different periodicals from your major or your intended profession. Make a list of the ways in which the two abstracts differ: length, style, word choice, readability. Write a brief paragraph pointing out any similarities or differences.

3. Read a cover article in one of the weekly magazines for the week of your birth. In no more than 200 words, write an abstract of that article.

4. Write a précis of one of the paragraphs in this book assigned by your instructor.

Writing a Paraphrase

11

Many people have the mistaken notion that paraphrase has importance only for students doing research papers. A paraphrase is a restatement of another person's words in your own words. When you tell someone a story a friend told you, you are paraphrasing. When you put in your own words some material from a book, you are also paraphrasing. The ability to transmit information accurately and coherently has great value, especially in college. Learning to paraphrase well will help you in almost all of your college classes.

Paraphrase, however, is not quotation. Quotation is exact word-for-word repetition of another person's words. Paraphrase resembles a summary or précis, but a paraphrase is approximately the same length as the original.

11.2 Process of paraphrasing

1. Read the passage, searching for the author's main idea. A dictionary or reference book should be used for unfamiliar words. Write out one sentence stating your idea of the writer's main point.

2. Read the passage again carefully, asking yourself these questions:

> ✐ How did you discover the author's main point?
> ✐ What material does the writer use to develop and support the main idea?
> ✐ How does the writer organize this material?
> ✐ If the material is complex, does an outline help you to see the main point and development clearly?

3. Now is the time to write down the meaning—entirely in the third person and in your own words. Keep the meaning, the logical order, and the tone the same. Use key words from the original. Do not copy phrases.

4. Reading your paraphrase out loud might help as you begin to revise the sentences for accuracy, complete-

ness, organization, and sense. The paraphrase should be in your own words, but take care to avoid the "thesaurus syndrome"—the use of preposterous synonyms and awkward phrasing to create a paraphrase. Writers have generally found the following strategies effective: (a) changing the length of sentences, (b) changing the word order, (c) changing verbs from active to passive or vice versa, and (d) changing *to be* verbs to active verbs. Meaningless abstraction should be avoided, and irrelevant words and phrases should be deleted.

11.3 Kinds of paraphrase

Writers generally use paraphrase for three common reasons: to simplify, modernize, or restate another author's words. The kind you choose depends on the original and also on your audience and your purpose.

a. Simplification

In simplification, the paraphraser takes a difficult passage and makes it simple for the average reader to understand. An example would be a paraphrase of Freud's distinction between *mourning* (normal grief) and *melancholy* (abnormal grief). Often, the material in scientific and scholarly publications is difficult. An effective writer makes the material accessible to the reader with minimum difficulty.

Original

> A set of drugs called tricyclic antidepressants were found to have considerable effect in treating depressed patients. These drugs prevented reuptake of norepinephrine and serotonin through the nerve

endings, where the biogenic amines would be in-active thus leaving them free to assert their full po-tency at the synapse, where one nerve is connected to another.

From Depression: The Facts
by George Winokur, p. 90

Rough draft of paraphrase

It is maintained that some drugs, antidepressants, help cure people suffering from depression. They do this by a complex chemical process in the brain in-volving norepinephrine and serotonin. The drugs work within the nerve cells in the brain preventing the passage of norepinephrine and serotonin, two components of every nerve cell, in the nerve endings, thus leaving the biogenic amines free to do their work at the synapse, where one nerve connects to another.

Later draft of paraphrase

Winokur claims that a new kind of drug, the tricyclic antidepressant, can help people suffering from depression. The drugs work deep within the nerve cells of the brain. To do this, the tricyclic antide-pressants influence the operation of two nerve cell components, norepinephrine and serotonin. By this influence on norepinephrine and serotonin, the tri-cyclics affect another set of chemicals called the bio-genic amines. As a result of this complex process, the biogenic amines are able to work at full efficiency. Their job involves connecting one nerve cell to an-other (90).

b. Modernization

Modernization, too, is for the reader. A text written in an earlier age may be difficult to follow. Often readers need help in understanding. In modernization, the paraphraser takes a passage written in an earlier time and makes the language and thinking accessible to a present-day reader. An example of this would be a paraphrase of a passage from a poem by John Keats, "On First Looking into Chapman's Homer."

Original

> Much have I travelled in the realms of gold,
> And many goodly states and kingdoms seen;
> Round many western islands have I been
> Which bards in fealty to Apollo hold.

Rough draft of paraphrase

> The first four lines of the poem mention that I have travelled to many wealthy countries and good states and kingdoms. It also mentions that I have visited many western islands where the poets are loyal to Apollo.

Later draft of paraphrase

> The first four lines of Keats's sonnet "On First Looking into Chapman's Homer" involve the idea of travel. The speaker claims to have visited wealthy kingdoms, large countries, pleasing states, and island cities whose poets are loyal to the Greek god of the sun, Apollo.

c. Restatement

In a restatement, the writer does not want to quote the original material. This is the most common use of paraphrase in college essay examinations, compositions, and research papers. In restatement, the writer restates the meaning of the original passage in his or her own words.

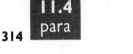

An example of this would be the passage by George Winokur on depressive symptoms in infants.

Original

Harlow demonstrated that infant rhesus monkeys that were separated from their mothers showed severe defects in their social activities. These infant monkeys were withdrawn and shortly developed a stage of "despair." This stage was characterized by decreases in movement, exploration, and social behavior such as play and vocalization. Something similar to this animal model of depression has been described in children.

From Depression: The Facts
by George Winokur, p. 73

Rough draft of paraphrase

Harlow showed that baby monkeys taken from their mothers developed serious problems in behavior. The baby monkeys became catatonic and despairing. They would not move. They would not explore. They would not engage in games or noise making. Some children seem to suffer the same kind of behavior.

Later draft of paraphrase

The psychologist Harlow showed that baby monkeys taken from their mothers developed serious behavioral problems. The baby monkeys became catatonic and despairing. They would not move, explore, play with toys, or even make noises. Psychiatrists have discovered that some children behave in an identical manner (Winokur 73).

11.4 Incorrect paraphrase: plagiarism

Avoid plagiarism. Be honest. Be careful. Credit all sources. If the words are not your words, let the reader know whose they are. If the ideas are not your ideas, let the reader know whose they are. Inform your reader with signals. The first signal may be an introductory phrase, such as "Professor Strand claims . . ." or "An early authority reported . . ." The second signal might be the author's name, a short title, or the page numbers in parentheses. If these signals are completely missing from a quotation, summary, or paraphrase, then plagiarism has occurred. Consult the appropriate MLA or APA form for parenthetical documentation in chapter 17 and the discussion of proper quotation in 22.7.

a. Examples of plagiarism

Some people imagine that the only form of plagiarism is deception. The student submits either a paper prepared by another person or material copied from a book or magazine. These crimes, of course, are the most severe forms of plagiarism, but they are not the only kind. There are several other ways to plagiarize:

- ✎ Omit the quotation marks around material taken in whole or part from any source: as few as two or three words. Omit the documentation.
- ✎ Omit the documentation for a summary.
- ✎ Omit the documentation for any paraphrase.

Original

Manic patients are frequently described as uninhibited, and this certainly appears to be so; however, the question of how much restraint the patient exercises over his behavior can give some measure of the internal control the patient has over his impulses. Accordingly the sexual behavior of the patient, i.e., whether or not he is promiscuous or acts in a socially unapproved fashion, can be considered a measure of this control.

From Manic Depressive Illness
by George Winokur, Paula J. Clayton,
and Theodore Reich, p. 74

Plagiarized version 1

Manic patients were frequently uninhibited. This certainly will appear to be so. There is, however, a question of how much restraint the patient exercises over his behavior. This can give some measure of the internal control the patient has over his impulses. Accordingly the sexual behavior of the patient, whether promiscuous or not, can be considered a measure of this control.

Nonplagiarized version 1

Winokur, Clayton, and Reich were interested in the relationship between mania, sexual promiscuity, and inhibition. They wrote, "Manic patients are frequently described as uninhibited. . . ." They were interested in "the question of how much . . . internal control the patient has over his impulses." The researchers concluded that "the sexual behavior of the patient . . . can be considered a measure of this control" (74).

Comment

The plagiarized version is copied mostly word for word. The writer omits any quotation marks and fails to indicate the authors, source, and page number. The nonplagiarized passage is introduced, and the authors are named. Quotation marks show where the quotation begins and ends. Ellipsis marks (. . .) indicate omissions. Documentation is provided. Note how the nonplagiarized version has coherent verb tenses.

Plagiarized version 2

Most doctors agree that manic patients are frequently uninhibited. The amount of inhibition can give a doctor some knowledge of patient self-control over his behavior.

Nonplagiarized version 2

Winokur, Clayton, and Reich mentioned that manic patients are "frequently . . . uninhibited." By studying whether the patients are promiscuous or not, they hoped to arrive at some conclusion about the degree of "internal control" patients have "over . . . impulses" (74).

Comment

The plagiarized sample copies a few words or phrases verbatim. No quotation marks appear. No documentation is provided. In the acceptable, nonplagiarized sample, a reader can easily identify the source of the quotation. A few words and phrases are quoted. Quotation marks appear. Documentation is provided.

Plagiarized version 3

It is a generally recognized fact that patients with mania act without any sexual inhibitions. The restraint shown by such patients gives a doctor an idea of how much control the patients have. Promiscuity or the lack of it is a good indicator of self-control.

Nonplagiarized version 3

Winokur, Clayton, and Reich indicate that many patients with mania act without any sexual inhibitions.

The restraint shown by such patients gives a doctor an idea of how much control the patients have. Promiscuity or the lack of it is a good indicator of self-control (74).

Comment

The plagiarized material is summarized, but the author is suppressed and no page number or source reference is given. In the nonplagiarized sample, the authors and the page number are indicated. Note that the paraphrase avoids any first- or second-person pronouns.

Plagiarized version 4

A person in a manic state is often said to be lacking in inhibition. Probably this is true. The amount of control demonstrated by such people indicates the level of interior methods of dealing with sexual desires. The presence or absence, then, of promiscuity gives some idea of the strengths of these inner controls.

Nonplagiarized version 4

Stating the obvious, Winokur, Clayton, and Reich indicate that manic people have few sexual inhibitions. Most observers would agree with this. They then go on to draw a connection between sexual promiscuity, manic states, and measured levels of internal self-control. The researchers maintain, not surprisingly, that promiscuity is linked not so much to mania as to lack of internal powers of self-control (74).

Comment

The plagiarized material is paraphrased, but the authors are suppressed and no page number or source reference is given. The nonplagiarized material is paraphrased, and both page documentation and authors are provided for the paraphrase.

Thinking Exercises

1. What do the following sayings mean? Write a few sentences explaining each. What is the difference between a proverb and a paraphrase?
   a. A stitch in time saves nine.
   b. The fox condemns the trap and not itself.
   c. He who loves pleasure will be poor.
   d. All the road to Heaven is Heaven.
   e. Hindsight is always twenty-twenty.

2. Choose one of the samples from 11.3 illustrating paraphrase and make a list of the differences between an early draft and a later draft.

3. Underline the passages in the following writing sample that show evidence of plagiarism.

> *Original source:* Scarcely had the midday bell rung in Assisi the next day, and the people were sitting at their tables, when Francis with his bowl in hand went on his circuit through the city. He knocked at all doors and got something at many of them—here a cup of soup, a bone with a little meat on it, a crust of bread, some leaves of salad, all sorts of things mixed together. When Francis had ended his begging trip his bowl was full, but of the most unappetizing mixture one could think of.
>
> From Saint Francis of Assisi
> *by Johannes Jörgensen, p. 53*

> *Writing sample:* When the midday bell rang, Francis with a bowl in his hand went on a circuit through the town.

Knocking at all doors, he got something at many of them: a cup of soup, some bones with a little meat on it, a piece of bread, and some leaves of salad (Jörgensen 53).

4.   Underline the passages in the following writing sample that show evidence of plagiarism. Revise to avoid plagiarism.

Original source: Daniel had never bought a book or borrowed one from the town library, and he read nothing but the magazine *Dirt Bike*—until his teacher piqued his interest with a new book, *About David* [by Susan Beth Pfeffer]. Daniel wrote a brief letter, saying he liked it "because it made me feil [feel] it happened to me. It was one of the first books I read that I enjoyed. Because I don't read much."

From Growing Up Writing
by Arlene Silberman, p. 135

Writing sample: Arlene Silberman writes about a student named Daniel who became interested in reading, even though he had never bought a book or borrowed one from the town library. He never read anything besides *Dirt Bike* until his teacher interested him in a new book, *About David* by Susan Beth Pfeffer. He told the teacher that he liked it because it made him feel it happened to him (Silberman 135).

Writing Assignments

1.   Paraphrase at least two sentences from each of the following passages, making sure in the revision that your work is accurate, complete, and in your own words. Begin

each paraphrase with a lead-in such as "Mack and Skjei maintain . . ." or "Kripke argues. . . ."

> a. As working writers, teachers of writing, and writing consultants ourselves, we have worked closely with scores of individuals from a spectrum of occupations—among them, students, teachers, salespeople, managers, accountants, ad agency executives, doctors, engineers, publicists, budding novelists, physicists, lawyers—who experience trouble with blocking. Whether they write occasionally or every day, whether they write for a living, for professional distinction and advancement, or from purely personal motivations—writing blocks are familiar afflictions to them all.
>
> *From* Overcoming Writing Blocks
> *by Karin Mack and Eric Skjei, p. 16*

> b. Of course, the body *does* exist without the mind and presumably without the person, when the body is a corpse. This consideration, if accepted, would already show that a person and his body are distinct.
>
> *From* Naming and Necessity
> *by Saul Kripke, p. 145*

> c. When Leo Tolstoy undertook to teach the children of his newly emancipated serfs to read and write, he discovered a principle of education that keeps getting lost, forgotten, or set aside. Tolstoy discovered there at Yasnaya Polyana what Socrates first taught and what anyone who has won freedom from the conventional wisdom can find out—namely, that the form-finding and form-creating powers of the human mind are the teacher's chief ally, once they are engaged, and that until they are engaged, no genuine learning can happen.
>
> *From* The Making of Meaning
> *by Ann Berthoff, p. 85*

d. And Francis bent down and laid his clothes of scarlet and fine linen at his father's feet, with a quantity of money. A mighty movement ran through the audience. Many began to weep; even the Bishop had tears in his eyes. Only Pietro de Bernardone was unmoved. With a face of stone, he stooped down, white with rage but without uttering a word, and took up the clothes and money. Then the Bishop stepped over to Francis, spread his cape over him, and clothed the naked young man in its white folds as he pressed him to his heart. From now on Francis was what he so long had wished to be—the servant of God only and a man of the Church.

> *From* Saint Francis of Assisi
> *by Johannes Jörgensen, p. 49*

2.   Make a copy of an editorial that you seriously disagree with. Paraphrase the main points of the editorial and then present some good reasons for opposing it.

3.   Look up the word *plagiarism* in the *Reader's Guide to Periodical Literature* from the past ten years. Read one of the articles. Write a brief summary paraphrasing it.

Writing in Journals

12

✍ **Student Comments on Writing**

I never thought writing could be valuable. Keeping a journal helps me believe in myself as a writer and it is also valuable. It was a delight to find out my grandparents kept a journal. Their journals are about life in Pennsylvania at the beginning of this century and are priceless and could never be replaced. This journal, which I plan to continue long after this course, will be a record of my activities.

Diane Renner

It was an eye opener for me to find how valuable a journal can be in doing this research project. I used the journal to write out my problems. The journal is a good listener. Sometimes, just the act of writing the problem out helped me solve the problem.

Ward Epson

People keep different kinds of journals or diaries and write in them on a regular basis. Some of these are simple and humble; others are quite complex and sophisticated. Some have entirely personal material in them, whereas others contain nothing personal. Some people keep journals just for themselves; others write for a wider audience.

Keeping a journal might lead to a bunch of boring, empty sentences, but if pursued with maturity and seriousness, a journal can offer several important advantages. First, it gives you the opportunity to record your observations and thoughts; both of these can be a rich source of material for your writing assignments. In addition, a journal can help you learn. It can help you discover things about yourself and help you learn in your college courses. A journal can also help you develop fluency in writing. It can provide the opportunity for practice, free from criticism and anxiety. You can benefit as a writer from knowing and experimenting with some different kinds of journal writing, such as the diary, the reading log, the observation notebook, the dialectical journal, and the personal journal.

12.1 Diary

A diary is, generally, a day-to-day abbreviated account of the life going on around the writer. The entries are usually short and the diary writer tries to present this material in a plain style. The puritan diarist, Samuel Sewell, wrote for July 8, 1677:

> In Sermon time there came in a female Quaker, in a canvas frock, her hair disshevelled and loose like a Periwig, her face as black as ink, led by two other Quakers, and two others followed. It occasioned the greatest and most amazing uproar that I ever saw. . . .

12.2 Reading log

The reading log is a form of diary writing that presents material read rather than people met or things done. Generally, it deals with material important in a course. The instructor will ask for a continuing series of reading responses. In a history class, for example, a teacher might ask the students to read a biography and then write in a journal on "some surprises about the character," "three things about style or sentence structure," or "three things about the narrative structure." Here is a selection from a student's reading log on a poem, "The Love Song of J. Alfred Prufrock," by T. S. Eliot. The particular assignment asked for comments on age in the poem.

> Eliot's poem "Prufrock" gives three good pictures of age. Prufrock constantly speaks of himself as an old man. He talks about his balding hair, his old style clothes, and he even tells the reader constantly that he is growing older and will live with his trousers rolled up like an old bum or a retired person on a beach. A second picture is the scene that Prufrock sees while out walking. He sees "lonely men in shirt-sleeves, leaning out of windows." He probably identifies with those ancient and solitary people. A third instance of something old is the "ragged claws" on the bottom of the ocean. This is a reference to a lobster or a crab or some such creature. They are the oldest kinds of things living and while they might not live as long as men, they have been on earth millions of years longer than human beings. In short, almost everything in the poem is ancient like the crab; antique like Michelangelo's art; or aged like Prufrock, who seems to be in a kind of hell.
>
> *Grant Walker*

12.3 Observation notebook

In addition to artists and sculptors who must look closely at things, people in many areas of scientific study such as archaeology, botany, geology, and zoology must use close observation. Often in such classes, instructors will assign field trips or observation exercises to train people to see better and to make better sense of what they see. Some students keep observation journals by drawing on the left page a sketch of the object with a list of observed characteristics, and then writing a paragraph pointing out the essential characteristics of that object on the right page. The following sample comes from a student's response to the request to write on something small and surprising, something out of the ordinary.

Last week a freaky warm spell wafted into southwestern Pennsylvania in January and the forsythia shrub in our yard began to blossom. I had never looked closely at these small, pale yellow flowers, but they stood out so that I found it interesting to look at them. Each tiny flower is about an inch long and an inch across. The color is a uniform yellow. From the front, the flower resembles a propeller on a plane. It has five petals flowing out of a funnel-shaped base. Each stem and branch of the entire shrub is covered with hundreds of these small flowers. Inside of each funnel-propeller-shaped flower is a tiny whitish stalk covered with pollen. If any bees are still around in the middle of winter, they might want to collect this pollen. The next day when I looked out at the forsythia, it was covered with snow and the temperature

outside was twenty getting ready to head down to
zero that night.

Sophie M. Cohen

two sides

12.4 Dialectical journal

Dialectical journal writing was invented by the writer Ann
E. Berthoff and asks for two things: careful observation and
thoughtful commentary on the thing observed or the act
of observing. The journal or notebook is divided into two
parts: right and left or top and bottom. In one place—
almost like a snapshot or a sketch—the object is observed.
It should be limited and focused. In another place on the
page is the writer's thinking about the object or the observation. Beginning writers find it easier to focus on just
one kind of thinking at first: comparing (similes, metaphors, analogies), contrasting, dividing into parts, showing
functions, giving examples, classifying, analyzing a process, defining, and so forth. It is important to understand
that grades are not assigned for right or wrong answers or
responses. Such a journal with its emphasis on close observation and writing can help a student prepare for a paper on the thing observed or learn material for an
examination on it. After describing her glasses, a student
prepared the following list as her commentary on them.

> I would be lost without my glasses. I need them to
> read the words on the blackboard. I need them to
> read the words on the pages of my textbooks. Without
> them, I would be lost. What else could I use them
> for if I had to? I might use them to start a fire. I would
> need some paper and a hot noonday sun. The moon
> would not do. I use my glasses sometimes as a paper-

weight to keep my papers from blowing away at the library. I have seen some people who look elegant and learned wearing glasses. I have used one part of my glasses to stir coffee. Some people say that glasses give people an air of authority and intelligence. I don't think that is true for me, but that might be a possibility.

Mary Martha Perdue

12.5 Personal journal

Many students keep personal journals. They report that writing in a journal becomes pleasurable. Journal writing might serve as a record of personal thought, feeling, and activity. In one sense, it might be an autobiographical narrative or a confession. In another sense, it might be material that has strongly influenced the writer. This is the kind of writing many people think of when mentioning a journal. Some students have found Peter Elbow's idea about freewriting a good device to help them write spontaneously about their experiences. (See 1.3e.) In freewriting, the author picks up a pen and begins writing without stopping for anything. The writer does not judge or evaluate what is being written down. He or she simply writes down the contents of a thought or an idea and then goes on to develop that as far as possible. Someone called this literary improvisation, and that is, perhaps, an apt description. Another way to label it is to call it "thinking on paper." One of the great advantages of this kind of writing is that a person is able to confront ideas and thoughts that may never have risen to the surface. The journal can be a device for self-discovery. It can also serve as a device for storing ideas and feelings until the time comes to use them, as the following example illustrates.

> I haven't eaten for a day and am getting quite hungry. See what a term paper can do to a poor student? I did this all by accident. First one thing and then another. I think I should try fasting for a day longer. How could anyone fast for forty days? Or even two days? I have been too busy to worry about eating. This could never happen while I am studying in my room because I would be close to a refrigerator and a pantry. But I have been working at the library the past few days on my research paper and I have missed meals because I am right in the middle of tracking something down and I really want to get all this material so I can begin writing the paper. Maybe the library and work in the library create chemicals in our bodies which drive hunger away. More likely, when a person is working hard, he or she is too busy to pay attention to the body's hunger signals. This idea is an unexpected and pleasant surprise. I now have a topic for my research paper in biology.
>
> *Ottavia Diaz*

Thinking Exercises

1. Ask some relatives if they have ever kept a journal. Ask them what they wrote about. If they reply that they have never kept a journal, ask them whether they wish they had written down some things to keep them alive in memory. Ask them what kinds of important family things should be recorded in a journal.

2. Read four passages from a journal in the library. What kind of material does the writer include in the journal? What is the writer's attitude toward the material?

3. Read your journal entries for one week. Imagine that you are a reader looking at it for the first time. Answer the following questions:

> a. How much information does the journal contain?
> b. How many examples does the journal provide?
> c. How many specific details does the journal contain?
> d. How predictable are the entries?
> e. What is the most interesting thing in the journal?
> f. How could you make the journal more interesting? More informative?

Writing Assignments

1. In a journal, write for two to four weeks a series of daily events that you would always keep private. If you feel this helps you, continue.

2. Write in a notebook twenty to thirty minutes every day for two to four weeks, following one of the five kinds of journals listed previously. Find a specific application for a journal to help you in another course.

3. Select an entry from your journal and revise it with examples and specific details.

13 Writing Essay Examinations

✍ **Student Comments on Writing**

During my interview for an internship, the personnel manager asked me if I liked to write essay exams. I told her yes and asked her why. She told me in her company that no one would prepare a multiple choice test to find out what I knew and that I would be expected to write memos which were a lot like essay exams.

Emily Underhill

13.1 Purpose of essay examinations

What is your purpose? Your instructor wants you to write an essay so the reader will say, "This student has read the material, understood the major points, and presented a clear idea with plenty of supporting material." Instructors assign these questions to test whether students have read the books, understood the material, and absorbed ideas presented in the lectures. In addition, essay examinations are important for another reason. Teachers believe that an essay provides a student the opportunity to connect ideas and make discoveries about the reading material. In other words, a well-designed essay examination provides students with an additional opportunity for further learning. Instructors who assign essay tests do not want minimal, parrotlike responses. They are looking for certain things, such as the following, in their students papers.

General statement. If an essay answer is of paragraph length or longer, a teacher is helped enormously by the presence of a general statement in the form of a topic sentence or a numbering sentence. (See 2.3.)

Primary material. Instructors want to see that the student has read and understood the important material in the primary texts. They want students to recognize and understand the main ideas and basic facts of the course. If outside reading is assigned, the important material there should form a part of the response. A student should understand how it relates to the central ideas in the course. An apt quotation in support of an idea usually receives a positive response from the reader.

Lecture material. Instructors want to see that the student has mastered the information and ideas given in lectures. Teachers emphasize certain material in class and usually expect students to know this. Students should ask the instructor for the precise contents of the material to be tested.

Key concepts. Teachers hope that their students will recognize and understand the meaning and importance of the key concepts in the course. Students should learn the definition of each important term and be able to provide a good example for the sake of illustration. It helps to know the origin of each term and to understand the situation or fact the term is designed to explain. Often fundamental ideas provide a guide to the kinds of thinking required in a course. These concepts can help develop an in-depth essay. Most instructors provide a list of these important terms, and the students then study the text or dictionary with the clearest definitions.

Thought. Instructors do not want parrots or tape recorders. They want their students to become autonomous, thinking individuals. Good essay writers use the question to begin thinking about the subject. They follow the directions in the question. If it asks for comparison, they compare. If it asks for definition, they define. In most cases, instructors appreciate a general statement supported by specific facts and details from the reading material.

Good organization. A clear statement of purpose at the beginning signals to the reader that the student is firmly in control of the material. It sets up a contract with the reader to expect certain material. A numbering sentence or a clear topic sentence at the very beginning of an essay can help both writer and reader.

13.2 Audience in essay examinations

The readers of essay examinations are teachers. They want to see the items mentioned above within student essays. Many readers also dislike certain things in essays. Because some teachers have strong ideas about writing, students can benefit from understanding different teachers' ideas. Teachers are always individuals, but generally they have a healthy dislike for the following problems that regularly appear in student examinations.

Illegible handwriting. Students who want to lower their grades, even if they know the material, can do so by writing illegibly. Teachers are not cryptographers. Neatness does count. If it helps, write on every other line and have margins.

Rambling digressions. Evading the question can become an art form. A digression that shows the teacher how much the student knows about the subject might earn a high grade. A digression that simply avoids the essay question will most likely earn a low grade. Ideas from other fields may illuminate the answer, but the reader will be looking for material presented in the course.

Major errors in English. It is hard to discover readers' pet peeves. The errors that bother most readers are garbled or meaningless sentences, lack of subject-verb agreement, run-on sentences, fragments, faulty logic, and incoherence. Students should spend the final two or three minutes proofreading the essay answer for errors.

Lack of organization. Student writers should remember that the picture inside the jigsaw puzzle box is complete but absolutely unintelligible. The essay reader does not have the time to organize the student's answer. Effective essays have a purpose statement, topic sentence, or numbering sentence at the very beginning of the answer. Specific examples and details can then develop that purpose statement.

Meaningless jargon. Students should write their sentences in clear English and avoid the use of complex terms to try to sound intelligent. Write simply and clearly about what you know, and your essay will be intelligent.

13.3 Writing in class

Read through the entire exam. Decide how much time to spend on each question. Decide which questions are easy and which are hard. Plan to answer the easiest questions first. That should help build up your confidence. Leave a few minutes at the end to check over what you have written.

Read each question carefully. As you come to each question, divide it into parts. Follow directions. Identify the primary focus of the question. Identify the key word: cause, effect, compare, classify, contrast, criticize, define, describe, evaluate, function, illustrate, interpret, justify, prove, summarize, or trace. If the word *discuss* or *explain* is used, try to determine the kind of thinking the teacher wants.

SAMPLE ESSAY QUESTION	Discuss the major differences between the Freudian and biochemical explanations of depression.
PRIMARY TOPIC	Freudian and biochemical theories of depression
DESIRED RESPONSE	Contrast of the two theories

Use scratch outlines. Quickly jot down the most important words and ideas you can think of related to that question. Refer to text, lectures, and supplemental work. Write a purpose statement to link key words in the question to your knowledge.

Organize your answer. Follow the pattern suggested by the key words in the question. Present the most important material first. Select the material that will most effectively develop your main idea. (See 2.5.)

NOTE: **Some professors keep a file of earlier essay questions on reserve in the library or they keep samples of student essay answers on file in the Writing Center. Inquire to find out whether you have access to these.**

Thinking Exercises

1.   Read the following essays given in response to the topic, "Discuss the relationship between the parent and child in the poem 'Mother Milking.' " This poem is found at the end of 3.1. The students knew ahead of time that they would be writing on that particular poem, and the examination gave a copy of the poem for the students to read. Decide which essay you believe is the better response to the question and make a list of the strong points about that writing. Then make a list of the weak points in the other essay.

> a. This is a beautiful poem. It captures perfectly the sense of wonder and awe a small child might feel in the presence of an older person. In this case, it is the relationship between the mother and her daughter. The images I remember the best are the white milk "warm and sweet/as the breath of a baby" and the chickens with their "soft cooing" and "shiny feathers" and how they almost magically float up "to the rafters like powder puffs." This is so true for most people do not have very much experience with things that happen in the country and on farms and a poem like this helps remind us what it would be like to grow up on a farm and to have to accompany a parent while the adult did the chores instead of the child.
>
> *B. L.*

b. This is a very soft and quiet poem. It is the exact opposite of a heavy metal rock song. The only human voice in the poem is the sound of the mother calling for quiet as she goes to "shush the hens" who make a little cooing sound. And then she might hear the sound of the cattle chewing their cuds and the sound of the milk squirting into the pail. It is against this vast background of silence that the relationship between the parent and the child is presented. The separation between the parent and the child is shown in four different ways. In the first sense, the parent and child do not communicate through speech. The small child simply trails after the mother and watches but does not speak a single word. Nor does the mother speak to the child who curiously asks the mother to "think thoughts I have no way of knowing." This separation in languages is one key difference between the two. The second point of difference is the question of activity. The mother is active. The child is passive. All the child does is watch. The mother goes about her job of going out to the old barn and milking the cows. Third, the mother is hurt and wounded. The child is naive and innocent, almost a baby. The mother has to wear a felt hat, something men usually wear, to keep out the sun. The mother has the experience of deep pain in some sense where the lines tell us of "the ache in the bone." The poem also refers to "the place over the heart" which is a roundabout way of saying a broken heart which is not full of good things any more. The child is being filled with these new, mysterious, and unforgettable impressions of the world which are "warm and sweet." The mother's heart is empty and its "fullness has flown" away. Fourth, and most important, the world of the mother is the world of work. It is the world of "barn," "cow," "muck," "felt hat," and "pail." The world seen by the small child is a magical world where the milk is "warm and sweet/as the breath of a baby." The child sees the chickens as "shiny feathers" that "rise to the rafters like powder puffs." The eggs inside the snake are imagined as "cocoons just before the butterflies/ emerge." The blue sky is imagined as a blue slat forming a side of the barn's wall. This child's world is magical. The adult's world is hard and even degrading. It may be no accident that both the mother who chews on her "rosy lips" and the cow which chews "its cud" are related in some way. The separation between the worlds of the adult and the child is clearly and beautifully presented in this poem.

R. H.

Writing Assignments

1.   Make a copy of an essay exam you have written in another class. Rewrite that essay to improve the content and the organization.

2.   Revise the following essay examination from a social studies class on the topic, "Discuss one of the following: (a) how local government works, (b) how local government helps the people, or (c) how local government can be changed."

There are many different ways that local government can work. There are the commission form, the strong mayor–city council form, and the city council–city manager form. If there is a commission, the people can pick whose idea they like best and vote for them. If there is a mayor council form, the people still get to decide whose ideas they think are best, but they must rely on the mayor whether or not they voted for him to choose a good, representative council that knows what it is doing. In the city council–city manager form, the people can pick many to form a good council, but they will have to trust them in their choice for the manager. The mayor, commissioners, or council members should want to help make the area they are governing a better and safer place for their people. They could fix roads, build new schools, or even fix up the old ones. They should have lots of good ideas for the city or county and I would want them to have past experience and a good reputation.

Business Writing: Letters and Résumés

14

14.1 Formal patterns

For personal letters, a writer may use any appropriate form. For business letters and letters of application, a writer needs to follow certain formal patterns or the letter will not be taken seriously.

Format. Follow the general directions in 1.11 for choosing paper, setting margins, typing, and general appearance. Avoid any hint of carelessness. Avoid all eccentricities and cleverness.

NOTE: The full block format is generally used for business letters. (See 14.2.) The indented format is generally used for letters of application. (See 14.3.) Whichever format you use, be consistent and avoid mixing them.

Heading block. Place a three-line heading with the writer's complete address and date at the top left or top right. Have at least a one-inch margin at the top and on the sides. Follow the form of the sample letter in 14.2 or 14.3.

Inside address. Type this exactly as it appears on the envelope. Except for common abbreviations such as the Mr., Mrs., or Ms. and state (TX), avoid abbreviating the inside address. Use full name, title (if known), and address.

Ms. Arla Nance	Name
Security Manager	Title
Xerxes Electronic Supply	Company
2345 Bosbey Road	Address
Rutherford, NJ 07071	City, State ZIP

Salutation block. Use the correct form and place it two spaces below the inside address in line with the left margin. Include a salutation followed by a colon. According to your information about the addressee, use one of the following forms:

Dear Ms. Nance: [proper for both Miss and Mrs.]
Dear Mrs. Schmiesing:
Dear Mmes. Jaoy and Teyu: [*Mmes.* is the plural of Mrs.]

Dear Professor Kern:
Dear Dr. Lambent:
Dear Messrs. Owen and Jones: [*Messrs.* is the plural of Mr.]

If you do not know the name of the person to whom you are sending the letter, use one of the following formalities. For forms not listed, consult "Forms of Address" in any good dictionary or a book of etiquette.

Dear Treasurer: [Title of person]
Dear Sir or Madam: [To avoid sexism]
Dear Sir: [If you know the person is a man]
Dear Madam: [If you know the person is a woman]
Dear Colleagues:

Paragraphs. Single-space the body using short, clear, precise, accurately stated paragraphs. Double-space between paragraphs.

Signature Block. After the body of the letter, skip two spaces and include a complimentary close such as *With good wishes*, or *Yours truly*. Then skip three spaces for room to sign your name, and type your name below the space for your handwritten signature. If a title is important, it should be included.

With thanks,

Milton Krassner

Milton Krassner
Personnel Manager

Yours truly,

Mrs. Judith Traxler

Mrs. Judith Traxler
Dean of Admissions

NOTE: If the letter is handwritten, sign your name, but do not print or rewrite your name under the signature.

NOTE: **Proper capitalization and a comma should be used with the different complimentary closes:**

Best regards,	*Cordially,*	*Cordially yours,*
Regards,	*Respectfully,*	*Sincerely,*
With good wishes,	*With thanks,*	*Yours sincerely,*

Envelope. Obtain a correct-size white envelope and address it accurately and completely. Try to use a standard envelope, $4 \times 9\frac{1}{2}$ inches. Do not use odd sizes or envelopes with curious colors. Include the return address in the upper left-hand corner—not on the back. Single-space on successive lines: name, title, organization, street address, followed by city, state, and zip code.

Gretchen Blake
1911 Woodmont Avenue
Omaha, NE 68131

        Ms. Desdemona Winters
        Managing Editor
        American Range Journal
        4980 South 25th Street
        Omaha, NE 68120

14.2 Business letters

People write business letters for all the different reasons that people write anything, but three kinds of letters appear most frequently: those asking for information, requests for action, and complaints. The strategies for completing such writing assignments resemble those for any other kind of writing, but the forms are very precise. Business writing has one important characteristic: It is precise and comes to the point quickly. It does not delay or digress. It must not waste the reader's time.

Do not evade the subject or apologize for writing. Come directly to your point. Be specific and use a plain style. Do not try to impress your reader with your knowledge, your greatness, or your fancy style. Do not try to curry favor with the reader by having a groveling attitude. Say what you mean quickly and give the person a good reason to act on your letter. By all means, present the facts in the case clearly and in good order.

Write the letter so that everything you have to say fits neatly on a single page. If you are unhappy about some situation, let the reader know that, but be polite. Honesty and rage are not the same things. Avoid anything that will cause the reader to dismiss your letter or not take it seriously. If the matter is urgent, indicate that in the letter. Follow the form of the following sample.

Sample Letter—Full Block Format

Heading   1638 Russell Avenue
block   Olympia, WA 98506
          May 1, 1990

Inside   Bob Green Shirts and Caps
address   11 Skyland Way
          Elko, NV 89154

Salutation   Dear Mr. Green:

Body
Our fraternity is in the market for a quantity of imprinted T-shirts and sweats. According to your advertisement in <u>Iron Horse</u> (May 1990), you offer high quality at low prices. Please send me a price list for T-shirts and sweats according to the following specifications. We need to purchase these items in navy blue with the Greek letters Δ, P, Γ imprinted in white: 50 short-sleeve crew-neck Ts, 50 hooded sweats, and 50 long-sleeved sweats. All sizes are large or extra large.

Please detail any possible discounts for quantities or any additional charges and indicate the time needed to process an order and ship the items.

Because we are unfamiliar with your company, we would appreciate your giving us the names of two organizations in our general area that have done business with you.

Thank you for your attention to our request.

Signature
block

Sincerely,
Jack Hammer
Jack Hammer
President
Delta Rho Gamma

Complimentary close
Signature
Typed Name
Title

14.3 Job applications and résumés

To apply for many good jobs, you need to write an application letter and create a résumé. The goal of these is to get you an interview for the job you are seeking. The letter shows an employer how your qualifications match the job description, and the résumé presents enough positive information to create a strong favorable impression. The following pages present the essential elements of application letters and résumés and also a few helpful hints for both of these forms of writing.

a. Elements of application letters

1. In the opening paragraph, indicate the specific job you are applying for. Indicate also how you learned about the job opening: through a friend, parent, or teacher, or through an advertisement. End this paragraph with a brief statement of your strongest qualification for the position.

2. In the second paragraph, you need to develop the background of your strongest qualification. Here is your chance to emphasize one of the following: (a) your interest in the kind of work, (b) your educational background that has prepared you for the job, and (c) the practical experience that prepares you for the job. Choose whatever will make the best impression on the employer.

3. In the third paragraph, develop the next strongest qualification. If you mentioned practical experience in paragraph, two, you might want to mention your education in this paragraph, or vice versa.

4. A fourth paragraph may be necessary if you have an additional strength that might impress the prospective employer.

5. A concluding paragraph is essential. You need to do the following: (a) mention your résumé, (b) indicate your availability for an interview, (c) specify when and where you will be so that an interview may be arranged, and (d) end on a polite and pleasing note expressing your honest interest in the job.

b. Hints for application letters

1. Be specific about the job you are applying for.
2. Be specific about your educational background that qualifies you for the job. Emphasize strengths.
3. Be specific about your previous work experience that has prepared you for this position. Emphasize strengths.
4. Be specific about those personal characteristics that would make you a good choice for the job. Emphasize strengths.
5. Be neat. Make your letter look, sound, and feel professional. Proofread the letter carefully several times. Use high-quality paper.
6. Be positive. Avoid criticizing any present or past employer, teacher, or employee of the company.
7. Be brief. Try to write a letter that will fit neatly on one page.

c. Elements of an effective résumé

1. Create a crisp, professional appearance. The résumé should look and feel like work completed by a mature, professional person.
2. Begin with personal information: your name, current address, phone numbers at work and at home.

3. Continue with your educational background. Focus on those aspects of it that relate to the job you are seeking.

4. Mention any significant work experience or volunteer activity.

5. List the names of at least two or three references who can comment on, in a specific way, your strengths as a learner, a worker, and a citizen.

d. Hints for an effective résumé

1. Avoid mentioning information about age, ethnic background, gender, height, health, marital status, religion, weight, and so forth unless the job description specifically mentions one or more of these as a qualification for employment.

2. Follow a clear chronological order when listing the details of your education or your job experience.

3. Avoid mentioning salary or benefits. This discussion can wait until the interview.

4. Provide information so the employer can clearly see how your education has prepared you for the job.

5. Provide information so the employer can clearly see how your previous employment has prepared you for this job.

6. Include—modestly—any honors, awards, or prizes that have a bearing on your education and experience and that relate to the job.

7. Create a professional appearance with high-quality paper and meticulous typing.

Sample Letter—Indented Block Format

Heading   1911 Woodmont Avenue
block   Omaha, NE 68131
                   May 11, 1990

Inside   Ms. Desdemona Winters
address   American Range Journal
block   4980 South 25th Street
             Omaha, NE 68120

Salutation Dear Ms. Winters:
block

          When I mentioned to you last
summer, while we were both judges for
several horse competitions at the State
Fair, my interest in working for your
magazine, I had no idea that a job for a
Body   writer would be available. Please
consider me for the position of reporter
and assistant to the editor mentioned in
the recent issue of American Range.

          As you can see from my résumé, I
have considerable practical experience
with horses, and my education includes
training in both writing and biology. I
have been trained in many of my college
courses to write in different forms for
widely differing audiences and for a
number of various purposes. To
complete a second major in biology, I
wrote my senior honors thesis on the
use of antibiotics by American and
Australian horse breeders.

Aside from extensive practice in academic writing, my experience includes the labor involved in preparing school yearbooks: as the head editor for two high school yearbooks and as yearbook editor at the college for the past two years. In addition, the duties of features editor and layout artist are familiar tasks to me after my work for the past three years on The Dodger, our student newspaper at the college.

I would love to work for your magazine and would feel flattered if you would request to see a portfolio of my writing samples. I am available for an interview at your convenience.

Sincerely,

Gretchen Blake

Gretchen Blake

Signature block

Sample Résumé: Example I

Gretchen Blake
1911 Woodmont Avenue
Omaha, NE 68131
(402) 555-3585

Job Goal: A position of responsibility that allows me to use my writing skill and my training in biology in the context of publishing related to ranching and the family farm

Education: Dodge University, B.A. 1988 with majors in biology and English and a minor in history

Experience: Veterinary assistant, Oppsmiff Animal Hospital
3562 Harney, Omaha, NE 68125, 1985–present
Features Editor, The Daily Dodger, 1985–1988
Layout artist, Daily Dodger, 1984–1988
Yearbook editor, Dodge University, 1987 and 1988
Yearbook editor, Howells High, 1983 and 1984
Horse trainer, Snow Road Ranch, Howells, 1981–1984

References: College Placement Office
Dodge University
Omaha, NE 68178

Sample Résumé: Example 2

Gretchen Blake

Permanent address: Current Address:
  Blake Land Ranch   1911 Woodmont Avenue
  Route 7, Box 311   Omaha, NE 68131
  Howells, NE 65410   (402) 555-3585
  (402) 820-3861

Position Sought: I would like a position where I could use my writing skills and my training in biology in dealing with topics of farming and the family farm.

Education: Dodge University, B.A. 1988
Majors: Biology and English
Minor: History

Honors: Omar Smith Writing Award, 1988
University Scholar, 1985–1988

Experience: Clinical assistant, Oppsmiff Veterinary, 1985–present
Layout artist, Daily Dodger, 1984–1988
Features editor, The Daily Dodger, 1985–1988
Yearbook editor, Dodge University, 1987 and 1988
Yearbook editor, Howells High, 1983 and 1984
Horse trainer, Howells, 1981–1984

Skills: Computer literate with MS–DOS, MAC, CP–M, UNIX
Experienced in layout programs such as Aldus
Good skill in using 35–mm camera and in working in a darkroom to develop prints

References: Available on request

14.4 Supplemental list on letters and résumés

If you would like additional material on letter writing, letters of application, résumés, and writing formats for nonacademic audiences, you might consult the following books.

Angel, Juvenal L. *The Complete Résumé Book and Job-Getter's Guide*. 3rd ed. New York: Pocket, 1990.

Barnett, Marva T. *Writing for Technicians*. Albany: Delmar, 1982.

Bolles, Richard N. *What Color Is Your Parachute? A Practical Manual for Job-Hunters*. Berkeley: Ten Speed, 1990.

Petras, Kathryn, and Ross Petras. *The Only Job Hunting Guide You'll Ever Need*. New York: Poseidon, 1989.

14.5 Letter to an editor

Writing to an editor is an excellent way for a person to inform the public. It takes no money for advertising or mailing. It takes no great energy to meet and talk to people. With only a pen or a typewriter, a person can alert an entire community to a problem or can express feelings on any topic of interest. Every newspaper in the country looks for good letters to the editor and is happy to publish them.

An effective letter has a number of important characteristics. First, the author must know and care about a subject. Second, the writer must have something interesting and important to say about one part of that subject. Third, the writer has to show the subject's importance to a reader.

Most important, the letter must focus on specific examples and contain concrete details.

Often letters to the editor are critical. Editors like to select these because they make interesting and informative reading. A letter can criticize an individual, an organization, or a policy, but it must contain specific examples. It cannot, however, be just an attack against some person. No responsible editor will print libelous material.

Thinking Exercises

1. Consider the following two letters to the editor complaining about the lax enforcement of the traffic laws within a city. If you were the editor, which would you print? Which is more effective in persuading a reader to take an interest in the problem?

a. To the editor: On the weekends you can drive out to the beach and see the cops lying in the sand asleep while their kids play in the water. This is on Sunday afternoon. That is probably what they are also doing on Monday and Tuesday and et cetera. I think it will take a little kid getting killed in this city to wake up the police to the fact that speeding drivers should be given big tickets and gotten off the road, especially around the intersections where schoolchildren have to cross twice a day. What will it take? A funeral to wake the police up to get them to perform their duties? Where are the policemen on Martin Road when every morning a whole band of cars speeds by sometimes at 50 mph? And this is in a 15 mph speed limit with the amber lights flashing to remind the drivers that kids are going to school! I think the police chief should have his head examined and that someone with some sense should give the go ahead to the police to write those tickets. Who needs it? Our children do. Do something, now, people, before it is too late.

Sid Robinson

b. To the editor: Last week I had to walk the two miles to school because my car was in the shop. It was one of the most frightening experiences of my entire life. I passed by three grade schools where 500–600 students attend school every day. At almost every intersection where a child might pass, I observed reckless driving by adults. The traffic laws simply are not enforced in this city. Speeders flourish. Some drivers seem to be drag racing through 15 mph zones. Sooner or later, a child will be seriously hurt. It is time for the police department to begin looking into this problem of crazy and reckless driving before something terrible happens. A few radar traps on a few mornings with some high fines for speeding in school zones should quickly put an end to this dangerous situation.

Daniel Bender

2. Study the examples of full block format in 14.2 and indented block format in 14.3. Which style is the more recent to appear? What technological advances might have made such a new style popular? Are there any other changes in writing style and writing format that may have been caused by new machines and new technologies?

3. In both sample résumés in this chapter, mention is made of work as a features editor. What effect might the following job description have on a prospective employer if it were added to the résumé?

Layout artist, <u>Daily Dodger</u>, 1982–1985: Solicited copy from advertisers, columnists, reporters; worked with copy editor; used various computer programs for graphics enhancement; with managing editors consent (and absence) made deletion decisions for copy length; designed page formats; delivered copy to printers under deadline pressures; served as graphics analyst for prospective clients; handled queries and complaints dealing with graphic clarity and layout.

Writing Assignments

1. Identify a serious problem in your community or at your school. Write a letter to the editor pointing out this problem. Use specific details and examples to get your point across.

2. Write an ironic letter to an editor, congratulating someone or some group for having done something you consider evil, stupid, or ignorant.

3. Write a paragraph describing a dream job you would like to have. Explain a few things about the job, especially the kind of work, the challenges, and the rewards. Then complete the following assignments:

    a. Write a help-wanted advertisement for the ideal job.

    b. Write a letter applying for your ideal job. Explain your qualifications and show how you have the necessary skills.

    c. Write two letters: one strongly recommending you and a second letter strongly not recommending you for the job.

4. Write a letter of complaint to a company, an individual, or a business that you or a friend is having a problem with. Include the following: (a) a clear statement of the problem and its background, (b) some hint of the level of your dissatisfaction, (c) a statement expressing what should be done, and (d) information about what you plan to do to receive legal satisfaction.

5. After reading the two résumés by Gretchen Blake, write a paragraph explaining the differences between them.

PART 5

Research and Writing

15 Libraries: Glossary of Terms

This chapter contains an alphabetical list of the most important elements in a library, and it also contains a few hints about some kinds of activities that can help you improve your reading and writing skills. It has been designed to assist college students who are required to complete reports, studies, papers, or research projects. Blank spaces follow many of the entries for you to fill in important information concerning your library in terms of availability and location of things. Be sure to fill in this information as you examine this chapter. Because understanding how to use a library invariably involves practical knowledge, this chapter will help you the most if it *is used in the library.*

Abstract. An abstract objectively summarizes the contents of an article. Most often an abstract presents the article's main idea and then explains the method of development. Abstracts appear in two separate places: in the periodical and in a separate volume published by an abstracting service. Reading an abstract can save valuable time. The abstract can let a reader know the importance of an article. If the article is valuable, it should be read. If it has no value, the phrase "Consulted—Of No Value" should be marked on the bibliography card. The following list contains some of the most important collections of abstracts.

- *Abstracts in Anthropology*
- *Abstracts of English Studies*
- *Biological Abstracts*
- *Book Review Digest*
- *Chemical Abstracts*
- *Dissertation Abstracts International*
- *Historical Abstracts*
- *Key to Economic Science*
- *Language and Language Behavior Abstracts*
- *Physics Abstracts*
- *Psychological Abstracts*
- *Religious and Theological Abstracts*
- *RILA (art)*
- *RILM (music)*
- *Science Abstracts*
- *Sociological Abstracts*

Most important for my research project: _____ .

Accuracy. Accuracy is essential in every stage of research and writing of papers. Many people, including the author of this book, have wasted hours or even days in library research because of a small error or a tiny omission. Accuracy is one of the key words in all labors of research. Tiny differences between a 1 and an l or between 0 and O make vast differences in the availability and location of scholarly material. Intelligent people make mistakes all the time, but they develop the habit of going over their work carefully to make sure that all information is copied correctly. People unwilling to learn the habits of accuracy often end up wasting time in boring and repetitive work. Students need to check their note taking and make sure their handwriting is correct and legible. It is important to use paper and pens that do not smear.

Audiovisual materials. This includes a collection of tapes, films, filmstrips, microforms, records, slides, and the machines necessary to use them.

Location: _____ .

Authorities in the field. In one sense, authorities are scholars with the most knowledge about a particular subject. Discover these by using the catalogs, bibliographies, and encyclopedias. In addition to these volumes, the reference librarian can help guide you to other specialists in your area of inquiry. The faculty at your school also contains numerous authorities in many different fields. Ask. Other possible authorities include advanced undergraduates and graduate students. At the beginning of your research project, search for the name of an important scholar in the subject, discover a central essay in the area, and find the most important anthology or textbook.

Background reading. A student needs to do background reading *before* any serious reading or note taking. You do this for three reasons: (1) to explore your interest in a topic; (2) to find out whether the library has enough material on the topic; and (3) to give a sense of direction to the library search for material dealing with your topic. Above all, you need to find a topic that interests you. You might find your subject in a newspaper, weekly magazine, or television interview. Many students have completed satisfying research projects by exploring matters of local interest.

Bibliography. A bibliography is a list of books or articles. Effective researchers know how to build a usable bibliography. Some excellent sources for a bibliography on a subject are the following:

- ✎ Library catalog: under author, title, subject
- ✎ *Guide to Reference Books*: at the reference desk
- ✎ Encyclopedias: at the very end of the article
- ✎ Reference bibliographies on certain subjects or persons
- ✎ Indexes and abstracts, such as *Bibliographic Index*
- ✎ Textbooks or scholarly books: in each chapter and at the end of book

Some important bibliographies are the following:

- ✎ Afro-American studies: *Black Bibliography*
- ✎ Arts and humanities: *Arts and Humanities Index*
- ✎ Education: *The Educator's Desk Reference*
- ✎ General: *A World Bibliography of Bibliographies*
- ✎ Film: *The American Film Institute Catalog*
- ✎ History: *Bibliographies in American History*
- ✎ Literature: *MLA International Bibliography*
- ✎ Philosophy: *A Bibliography of Philosophical Bibliographies*

- Psychology: *Harvard List of Books in Psychology*
- Science: *Science Citation Index*
- Social sciences: *Social Science Citation Index*

Biography. Often encyclopedias do not contain enough information about a writer or a public figure. The following volumes provide important sources of biographical information:

- *American Men and Women of Science*
- *Contemporary Authors*
- *Current Biography*
- *Dictionary of American Biography*
- *Dictionary of American Negro Biography*
- *Dictionary of Canadian Biography*
- *Dictionary of National Biography*
- *McGraw-Hill Encyclopedia of World Biography* (1973)
- *Who's Who*
- *Who's Who in America* (1899–   )

Books. Get in the habit of inspecting books carefully before you read them. Find out whether a book will help your research. Check the date, because in most fields recent books are the most useful. Identify the author, and try to determine if the person is an authority in the field. Reference books such as *Who's Who* or *Dictionary of American Scholars* should give you some indication. Then examine the book itself. Skim through the table of contents. Leaf through the introduction, preface, or foreword. Check the index. Notice whether the book contains any bibliography. Copy any interesting leads. Open the book at random to see the level of writing and scholarship. Is the book written for a general audience or for a research scholr? Before reading the book, try to find out how much it can help you in your research project. If the material is valuable, withdraw the book from the library or make a copy of the important information in it. If the material is of no value, mark on the appropriate bibliography card: "Consulted—Of No Value."

Browsing. Another phrase for browsing is "keeping your eyes open." You will learn much from the card catalog and the indexes. However, not everything the library has on your subject will be found by your searching the catalog or the indexes. Whenever you are in the reference area, look for volumes related to your subject. While in the stacks, stop and look for a moment on your way to get a book. When in the periodical section, stop for a minute or two to see what is in some other journals. Of course, you are pressed for time, but the habit of browsing can prove valuable. Browsing will also give you a better sense of location. Your next visit will be easier. No library feels comfortable until a person has used it a dozen times. Browsing will make your library visits less intimidating and more pleasurable.

Call number. Obtain the sheet or the information from your library regarding the system of call numbers, which are the particular ID numbers for each item in the library. Call numbers are found on cards in the catalog or on the screen of a terminal. On a card, they are in the upper left-hand corner. On a screen the call number is often one of the first items to appear. (See the examples on page 374.) Each item in the library has a unique call number. Whether you use the catalog or the terminal screen, accurately copy the call number including *all* words, *all* letters, and *all* numbers. Copy them in the exact order they appear on the card or the screen. If they are on different lines, write the symbols on different lines. Locate the item by consulting the map of your library. (See *Classification systems* in this chapter.) The following examples show three different call numbers for the same book, the *MLA Handbook for Writers of Research Papers*:

LC Number	LC Number	Dewey Number
Reference	LB	808′
Z	2369	.02
LB	.G53	
2369	1988	
.G53		
1988		

Card catalog. Using the card catalog is easy, but keep in mind four facts about the way it is arranged:

1.   The cards are arranged alphabetically. However, the cards on an author or a subject may be arranged both alphabetically and chronologically. For example, Shakespeare's play *Macbeth* precedes his play *Measure for Measure*. However, the editions of *Macbeth* are arranged in chronological order, whereas the critical books on *Macbeth* are arranged alphabetically. To make your search complete, locate the first card on the author or subject and the last card. Be sure to go through all relevant cards in between.

2.   Some authors and subjects have cards filed under an old system and a new system. Pay close attention to a reference card telling you to see another heading.

3.   Material is listed according to a standardized set of subject headings. Before looking up a subject, consult the *Library of Congress Guide to Subject Headings* at the reference desk. That will direct you to the proper heading.

4. The card catalog contains three important kinds of cards: author cards, title cards, and subject cards.

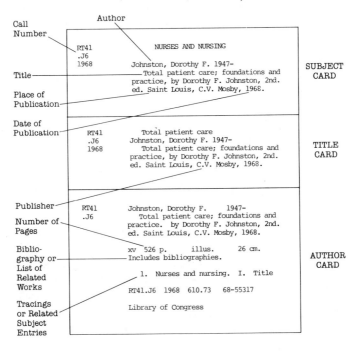

The following bibliographic card was created from the material on a card in the card catalog.

[Health Science library]

RT 41
J6
1968

Johnston, Dorothy F.

Total Patient Care:
Foundations and Practice

2nd ed. St Louis:
C.V. Mosby, 1968.

[Has Bibliographies]

NOTE: In some libraries, the computer terminal contains only material published *after* a certain date. If this is the case at your library, you need to learn the date that separates the material in the card catalog from the material on the computer terminals. You may have to use both catalogs. Date: _____ .

Catalog. The catalog lists the contents of the library. Using the catalog, you can prepare a bibliography card that includes author, title, publication information, and call number. Because of new technologies, most libraries have been changing, and the catalog now exists in two forms. One is the familiar card catalog. A second is a central data base accessible through a computer terminal. (See both *Card catalog* and *Computer catalog* in this chapter.)

Catalog form in your library: _____ .

Location(s): _____ .

Circulation desk. This desk serves as one of the central points of the library. Students need to know its location and its importance. You will use it for the following: (1) checking out books, (2) requesting books in a closed stack system, (3) searching for volumes not on the shelves, (4) reserving books, (5) paying fines, and (6) information.

Location: _____. Hours: _____.

Classification systems. To classify, label, and shelve books, most American libraries use one of two systems: either the Dewey Decimal or Library of Congress system.

System used at your school: _____.

The Dewey Decimal System, based on the number 10, has ten categories. This system shelves nonfiction books numerically. Fiction books are shelved alphabetically by the author's last name.

000–099	General works	500–599	Pure science
100–199	Philosophy	600–699	Technology
200–299	Religion	700–799	The arts
300–399	Social sciences	800–899	Literature
400–499	Language	900–999	History

The Library of Congress System omits the letters I, O, W, X, and Y. It shelves books alphabetically and then numerically.

A	General works
B	Philosophy, psychology, religion
C	History
D	History: general and European
E–F	History: North and South America

G	Geography, anthropology, recreation
H	Social sciences
J	Political science
K	Law
L	Education
M	Music
N	Fine arts
P	Language and literature
Q	Science
R	Medicine
S	Agriculture
T	Technology
U	Military science
V	Naval science
Z	Bibliography and library science

Computer catalog. In addition to the card catalog, information about the call number, author, and title of a book is available on the computer catalog. Most libraries provide printed instructions about the computer terminals or have librarians available for assistance. Using the computer terminal is different at first but not difficult. A knowledge of typing is not required, but patience and precision are necessary. You can solve most problems involving the computer catalog by reading the library's printed instructions or by asking a library worker for assistance. The instructions on the screen must be followed exactly. Most computer terminals display on the screen preliminary information (the material is called a *help menu*) such as that shown here. Notice that the instructions give information about author, title, call number, subject, and holdings. To search for an author, type in A/, but to search for a title, T/ is typed in.

```
The system may be approached using the following commands:

    Author Search    Enter A/ and the author's name (last name first)
                     EXAMPLE: A/Hemingway, Ernest

    Title Search     Enter T/ and the title.
        (omit any leading articles: THE,A,AN,LA,L',DER...)
                     EXAMPLE: T/Sun also rises

    Call Number Search Enter C/ and the call number.
                     EXAMPLE: C/TL725.3 T7 J6

    Subject Search   Enter S/ and the subject term(s).
                     EXAMPLE: S/Metals

    KEYWORDS: AUTHOR,TITLE,CALL,SUBJECT,
```

The preceding help menu tells the viewer that catalog information can be found by typing in either *A/, T/, C/,* or *S/* followed by author, title, call number, or subject. The following information appeared on the screen after *A/ CONRAD, JOSEPH* was typed in.

```
1. Title ------- LORD JIM BY JOSEPH CONRAD INTRODUCTION BY J DONALD
                 ADAMS
   Main author - CONRAD JOSEPH 1857-1924
   Pub. data --- NEW YORK THE MODERN LIBRARY 1931

2. Title ------- NOTES ON LIFE AND LETTERS
   Main author - CONRAD JOSEPH 1857-1924
   Pub. data --- GARDEN CITY N Y DOUBLEDAY PAGE 1925 1921
```

Notice that the screen presents a numbered series of books by Conrad. Notice at the bottom of the screen that *NS* is an abbreviation for *Next Screen*. If *NS* is typed in, the screen will continue to display titles of books by Conrad. If the number *1, 2, 3,* or *4* is typed in, the screen will display information about that item.

```
3. Title ------- PORTABLE CONRAD EDITED AND WITH AN INTROD AND
                 NOTES BY MORTON DAUWEN ZABEL
                 REV ED BY FREDERICK R KARL
   Main author - CONRAD JOSEPH 1857-1924
   Pub. data --- NEW YORK VIKING PRESS 1969

4. Title ------- SECRET AGENT A SIMPLE TALE
   Main author - CONRAD JOSEPH 1857-1924
   Pub. data --- GARDEN CITY N Y DOUBLEDAY 1953
                                                 Enter 'NS' for more
Please enter NEW COMMAND or LINE # of selection
```

Notice that the following screen lists two items by Joseph Conrad with the title *Lord Jim*. If the number *1* is typed in, a screen such as the following will appear.

```
MARSHALL UNIV. LIBRARIES- - - - - - V T L S - - - - - - - -
  1. Lord Jim, by Joseph Conrad; introduction by J. Donald
     Adams.
  2. Lord Jim.

  Please enter NEW COMMAND or LINE # of selection


MARSHALL UNIV. LIBRARIES- - - - - - V T L S - - - - - - - - - -

CALL NO: PZ3 C764 L20
AUTHOR: Conrad, Joseph, 1857-1924.
TITLE: Lord Jim, by Joseph Conrad; introduction by J. Donald
  1) Item Number - 1170154734
  2) Copy Number -     1          7) Units ----
  3) Loan Period -    90          8) Price ----
  4) Circ. Count -     5          9) Location - MORROW LIBRARY
  5) Entry Date  - 22Jun85       10) Temp. at -
  6) Item Class  -               11) Last Checked in on -   2May86
 12) Circulation Count  - Since - 22Jun85 is -      5
Status: AVAILABLE
Please enter NEW COMMAND or 'HELP' for assistance
```

Much information presented on such a screen interests only librarians, but the following information is especially valuable: call number, author, title, location, and status. The word *Available* beside the word *Status* indicates that the book should be on the shelf.

Computer search. A trained librarian can use a computer to prepare a comprehensive bibliography on your subject. Many libraries will, for a fee or occasionally for free, conduct a computer search through an available data base. Ask the reference librarian whether this service is available. You will need to have a list of precise words, called "descriptors," to locate the information.

Computer terminals. When using the terminal, follow the instructions precisely. For correct subject headings, consult the *Library of Congress Subject Headings*. Know precisely too whether the terminal has access to all of the holdings in the library or just a part.

Percent of library items in data base: _____ .

Location of computer terminals: _____ .

Copying services. Copiers have removed some drudgery from scholarship and research. In addition to copiers, most libraries have machines to make copies of microforms. Ask the librarian for assistance. When copying material, keep the following ideas in mind: (1) avoid damaging any book or magazine by bending it sharply; (2) copy only what you need—do not copy blindly; (3) observe the copyright laws—copy only for *your* research purposes; (4) immediately record on the copy the page number and all the information needed to identify the source.

Location of microform copiers: _____ .

Location of copiers: _____ .

Cost: _____ .

Data bases. A data base is a central computerized collection of information. On almost any subject of interest today, you can find a data base. Most of them are private companies that have collected enormous amounts of information. To obtain this information, you need a phone, a computer, a modem, and access to one of the different data bases. Some university libraries and departments have access to the data bases. The following books give valuable information on two different data bases.

- Bowen, Charles, and David Peyton. *How to Get the Most out of CompuServe.* 3rd ed. New York: Bantam, 1987.
- Bowen, Charles, and David Peyton. *How to Get the Most out of Dow Jones News-Retrieval Service.* New York: Bantam, 1986.

If you plan to use a data base, make sure you copy the relevant information that refers to the printed source. This bibliographical information will be presented on the screen either before or after the data.

Dictionaries. Dictionaries are commonly divided into three different classes: unabridged, abridged, and special dictionaries. An unabridged dictionary is a large, comprehensive dictionary that is not based on another text. The most common examples of unabridged dictionaries are the twenty–volume second edition of the *Oxford English Dictionary*, the one-volume *Webster's Third New International Dictionary of the English Language*, with 2,662 pages, and the *Random House Dictionary of the English Language*, with 2,478 pages.

Call numbers of unabridged dictionaries: _____ .

A second kind of dictionary is an abridged dictionary, which is based on a larger one. *Webster's Ninth New Collegiate Dictionary* is a standard college dictionary based on *Webster's Third New International*. Similarly, the *Random House College Dictionary* is based on the larger unabridged *Random House Dictionary of the English Language*. The other standard college dictionaries are listed at the beginning of 21.2.

A third kind is a dictionary specialized for a particular area of knowledge. These are valuable reference sources for information on subjects such as medicine, psychology, religion, physics, and other disciplines. A list of commonly used special dictionaries on language and usage can be found at the beginning of 9.3.

Most valuable for my research: _____ .

Call numbers: _____ .

Encyclopedias. Everyone is familiar with the standard encyclopedias: *Collier's Encyclopedia, Encyclopedia Americana, New Encyclopaedia Britannica, New Columbia Encyclopedia.* As a researcher, you need to be aware of the aid these volumes can give you. They can help in developing a bibliography and in providing important background information. In terms of bibliography, consult the reading list at the end of each entry. Also note the author of the article. Pursue each of these leads. For background information, identify the specialized encyclopedia with the most up-to-date information on your subject. Here are a few of the many important specialized encyclopedias:

- *Cambridge Atlas of Astronomy*
- *Cambridge Guide to World Theatre*
- *Cambridge History of English Literature*
- *Chambers Dictionary of Science and Technology*
- *Dictionary of American History*
- *Encyclopedia Judaica*
- *Encyclopedia of Southern Culture*
- *Grove's Dictionary of Music and Musicians*
- *Grzimek's Encyclopedia of Mammals*
- *International Encyclopedia of the Social Sciences*
- *McGraw-Hill Encyclopedia of Science and Technology*
- *Oxford Companion to Classical Literature*
- *Women's Studies Encyclopedia*

Location of encyclopedias: _____ .

Most important encyclopedias on my subject: _____ .

ERIC. This is the acronym for Educational Resources Informational Center. Often this is separate from the main library at many schools. ERIC is a center specializing in sources dealing with education. It can provide a bibliography on a selected topic and it may have a microfiche copy of the relevant materials.

Location: _____ . Hours: _____ .

Government documents. The largest publisher in the world is the United States government. If your library has a government documents collection, use it. Inquire, especially if your topic has anything at all to do with public affairs. The federal government has a unique filing, coding, and numbering system. To use government documents, you need to ask the documents librarian for assistance.

Location: _____ .

Hours: _____ .

Indexes. An index will help you find the library's periodicals on your topic. Learn the different kinds of indexes.

1. Library index: Your library has a special volume or catalog listing all its magazines and periodicals with a title such as *Serials Holdings File* or *List of Serial Holdings*. It indicates how many back copies of any periodical the library has. It also indicates missing volumes and lets you know whether the material is in print form or microform.

Location: _____ .

2. Newspaper indexes: These give information on material published in newspaper form. Some of the newspapers that index their contents are the *London Times, New York Times, Wall Street Journal*, and *Christian Science Monitor. Newspaper Index* combines material from

four papers: the *Chicago Tribune, Los Angeles Times, New Orleans Times-Picayune*, and *Washington Post*.

Location: _____ .

    3.   General indexes: Earlier versions are *Poole's Index to Periodical Literature: 1802–1881, Nineteenth-Century Readers' Guide*, and *International Index*. Used today are *Readers' Guide to Periodical Literature, Magazine Index, Essay and General Literature Index*, and *Catholic Periodical Index*.

Location: _____ .

The following sample entries from *Readers' Guide* illustrate author, subject, and cross-reference entries.

Subject ——— REGATTAS
    Master mariners race; annual regatta in San
    Francisco Bay. W. E. Vaughn. il Motor B
    125:54-6+ My '70 ——— Date
    See also
    Yacht racing

    REGGE trajectories
    Serpukhov data are highlight at Regge-pole
    conference. M. Bander and G. L. Shaw. il
    Phys Today 23:83+ My '70
Pages ——— REGIONAL library associations. See Library— Crosslisting
    associations

    REGIONAL planning
    Let's sing Auld lang syne for the upper
Volume ——— Brandywine. L. B. Leopold. il Natur Hist
    —79:4-6+ Je '70

    REICHLIN, Seymour. See Martin, J. B. jt. auth.

    REID, W. Stanford
    Christianity: the true humanism. Chr Today — Periodical
    14:9-11 Je 19 '70 Title

    REIF, Rita
    Home (cont) il N Y Times Mag p66-7 Mr 1;
    92-3 Mr 8; 82-3 Mr 22; 104-5 Ap 5; 76-7 Ap
    19; 74-5 My 10; 50-1 Je 21 '70

Author ——— REIGER, George W.
    Hustler: a new breed of Arkansas traveler. Il
    Pop Mech 133:98-100 My '70 Cross
    REILLY, Christopher T. See Bird, L. P. jt. auth.— reference
    REINERT, Jeanne
Article Title ——— Would you obey a Hitler? il Sci Digest 67:
    34-9 My '70

The following bibliographical card was created from the material listed in the *Readers' Guide*.

SAMPLE BIBLIOGRAPHY CARD

Reinert, Jeanne

"Would You Obey a Hitler?"

Science Digest

Volume 67, pages 34-9
May 1970

---

4. Specialized indexes: These are special indexes for separate academic disciplines.

Art	*Art Index*
Arts and humanities	*Arts and Humanities Citation Index*
Bibliography	*Bibliographic Index*
Biography	*Biography Index*
Biology	*Biological and Agricultural Index*
Book reviews	*Book Review Digest*
Business	*Business Periodicals Index*
Chemistry	*Index Chemicus*
Classical studies	*L'Année Philologique*
Education	*Education Index*
	Current Index to Journals in Education

Engineering	*Engineering Index*
General	*Bibliographic Index*
Health sciences	*Index Medicus*
Humanities	*Humanities Index*
Law	*Index to Legal Periodicals*
Library science	*Library Literature*
	Ulrich's International Periodicals
Literature and language	*MLA International Bibliography*
Music	*Music Index*
Philosophy	*Philosopher's Index*
Political science	*ABC: Political Science*
Religion	*Religion Index*
Science	*General Science Index*
	Science Citation Index
Social sciences	*Social Science Index*
Technology	*Applied Science and Technology Index*

Most important on your topic: _____ .

Location: _____ .

Instruction. Libraries are complex tools for acquiring, holding, and sharing knowledge. New students may find a college library difficult or even impossible. To help students, most libraries publish maps, guides, and pamphlets on the use of the library. Also they may offer helpful lectures, tours, and workshops in library skills.

Location for library instruction: _____ .

Times: _____ .

Interlibrary loan services. If you cannot obtain a needed book or periodical, you may be able to obtain the material through interlibrary loan. To do this, you need to consult with the reference librarian, fill out the necessary paperwork, and pay any required fee. Some libraries may not offer this service to undergraduates. Some material may take two to three weeks or longer. The librarian will help you arrange the loan, if possible.

Location: _____ . Hours: _____ .

Availability: _____ . Cost: _____ .

Librarians. Not everyone who works in a library is a librarian. Librarians are professionals with wide training and different skills. Some work in acquisitions; some work in cataloging; some work in manuscripts; other librarians work in reference departments. Reference librarians will be able to help you the most. Discover the different kinds of library workers.

Find out who are the shelvers. Shelvers are often students who have little training in the contents of the library. These people may be able to help you find a certain part of the library or locate materials such as large or small size materials. Find out also who are the circulation clerks. These people will be able to check out books for you. In addition, they can trace the location of a book or indicate when a checked-out book might be available. They can reserve the book for you or, in certain cases, recall a book for your use.

Above all else, discover the reference desk and the reference librarians. These people will prove the most valuable to you. They know the location of almost everything in the library. When you have a question about places to find information on your subject, ask them. They will be able to direct you with very little effort to the best available source. They may also arrange for or direct you to interlibrary loans and, when available, computer searches.

Location of reference desk: _____ .

Hours: _____ .

If you have to use one of the special sections in the library, discover who is in charge. Your library may have special sections for rare books, government documents, periodicals, audiovisuals, or other collections. In that case, you will be able to acquire specialized information from the person in charge of any of those sections. Remember that the central goal of any library is the passing on of information. A question is the best way to discover information. Do not hesitate to ask questions.

Library of Congress Guide to Subject Headings. This volume stays at the library's reference desk. Using it, a student can look up the correct subject headings in the appropriate indexes and in the card or computer catalog. This volume contains the correct headings in the catalogs and can help save time.

Location: _____ .

Map. Obtain a copy of the map of your library. Keep it in a convenient place and use it when needed.

Microforms. Pay particular attention to the call numbers in the card catalog, for they often indicate microfilm or microfiche. Both of these require special devices to be read. Ask for information if you do not know the different kinds of machines or how to operate them. Note also which machines are capable of making copies of microform materials.

Location: _____ .

Newspapers. You will find these in three different places: (1) the most current are generally kept in a reading room; (2) less recent issues are often in the stacks; and

(3) earlier issues are on microfilm or microfiche. Material in newspapers is found in the various newspaper indexes.

Location of current issues: _____ .

Location of back issues: _____ .

Other sources. Some students' research projects have led them to museums, newspapers, courthouses, businesses, labor unions, government offices, historical societies, archives, private libraries, churches, and other sources of information. If you find that your project might benefit from these kinds of inquiry, a phone call or a letter is generally essential. As always in research and scholarship, honesty and politeness are their own rewards, but they reap substantial benefits.

Pamphlets. Some pamphlets are catalogued in the main catalog. Government pamphlets are in Government Documents and can be found with the help of the documents librarian. Many other pamphlets on topical subjects are collected in the *Vertical File Index.*

Location: _____ .

Periodical articles. Obtaining these involves a four-step process:

1. Determine the most suitable indexes or abstracts for your topic. If available, consult *A World Bibliography of Bibliography* and *Bibliographic Index.* Search the indexes for your subject. Pay careful attention to all cross-references.

2. Make a bibliography card for each appropriate citation: author, title, publication, date, volume, and pages.

3. Determine whether the library has the periodical. Check the periodicals desk or the library's *List of Serial*

Holdings. If the library does not have the article and you need it, you will have to obtain it through interlibrary loan. If the library does have the article, mark down the location: on the shelves, on microform, or in the reading room.

4.   Find the periodical. Check to see whether the issue contains an abstract of the article you need. If available, study the abstract first to let you know whether you want to read the entire article.

Periodicals room. Generally, such a room contains the most recent issues of various periodicals. Earlier items are either bound and in the stacks or microfilmed.

Location: _____ .

Questions. Get in the habit of asking questions. A library is a research tool, a complex device for providing information. A library, however, can give only as much information as it is asked to. Questions are essential to the success of any writing assignment. The questions change as the writer proceeds in the assignment. The important questions at the beginning include the following: What is your subject? How will you narrow it? Does the library have enough material? Library work is more efficient and pleasant if the student-researcher prepares a list of five to ten questions before each library visit. Writing down such questions sets specific goals and helps direct the researcher's energies. Above all, students should not hesitate to ask librarians, especially reference librarians, for help.

Reference guides. These volumes are never checked out. They are used for reference only. Specialized guides to reference material in all fields are Eugene P. Sheehy's *Guide to Reference Books*, and A. J. Walford's *Guide to Reference Material*.

Reference room. This part of the library contains non-circulating material, such as bibliographies, encyclopedias, indexes, and abstracts. It also contains a group of helpful people: the reference librarians.

Location: _____ . Hours: _____ .

Reserve desk. Often a teacher may need to reserve certain volumes for an entire class. To do this, a book is placed on reserve for a limited period of time, such as an hour or overnight. The book may be used for that short period of time and then checked back in again.

Location: _____ . Phone: _____ .

Hours: _____ .

Reviews. You may want to know what others thought about a book. Books are generally reviewed in the four years after the first publication. The following sources include both popular and scholarly reviews in various periodicals: *Book Review Digest, Book Review Index, An Index to Book Reviews in the Humanities*, and in recent volumes in the "Book Reviews" section following the main body of the *Readers' Guide to Periodical Literature.*

Skimming. Skimming is quick reading for general, not specific, content. After skimming, a researcher is able to form a quick judgment about the worth of the material. This practice, once learned, can save enormous amounts of time and energy and as such is a valuable skill. The most important keys to skimming involve using the abstracts for periodicals and reading the index, table of contents, and introduction of a book.

Sources. Scholars refer to the origin of something in writing as a source. Sources are either primary or secondary. A primary source is a work *by* a writer. Herman Melville's *Moby Dick* is a primary source. Primary sources include material such as interviews, eyewitness accounts, historical documents, letters, documentary films, and manuscripts. A secondary source is a book *about* a writer or a subject. Leon Howard's book, *Herman Melville: A Biography*, is a secondary source. Secondary sources discuss primary source material.

Stacks. In the earliest libraries, the shelves were stacked on top of each other. That section of the library containing the main collection of books is called the stacks. Stacks are either *open* or *closed*. In an open stacks system, people can wander anywhere throughout the library and take the books off the shelves to read or check out. In a closed stacks system, people fill out forms with accurate information, requesting certain material. The forms are turned in at the circulation desk. The books are then delivered to the desk and checked out.

System at your school's library: _____ .

Tracings. On cards in the card catalog, tracings appear after most of the other information. The tracings list the subject headings for a book. Mark them down when you see them. They can be a valuable method for tracking information. See the example of the tracings reference on the card under the entry for *Card catalog*.

Library Exercise

1. Create a separate bibliography card for each of the following items.

a. A reprint published by the Green Press in Lincoln, Nebraska, in 1985 of Ted Smith's book of poems, *Night on the River Styx*, published in 1935 by Martin Press in New York City.

b. An essay by Ann Chatres with the title "Searching for Cheap Antiques" published in the magazine *Curios* in November 1972, volume 23, on pages 11–24.

c. A book by Ann Chatres with the same title as above that was published by the Rumbleseat Press in Charlotte, North Carolina, in June 1984.

d. A letter you wrote that appeared in *Dialectical Studies*, volume 13 on page 33 in 1989.

e. The entry for the word *sun* in the *Encyclopaedia Britannica* copyrighted in 1974.

f. The essay by Regenia Lucas that appears at the end of chapter 9 in this book.

g. A statement made by one of your professors in a class you are taking now.

2. Using the following information, prepare entries for a list of works cited. Study the sample at the end of 17.5, and follow the MLA format presented in 17.6.

a. An article in the *Washington Post* by Paul Richard with the title "Down the Garden Path" that was published on Saturday, March 31, 1990, in Section D. The first part of the article appears on page 1, and it continues on page 7.

b. An unsigned article in the *Washington Post* with the title "Washington Area Real Estate Trends" that appeared on page 5 in Section E on March 31, 1990.

c. An article by Igor Lukes that appeared in the March/April issue of *Bostonia* in 1990 with the title "The Wall in Our Heads" that begins on page 21 and continues to page 23. (Note: Use Mar.–Apr. 1990: to indicate the publication months.)

d. An unsigned article on roller blading with the title "Roll With It, Baby" that appeared on pages 272 and 273 of *Seventeen* in March 1990.

e. An article by Douglas H. Lamb and Glenn D. Reeder with the title "Reliving Golden Days" that appeared in *Psychology Today* and began on page 22 but continued throughout that issue on numerous pages in June 1986. (Use 22+ to indicate page numbers.)

f. The first article in the March 1990 issue of *PMLA* that began on page 197 and continued to page 208 by Andrew Galloway with the title "*Beowulf* and the Varieties of Choice." That issue was volume 105, Number 2. (Note: *PMLA* is a scholarly periodical with continuous paging from issue to issue. The first page of the March issue is page 185.)

g. The article by Cynthia Kadohata with the title "Breece D'J Pancake" on pages 35 to 61 of the *Mississippi Review* published in 1990 at the University of Southern Mississippi that was number 1 of volume 18. (Note: *Mississippi Review* is a periodical without continuous paging from issue to issue. In other words, each issue begins on page 1 and continues to the last page.)

h. The poem by William Stafford entitled "Several Dances" that appeared on page 35 of *Granite* and was published in Spring 1973, issue number 5. (Note: *Granite* is a periodical with issue numbers only and without any volume numbers.)

16 Research

✍ **Student Comments on Writing**

I know that if I finish this research paper I deserve
to graduate. At first I was overwhelmed and almost
despaired. Then I saw the whole assignment in
terms of a process with stages and chances to undo
any mistakes or to improve what I had done. Then
I calmed down.

Kenneth Hawkins

I don't want to sound like a radical, but I have a
different way of writing a research paper. I think it
is easier than the way in the book. What I do is
pick a topic and narrow it down very tightly: a tiny
little area to explore. Last year I did a paper on
"The Building of Central Park in New York City."
What I do then is read and read and read. I read
until I know enough about the subject so I could
explain it to someone. Then I write the rough
draft. I write it without looking at any books or any
notes. I know this seems curious. Some parts I can
only remember in bits; for other parts I know I
need to quote something to make my point. After I
have finished the rough draft, I go back and fill in
the blanks with some quoting and summarizing.

Helen Chase

The preceding student comments show two different approaches to the work involved in a research project. One writer mentions a "process with stages," whereas the second author emphasizes reading and writing. These writers seem experienced when it comes to doing research, but many students in college writing courses feel uncomfortable when confronted with research assignments. If you have previously written a research paper, you will know your strengths and weaknesses. If you have not, you can use the material in this chapter to guide you through a process that is remarkably similar to that followed in most other writing assignments. The three ingredients for a successful and informative research paper are (1) an interesting topic, (2) sufficient time, and (3) sufficient energy to complete the work. No teacher can deliver these three things to you. You must find them within yourself. What this chapter can do is show you what steps you need to follow and what choices you need to make in order to write a research paper on a selected topic.

16.1 Creating an assignment

Think of your research assignment as more than the summary of various comments about a topic. Think of it as something that can help you in this course, in your other courses, in your college career, and in the life you will live after college. To do that, you need to think of research as something completely different from the exercise of finding information in an encyclopedia and reporting that information back to your teacher in a summary or quotations. To think in this new way, you have to *use* your research to do one of the following:

- ✎ Solve a problem in your life or in the life of another person or group
- ✎ Discover an answer to a question about something that has interested, fascinated, or bothered you
- ✎ Discover what you really think about some specific person, place, or thing
- ✎ Help you learn important information about a topic connected to another course you are taking

The following are some student journal entries discussing the selection of a topic for a research paper.

I went to a boarding school for the last two years in high school and I could never understand what happened to my roommate. He became very strange when before he had been perfectly normal. He had to drop out of school because he was suffering from depression. My research question came out of my bafflement. How could that happen to my friend? What is depression?

Ward Epson

A professor in another class, Dr. Deutsch, had the greatest idea. I got this from my roommate, and I guess it is okay to use. The teacher asked each student to write out three questions he or she had been most curious about. I only had two questions: I wanted to know how the universe was created and I wanted to know how they built the pyramids. I ended up writing a paper on the "Big-Bang" theory. I actually enjoyed writing the paper.

Drueena Jenkins

Writing helps learning! When I took a fine arts course, I needed to understand what classical music was, so I did a research paper on the piano sonata form. The paper helped me learn about music and understand what a serious musician was doing. I felt that I *under-stood* music instead of just knowing some facts. Writing did help me to learn.

Hillary Davies

Thinking Exercise

1. Discover the answers to the following questions in reference to the research paper you will be working on in the next few weeks. These questions will help you accomplish your task efficiently and effectively.

    a. Will the instructor accept a report paper?

    b. When is the rough draft due? The final draft?

    c. What is the minimum length? The maximum length?

    d. Are the rough drafts to be typed? Handwritten?

    e. What is a reasonable schedule for completing the paper?

    f. Must the final draft be typed? Handwritten?

    g. What is the penalty for plagiarism?

    h. Is the original to be turned in? Or a photocopy?

    i. How many parenthetical documentations are required? Minimum? Maximum?

    j. Must the bibliography contain a minimum number of sources? Maximum?

    k. Are diagrams, statistics, illustrations allowed? Required?

    l. Is the rough draft or drafts to be turned in? When?

    m. Are the note cards to be turned in? When?

    n. Will any material be returned?

o. Will the instructor assign the topic? Approve the topic?

p. When are the deadlines for (1) topic narrowing and approval, (2) preliminary bibliography, (3) note cards?

q. Are magazines and journals required? Any specific number?

r. Are any specific sources required? Are any sources to be avoided?

s. Must all the material used come from the school library?

t. May this paper satisfy the requirements for another course?

u. Are any other things required?

16.2 Finding and narrowing the topic

Plan to use the library. Make sure your topic requires the use of the library. The material in your paper must come from sources outside yourself: mainly books, journals, and reference material, perhaps an interview or alternative sources. Students who have some idea about their topic *before* they go to the library generally feel better than students who are confused about the topic. Read and study chapter 15.

Create interest for yourself. The best topic is one about which a student has a lively curiosity—a topic of personal, intellectual, or professional interest. Because research involves frustrating delays, an active interest in the subject is essential. Otherwise, the work of preparing a research paper can become boring, even impossible. Because you are the researcher, you know the level of your interest. If you have no interest or if you lose all interest in a topic, immediately choose another topic to explore.

Narrow your topic. A narrowed topic helps you focus your energies; however, a broad topic leads to unnecessary work and delay. An early narrowing of the topic has numerous advantages: (1) you banish uncertainty; (2) you stake out a limited area for research; (3) you exclude thousands of interesting, but irrelevant, sentences; (4) you can concentrate on one topic with undivided concentration; and (5) you simplify your work and save time. This narrowing is identical to that discussed in 1.2 and 1.4. Carefully reread those pages.

Turn your topic into a question. A topic by itself is not good enough. Source material by itself is not enough. A good original question about a topic will challenge and interest you. Although good questions demand answers, boring questions put people to sleep. Select a topic that leads you to ask questions and search for answers. A good question can energize and direct an entire research project from beginning to end. You cannot write an acceptable research paper on a topic as vast as "The Variety of Wars," "A Study of Drugs," or "The History of Sex." Think of good questions such as the following: What kind of navy did the Confederacy have during the Civil War? Are tranquilizers safe? What ideas did the Romans have toward virginity and chastity?

Seek direction. Ask for direction at the start. Ask your instructor, someone who knows a great deal about the subject, or the reference librarian. You are looking for names—the names of recognized authorities and the titles of the most important books, articles, and pamphlets. You want the names of important indexes, bibliographies, and periodicals. After choosing a particular subject to work on, you may profit enormously from a brief conversation with an authority.

Create a challenge. Some students think the best way to approach a research paper is to find some easy and safe topic that completely lacks any challenge. Simple, meaningless tasks create boredom and frustration. Although it helps to know something about the subject, it is better to avoid a topic you have already researched. Going over what you have done earlier may seem attractive, but repeating and plagiarizing your own work will not help you grow intellectually.

Avoid certain topics. Some kinds of topics present problems that lead to weak papers or writing blocks. The following usually present serious problems for student researchers:

✎ *Autobiographical and subjective topics:* A research assignment is an objective enterprise. Its main point and interpretation are yours, but the material in the paper, quite simply, must come from sources outside yourself and your experience. If you feel that you are writing about yourself and your experiences, the writing may be valuable, but it will not be a research assignment. For example, avoid a topic such as "My Feelings about Teenage Suicide" and instead work on a paper dealing with "Teenage Attitudes toward Suicide."

✎ *Vast topics:* Avoid topics that attempt to include everything or to say everything. Instead of a vast topic such as "A History of Painting" or "Evolution," limit the scope of the topic and focus on a paper such as "Picasso's Early Styles of Painting" or "Theories of Evolution before Darwin."

✎ *Purely emotional topics:* Avoid topics that inflame your emotions. Find an interesting topic that will allow you to be objective, reasonable, calm, and fair. Such advice is not asking you to turn into an emotionless zombie, but a research topic must be the starting point for a rational investigation rather than an emotional experience. Avoid a topic such as "The Contemptible Nature of Apartheid in South Africa." Select a topic that can be developed with facts, such as "Native White Critics of Apartheid in South Africa."

✎ *Inadequate topics:* Avoid topics with one source or with sources that only repeat each other. If you can find only a few paragraphs on the topic or if everything written may be found in a single place, choose another topic. Make sure that your library has enough of this material. If the material is inadequate or inaccessible, change topics immediately. For example, the topic "The Early Days of Boy Scout Troop 100" is probably too limited. However, a topic such as "Three Important Forces in the Founding of Scouting in America" would lead to a more adequate research paper.

✎ *Specialized topics:* Avoid topics such as "The Phenomenology of Religious Consciousness in Post-Khomeini Iran." Wait until later to write a master's thesis. Select a more manageable topic such as "Examples of Religious Fervor in Iran." Avoid topics that would lead to papers containing only complex definitions of specialized terms or papers that need numerous footnotes to explain difficult theories and concepts. Consider your audience as average, intelligent undergraduates, not professors at the doctoral level.

Thinking Exercise

1. Read through the following explanations of different kinds of research projects. Decide which one most closely fits the kind of research you intend to do.

a. Report paper

The report paper might be compared to an article in a comprehensive encyclopedia. It gives a recital of facts. Its primary purpose is information. It deals with a very limited topic and presents the author's knowledge and discoveries.

REPORT PAPER A report on the earliest computer

REPORT PAPER A description of five different paintings by Cézanne

REPORT PAPER A report on the different kinds of depression

Another way to think of a report is in terms of question and answer. Although a writer might choose to report on a number of questions about a certain topic, generally such papers include a discussion that attempts to answer particular questions.

QUESTION REPORT How are robots used in modern medicine?

QUESTION REPORT What opinions did Cézanne have
toward his contemporaries?

QUESTION REPORT How do antidepressant drugs work?

b. Dialectical paper

The dialectical paper explores both sides of a controversial issue and then attempts, if possible, to reach an informed conclusion about the topic. This approach resembles a debate. It presents what scholars and eminent authorities have to say on a particular topic. The dialectical paper appeals to students interested in history, government, and current affairs. It also creates excellent assignments in response to different artistic problems, in such works as novels, movies, paintings, and musical compositions.

DIALECTICAL PAPER The debate over jobs for robots and
jobs for people

DIALECTICAL PAPER The controversy over Cézanne's influence on modern art

DIALECTICAL PAPER The conflict between psychology and
psychiatry in the treatment of
depression

c. Problem-solution paper

The problem-solution paper generally has three parts, all of which can come from library research. First, the problem is identified and background material is presented to show the nature and significance of the problem. Second, the causes and/or effects of the problem are presented. Third, various solutions are explored or recommended, and the advantages and disadvantages of each are explained.

PROBLEM-SOLUTION PAPER The problems that robots create for workers in automobile factories

PROBLEM-SOLUTION PAPER The problems that some critics had in understanding Cézanne's later paintings

PROBLEM-SOLUTION PAPER The effects that depression has on the job performance of factory workers

d. Evaluation paper

The evaluation paper presents as its thesis a judgment or critical analysis of some created object: a movie, a poem, a story, a building, an invention, and so forth. The writer generally presents background material to explain the topic and then analyzes it. In the paper, the writer sets up criteria and then evaluates the created work in terms of the criteria.

EVALUATION PAPER Robots improve product quality in factories.

EVALUATION PAPER Picasso's early paintings are excellent examples of realism in art.

EVALUATION PAPER T. S. Eliot's poetry paints accurate and moving portraits of depressed people.

16.3 Compiling a preliminary bibliography

Use as many sources as possible. Your instructor will give you some idea of how many sources the final paper should have. Prepare a separate 3″ × 5″ bibliography card for each source you discover. See the sample on page 380. While gathering your bibliography, begin background reading on the topic. Skim books, articles, and other reference material. Write down any questions you might have. Postpone close reading and note taking until later.

Encyclopedias and handbooks. Search the general encyclopedias for background information about your topic. Skim the material. Check significant cross-references found at the end of an article. You can discover the names of the relevant reference volumes by consulting Marion Bell and Eleanor Swiden, *Reference Books: A Brief Guide*, or Eugene Sheehy, *Guide to Reference Books*. Read the following entries in chapter 15: *Background reading, Bibliography, Biography*, and *Encyclopedias*.

Card catalog and/or computer terminal. Search your topic under author, title, and subject. Consult the *Library of Congress Guide to Subject Headings*. Follow all cross-listings and all tracings at the bottom of each card or screen. See *Card catalog* and *Computer catalog* in chapter 15.

Indexes. Begin with *Bibliographic Index*. Search the different indexes and abstracts. Use the best indexes for your topic. Consult the reference librarian. If your subject is confined to a specific time, refer to that time in your search. If not, begin with the most recent issues and work back. Make a separate bibliography card for each item. See *Indexes* in chapter 15.

Computer search. Find out whether your library offers this service. Consult the reference librarian and prepare a list of key words that describe your topic. Because most searches cost money and may take a week or two, you need to plan accordingly.

Authorities. Certain researchers, teachers, or students at your school may know a great deal about your subject. Inquire. A knowledgeable and polite request for direction at the beginning of a research project may yield valuable information. Scientific and intellectual life involves the sharing of information. See *Authorities in the field* in chapter 15.

Reference librarians. Take advantage of any tours, workshops, or services your library offers. Consult information packets prepared by the library staff. At the beginning and especially at the first hint of confusion or trouble, consult the reference librarian for direction and assistance. Do not hesitate. Librarians cannot write your paper for you, but they can help you plan research. They will direct you to the best materials and show you how to take full advantage of the library's resources. See *Librarians* in chapter 15.

Textbooks. These are great places to begin. They yield important background information. The bibliographies they contain can give valuable leads.

Government documents. The most prolific publisher on earth is the U.S. Government Printing Office. If you have a Government Documents Collection, use it. You will need the assistance of the documents librarian, but that person will be glad to help.

Other sources. Interview people if that will yield valuable information. Think of alternative sources of information: museums, newspapers, courthouses, businesses, labor unions, government offices, historical societies, archives, private libraries, and churches. See *Other sources* in chapter 15.

Changing topics. If you cannot find enough material on your subject or if your library does not contain the needed material, you must change your topic immediately.

16.4 Clarifying the purpose

You know your subject, but what is your idea about that subject? Discovering your main idea is perhaps the most important step in the entire research project. You need to pause, step back from your reading and research, and ask the question: "What am I doing?" Up to this time, you have been gathering a bibliography, reading material, and narrowing your topic. Now you must ask two related questions:

✎ What is your main point about the subject?

✎ What questions do you want the paper to answer?

Until you have the answers to these questions, everything is risky. Once you have these answers, you can begin close reading and serious note taking. You should also be able then to write a tentative statement of purpose. Such a statement is identical to those discussed in 1.4. What is *your* idea about the topic? Do not worry whether your idea is large or small, popular or unpopular, humble or sophisticated. Your idea is important because it expresses your interest and your reading. Limit the scope of your inquiry. Take a stand. State clearly your idea about the topic, for or against.

VAGUE I am going to write on Indians.

CLEAR   Some Indian reservations have helped preserve
        Native American cultures.

VAGUE   I am going to write on the atom bomb.

CLEAR   Einstein had little to do with the development of
        the atomic bomb.

VAGUE   I am going to write on education.

CLEAR   Public education in the first quarter of the 19th
        century was ineffective and quite limited.

Thinking Exercise

1. Formulate in one clear sentence your main idea
about your topic.

16.5 Evaluating the sources

You need to discover whether the books and periodicals
you have included in your preliminary bibliography are
valuable to you. You may discover you have an abundance
of material. In that case, you will need to exclude all material of lesser importance. You can do some of this excluding at the card catalog by checking on readability,
date, and publisher. First, check for readability, and exclude unreadable material on the basis of highly technical
titles. Second, check for recent publication. Exclude outdated material in light of the fact that recent material will
be more knowledgeable. Third, check the publisher. Exclude material by keeping in mind that books by prestigious institutions and publishing houses probably have

more value than other kinds of publications. If you have any doubts about excluding a book, it may be better to keep it on your list until you have checked a review of it. If you have too few bibliography cards, you may need more material. If you cannot find enough information on your topic and main idea (even after consulting an authority in the field), you must change subjects immediately. Consult your professor for advice.

During this evaluating stage of the research assignment, you will decide which material seems central to your research interests. Not all the material has value for you right now. The following hints can help you decide which are your most important sources.

Use only material related to your main idea. No matter how interesting or well written it may be, pay no attention to material not closely tied to your main idea.

Check the publication date. Is the material recent and is it the latest edition? If a renowned authority wrote material or if the book is the standard text in the field, use it, too. As a general wise rule, however, use the most recent material. When in doubt, ask an authority.

Check scholarly reputation. Distinguish between popular magazines such as *People* and scholarly publications such as *Journal of Popular Culture*. Always place more value on the scholarly material. In terms of books, distinguish between the publications of commercial or private presses and the publications of prestigious institutions. For accuracy and authoritative opinion, academic books are generally more reliable than others. For example, the University of California Press generally publishes more authoritative books than Lurid Publications or Nick's Notes. Check the scholarly apparatus in the book. Does the volume have a good index, scholarly notes, and an up-to-date bibliography? Check other reference books (*Who's Who* or *Notable American Women*) to determine whether the writer is an authority on the subject. If you are puzzled about the value of the book, read various reviews. To locate reviews, consult *Book Review Index, Current Book Review Citations,* or *Index to Reviews in the Humanities*. These will direct you to the original sources or to *Book Review Digest*.

Read the periodical abstracts. You can often find the abstract at the beginning of the issue or at the beginning of the article. Some abstracts, such as *Psychological Abstracts*, will be available in your library. Reading the abstracts will save an enormous amount of time. An abstract will quickly let you know the content and the value of the material. See *Abstract* in chapter 15.

Scan the contents. Check the table of contents and index. Skim the introduction and preface. Try to connect the material to your subject. If it lacks relevance, return it. If it has value, put it aside for further reading. You might make a photocopy of any promising periodical.

Read a sample of the writing. Is it readable? Some things are impossible to read because the material is too technical or the author is unintelligible. Give the material a chance. See whether you can begin to understand the material, and if you can, keep it. However, if it is impenetrable, return it.

Use your common sense. Judge for yourself whether the work is competent and thorough or uninformed and skimpy. Is the author logical? Does he or she respect evidence? Does the author distinguish between fact and opinion? Be alert for bias and special interest.

Use primary sources when possible. A primary source gives "the thing itself" by the actual author or creator. It may be a speech, photograph, letter, essay, book, song, or article. Secondary sources explain and comment; they present writing about writing. If the same material appears in available primary and secondary sources, use the material from the primary source.

NOTE: **Each time you do some preliminary reading and decide not to use the material, be sure to mark this fact. Write on your preliminary bibliography card the words: "Examined—Of No Value." This will save you an enormous amount of time later on.**

16.6 Reading and taking notes

Read as much as you can on your topic. Figure out the most important sources and go through those carefully in the order you think them most valuable. In your reading, search for ideas and information. Focus on one source at a time—that is, read the material in that source; determine its value. Take notes. Then go to the next important source.

Read widely, but plan to relate your notes to your main idea. Anyone can copy words down on a page or use a copier. Note taking should be efficient and purposeful. Blind, pointless copying will make you hate your entire project. Keep your main idea clearly in mind, and relate all of your note taking to your central purpose. Be practical and efficient. The materials for a research project are complex and numerous.

Each note card should have a purpose: It should record important information relating to the main idea. Note cards enable a writer to record a multitude of information, piecemeal, on one small part of a topic. By forming a small library of source material on each part of the topic, you will find that your note cards are valuable when the time arrives to write the research paper. Then they can be rearranged at will and used as support and evidence for the main idea. Think of note cards as tools to develop various aspects of your main idea.

a. Problems in note taking

✎ *Inaccuracy:* Take down quotations word for word. Be accurate, precise, complete, and thorough. If you add anything, put that in brackets [ ]. If you omit anything, use three-dot ellipsis marks (. . .).

✎ *Incompleteness:* On each note card, always indicate author, title, and page. Some people prefer to use a code to indicate such information. Be especially careful in dealing with the second or third pages of any notes. When taking notes that span several pages, use double slash marks [79// 80] to indicate a new page.

✎ *Disunity:* Keep the material on each note card unified: only one author, only one subject, only one quotation, only one note on each card.

✎ *Confusion:* Mark clearly on each card whether the material is a quotation, a summary, a paraphrase, a fact, or an outline.

✎ *Excess:* Be selective in your notes. Write down only material connected and important to your main idea. Avoid repeating material already noted.

✎ *Haste:* Take notes only *after* you have read carefully and understand the material. Avoid blind, pointless note taking and meaningless photocopying. Do not write so quickly that you become careless and sloppy. Who will be able to use an illegible note card with brilliant ideas on it?

b. Kinds of note material

- *Fact:* This provides primary, accurate information about the subject. It may include observations, memories, statistics, information, or explanations.

- *Opinion:* This consists of interpretation. It represents one person's ideas about facts or reality. Opinion ranges widely between informed opinion and uninformed opinion. As a writer, you need to be able to distinguish carefully between opinion and fact. Make clear who gave the opinion, and supply some context for the idea. Much of your research may be finding different opinions and evaluating them.

- *Précis or summary:* As a reader, you will summarize many different kinds of writing: narratives, arguments, descriptions, explanations, definitions, experiments, and opinions. Summaries should be clear, orderly, readable, and accurate, always with fewer words than the original. A précis gives a condensed summary—often in one or two sentences. It will help you to get in the habit of writing a précis to express the entire meaning and content of a selection. (See chapter 10.)

- *Paraphrase:* This is, simply, putting in your own words the words of another person. (See chapter 11.) Paraphrasing provides good practice for learning to read carefully, but it is overemphasized in note taking. Avoid paraphrase in your notes. Instead, quote important material that you can later summarize or paraphrase.

✎ *Outline:* This form of summary may consist of a topic outline or a sentence outline. Readers use outlines to remember structure, main points, and meaning in a passage. An accurate outline can help a reader condense large amounts of material into a short space. (See 1.7.)

✎ *Direct quotation:* In your notes, quote important material connected to your main idea. Having the important material in the form of direct quotation will help you write the paper later on. Then you will be able to decide whether you want to summarize, paraphrase, or quote. Use your common sense when it comes to copying machines. If you can save time by using a copier and your teacher approves, then make your note cards using copies. In all cases, be sure to include the author, title, and page numbers.

✎ *Personal notes:* Write notes to yourself! Write directions and reminders for your own use. Keep a separate pile of note cards for problems and questions. Ask yourself questions while you are reading. Remind yourself to read a certain article, find the definition of a word, ask someone for advice, inquire about a book, telephone someone for advice. If you are puzzled, write down what is bothering you. If something in a source confuses you, make a note of it. If you find contradictions in different places, write them down. If an idea or a question comes that you cannot deal with right then, write it down. See the ideas about a reading log in 12.2. See also in 16.10 the journal Ward

Epson wrote while working on his research project.

c. Taking notes

✎ *Know the difference between your subject and your main idea.* (See 1.4.) Do not take random notes on the subject. Take notes to develop your idea about the subject.

✎ *Read carefully before taking notes.* Make sure the material is important and related to your main ideas before you take notes. Remember—your goal involves writing to develop a main idea rather than copying.

✎ *Have a purpose in your note taking.* Connect your reading and your note taking to various aspects of your main idea. Keep these ideas in mind. Take notes for commonsense reasons. Take notes to prove something, offer evidence, answer a question, or solve a problem.

✎ *Copy only what you need.* Select the most valuable material in terms of developing support for your main idea. Exclude everything unimportant.

✎ *Feel free to write your responses to the material.* You might discover that you are writing parts of your paper as you take certain important notes. Some writers report that taking notes energizes their minds. They use separate note cards for commentary on the subject.

✎ *Quote directly.* Outline carefully. Summarize accurately. Record information or statistics.

✎ *Unify each note card in terms of kind.* Make each note card a summary, a précis, a quotation, or another particular kind. Do not mix different kinds of notes on the same note card.

✎ *Unify each note card in terms of subject or idea.* Do not present two different points or ideas on the same note card. Make separate note cards for different points or ideas.

✎ *Unify each card in terms of author.* Do not have material from two different authors on one single card. Make two separate cards.

✎ *Unify each card in terms of source.* Do not have material from two different sources on the same note card. Make individual cards for each different source.

✎ *Unify each card in terms of rhetoric.* Confine each card to one rhetorical mode: example, definition, comparison, analysis, or some other pattern.

✎ *Do not throw away any note cards!* Keep your note cards until your final draft is returned.

✎ *Use uniform note cards.* Throughout the entire project, use 3″ × 5″ cards to compile your bibliography. Use 4″ × 6″ cards for everything else.

✎ *Write on only one side of the note card.* If you need to put continuous material on two cards, staple them together. Indicate the page numbers on both cards.

✎ *Write in ink.* Pencil will smear and become illegible.

d. Making quotation cards

As the following examples show, each note card should be accurate and should follow a common pattern. As you develop as a researcher and scholar, you will find your own ways to become a productive note taker. Whatever technique you develop, you will need to include important information such as the following: title, author, summary label, page number, and—of course—quotation marks.

Grief reaction
P.4

" Schuyler   Spectrum

It is well within the realm of normal experience to sustain the loss of a significant other through death. The reaction commonly observed in some form in most survivors has been called "grief." It is the general consensus that this grief is entirely normal and in fact it may be detrimental to one's subsequent mental health not ~~to~~ [author's emphasis] to mourn."

QUOTE

Notice how the examples observe the following instructions:

✎ *Identify each card.* Leave a space at the top for a summary label to help you sort out the cards. These labels may be organized according to various points relating to the main idea, various parts of the main idea, various kinds of proof or evidence for the main idea, and so forth.

✎ *List bibliographical information.* On the next line, write the author's last name, one key word from the title, and the page of the beginning quotation. When you move to a new page in your quoting, include that in your note card in parentheses. If you want to devise a coding system for the bibliography cards, you might use that code and the page number. After you have finished quoting, proofread the card twice: check once for clarity and legibility; check a second time for accuracy. Make sure you have put quotation marks around all quoted material. At the end of the quotation, write "Quote." Last, at the top—in pencil—include a summary heading for the contents of the note card.

✎ *Note all changes.* If you add or change anything when quoting a source, use a [pair of brackets]. If you omit anything when quoting, even the smallest items in any source, indicate the omission by a three-dot ellipsis mark (. . .). (See 22.7g.) If the material you quote contains an error, indicate the mistake by using *sic* in brackets or parentheses. (See 16.8b and 22.7l.)

ORIGINAL: Pharmacotherapy for depression is at least as ancient as Homer, who related in *The Odyssey* that Penelope took a drug to dull her grief for her long-absent husband.

NOTE CARD:

Chemotherapy

Beck   Diagnosis   p. 81

"Pharmacotherapy [chemotherapy] for depression is at least as ancient as Homer, who related in *The Odyssey* that Penelope took a drug to dull her grief...."

QUOTE

✎ *Indicate nature of note card.* If you do not quote, mark whether the material is a summary, list, outline, or statistic. Record the information accurately. Be sure to indicate the source.

16.7 Planning a strategy

✎ *Pause to organize.* Arrange your thoughts by writing at least one sentence in response to the following questions: What is your main idea about the topic? What question do you want the paper to answer? What problem do you want the paper to solve?

✎ *Read.* Examine all your notes and group·related cards together. Decide whether you have enough note cards to develop your main idea.

✎ *Think of answers.* Without referring to your notes, write a short two-page paper answering this question: "What are the four most important things I have learned about my topic?" This short paper may form the basis for your longer paper's organization.

✎ *Outline.* Develop a preliminary outline. In it follow any thinking pattern you have been using to organize your notes or your discussion, such as cause-effect, contrast, or question-answer. (See 1.7b.)

16.8 Writing the rough draft

The rough draft forms an important step in the composing process. You might review the ideas about drafting in 1.8. The rough draft asks for a definite commitment, and some things are absolutely necessary.

✎ *Time and energy:* These are two essential items. Do not even imagine that you can write the draft in fewer than four or five hours. Plan to write the draft well ahead of the deadline, so you will have plenty of time to reread the paper, gather further material if necessary, revise several times, and improve meaning and content.

✎ *Clear statement of purpose:* This will guide and direct the entire writing process. Have this on a small note card immediately in front of you so you will have a clear purpose in all your writing.

✎ *Note cards:* Read your cards again in light of your main idea about the subject. Place to one side all note cards not directly linked to your central idea and purpose. Avoid the idea that you have to use all the notes you have gathered. Arrange and rearrange the cards until the order expresses your main idea most effectively.

✎ *Some kind of outline:* This will guide your writing. It should help you think in terms of paragraphs or blocks of thought and in terms of general statements and specific support. Writing an outline forces you to both think about the overall shape of your paper and confront the necessity for an introduction and conclusion. At this time, you should be thinking of a rhetorical pattern that can help you develop and support your main idea: chronological narrative, general statement-specific examples, problem-solution, question-answer, comparison-contrast, cause-effect, induction, deduction, or another pattern.

a. Ideas about starting the draft

Writers have different ways for getting started. Some ideas about drafting are presented in 1.8, but writers have indicated that the rough draft of a research paper poses unique problems. The following section gives hints, not rules. Other writers have found the following strategies effective to begin the draft and move into the flow of effective writing.

✎ *Write the introduction first.* If you follow this advice, give your reader reasons to believe the topic has importance and worth. Provide information so that the reader will want to continue reading. State clearly your main idea in one of the different forms of a statement of purpose. Let your reader know what kind of overall rhetorical strategy you plan to use. You may discover that sharing this information with your reader will increase your energies and commitment to writing an excellent paper. (Reread 5.1–5.4.)

✎ *Write the conclusion first.* Many conclusions emphasize the main points of the paper and summarize important material. With clear order and good emphasis, such a conclusion often stresses the key ideas one final time. Or to help the reader, the central idea and purpose of the paper can be restated. Such a writing exercise to begin the draft can give a writer a clear idea of the work to be done in writing the paper. (See 5.5–5.7.)

✎ *Avoid delaying.* Whatever strategy you pursue, you need to write. Do not stall. Do not sit and meditate. Think, using your pen or typewriter. Write. Get your ideas down in front of you. Do not worry about the perfect paper. Do not write one sentence only to erase it a moment later. Do not worry about correctness or neatness, and do not even entertain the idea that any part of your rough draft will be anything but rough. Accept imperfection for a while. Reconcile yourself to a good draft and write your ideas down on the page as clearly and effectively as possible. If you need to look something up in the library, make a note of that, but continue writing. Do not interrupt the flow of your writing. If you come to a difficult place and sense that you are stalled, push on. You can always improve the draft by revision, but if there is no draft, revision is impossible.

✎ *Write what you know.* Let the note cards guide and help you, but do not let them dictate to you. You may remember something important to your main idea that is not on a note card. Write that information down. Later on, go and research that point. Think of yourself right now as a writer, not a reader. If you absolutely need to look something up to continue your paper, do it, but avoid being sidetracked.

✎ *Quote as little as possible.* You can write an effective research paper without using a single quotation. Think of the paper as the development of your main ideas on a particular subject. Get away from the idea of the research paper as a string of quotations glued together by a random or occasional transitional sentence. Write the paper in your own words. Do not stare at a note card, trying to put the material in your own words. After reading the note card, turn it over. Write down in your own words the important information in the note.

✎ *Think in terms of blocks of thought or paragraphs.* Think of the introduction as a unit, perhaps one single paragraph. Think of the conclusion as a unit, one moving and effective paragraph. Think of the body as a string of supporting paragraphs, or chunks of thought, each one exploring and discussing an important aspect of the main idea.

✎ *Design paragraphs in terms of a general statement and supporting evidence.* Set forth a general idea and then develop that idea with supporting evidence. Use a variety of patterns to develop your ideas. Use, when needed, examples, narration, description, explanations, definitions, comparisons, contrasts, quotations, classification, analysis, process, evaluation, and causality.

b. Common questions on the rough draft

✎ *What should I avoid?* Avoid waiting for inspiration. Begin writing. Avoid stringing together a series of quotations. Avoid giving your personal opinions and experiences. Avoid wandering away from the topic.

✎ *What should I do?* Write the rough draft, following the directions in 16.8a. After you finish it, read it closely noting the various parts that need to be revised and why. (See 1.9.) After you have revised the paper as skillfully as you can, prepare a final good copy that you have carefully proofread.

✎ *How much should I quote?* Quote only when necessary. If you can paraphrase or summarize the material effectively, do so. Only a few situations require quotation:

1. When the quotation has unique style or expression
2. When the quotation is easier to understand than a paraphrase
3. When the quotation is definitive or authoritative
4. When the quotation is required for exact meaning

Without distorting the meaning of a quotation, writers omit inessential words, phrases, sentences, and whole paragraphs, but they always let the reader know of the omission. Ellipsis marks indicate omissions: three dots (. . .) between words; three dots and a period (. . . .) to end a sentence. Similarly, when quoting material containing errors of logic, fact, spelling, mechanics, or grammar, use *sic* in brackets inside a quotation or *sic* in parentheses outside a quotation to let the reader know that you did not make the mistake. Doctor Bartok wrote, "Mark Twain was borne [sic] in Missouri." Because Doctor Bartok misspelled a word, the *sic* in brackets is used to indicate the source of the error. For further discussion of proper quotation, see 22.7.

✎ *How should I go about writing the various drafts?* Have plenty of paper. Write or type on every third line. Have wide margins for notes and revisions. Write to develop your main ideas. Follow the outline. Have the note cards handy. Do not behave like a dog led on a leash. Avoid a slavish copying of the note cards. *You* are the one using the note cards to develop *your* ideas and to prove *your* points. You should have the sense that you control the material. Write your ideas down and use the note cards for support.

✎ *How can I save time?* Two practices may help you write the paper more quickly. First, instead of copying material word for word from a note card or a photocopy, tape or staple the information onto the page. Second, at the end of each source, list only author, title, and page, not full documentation.

✎ *How can I avoid repetitive lead-ins?* Find other lead-ins besides "She said . . . ," "He says . . . ," "It says. . . ." Vary the introductions. Use the following comparable expressions precisely and idiomatically: affirm, argue, ask, assert, believe, bemoan, broadcast, claim, comment, complain, contend, declare, define, deny, describe, estimate, explain, express, hold, hypothesize, indicate, inquire, insist, maintain, mention, note, point out, present, prove, publish, quote, recite, refer to, remark, repeat, report, reveal, set forth, speak, specify, speculate, state, suggest, think, understand, urge, utter, write, verify, begin with, continue on with, end with.

✎ *What kind of a style should I use?* Your own. Except for quotation, make the language your own words. Write to be read. Avoid shifting needlessly from past to present to future. In literary analysis use the present tense to discuss a literary text. Make your writing interesting. Avoid informal and colloquial language. Avoid jargon and pretentious language. If a word or phrase is unfamiliar, define it.

✎ *How should I deal with references in the draft?* Put them in while writing. In parentheses list author, short title, and page. Place the source immediately after the material, whether quotation, summary, or paraphrase. Later on, when you prepare the final draft, you will use the correct form, but right now include the material correctly.

✎ *How can I indicate quotation?* Be sure to use quotation marks. For longer quotations, some writers use a system of taping or stapling note cards on the page to avoid needless copying.

16.9 Revising the paper

Begin your revising by reading your paper and making an outline right after you have finished it. Be sure to include each paragraph and main point in your outline. Put the paper aside for a day or even longer before doing any further work. While waiting, go back and reread 1.9. Those principles of revision should guide you in revising the rough draft. Remember that a research paper should be as well organized and carefully written as any other paper. You might also study chapters 4 and 19.

Later, without looking at your paper, state your main idea in one sentence and list the five most important things about the topic. Compare this list with your outline. Study the paper carefully. Use any strategies you have developed to help in revision. Then read the paper again, thinking of the following questions. Make any changes needed.

- ✎ Does the paper make sense?
- ✎ Does the paper have a main idea?
- ✎ Does the main idea have enough support?
- ✎ Does the paper have too much of anything?
- ✎ Does the paper have a clear organization?
- ✎ Do any parts need to be rearranged?
- ✎ Are the quotations correct?
- ✎ Have you documented each source?
- ✎ Is the material accurate?
- ✎ Are the citations and documentation accurate?
- ✎ Does the paper have a beginning, middle, and end?
- ✎ Do the paragraphs flow together?
- ✎ What three things would improve the paper?
- ✎ Have you proofread the paper?

16.10 Using a journal in research

Using a journal has helped many students clarify the work done in completing a research project. Ward Epson, the author of the research paper on depression, devoted a part of a notebook to ideas and questions about his research project.

2/3/85: I have been doing what the teacher calls "background" reading. Encyclopedias, textbooks, general articles in magazines. I think I have some vague understanding of my subject which has the fancy name not "depression" but "affective" or "mood" disorder. That is one problem—all the specialized vocabulary. Some of the things are absolutely beyond me. Written for PhDs or MDs.

2/4/85: Accident? Good luck? I found a great review of some great books related to my subject. I was browsing in the library and I found the review.

2/12/85: The paper is falling into place. I am learning to understand what I am reading. Before, when I did a "research paper," all it was was a copying exercise. I don't think I had to think for more than six minutes. Only thought of correctness in footnotes, bibliography, and quotations. Here I sense that I am learning something. This paper is all I am doing it seems. It seems like I keep running into things in newspapers, magazines, on TV that are connected to my topic of depression. It is kind of spooky. I guess I am just extra sensitive to the subject, but I can't believe the volume of material on this subject!

2/19/85: Teacher has always been harping on the idea of numbering sentences, question-answers, problem-solutions, hypothesis-proof, thesis-evidence. Asked us to phrase the research question in several different ways. I have come up with: What is the biological explanation of mental (or depressive) illness? What three or four things serve as evidence to support the biological theory of depression? I can see in my mind what the paper will look like: beginning, middle, and end.

2/20/85: Yesterday I wrote out the exercise, "The four or five most interesting things I have learned about my subject." That helped me clarify better what my paper will be. This afternoon, I sorted out all my note cards and all my Xerox copies and began writing the rough draft. It felt good not to have to worry about footnotes. The parenthetical documentation is a cinch. It felt great knowing that this did not have to be perfect and that it could be improved substantially in a week or two. The draft is pretty good.

2/25/85: We shared papers in class. It was a good thing to see how another student did his work. I don't want to feel too smug but I hope my comments about his paper helped him. The comments my reader made on the reading sheet are really good. It was hard for me to look at my paper and criticize it right away. Time makes that easier. I see that I have really confused my main idea and have two or three main ideas. I need to unify my main idea.

Commentary on Sample Research Paper

1. FORMAT: The proper format for the heading of a research paper places the writer's name, the instructor's name, the course number, and the date on separate lines, double-spaced on the left margin. The title is centered and double-spaced. There are two spaces between the left heading and the centered title. Double-space between the title and the first line of the paper.

2. INDENTATION: Note how each paragraph is indented five spaces.

3. MARGINS: One-inch margins allow for commentary and questions.

4. INTRODUCTION: The author has used questions (see 5.4c) in the introduction to create interest; at the same time, he is introducing the topic. Study the strategies for effective introductions and conclusions in chapter 5.

5. QUOTATIONS: All quotations in the paper have a lead-in to the quoted material. There are no free-floating, unidentified quotations in the paper. See 16.8b. Some lead-ins used by Epson are the following verbs: *defines, presented, refers to, writes of, describes,* and *speak of.*

NOTE: **The sample research paper by Ward Epson follows the MLA format that is presented in 17.2–17.6.**

16.11 Sample research paper

Epson 1

1 Ward Epson
Professor Fingel
English 102
3 April 1985

Depression: The Medical View

2   Many people do not know the answers to the
3 following questions.   What illness afflicts millions
4 of people in America and leads to many suicides a
year?   What illness has been called "the most
untreated of all major diseases" (Kline 19) and
labelled "the most treatable condition in
psychiatry"? (Goodwin 40)   The answer is
depression.   Medical doctors use the term to refer
to a disorder in mood or feeling.   The disorder
may be so severe that people simply lose the will to
5 live.   In the words of a person who suffered
through a depression, "It was an effort to get up in
the morning. . . .   I felt like I was all wrapped

6. QUESTIONS: Notice that the remainder of the paper develops answers to these questions presented here in the introduction. See 5.4c.

7. AUDIENCE: The author has indicated that the audience for the paper is generally students.

8. DEFINITION: The second paragraph contains a definition to help the reader understand specifically the subject of the paper. Notice it is an authoritative definition. The following note cards show how the writer incorporates material from Schuyler and Trafford into a paragraph. The three-dot ellipsis marks in the paper indicate material omitted from the quotation on the note card.

Definition

Schuyler _Spectrum_ p. 2

"Depression is an emotional state of dejection and sadness, ranging from mild discouragement and down-heartedness to feelings of utter hopelessness and despair."

Nat'l Assn. for Mental Health made this def.

Epson 2

in wool—everything was blunted, dull.   I felt like
I was wearing concrete boots" (Conkling 1).   If
untreated, depression may lead to suicide.   But
what specifically is depression?   What are its
6   causes and effects?   What are its symptoms?
Can it be treated and how?   The answers to these
7   questions should help many students understand a
disease that literally destroys lives.

8   Most specialists agree that depression is a
serious emotional state marked by persistent
sadness, negativity, and self-hatred.   The National
Association for Mental Health defines depression as
"an emotional state of dejection and sadness,
ranging from mild discouragement . . . to feelings of
utter hopelessness and despair" (Schuyler 2).
Many famous people have suffered from severe
depression such as Ernest Hemingway, Abraham
Lincoln, and Queen Elizabeth I (Trafford 40).

Since millions of people suffer from this

9. STATISTICS: Epson has used statistics to show the significance of the subject.

10. QUOTATIONS: Note the introduction to the longer quotation from *Rolling Stone*. The entire block quotation is indented uniformly ten spaces. For further information on quotation format, see 22.7. Note the slight difference between the documentation at the end of the third and fourth paragraphs.

Famous Depressives

Trafford p. 40

    Hemingway, Lincoln, Queen
    Elizabeth I

    [See Fieve book which has a
    chapter on Roosevelt, Lincoln,
    and Churchill.]

Epson 3

illness, it is important to stress the connection
between depression and suicide. The National
Institute of Mental Health estimates that 75% of
suicides are depressed people. Because some
suicides are disguised as accidents, figures on
suicides may vary. The minimum figure is 20,000
actual suicides a year in American (Greist 10).

9   Such a statistic is terrifying because the number of
suicide attempts far exceeds the number of actual
suicides. A recent issue of Rolling Stone
presented some grisly statistics about adolescent
suicide:

10   While suicide rates for adults have
remained static, rates for adolescents and
young adults fifteen to twenty-four years
old began rising in the middle 1950s and
had tripled by 1978. Some 5000
adolescents now take their lives each year.
For every adult suicide there are ten

11. DOCUMENTATION: Note the two different quotations from Schuyler, one in the second paragraph and another in the fourth paragraph. In the fourth paragraph, the author of the quotation is identified in the lead-in sentence. In the second paragraph, Schuyler's name is mentioned in the parentheses. See 17.3.

12. SPECIAL TERMS: Quotation marks are used around the two words by Freud because they have a special meaning given to them by Freud.

13. SOURCES: Note the use of Arieti's name as the source containing Freud's comments.

Epson 4

suicide attempts, but for every adolescent
suicide there are fifty to one hundred
attempts—up to a half million a year.
(Girls attempt suicide three times more
frequently than boys; boys succeed four
times more frequently than girls.)   Suicide
rates for ten to fourteen-year-olds have
tripled as well. . . . (Breskin 26)

Depression is not sadness or grief.   It is
something much more.   Some distinction is
important.   Schuyler refers to the "important
boundary between grief and depression" (6).
Freud distinguished between "mourning," which is
normal grief following serious loss, and
"melancholia," which is a serious depression
(Arieti 21).

Essentially there are three types of
depression with three different sorts of causes.
One depression is a state of sadness or grief

14. ORGANIZATION: Study the topic sentences in the sixth through ninth paragraphs and examine the relationships between the paragraphs and the outline that is presented at the end of 16.11. See 1.4 and 2.3.

Epson 5

caused by loss of a loved object, Freud's
"mourning."   This might be referred to as "the
blues" or a "grief reaction" (Schuyler 2).   A
"grief reaction" is caused by the loss through
death of an important and significant person.   In
such a case, it is thought, "grief is entirely normal
and in fact it may be detrimental to one's
subsequent mental health *not* to mourn" (Schuyler
4).   Neither the blues nor grief is a serious
depression.   Both are temporary and do not
destroy a person.   Such a reaction to loss will
disappear with time.   It is labelled a reactive
depression.

14   Another sort of depressive state of physical
and psychological discomfort can be brought on by
illness, allergy, or chemicals.   For example, the
chemical reserpine, often prescribed for high blood
pressure, can bring on a serious case of depression.
A second, more common example involves

15. SUMMARY: This single paragraph summarizes material found on three pages in the original source. See chapter 10.

Epson 6

alcohol in that secondary depression occurs in large numbers of chronic alcoholics (Winokur, "Alcoholism").   However, when the chemical, illness, or allergy is removed, the depression will disappear.   This is labelled a secondary depression (Beck 73–74).

15

A third sort of depression, the subject of this paper, can develop suddenly and internally with no outside precipitating event.   This kind of depression, researchers have discovered, is caused by chemical imbalances in the human body.   It is labelled endogenous depression (Beck 63–65).

The word "endogenous" means growing from inside.   This interior quality sets it off from the other two kinds mentioned above.   This is not, however, a Freudian theory.   The most recent and advanced thinking seems to have avoided Freud's theories.   The new thinking concentrates on

16.11
res

16. MULTIPLE SOURCES: Note the three different uses of material by Winokur from three different sources. Two of them are in this paragraph.

16

biological and chemical processes in the brain and central nervous system (Winokur, <u>Depression</u> 5).   Scientists have discovered that some people are predisposed to depression.   This predisposition is passed on genetically, the way eye color or body shape is passed on (Winokur, Clayton, Reich). Scientists have also, more importantly, discovered that certain biochemical processes are at work in a person who suffers from depression (Kline 90–105).

Depression shows itself in certain symptoms. An ill person will go to a doctor or a clinic.   The doctor will conduct a physical examination and then talk to the person.   One common tool for diagnosis is the "Beck Depression Inventory" (Beck, et al.).   The list of 21 questions tries to identify symptoms, severity, and time span. To make a valid diagnosis, the doctor needs to know three things: (1) that the patient is really

17. SUMMARY: Epson has summarized six pages of material from the book by Greist and condensed it into a single paragraph.

18. SUPPORT: This paragraph contains material that the author has taken from a short story. Epson read the story in another course and found it relevant to his topic. Note the ellipsis marks that indicate omissions from the original text.

19. SUPPORT: Though research papers generally avoid the author's personal experiences, this paper uses the relevant comments of a depressed teenager to make a significant observation about the topic.

Epson 8

suffering; (2) that this suffering has lasted one or
two weeks; and (3) that the person's life has
changed for the worse and is marked by tiredness,
negativity, sadness, crying, hostility, irritability,
anxiety, fear, worry, hopelessness, guilt, insomnia,
and recurring suicidal thoughts or planning (Greist
44–50).

The experience of depression is uniformly
unpleasant.   D. H. Lawrence in his story "The
Blind Man" writes of depression as "devastating
fits . . . which seemed to lay waste his whole
being . . . black misery, when his own life was a
torture" (71–72).   A teenager who twice tried to
kill herself describes her depression:

> It was a black cloud of depression.   It
> envelops you.   You cannot get out.   You
> don't think life will ever get better.   You
> can't conceive of it.   You can't imagine it.
> You can't even dream it.   And you're

20. ANALOGY: This paragraph focuses on the main aspect of the topic, the biochemical explanation of depression. To help develop his ideas, Epson makes an analogy between the understanding of diabetes and the understanding of depression.

Epson 9

gonna die anyway; life's this long corridor
with all these doors, and death is the last
one, so why not now?   It's so painful to
live that it seems less painful to die.   I felt
great satisfaction.   I felt great calmness.
It was real decisive.   I was finally taking
fate in my own hands. I had some control.
As opposed to being a victim. (Breskin 78)
In the past, everything from egos to
demons has been used to try to explain the cause
of depression.   The most recent and widely
accepted theories involve biochemistry (Science
Digest).   Just as doctors understand diabetes now
as an imbalance of insulin in the body, so too do
researchers understand depression as a result of
the presence or absence of minute amounts of
ordinary biochemical substances in the brain.
Such substances are labelled neurotransmitters.
The chemical neurotransmitters send impulses

21. BOOK REFERENCE: The reference to an entire book is indicated by the use of the author's name and the absence of page numbers.

22. TRANSITION and LINKAGE: Epson has linked the paragraphs together by transitional devices. In this paragraph, notice the repetition of key words and ideas. See 2.7d for several different methods of paragraph linkage.

Epson 10

and messages in the brain.   To function properly,
the brain needs certain chemicals.   Depressed
people lack these chemicals in the central
nervous system.   These materials are absolutely
essential.   The neurotransmitters in the brain
need them to function in carrying their
messages.   If the chemical conditions are not
right, a person manifests a variety of physical and
psychological symptoms known as depression
(Kline 90-109).   Doctors have had enormous
success in treating this third type of depression.
They call this use of medication chemotherapy
21   (Baldessarini).

22   Although there are some opponents and
some exceptions, doctors today treat people
suffering from depression with antidepressant
medications.   These medications, discovered only
thirty years ago, are highly effective (Prange).
They are not, as some might think, tranquilizers.

23. INTEGRATING QUOTATIONS: Note the integration of a quotation that is an entire sentence within the sentence at the end of this paragraph. See 22.7.

Epson 11

They work by changing, somehow, a chemical
imbalance in the body (Kline 110–41).   Their
effectiveness cannot be disputed; they work in 70
percent of all cases of endogenous depression
(Greist 142).   They have been called miracle drugs
and compared to the antibiotics.   They are not
magic, however, and they do not solve every
problem that a depressed person might have.
Many doctors prescribe the medication and also
recommend counseling.   The medications alleviate
the symptoms.   They eradicate the illness.
23   People commonly speak of cures with statements
such as, "Although it took me four years to get
everything sorted out, I feel as if I completely
rewrote my life" (Trafford 39).

The exact mechanism of the drug's activity is
a mystery.   Scientists have some general ideas
about the activity of these medicines.   The effects
take place within each of the nerve cells inside of

24. SUMMARY: This paragraph summarizes a large amount of material from the book by Kline.

25. CONCLUSION: The conclusion presents some of the author's opinions about different aspects of depression and how differently people respond to it. The author makes a prediction (see 5.7c) and asks the reader to take a certain attitude toward the subject.

Epson 12

the brain.   In order for the brain to respond to
information, nervous impulses must pass from one
nerve cell to another nerve cell which connect at
locations called synapses.   These small chemical
messengers in the brain are called
"neurotransmitters."   For normal functioning,
the brain must have enough of the right kind of
neurotransmitters.   They must also be in the
right place in the brain.   These processes are
microscopic, incredibly rapid, and complex.   They
puzzle even the most knowledgeable scientists.
To simplify vastly, the brain needs certain
chemicals to work properly.   Depression is caused
by the absence or presence of certain chemicals in
the body.   Or it may be caused by a defect in how
the body processes these chemicals.   In other
words, medical depression has an interior chemical
basis within our bodies (Kline 110–41).

The amount of fear and ignorance that

24

25

Epson 13

surrounds emotional illness is amazing.   People
are afraid of it.   They are afraid to discuss it.
They are afraid they might catch it.   They are
afraid of contact with other humans who suffer
from emotional illness.   All this will, one hopes,
slowly begin to change for two reasons.   One,
doctors have shown that emotional illness is
directly related to biochemical processes in the
human body.   Two, doctors have had remarkable
success in treating this illness with readily
available medication.   What this country needs
right now is a vast educational endeavor dedicated
to informing the general public of the nature and
treatment of depressive illness.   Until the ghosts
of fear and ignorance are driven away, millions of
people will suffer needlessly from a common and
easily treated illness, depression.

26. PAGING: Page numbering continues, preceded by the author's last name, placed one-half inch from the top.
27. TOP MARGIN: The words *Works Cited* are centered and placed one inch from the top of the page.
28. BIBLIOGRAPHY: Epson lists the works actually used in the paper. An alternate form might include all the works looked at, which would then be a list of works consulted.
29. INDENTATION: The indentations are uniformly five spaces.
30. SPACING: Two spaces are placed after the periods following names and titles.
31. SUBTITLE: The subtitle of the book by Beck is included after the colon and is underlined also.
32. ORDERING: Epson follows the correct order of presenting a book in the list of works cited. He follows alphabetical order and then lists (a) the author (last name first), (b) title (underlined), (c) place of publication, (d) publisher, and (e) date.
33. DIFFERENCES: Magazine citation differs from book citation. See 17.4. Notice further the differences between the formats of *Rolling Stone* and *Archives of General Psychiatry.*
34. PAGE NUMBERS: The page numbers in the *Rolling Stone* article are given as 26+ because they extend over various pages 26–35 and 78–79. Contrast with the paging in the *Science Digest*, which is 89–90.
35. NEWSPAPER: The reference to the newspaper article by Conkling contains the section.

Epson 14

26

27   Works Cited

28

Arieti, Silvano, and Jules Bemporad.   Severe and

29   Mild Depression: The Psychotherapeutic

            Approach.   New York: Basic, 1978.

30   Baldessarini, Ross J.   Chemotherapy in

            Psychiatry.   Cambridge: Harvard UP, 1977.

31   Beck, Aaron T.   Depression: Causes and Treatment.

32   Philadelphia: U of Pennsylvania P, 1970.

     Beck, Aaron T., et al.   "An Inventory for

            Measuring Depression."   Archives of

            General Psychiatry 4 (1961):561-571.

33   Breskin, David. "Teen Suicide."   Rolling Stone 8

34   Nov. 1984:   26+.

35   Conkling, Winifred.   "Therapy Eased the Fears,

            Let Her Accept Who She Is."   Herald

            Dispatch [Huntington, WV] 2 Sep. 1984:

            D1+.

36. UNSIGNED ARTICLE: The article from *Science Digest* is unsigned. Such an article is alphabetized by the first word in the title excluding *the*, *a*, or *an*.

Epson 15

36

"Depression: Brain Chemistry Gone Awry."
Science Digest Dec. 1982: 89–90.

Fieve, Ronald R. Moodswing: The Third
Revolution in Psychiatry. New York:
Bantam, 1976.

Gibson, Robert W. "Planning a Total Treatment
Program for the Hospitalized Depressed
Patient." Depression: Biology,
Psychodynamics, and Treatment. Eds.
Jonathan O. Cole, Alan F. Schatzberg, and
Shervert H. Frazier. New York: Plenum,
1978. 229-42.

Goodwin, Frederick K. "Interview: What Causes
Mental Depression and How to Cope." U.S.
News and World Report 8 Oct. 1979: 39-40.

Greist, John H., and Thomas H. Greist.
Antidepressant Treatment: The Essentials.
Baltimore: Williams, 1979.

37. ANTHOLOGY: Work quoted from Lawrence is contained in a book edited by others.

38. ABBREVIATIONS: The publisher's name is shortened. Instead of writing out *Holt, Rinehart, and Winston*, Epson uses the one word *Holt*. Notice also the use of abbreviations: *Oxford UP* for *Oxford University Press* and *Jan.* for *January*. See *Abbreviations* in 17.14.

39. MULTIPLE EDITORS: The edition of the *American Handbook of Psychiatry* is mentioned and the multiple editors are named. If an entry has four authors or editors, use *et al.* and the first author's name.

Epson 16

Kline, Nathan S.   From Sad to Glad: Kline on
    Depression.   New York: Putnam's, 1974.

37 Lawrence, D.H. "The Blind Man."   Studies in the
    Short Story.   Eds. David Madden and Virgil

38   Scott.   6th ed.   New York: Holt, 1984. 71–
    85.

39 Prange, Arthur J., Jr.   "Antidepressants."
    American Handbook of Psychiatry.   2nd ed.
    Eds. Silvano Arieti, Daniel X. Freedman, and
    Jarl E. Dyrud. Vol. 5. New York: Basic, 1975.
    476-89.   7 vols.

Scarf, Maggie. "The More Sorrowful Sex."
    Psychology Today Apr. 1979:   45+.

Schuyler, Dean. The Depressive Spectrum.   New
    York: Aronson, 1974.

Trafford, Abigail.   "New Hope for the Depressed."
    U.S. News and World Report 24 Jan. 1983:
    39-42.

40. BOOKS BY SAME AUTHOR: If two items by the same author are listed, the author's name is given in the first entry only. In place of the name, type three hyphens and a period. After skipping two spaces, give the title.

41. COAUTHORS: George Winokur, the author of two items listed, has coauthored with two others the book *Manic-Depressive Illness*.

42. MULTIPLE AUTHORS: When two authors have written a book or article, the name that comes first on the title page is the first name in the bibliography.

Epson 17

Winokur, George.   "Alcoholism and Depression."
        Substance Alcohol Actions/Misuse 4 (1983):
        111–19.

---.   Depression: The Facts.   London: Oxford UP,
        1981.

Winokur, George, Paul J. Clayton, and Theodore
        Reich.   Manic-Depressive Illness.   St. Louis:
        Mosby, 1969.

Yalom, Irvin D., and Marilyn Yalom.   "Ernest
        Hemingway: A Psychiatric View."   Archives
        of General Psychiatry 24 (1971):   485–94.

TITLE PAGE: Your instructor may ask you to prepare a title page that should follow an acceptable format such as the following:

Depression: The Medical View

By
Ward Epson

English 102, Section 117
Dr. Brad Fingel
March 1, 1985

OUTLINES: Many writers use outlines to help them guide the organization and direction of the writing. Some instructors require an outline such as the following to be submitted with the paper.

Epson i

Outline

<u>Thesis Statement</u>: Depression, a common yet serious medical illness with three major kinds, shows itself in certain symptoms and responds well to a readily available form of treatment. Introductory Material: This involves several quotations about depression and asks several important questions.

  I. Depression is a serious medical illness.

    A. It has a certain definition.

    B. It afflicts millions of Americans.

    C. If untreated, it may lead to suicide.

  II. Depression has three different forms.

    A. A grief reaction is a normal response to loss.

    B. A secondary depression is caused by elements in the environment.

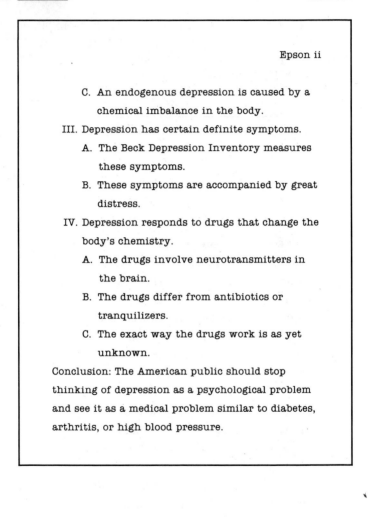

Epson ii

    C. An endogenous depression is caused by a
       chemical imbalance in the body.
  III. Depression has certain definite symptoms.
    A. The Beck Depression Inventory measures
       these symptoms.
    B. These symptoms are accompanied by great
       distress.
  IV. Depression responds to drugs that change the
     body's chemistry.
    A. The drugs involve neurotransmitters in
       the brain.
    B. The drugs differ from antibiotics or
       tranquilizers.
    C. The exact way the drugs work is as yet
       unknown.
Conclusion: The American public should stop
thinking of depression as a psychological problem
and see it as a medical problem similar to diabetes,
arthritis, or high blood pressure.

17 Parenthetical Documentation

17.1 Using parenthetical documentation

For most college research assignments, teachers require the final drafts of papers to appear in either MLA (Modern Language Association) style or APA (American Psychological Association) style. In this chapter, sections 17.2 through 17.7 focus on MLA format, and the guidelines for APA format begin in 17.8.

17.2 Using MLA format

If your teacher requires the use of MLA format in your research paper, acknowledge all sources and document your research paper according to the guidelines presented in the most recent edition of the *MLA Handbook for Writers of Research Papers*. The MLA style uses parenthetical documentation in the paper and a list of works cited at the end of the paper to identify all sources of material.

17.3 Material to acknowledge

In addition to direct quotations, a writer must let the reader know the source of all information, whether summary or paraphrase. Full acknowledgment in the text includes author, title, and page. In essence, this means that all borrowed material from any source whatsoever must be acknowledged with the following exceptions:

a. *Acknowledge interpretations of common knowledge, but not common knowledge itself.*

Common knowledge   On April 14, 1865, while attending Ford's Theater in Washington, Abraham Lincoln was shot by the actor John Wilkes Booth.

Interpretation   Emerson, according to Carl Sandburg, believed that Lincoln had been shot because he was not following the orders of Divine Providence (378).

b. *Acknowledge specialized knowledge and explanations, but not common facts.*

Common fact   A small number of people have severe reactions to bee stings, sometimes including death.

Explanation   Anaphylaxis is a serious medical condition involving shock to the body. It is caused by the reaction of antigens and antibodies on affected tissue systems within

the body. This condition is dangerous and can result in
death if ignored and not treated properly (Myers 194).

c. Acknowledge special definitions, but not the common use of a word.

Common use   It was a tragedy when the plane carrying the
entire Marshall football team crashed into the mountain.

Special use   Aristotle defines tragedy as the imitation of a
unified action which arouses the emotions of pity and fear
(7).

d. Acknowledge research, theories, and explanations, but not common ideas.

Common idea   Many people who drink heavily are
depressed.

Special research   Winokur discovered that secondary
depression occurs in a large number of chronic alcoholics
(111–19).

17.4 Options in MLA format

The following examples show some ways to use parenthetical documentation to acknowledge sources. The MLA
format requires the use of parentheses around identifying
information. A reader must be able to use the information
within the parentheses and in the text to refer to any source
in the list of works cited. The elements in documentation
are author or title, and page. Notice that the following
examples show some degree of flexibility and variety, particularly in terms of information contained within the
parentheses.

Author and page in parentheses   Churchill has been described as "impulsive . . . insolent and domineering" (Fieve 112).

Author named in text, page in parentheses   Fieve maintained that Churchill was "impulsive . . . insolent and domineering" (112).

Author and short title in text, page in parentheses   Fieve claims in <u>Moodswing</u> that Churchill was "impulsive . . . insolent and domineering" (112).

Author, short title, page in parentheses   One author sees Churchill as "impulsive . . . insolent and domineering" (Fieve, <u>Moodswing</u> 112).

Note that all three items (author, title, page) are necessary only if another source by the same author appears in the paper. In most cases, mentioning the author and the page number of the source is adequate. Note also that in all cases parentheses are placed as close as possible *after* the borrowed material. They are inserted at a natural break in the sentence or at the end. They are never placed before any borrowed material. The reader of a research paper must be able to find in the list of works cited at the end of the paper a complete bibliographical entry for each source used in the paper. This will include information on author, title, and publication. For the references above, here is what the bibliographical entry at the end of the paper would look like:

Work Cited

Fieve, Ronald R.   <u>Moodswing: The Third Revolution in Psychiatry.</u>   New York: Bantam, 1976.

17.5 Examples of MLA documentation and citation

This section focuses on the form of documentation required in research. To illustrate this form, the section includes two connected parts: (1) a collection of model citation forms commonly used in the body of a paper and (2) a list of works cited such as would appear at the end of a paper. It is important to study and understand how these two parts are connected. Examine each of the following borrowings. Then inspect the material in the following list of works cited.

Author—MLA   Linda Flower, an authority on composition, writes, "So, the myth says, if you weren't born with talent or don't feel inspired, there's nothing much you can do. Secondly, in addition to being discouraging, this myth is just plain wrong about what actually happens when people write" (2).

Two authors—MLA   Cowan and Cowan describe a writing process called "looping" in which a student starts with a subject and writes down without stopping anything that comes into the mind (9).

Three authors—MLA   Leggett, Mead, and Charvat stressed in their book on writing the importance of the topic sentence. They claimed that every paragraph contains a topic sentence. Such a sentence is either at the beginning of the paragraph or at the end (117–19).

Four or more authors—MLA   One popular theory about writing is stated in this manner: "The composing process is a series of stages that can vary in sequence and are often recursive, even though they must be ordered in certain ways in a text" (Lauer et al. xv).

Government or corporate author—MLA   The report prepared by the Instructional Resource Center of the City University of New York commented on remedial instruction: "A substantial percentage of incoming freshmen are viewed as requiring assistance in the basic skills areas—28% in reading, 31% in basic writing, and 32% in basic mathematics" (1).

Anonymous author—MLA   One person, Harold C. Cannon, destroyed an old and rare book by simply crumpling the pages in his fingers. He did this to illustrate the problem of the millions of items deteriorating in libraries throughout the country. The book in question had been microfilmed earlier ("Footnotes" 5).

Author with two or more works used in the paper—MLA   Mark Strand's first book of poems, <u>Reasons for Moving</u>, contains twenty-two poems. One of them is an imitation of a poem by Carlos Drummond de Andrade with the title, "The Dirty Hand" (28). Mark Strand's poem, "The Way It Is," presents a caricature of the average American with the lines: "His helmet in a shopping bag,/ he sits in a park, waving a small American flag" (Darker 45).

Reference to entire work—MLA   Ross Baldessarini's book gives an excellent survey of the effectiveness of various drugs on the treatment of psychiatric illnesses.

Reference to an article—MLA   George Orwell composed his novel <u>1984</u> while mortally ill with tuberculosis. He wrote the book in a solitary cottage on the deserted island of Jura off the west coast of Scotland (Lockwood 66–67).

The Bible—MLA   Toward the end of one letter, Paul reminds his readers to think beyond themselves: "Whatever is true, whatever is honorable, whatever is just, whatever is pure, whatever is lovely, whatever is gracious, if there is any excellence, if there is anything worthy of praise, think about these things" (Philippians 4, 8).

Literary works—MLA   When Macbeth first meets the three witches at the beginning of the play, he notices their "choppy finger[s]," "skinny lips," and unladylike "beards" (1.3.44–48).

Book from a series of volumes—MLA   In the medieval period, people celebrated May Day in England as a village festival. People gathered together and put on shows and

dances. Records indicate that some people dressed in
elaborate costumes covered over with fresh flowers and
new green leaves (Chambers 1:64–66).

Secondary quotation: source in another book—MLA

It was Ludwig Wittgenstein who said, "Everything that can
be thought at all can be thought clearly. Everything that
can be said can be said clearly" (qtd. in Williams 1).

**NOTE: Examine the following alphabetized list and notice
how each entry is linked to a parenthetical documentation
immediately above. It is essential that works mentioned in
the text of a research paper must match up with those in
the list of works cited. Be sure to cross-check names, titles,
and dates.**

Works Cited

Baldessarini, Ross J. Chemotherapy in Psychiatry. Cambridge:
    Harvard UP, 1977.

Chambers, E. K. The Medieval Stage. 1903. Vol. 1. London:
    Oxford UP, 1967. 2 vols.

City University of New York. Assessment and Improvement of
    the Academic Skills of Entering Freshmen Students: A
    National Survey. New York: Instructional Resource
    Center–CUNY, 1983.

Cowan, Gregory, and Elizabeth Cowan. Writing. New York:
    Wiley, 1980.

Fieve, Ronald R. Moodswing: The Third Revolution in
    Psychiatry. New York: Bantam, 1976.

Flower, Linda. Problem Solving Strategies for Writing. New
    York: Harcourt, 1981.

"Footnotes." The Chronicle of Higher Education 3 Apr. 1985:
    5.

Lauer, Janice M., et al. Four Worlds of Writing. New York: Harper, 1981.

Leggett, Glenn, C. David Mead, and William Charvat. Handbook for Writers. 2nd ed. Englewood Cliffs: Prentice, 1954.

Lockwood, Allison. "George Orwell and 1984." British Heritage Apr.–May 1984: 66+.

May, Herbert G., and Bruce M. Metzger, eds. The Oxford Annotated Bible with the Apocrypha. New York: Oxford UP, 1965.

Shakespeare, William. Macbeth. Ed. Sylvan Barnet. New York: NAL, 1963.

Strand, Mark. Darker. New York: Atheneum, 1970.

———. Reasons for Moving. New York: Atheneum, 1969.

Williams, Joseph. Style: Ten Lessons in Clarity and Grace. 2nd ed. Glenview: Scott, 1985.

17.6 MLA citation forms

To illustrate proper bibliography at the end of a research paper, this section is divided into four separate parts: (1) a list of the proper forms for books, (2) a list of the proper forms for encyclopedias and dictionaries, (3) a list of the proper forms for periodicals, and (4) a list of the proper forms for other nonprint sources. To have an idea of how such a list appears at the end of a research paper, examine carefully the list prepared by Ward Epson at the end of his paper (see 16.11). Notice how Epson's list combines both books and periodicals in alphabetical order.

a. Books

Anonymous book

Dictionary of Ancient Greek Civilization.　London: Methuen,
　　1966.

Books with one author

Flexner, James Thomas.　A Short History of American Painting.
　　Boston: Houghton, 1950.

Tennyson, Alfred Lord.　In Memoriam.　Ed. Robert H. Ross. New
　　York: Norton, 1973.

Books by the same author

Kooser, Ted.　Official Entry Blank.　Lincoln: U of Nebraska P,
　　1969.

---.　Sure Signs: New and Selected Poems.　Pittsburgh: U of
　　Pittsburgh P, 1980.

Book with two authors

Gebhardt, Richard C., and Dawn Rodrigues.　Writing: Processes
　　and Intentions.　Lexington: Heath, 1989.

Book with three authors

Winokur, George, Paul J. Clayton, and Theodore Reich.　Manic
　　Depressive Illness.　St. Louis: Mosby, 1969.

Book with four or more authors

Mussen, Paul, et al.　Psychology: An Introduction.　Lexington:
　　Heath, 1973.

Book or pamphlet by committee, organization, or corporation

Commission on the Humanities. The Humanities in American
Life: Report of the Commission on the Humanities.
Berkeley: U of California P, 1980.

Book in second or later edition

Flower, Linda. Problem Solving Strategies for Writing. 2nd ed.
San Diego: Harcourt, 1985.

Book in a series

Singer, Marcus G., ed. American Philosophy. Royal Institute
of Philosophy Lecture Series 16. Cambridge: Cambridge
UP, 1985.

Dissertation

Merker, Kyle. "Deconstructionist Readings of Hoto Tanka's
Later Poetry." Diss. Walsh U, 1989.

Reprint

Willey, Basil. The Eighteenth Century Background. 1940.
Boston: Beacon, 1961.

Work in several volumes

Pickard, John B., ed. The Letters of John Greenleaf Whittier. 3
vols. Cambridge: Harvard UP, 1975.

NOTE: List the total number of volumes in the work if you
use more than a single volume. If you use only a single
volume, list that volume's number, using *Vol.* after the title.

Translation

Picard, Max. Man and Language. Trans. Stanley Godman.
Chicago: Regnery, 1963.

Editor or compiler

Hindle, Brooke, ed.   Material Culture of the Wooden Age.
    Tarrytown, NY: Sleepy Hollow, 1981.

Anstey, Sandra, comp.   Critical Writings on R. S. Thomas.
    Bridgend, Wales: Poetry Wales, 1980.

Anthology

Yeats, William Butler.   "Ireland and the Arts."   Essays and
    Introductions.   New York: Collier, 1968.   203–10.

Frye, Northrop.   "Blake After Two Centuries."   University of
    Toronto Quarterly 27 (1957): 10–21.   Rpt. in English
    Romantic Poets: Modern Essays in Criticism.   Ed. M. H.
    Abrams.   London: Oxford UP, 1960.   55–67.

Introduction, Foreword, Preface, or Afterword

Wilson, Gay Allen.   Introduction.   Leaves of Grass.   By Walt
    Whitman.   New York: NAL, 1955.   v–xx.

Pamphlet

Gerber, William.   Future of Psychiatry.   Washington, DC:
    Editorial Research Reports, 1969.

b. Encyclopedia or dictionary

Little, Donald P.   "Circassians."   Dictionary of the Middle Ages.
    New York: Scribner's, 1983.

"Omaha Indians."   Encyclopedia Americana.   1980 ed.

**NOTE: If a dictionary or encyclopedia is organized
alphabetically, the volume and page numbers may be
omitted.**

c. Periodicals

Daily newspaper: Signed, unsigned

Radcliffe, Donnie. "Mrs. Bush's Summit Overlook."
Washington Post 12 July 1990: 1B+.

"Mining Company Reports Lost Equipment." Daily Ledger
[Crandall, NE] 13 July 1990: 7–8.

Editorials: Signed, unsigned

"Continuing Targets." Editorial. Herald-Dispatch [Huntington,
WV] 21 Feb. 1985: 4.

Corr, Robert. "More Than Pretty Pictures." Editorial. PC 8
Jan. 1985: 91.

Reviews: Signed, unsigned

Gilliatt, Penelope. Rev. of Guernica, by Arrabal. New Yorker 7
June 1976: 119–25.

Rev. of Lyndon Johnson and the American Dream, by Doris
Kearns. New Yorker 7 June 1976: 136–37.

Lawrence, Charles. Rev. of Radikale Reformatoren, by Hans-
Jürgen Goertz. Sixteenth Century Journal 12 (1981):
122–23.

Periodical with continuous paging from issue to issue

Howe, Irving. "Strangers." Yale Review 56 (1977): 481–500.

Periodical with issue numbers only

Wright, Charles. "Improvisations on Montale." Field 27
(1980): 47–54.

Periodical without continuous paging from issue to issue

Hass, Robert. "James Wright." Ironwood 5.2 (1977): 74–96.

Weekly or biweekly magazine: Signed, unsigned

Greider, William. "The Fools on the Hill." Rolling Stone 8 Nov.
1984: 13–15.

"Energy." National Review 27 Apr. 1973: 451.

Monthly magazine

Nunberg, Geoffrey. "The Decline of Grammar." Atlantic Dec.
1983: 31–46.

d. Other nonprint sources

Art

Luks, George Benjamin. The Miner. National Gallery of Art,
Washington, DC.

Computer software

EasyWriter. Computer software. Information Unlimited, 1980.
CP/M-86/80, 128 KB, disk.

Material from a computer service

Laskell, George. "The Price of Victory." Woonsocket Review of
the Arts Dec 1989: 23+. Access file 0297, item 51142
50842.

Film, filmstrip, slide

Angyal, Jennifer. Enzymes. Filmstrip. Burlington: Carolina
Biological Supply, 1979.

Police: The Human Dimension, Stress. Film. Northbrook: MTI
Teleprograms, 1975.

Play performance

Kate's Diary. By Kathleen Tolan. Dir. David Greenspan.
Public Theater, New York. 8 Dec. 1989.

Motion picture

The Deer Hunter. Dir. Michael Cimino. With Robert DeNiro,
Christopher Walken, John Cazale, John Savage, and Meryl
Streep. Universal-EMI, 1978.

Kurosawa, Akira, dir. Rain. With Tatsuya Nakadai and Akira
Terao. Greenwich Film, 1985.

NOTE: **If you intend to emphasize one person connected
with the film, as the citation for Kurosawa emphasizes the
director, create your citation with that emphasis first.**

Interview

Redford, Robert. Interview by Dodie Kazanjian. Arts Review
2.2 (1985): 2+.

Webster, W.G. Personal interview. 18 Oct. 1984.

Lecture, speech, talks

Boyer, Ernest L. Address. General Sess. SAMLA Convention.
Atlanta, 6 Nov. 1980.

Vendler, Helen. Class Lecture. English 475. Boston
University. 14 July 1975.

Letter

Lindsey, Jim. Letter to the author. 18 Jan. 1985.

Singer, Ben. Letter. Atlantic Dec. 1983: 4.

Radio or television program

Keillor, Garrison. "Monolog." Prairie Home Companion. PBS.
WPBY, Huntington, WV. 23 Feb. 1985.

The Precious Legacy. PBS. WPBY, Huntington, WV. 22 Feb.
1985.

Recordings

Watkins, Ronald, Ann Morris, and Peter Orr. The Speaking of
Shakespeare's Verse. Spoken Arts, SA 1022, n.d.

Appalachian Writers. NPR, OP-800716.01/01-C, 1981.

Palmer, D. J. A Lecture on Shakespeare's "Hamlet." Norwich
Tapes, 1978.

**NOTE: For additional information regarding nonprint
materials, consult Eugene B. Fleischer. A Style Manual for
Citing Microform and Nonprint Media. Chicago: ALA,
1978.**

Government documents

Cong. Rec. 11 May 1984: 5635–74.

Charache, Samuel, Bertram Lubin, and Clarice D. Reed, eds.
Management and Therapy of Sickle Cell Disease.
Washington, DC: GPO, 1984.

United States. Dept. of Justice. Computer Crime: Computer
Security Techniques. Washington: GPO, 1986.

**NOTE: Writers often discover the need to add to or combine
models. For example, to list a book with two translators it
would be necessary to add to the form for a translation in
light of the form for a book with two authors. When in
doubt, consult your instructor or the latest edition of the
*MLA Handbook.***

Thinking Exercises

1.   Refer to the exercise at the end of chapter 15. For
each bibliography card, prepare an entry according to MLA
form for a list of works cited.

2.   Study the examples of MLA citation form in 17.5, paying particular attention to the names of publishers. How are the names of the following publishers listed? (a) Harcourt Brace Jovanovich, Publishers, (b) Houghton Mifflin Co., (c) Harvard University Press, (d) Scott, Foresman and Company, (e) John Wiley and Sons, (f) Harper & Row, Publishers, (g) New American Library.

17.7   Footnotes and endnotes

Footnotes and endnotes are occasionally used for commentary or for bibliography. An endnote may be placed at the end of the paper to include significant material not centrally connected to the main points of the paper. A footnote is placed at the bottom of the page and may be used for bibliographical reference. To signal the note, a number is positioned a half space above the line and placed immediately after a significant word or at the end of a sentence. The note itself is double-spaced and the first line is indented five spaces. The following examples illustrate several notes that Ward Epson might have included in his research paper on depression. Each source in a footnote or endnote is included in the list of works cited.

Paper   The seriousness of student suicide is often hidden from the general public and especially from the students themselves.[1]

Footnote   [1] The problem of student suicide is discussed from different perspectives in Hendin 204–19; Klerman 318–23; Nicoli 105–12; Davis, Hall, Cadoret 241–46; Grofe 197–209; Oneil, Marzialli 477–81; and Jacobziner 7–11.

Paper   Elaborate systems of classification and naming have been developed over the years in an attempt to make some

sense out of the term this paper is referring to as
"depression."[3]

Endnote [3] Fieve explains how doctors in the past have
completely misdiagnosed depression by labelling it as
"mania," "schizophrenia," "personality disorder," or
"neurosis" (167–76). Becker gives an excellent review of
the "subtypes of depression" (16–17) and then goes on to
identify nine different kinds of depression (17–33).
Winokur represents the most advanced thinking on the
subject when he uses the term "mood disorder" to refer to
both depression and its opposite, mania (Depression).

17.8 APA style guidelines

In addition to the MLA guidelines, another common system is presented in the third edition of the *Publication
Manual of the American Psychological Association.* APA
format uses the author-date method of citation. The bibliography or list of works cited is called "References," and
APA form observes a distinctive pattern for citation and for
reference.

If your instructor asks you to prepare your research
paper following APA format, you need to observe the following guidelines. If any questions arise, consult the most
recent edition of the *Publication Manual of the American
Psychological Association.*

1.   Include a separate title page with the four following elements: (a) a short title made up of the first one or
two words of the whole title, (b) the page number (count
the title page as page 1), (c) the paper's title, and the
author's name and affiliation centered on the page, (d) at
the bottom of the page the words *Running Head* followed
by a colon and an abbreviated title with a maximum of fifty

characters in capital letters. See the example in Thinking Exercise 1 following 17.12.

2. If your teacher requires an abstract of the paper, add this on a separate page after the title page. An abstract is generally a single paragraph of between 50 and 150 words summarizing the main points of the paper. See chapter 10.

3. Include the following elements in the development of the entire paper: (a) introduction that states the topic, (b) presentation of the hypothesis or thesis, (c) explanation of methodology, (d) statement of context or background, (e) statement of procedures used, (f) statement of results, and (g) interpretation of information or results.

4. Use APA author-date format in the text of the paper. For summary, paraphrase, and quotations, include author, date, and page numbers.

5. Use headings in the paper to correspond to the main divisions and subdivisions of the paper.

6. Include after the paper a list of sources used and identify this with the word *References*. If your instructor asks you to list sources used and sources consulted, identify the page with the word *Bibliography*. Study the sample entries in this chapter and refer to the discussion in 17.12.

7. Follow these special typing notes: (a) Use a typewriter or printer that provides a dark, clear, readable type. Avoid a typeface made up of dots unless it is clear and legible. (b) Double-space. (c) Have margins of 1 1/4 inch.

17.9 Citations in APA author-date style

Short quotation of fewer than forty words

A recent pamphlet on writing anxiety states, "High apprehensives are characterized by tortuous writing marked by many pauses as the writer strives for perfection" (Smith, 1984, p. 9).

Long quotation of more than forty words

Smith (1984) gives the following advice to teachers:

> If teachers break down the writing task and prepare students for each element of the task, students can perceive assignments as a series of conquerable steps instead of insurmountable obstacles. If students have been adequately prepared to meet the demands of an assignment, they will write with confidence. (p. 11)

Paraphrase Smith (1984) mentions that anxious writers want their sentences to be perfect and hence delay and agonize over their writing (p. 9).

17.10 Book references in APA style

Book: One author

Smith, M. W. (1984). Reducing writing apprehension. Urbana:

ERIC-NCTE.

Book: Later edition

Strunk, W., Jr., & White, E. B. (1979). The elements of style

(3rd ed.). New York: Macmillan.

Book: Two or more authors
Coles, W. E., & Vopat, J. (1985). What makes writing good.

Lexington, MA: Heath.

Book: Edited
Rose, M. (Ed.). (1984). Writing process problems: Writing

blocks, writing anxiety, writing apprehension. New York:

Guilford.

Book: Second by same author
Hillocks, G. (1975). Observing and writing. Urbana: ERIC-RCS.

Hillocks, G. (1986). Research on written composition. Urbana:

NCRE-ERIC.

Chapter or section from an edited book
Keith, S. (1989). Exploring mathematics in writing. In

P. Connolly, & J. Kobler (Eds.), Writing to

learn mathematics and science (pp. 134–146). New York:

Teachers College Press.

Government document
U.S. Bureau of the Census. (1987). Census catalog guide: 1987.

Washington, DC: U.S. Government Printing Office.

Section in anthology, volume, or collection
Berdoulay, V. (1981). The contextual approach. In D. R.

Stoddart (Ed.), Geography, ideology and social concern

(pp. 8–16). Oxford: Blackwell.

17.11 Periodical references in APA style

Periodical with continuous paging from issue to issue

Howe, I. (1977).   Strangers.   Yale Review, 56, 481–500.

Periodical without continuous paging from issue to issue

Hass, R.   (1977).   James Wright.   Ironwood, 5(2), 74–96.

Monthly, biweekly, or weekly periodical

Greider, W.   (1984, November 8).   The fools on the hill.

　　　Rolling Stone, pp. 13–15.

Anonymous article

Energy.   (1973, April 2).   National Review, p. 451.

Daily newspaper: Signed

Howe, R. F.   (1990, July 13).   Justice plea gains a life of its own.

　　　Washington Post, pp. B1, B6.

Daily newspaper: Unsigned

More Greyhound buses targeted.   (1990, April 15).   Washington

　　　Post, sec. A, p. 20.

Interview

Greene, P.   (1961, November).   Talking with a teacher [Interview

　　　with Leo Jacks].   Greene's Journal, pp. 32–37.

17.12 Notes on APA references page

1. Use a separate page after the paper. Center the word *References* at the top of the page, double-space, and begin your list at the left-hand margin. If the entry goes on to the next line, indent three spaces. Double-space the complete list.

2. Alphabetize by authors' last names. Anonymous works are alphabetized by titles (excluding *A*, *An*, or *The*). Multiple works by the same author are listed in chronological order with the earliest work first.

3. Indicate in parentheses the year the work was copyrighted. For periodicals include year, month, and day, if any.

4. For the titles of periodicals, capitalize the first word and all nouns and adjectives. For the titles of books and articles, capitalize only the first word of the title, the first word of the subtitle, and any proper noun or adjective.

5. Underline the complete title of a periodical and the volume number, if any. Underline the complete title of any book.

6. For books, include the following publication information: (a) city of publisher; (b) publisher's name, omitting unnecessary material such as *Inc.*, *Corp*, and so forth; (c) the complete spelled-out name of a university publisher, and (d) the name of a state or country if most readers would find the city unfamiliar.

7. Do not hyphenate at the end of lines. Type a line short or extend it one or two spaces beyond the margin.

Thinking Exercises

1. Besides the fact that APA format requires a separate title page done in the following style, what are the major differences between the following title page and the titling used in the MLA format presented at the beginning of 16.11?

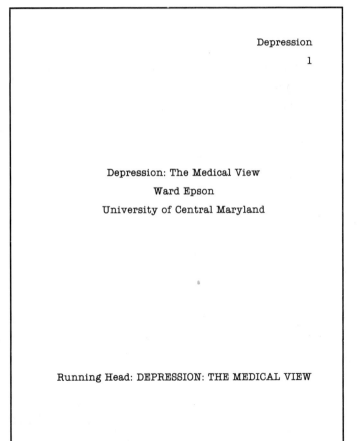

Depression

1

Depression: The Medical View

Ward Epson

University of Central Maryland

Running Head: DEPRESSION: THE MEDICAL VIEW

2. What are some differences between the parenthetical documentation of the following page, which is done in APA style, and the corresponding section from page 426 done in MLA style?

Depression

6

A second, more common example involves alcohol in that secondary depression occurs in large numbers of chronic alcoholics (Winokur, 1983). However, when the chemical, illness, or allergy is removed, the depression will disappear. This is labelled a secondary depression (Beck, 1970, pp. 73–74).

A third sort of depression, the subject of this paper, can develop suddenly and internally with no outside precipitating event. This kind of depression, researchers have discovered, is caused by chemical imbalances in the human body. Beck (1970) labelled this "endogenous depression" (pp. 63–65).

3. What are the main differences between the following *References*, which follow APA style, and the corresponding entries in the list of *Works Cited* following the sample research paper in 16.11?

References

Arieti, S., & Bemporad, J. (1978). Severe and mild depression: The psychotherapeutic approach. New York: Basic.

Breskin, D. (1984, November 8). Teen suicide. Rolling Stone, pp. 26–35, 78–79.

Conkling, W. (1984, September 2). Therapy eased the fears, let her accept who she is. Huntington Herald Dispatch, sec. D, pp. 1, 5.

Depression: Brain chemistry gone awry. (1982, December). Science Digest, pp. 89–90.

Gibson, R. W. (1978). Planning a total treatment program for the hospitalized depressed patient. In J. O. Cole, A. F. Schatzberg, & S. H. Frazier (Eds.), Depression: Biology, psychodynamics, and treatment (pp. 229–242). New York: Plenum.

Prange, A. J. (1975). Antidepressants. In S. Arieti, D. X. Freedman, & J. E. Dryud (Eds.), American handbook of psychiatry (Vol. 5, pp. 476–489). New York: Basic.

Winokur, G. (1981). Depression: The facts. London: Oxford University Press.

Winokur, G. (1983). Alcoholism and depression. Substance Alcohol Actions/Misuse, 4, 111–119.

17.13 Other systems of documentation

Not all instructors require the use of the MLA style guidelines or the APA format. If your instructor requires a different system, use a copy of the latest edition of the recommended style manual. These can generally be found in the Reference Room in your school's library. Other common forms of documentation appear in the following books:

- ✎ *Associated Press Stylebook.* Dayton: Lorenz, 1980.
- ✎ *CBE Style Manual.* 5th ed. Bethesda: Council of Biology Editors, 1983.
- ✎ *The Chicago Manual of Style.* 13th ed. Chicago: U of Chicago P, 1980.
- ✎ *Handbook for Authors.* Washington: American Chemical Soc., 1978.
- ✎ *A Uniform System of Citation.* 14th ed. Cambridge: Harvard Law Rev. Assn., 1989.

17.14 Abbreviations in research

Unless they are within parentheses, avoid using abbreviations in the body of a research paper. Use correct abbreviations when appropriate in the list of works cited. Avoid using abbreviations that might puzzle a reader. Further information on the use of abbreviations in research may be found in section 6 of the *MLA Handbook for Writers of Research Papers* or in 3.19–3.27 in the APA *Publication Manual.*

anon.	anonymous
abr.	abridgement
Acad.	Academy
app.	appendix
Assn.	Association
Aug.	August
biog.	biographer, biographical, biography
bk.	book
bull.	bulletin
ch. chs.	chapter, chapters
comp.	compiler
Cong. Rec.	*Congressional Record*
dir.	director
diss.	dissertation
div.	division
ed., eds.	edition, editors
enl.	enlarged
et al.	and others
f., ff.	the following
fig.	figure
fwd.	foreword
gen. ed.	general editor
govt.	government
GPO	Government Printing Office
i.e.	that is
illus.	illustration, illustrator
Inst.	Institute
intl.	international
introd.	introduction
jour.	journal
l., ll.	line, lines
mag.	magazine
ms., mss.	manuscript, manuscripts
n., nn.	note, notes
natl.	national
n.d.	no date given
no., nos.	number, numbers

n.p.	place of publication not listed
	publisher not listed
n. pag.	no page numbers
P	Press
pref.	preface
proc.	proceedings
pseud.	pseudonym
pt., pts.	part, parts
rept.	report
rpt.	reprint
sec., secs.	section, sections
ser.	series
sic	thus, so
Soc.	Society
supp.	supplement
trans.	translation, translator
U	University
vol., vols.	volume, volumes

PART 6

Writing Sentences

18 Sentence Grammar

An understanding of sentence grammar can assist a writer in several ways. In one way, a knowledge of grammar can help a writer see the different possibilities of sentence structure. In this sense, then, grammar is a practical art. It gives the writer tools or different ways to present the same material, extending the writer's range and thereby increasing sentence grace and variety. In a second way, a knowledge of grammar can help a writer in the revising stage of the writing process. Often during that stage, a writer will find tangled and confused sentences. By analyzing the tangle and discovering purpose and meaning, a writer is able to effectively revise confusing sentences. In both writing and revising, grammar is seen as an aid in composing instead of as a set of rules. With the goal of expanding a writer's options, the following sections give a glimpse of the most common functions in an English sentence.

18.1 Nouns

Nouns are naming words. They name whatever is—including persons, animals, places, things, qualities, ideas, emotions, and actions (*Mike, spider, Nevada, circle, viciousness, socialism, fear, bowling*). Most nouns change their forms in some way to indicate plural number (*man/ men, hat/hats*). In sentences, nouns have different functions. Two verb forms can be made to function as nouns: the infinitive (for example, *to swear*) and the gerund (for example, *dancing*).

a. Noun functions

Subject

A noun can function as the subject in a sentence or a clause. A subject is that word or word group in a sentence about which the verb asks or states something.

> *Mike* hates to study history.

> Did the *lightning* frighten the child?

Subject complement

A noun functions as a subject complement when it is the word or word group following a linking verb (for example, *to be, seems*) that completes the meaning of the subject and the linking verb. Unlike a direct object, a subject complement is related to the subject rather than the verb. The subject complement as a noun form is called the predicate noun, or predicate nominative.

> Abdul is *king*. [*King* is the subject complement, predicate noun.]

> Jason will always be a *thief*.

Object complement

A noun functions as an object complement in a sentence when it is the word or word group that completes the meaning of an object and its verb.

> The basketball team elected Rhonda *captain*. [*Rhonda* is the object of the verb *elected* and *captain* is the object complement that completes the meaning of the object and its verb.]

Direct object

A noun functions as a direct object when it receives the action of the verb. In a sentence with a transitive verb in the active voice, the direct object always receives the action of the verb. Use this test to determine the direct object: "Verb + Whom or What?"

> Joan kissed *Robert*. [In the sentence, Robert receives the action of the verb. Whom did Joan kiss? *Robert* is the direct object.]

> The teacher expects *perfection*. [What does the teacher expect? *Perfection* is the object of the verb *expects*.]

Indirect object

A noun functions as an indirect object in a sentence with a transitive verb such as *give*, *present*, *offer*, *pay*, *make*, *bake*, *read*, *teach*, *sing*, or *award*. The indirect object is the recipient that is not preceded by a preposition.

The direct object specifies that which is given to the recipient.

> The pitcher threw *Smith* a slow curve. [*Smith* is the indirect object, the recipient. *A slow curve* is the direct object.]

> Mike gave his *mother* a map. [*Mother* is the indirect object. *Map* is the direct object.]

Object of preposition

A noun functions as the object of a preposition when it is the word or word group following a preposition and creating a prepositional phrase.

> That man on the *bridge* will jump. [*Bridge* is the object of the preposition *on*.]

> The bird crashed into the *window*. [*Window* is the object of the preposition *into*.]

Appositive

A noun functions as an appositive when it is the word referring to and explaining a preceding noun.

> Mr. Becker, *the lawyer*, was indicted. [*The lawyer* is in apposition with the subject, *Mr. Becker*.]

> The students know only one emotion, *terror*. [*Terror* functions as an appositive.]

Direct address

A noun functions as direct address when added to a sentence to indicate the person or group addressed.

> *Students*, begin the exam!

> *Marge*, this pizza is delicious.

Practice 1: Write two sets of eight sentences each—illustrating each of the eight different kinds of noun functions (subject, subject complement, object, and so forth). Choose from this list of nouns: Thanksgiving, danger, love, wombat, record, skirt, pot, dinner, table, child, park, mattress, car, bike, lawn, spider, game, killing, stairs, TV show, glass. Identify the function of each noun used from the list.

b. Noun classes

PROPER NOUNS   Mark Twain, Hamlet, Iowa City, Russia, Mars [Proper nouns refer to one person, place, or thing.]

COMMON NOUNS   writer, actor, city, country, planet [All nouns that are not proper nouns are common nouns.]

CONCRETE NOUNS   paper, bat, blanket, catsup, apple [Concrete nouns name things that are known to the senses.]

ABSTRACT NOUNS   charity, gravity, goodness, evil, feminism [Abstract nouns refer to relationships, ideas, concepts not accessible to the physical senses.]

COUNT NOUNS   spoon/spoons, spot/spots, bus/buses [Count nouns have both singular and plural forms.]

MASS NOUNS   silverware, dust, transportation [Mass nouns generally do not have plural forms.]

COLLECTIVE NOUNS team, orchestra, audience [If a collective noun refers to the group as a whole, it takes a singular verb. If a collective noun refers to the individual members of the group, it takes a plural verb. See 20.3e.]

c. Verbal nouns

Certain forms of the verb, such as the gerunds (*kissing, being kissed, having kissed, having been kissed*) and the infinitives (*to kiss, to be kissed, to have kissed, to have been kissed*) are commonly used as nouns and can fulfill any of the noun functions in a clause or sentence.

INFINITIVE *To read* the book is my goal. [*To read* functions as the subject of the verb *is*.]

INFINITIVE Patty wants *to be admired*. [The infinitive, *to be admired*, functions as the direct object of the verb *wants*.]

GERUND   *Winning* is not everything. [The gerund *winning* functions as the subject of the verb *is*.]

GERUND   The coach hated *losing*. [*Losing* functions as the direct object of the verb *hated*.]

Practice 2: Write five sentences using the gerund form (that is, *loving*) of each of the following verbs: *love, lose, defend, type, yell.* Then write an additional five sentences using infinitive forms (that is, *to love, to be loved*) of those verbs.

18.2 Verbs

Verbs indicate action, occurrence, or state of being. They signal time or tense by means of auxiliaries (*help/will help*), inflections (*help/helped*), or change in spelling (*go/went/gone*). A verb is one of two building blocks in the creation of sentences. The other is the subject. All complete sentences contain verbs of one kind or another. There are three classes of verbs: linking, transitive, and intransitive. In addition to these, there is also the class of auxiliary or helping verbs.

a. Classes of verbs

Linking verbs

Linking verbs indicate states of being and include forms of *to be* (*am, is, was, were*), *appear, become, remain,* and *seem.*

> Mike *is* a thief. [*Is* is a linking verb. It links *Mike* to the noun *thief,* the subject complement.]

> Mike *seems* embarrassed. [*Seems* is a linking verb. It links *Mike* to the adjective *embarrassed,* which functions as a subject complement.]

Besides the verbs listed above, a few sensory verbs (*feel, look, sound, smell,* and *taste*) can function as linking verbs. These verbs link the subject to a subject complement.

> These grapes *taste* sweet. [Compare with *These grapes are sweet.* Contrast with *The cook tasted the sauce.*]

Transitive verbs

Transitive verbs indicate action passing from the subject to the object. A transitive verb always has an object.

> Jake *painted* the wall. [*Wall* is the direct object of the transitive verb *painted*.]

Intransitive verbs

Intransitive verbs indicate the action of the subject. An intransitive verb does not have a direct object.

> Leslie *drew*, but Jake *painted*.

Auxiliary verbs

An auxiliary verb is a helping verb (*do, be, have*) in that it is used with a form of the main verb to express tense, number, voice, person, or mood.

TENSE   Our team *did* win. [Past tense]

NUMBER   Our teams *are* winning. [Plural number]

VOICE   The game *was* won. [Passive voice]

PERSON   I *am* now playing on the team. [First person]

MOOD   If I *were* playing on the team, I would be happy. [Subjunctive mood]

Other helping verbs are the modal auxiliaries *can, could, may, might, must, shall, should, will,* and *would*.

Phrasal verbs

When a verb is combined with a word such as *across, by, down, in, of, out, with,* and so forth, a phrasal verb may be created.

VERB   After slowing down, the driver *turned*.

PHRASAL VERB The artist *turned out* a suitable likeness of
    the president.

PHRASAL VERB My sister *turned down* Mike's invitation.

Practice 3: Write a sentence for each of the following
verbs; use each as a transitive verb taking a direct object:
smell, taste, and *feel.* One example would be the sentence,
The dog smelled its dinner.

Practice 4: Write a sentence for each of the following
verbs; use each as a linking verb taking a subject complement: *smell, taste,* and *feel.* One example would be the
sentence, *The dog smelled terrible.*

b. Recognizing verbs

Verb recognition is important in revising sentences. Two
methods might help a writer recognize the verb in a sentence. First, find the word or word group in the sentence
that indicates state of being, occurrence, or action. Make
sure the word or word group is not a noun.

BEING   My car *is* in the street.

OCCURRENCE The windshield *glows* in the moonlight.

ACTION   The neighbor boy *stole* the hubcaps.

    Second, search for the word or word group in the sen-
tence that changes form to express a sense of the past,
present, or future. Verbs change tense to express past, present, or future. For example, the word *today* expresses time
but does not change form to express time; however, the
verb *say* changes to *said* in the past tense.

PAST The dog *ate* the frog.

PRESENT The cat is *eating* a mouse.

FUTURE I *will eat* some pizza.

Practice 5: Write five different sentences. Have each sentence include forms of the verbs in the following groups. One example would be the sentence, *In his story Mark said that the prince kissed the toad.*
a. *kiss* and *say*
b. *see* and *laugh* in the past tense
c. *fight* and *resist* in the future tense
d. *want* and *prepare* in the present tense
e. *drip*, *freeze*, *burst*, and *scream*

18.3 Pronouns

Pronouns are words that take the place of nouns. As noun substitutes, they are able to function in sentences in many of the same ways that nouns function. Also like nouns, pronouns can be grouped into a number of different categories depending on their functions in sentences.

a. Pronoun functions

SUBJECT	*Who* wants to go to the game? Ted knows *he* is good-looking.
SUBJECT COMPLEMENT	The wound is *nothing*. It was *she* who caused the accident.

Object complement	Lem considers the books *his*. We have to name the team *something*.
Direct object	The coach warned *us*. The teacher lost *everything*.
Indirect object	That owner gave *himself* the grand prize. Mr. Noodle told *them* to shut up.
Object of preposition	What does this song mean to *you*? The pilot laughed at *something*.
Appositive	I *myself* am going. You *yourself* know the answer.
Direct address	*Someone*, help! *You* clown, bring me a beer.

b. Pronoun classes

| Personal pronouns | I, me, my, mine, we, us, our, ours, you, your, yours, he, him, his, she, her, hers, it, its, they, them, their, theirs [The personal pronouns refer to individual people and animals and also to things and places: My cat loves *me*.] |
| Reflexive pronouns | myself, ourselves, yourself, yourselves, himself, herself, itself, themselves [Reflexive pronouns refer back to a person or thing already mentioned: Joe kissed *himself* in the mirror.] |

INTENSIVE PRONOUNS

These are identical to the reflexives. [Intensive pronouns function as appositives for emphasis: Patrick *himself* will have to solve his own problems.]

DEMONSTRATIVES

this, that, these, those [Demonstratives are pointing pronouns: *That* is a mistake!]

RELATIVE PRONOUNS

who, whom, whose, whoever, whomever, that, which, what [These pronouns link a subordinate relative clause to the main clause as in the sentence, I know *who* lives here.]

INTERROGATIVES

who, whom, whoever, whomever which, what [These introduce questions such as *Who* lives here?]

INDEFINITE PRONOUNS

another, anyone, anybody, anything, any, each other, either, enough, everybody, everyone, everything, few, less, more, much, nothing, no one, nobody, someone, somebody, something [These function in sentences such as *Everyone* wants to pass the test.]

RECIPROCAL PRONOUNS each other, one another [Use *each other* with two people: Jane and I praised *each other.* Use *one another* with more than two: The team members get along well with *one another.*]

Practice 6: Underline each noun and pronoun in the following sentences. For each pronoun, identify the kind of pronoun and its function in the sentence. After you have finished, write a series of ten sentences imitating the following.

a. Simon dreamed of pouring himself a double martini and of drinking it very slowly.

b. Simon, who was thinking about his chemistry final, wandered aimlessly up the stairs to his room.

c. The teacher had told her students that they needed to review their lecture notes.

d. Simon had to admit to himself that he had not studied very hard.

e. Was he trying to fool himself or his dad?

f. Something kept bothering him.

g. A small voice inside said to him, "You can do it. Go over to Mike's dorm room and get his notes. Don't quit."

h. This had never happened before.

i. Simon grew tired of thinking about himself.

j. He had had enough of these negative thoughts, so he went to find out what was on at the movies.

18.4 Adjectives

Adjectives are modifiers of nouns and pronouns. They change in some way the meaning of a noun, as illustrated by the different adjectives in *old dress* and *new dress*. Adjectives appear as a number of different kinds, and they also have comparative and superlative forms to indicate differences in degree.

a. Classes of adjectives

DESCRIPTIVE | long, short, silly, thin, green, good [Descriptive adjectives indicate a particular quality or state about a noun or pronoun.]

PROPER | Shakespearean, French, Indian [Proper adjectives are derived from proper names and are always capitalized.]

VERBAL | winning, crying, rejected, worried [Present participles such as *falling* and *caring* are often used to modify nouns or pronouns: The *falling* box smashed Mary's toe. Past participles are also used as modifiers: The *lost* dog has been away for two weeks now.]

POSSESSIVE | my, your, his, her, its, our, your, their, Mike's

DEMONSTRATIVE | this, that, these, those

NUMERICAL | one, two, three, ninth, tenth [The cardinal numerals indicate quantity: *one, two, three*. The ordinal numerals indicate position: *first, second, third*.]

INDEFINITE	another, any, both, few, many, no, and so forth
INTERROGATIVE	what, which, whose [*What* book do you want?]
ARTICLES	a, an, the
RELATIVE	what, whatever, which, whichever, whose [I know *which* book you want.]
ABSOLUTE	dead, unique, perfect

NOTE: Some noun forms function as adjectives to modify other nouns as in the following: *house* rules, *honor* code, *Saint Mary's College* campus.

b. Comparison of adjectives

Descriptive, proper, and verbal adjectives can change form to show degrees of difference in manner, quality, and quantity. English grammar possesses three degrees: positive, comparative, and superlative.

Positive	**Comparative**	**Superlative**
good	better	best
possible	less possible	least possible
filthy	filthier	filthiest
loving	more loving	most loving

NOTE: Short adjectives form comparative and superlative forms with *-er* or *-est* (*sad, sadder, saddest*). Long adjectives add *more* or *most* (*democratic, more democratic, most democratic*). When in doubt, consult a standard dictionary.

18.5 Adverbs

An adverb is a word or word group that modifies in some way a verb, verbal, adjective, adverb, or clause. Most often, adverbs answer the questions *when, where, why, how,* or *to what extent.* Adverbs made from adjectives end in *-ly,* as in *rudely.* Like adjectives, adverbs indicate degrees of comparison.

a. Classes of adverbs

ADJECTIVAL ADVERBS ENDING IN -LY	safely, lovingly, dejectedly, and so forth [The child arrived *safely* home.]
ADJECTIVAL ADVERBS NOT ENDING IN -LY	last, long, later, high, hard, far, and so forth [The kite sailed *high* in the sky.]
PREPOSITIONAL ADVERBS	up, down, in, around, off, and so forth [The wall fell *down.*]
PHRASAL ADVERBS	out, in, up, down, and so forth [Mike ran *down* his opponent. A phrasal adverb is a part of a verb-adverb combination. Contrast: Mike ran *down* the road.]
INTERROGATIVE ADVERBS	when, where, why, how [Interrogative adverbs ask questions: *When* will it rain?]
RELATIVE ADVERBS	when, where, why, how [Relative adverbs introduce relative clauses: I remember the time *when* the creek flooded.

CONJUNCTIVE ADVERBS	however, nevertheless, therefore, and so forth [The bomb exploded; *however*, no one was injured.]
MISCELLANEOUS ADVERBS	already, also, always, ever, indeed, maybe, never, quite, so, then, there, too, very, well, daily, early, weekly, and so forth [The room was *so* filthy that no animal would live *there*.]

b. Functions of adverbs

Adverbs express a number of different kinds of meaning. The following list contains some important functions performed by adverbs in sentences.

AFFIRMATION	The coach *certainly* has prepared the team for the next game. [*Certainly* modifies the verb *has prepared*. Contrast with Negation below.]
DEGREE	This lecture is *too* long. [*Too* is an adverb of degree, explaining how long.]
FREQUENCY	Jerry went fishing *twice*. [The adverb *twice* explains how often Jerry went fishing.]
INTENSITY	That person is *extremely* cruel. [The adverb *extremely* explains the intensity of the adjective *cruel*.]
MANNER	The students *blindly* follow that teacher. [The adverb *blindly* explains the manner in which the students follow the teacher.]

NEGATION   Keith will *never* be able to finish this course.

PLACE   Opel threw the dead mouse *there*.

QUALIFICATION *Perhaps* this plan will fail.

TIME   Rodney ate twelve hamburgers *yesterday*.

c. Comparison of adverbs

Descriptive and verbal adverbs can be changed to show degrees of difference. English grammar possesses three degrees: positive, comparative, and superlative.

Positive	Comparative	Superlative
lovingly	more lovingly	most lovingly
quickly	more quickly	most quickly
quickly	less quickly	least quickly

NOTE: The suffix *-ly* clearly signals the adverbial form. Most adverbs form the comparative and superlative forms with *more/most* or *less/least*.

Practice 7: Write nine sentences, each one illustrating one different kind of adverb function listed in 18.5.

Practice 8: In the following sentences, underline each adjective once and each adverb twice. Draw an arrow from each adverb or adjective to the word it modifies. Then write eight sentences of your own using those adjectives and adverbs.

 a. Hector gains weight quickly because he always devours junk food.
 b. If you have a serious health problem, you should immediately see a good doctor.

c. Earl waved at the unruly spectators below.
d. The vicious killer easily escaped from the overcrowded jail.

18.6 Prepositions

a. Prepositions always have objects

A preposition is a function word that combines with a noun, pronoun, or noun substitute to create a prepositional phrase that generally functions as an adverb or an adjective in a sentence.

> The thin man placed a book *on* the desk. [*On* is a preposition. *On the desk* is a prepositional phrase modifying the verb *placed*.]

> The thin man read a book *on* elephants. [*On* is a preposition. *On elephants* is a prepositional phrase modifying *book*.]

Common prepositions

about	below	from	since
across	between	in	through
against	but	into	to
around	by	near	under
as	down	of	until
at	during	off	up
before	except	out	with
behind	for	out of	without

Phrasal prepositions

according to	by means of	with the exception of
apart from	in place of	because of

Practice 9: Explain the differences between the italicized words in the following sentences. Identify all prepositional phrases. Use the dictionary if necessary.

a. Jack struck *out* nine batters. Jack ran *out* the door.

b. The waiter passed *out* free champagne. The waiter passed *out*.

c. The student handed *in* a paper. The student saw the notice *in* the paper.

d. The hunter ran *down* the fox. The runner ran *down* the highway.

e. Kerns loves to make *up* stories. These toys are made *up* the road at the new factory.

f. Jack is tired *of* working. *In spite of* working fifty hours a week, Jack is very poor.

g. Mike is *out* to earn money for college. Mike walked *out of* the room.

18.7 Conjunctions

A conjunction is a connective within a sentence joining together words, phrases, or clauses. There are four main classes of conjunctions: coordinating, correlative, subordinating, and adverbial.

JOINING WORDS   The cats *and* dogs fought constantly *and* loudly. [The coordinating conjunction *and* joins together two nouns and two later adverbs.]

JOINING PHRASES	The trees in the parks *and* along the highways will all have to be sprayed with insecticide. [The coordinating conjunction *and* links together two prepositional phrases, one beginning with *in* and the other beginning with *along*.]
JOINING CLAUSES	*When* I go downtown, I have an urge to squander money, *but* I have none to spend. [The subordinating conjunction *when* joins the subordinate clause, *when I go downtown*, to the main clause, *I have an urge to squander money*, and the coordinating conjunction *but* joins the two main clauses together.]

b. Classes of conjunctions

Coordinating conjunctions

Coordinating conjunctions join elements of the same rank within a sentence. They are *and*, *but*, *or*, *nor*, *for*, *so*, and *yet*.

AND	The lion *and* the lamb both live in the zoo.
BUT	The cup is broken *but* easily repairable.
OR	Would Lance dress formally *or* informally?
NOR	The teacher didn't care, *nor* did the students.
FOR	Hank was quiet, *for* his father was very ill.

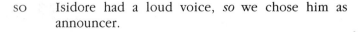
SO   Isidore had a loud voice, *so* we chose him as announcer.

YET   Pete worked six days, *yet* his boss paid him only for five.

Correlative conjunctions

Correlative conjunctions are word pairs used to link sentence elements that are grammatically equivalent: *both . . . and, either . . . or, neither . . . nor, whether . . . or, not only . . . but also.*

BOTH . . . AND   Janey ordered *both* snails *and* cheeseburgers.

EITHER . . . OR   *Either* I pass this course, *or* I drop out of school.

NEITHER . . . NOR   Lambert mows the lawn once a week *neither* willingly *nor* quickly.

WHETHER . . . OR   *Whether* a book is commercially successful *or* not has almost nothing to do with its literary merits.

NOT ONLY . . .   *Not only* is this book boring, *but* it is
BUT ALSO   *also* obscene.

Subordinating conjunctions

Subordinating conjunctions introduce dependent (subordinate) clauses and link them to an element in the main clause. The different kinds and functions of clauses are presented in 18.9. Some common subordinating conjunctions are the following:

after	if	since	when
although	in case	so that	whenever
as	in order that	than	where
as if	in that	though	wherever
because	now that	unless	whether
how	once	until	while

In addition to the preceding conjunctions, the relative pronouns *who*, *that*, and *which* also function as signals of subordinate clauses and as links to elements in a main clause.

Adverbial conjunctions

Adverbial conjunctions, or conjunctive adverbs, are connectors and sentence modifiers, such as *thus*, *nevertheless*, and *however*. Such a conjunction links main clauses and, regardless of placement, signals the meaning relationship between the independent clauses.

Bill failed the test; *therefore*, he will drop the class.

Bill failed the test; he will, *therefore*, drop the class.

Conjunctive adverbs

also	however	nevertheless
anyway	incidentally	nonetheless
besides	indeed	on the contrary
consequently	instead	otherwise
finally	likewise	still
for example	meanwhile	then
furthermore	moreover	therefore
hence	namely	thus
in addition	next	yet

Besides conjunctive adverbs, writers use transitional phrases to join independent clauses together.

Transitional phrases

after all	by the way	in the second place
as a result	even so	on the contrary
at any rate	in addition	on the other hand
at the same time	in fact	

18.8 Phrases

A phrase is a group of grammatically connected words with either a noun or a verb but not both. Phrases have definite functions within sentences such as subject, verb, complement, object, or modifier. Depending upon its components, a phrase can be classified as a noun phrase, verb phrase, verbal phrase, prepositional phrase, or absolute phrase.

a. Functions of phrases

SUBJECT   *The large, moth-eaten blanket* was sold for $500. [The noun phrase, *the large, moth-eaten blanket*, functions as the subject in the sentence.]

VERB   In the past few days, the spider *has been weaving* a gigantic web on the back porch. [The verb phrase, *has been weaving*, functions as the verb.]

COMPLEMENT Brenda's hobby is *collecting stamps*. [The verbal phrase, *collecting stamps*, functions as the subject complement.]

OBJECT   Glenn decided *to buy a motorcycle*. [The infinitive phrase, *to buy a motorcycle*, functions as the object of the verb *decided*.]

MODIFIER   The child threw the bottle *on the floor*. [The prepositional phrase, *on the floor*, functions as an adverbial modifier of the verb *threw*.]

b. Classes of phrases

Noun phrases

A noun phrase consists of a noun or a pronoun and all its modifiers.

NOUN PHRASE   *The cowboy* fell asleep.

NOUN PHRASE   *The weary cowboy* fell asleep.

NOUN PHRASE   *The weary cowboy from Nebraska* fell asleep.

Verb phrases

A verb phrase consists of the main verb and its auxiliaries.

VERB   The twins *work* on Sunday.

VERB PHRASE   The twins *must be working* on Sunday.

VERB + AUXILIARY   The twins *will work* on Sunday.

Verbal phrases

A verbal phrase consists of a nonfinite verb form (gerund, participle, infinitive) and its object(s), or complement(s), plus any modifiers.

GERUND PHRASE   *Stealing the phone* caused all the problems. [The gerund phrase, *stealing the phone,* functions as the subject of the verb *caused.*]

PARTICIPLE PHRASE   The boy *chasing the cat* tripped and fell. [The participle phrase, *chasing the cat,* modifies the noun *boy.*]

PARTICIPLE PHRASE   Todd saw the house *destroyed by fire.* [The participle phrase, *destroyed by fire,* modifies the noun *house.*]

INFINITIVE PHRASE   The girl wanted *to study Latin.* [The infinitive phrase, *to study Latin,* functions as a direct object of the verb *wanted.*]

Prepositional phrases

A prepositional phrase is a group of words consisting of a preposition and its object and any modifiers. Prepositional phrases generally function as adjectives or adverbs within a sentence.

PREPOSITIONAL PHRASE   Oakley Jakobsen swam *at night.* [The prepositional phrase, *at night,* functions as an adverb modifying the verb *swam.*]

PREPOSITIONAL PHRASE   I like the texture *of chocolate ice cream.* [The prepositional phrase, *of chocolate ice cream,* functions as an adjective modifying the noun *texture.*]

Absolute phrases

An absolute phrase is a special kind of verbal phrase consisting of a participle with its subject, object, or modifiers.

ABSOLUTE PHRASE   *The weather being snowy and icy,* school has been cancelled. [The noun *weather* is the subject of the participle *being. Snowy* and *icy* are adjectives modifying *weather.* Together they make up the absolute phrase, *the weather being snowy and icy,* which modifies the rest of the sentence.]

Practice 10: Create a sentence using each of the following word groups as a phrase:

a. in a weak condition
b. with strange music
c. a dangerous wounded animal
d. running down the highway
e. walking across the street
f. to France next year
g. for a bad reason
h. was calling to tell
i. having spent all his money
j. away from school for a while

Identify the phrases in each sentence you composed, and indicate their kind (noun, verbal, and so forth).

Practice 11: Write sentences of your own illustrating each of the five different kinds of phrases discussed in 18.8.

18.9 Clauses

A clause is a group of words containing a subject and a finite verb. Clauses are either independent or dependent.

a. Independent clauses

An independent clause can stand by itself as a complete sentence, or it can function in a sentence as a main clause.

SENTENCE   Brad dropped his pencil. [The entire sentence is an independent clause. *Brad* is the subject. *Dropped* is the main or finite verb.]

MAIN CLAUSE   Just after class began, *Brad started coughing.* [*Brad started coughing* is a main or independent clause that could function as a sentence by itself.]

b. Dependent clauses

A dependent (subordinate) clause functions as a part of a sentence, as either a noun or a modifier (adverb, adjective).

NOUN CLAUSE   I know *that the doctor left the room.* [The noun clause, *that the doctor left the room*, functions as the object of the verb *know.*]

NOUN CLAUSE   *Whoever stole the doughnuts* is in big trouble. [The noun clause, *whoever stole the doughnuts*, functions as the subject of the verb *is.*]

ADJECTIVE CLAUSE   The boy *who bought the rose* was stuck by a thorn. [The adjective clause, *who bought the rose*, modifies *boy*.]

ADVERB CLAUSE   *If you like to write*, you will enjoy that class. [*If you like to write* is an adverb clause modifying the verb phrase *will enjoy*.]

Practice 12: Write a set of five sentences, each of which contains one of the following clauses:
a. when the small kittens were attacked by the Doberman
b. who is able to cook a meal for twenty-five people
c. whose swimming pool was full of soap suds.
d. after the screaming had stopped
e. although I am afraid

Practice 13: Combine each of the following pairs of sentences by turning one into a subordinate clause. Remove or add words if necessary. Use conjunctions listed in 18.7b.

SAMPLE   The mower is broken. The grass is uncut.

COMBINATION   Because the mower is broken, the grass is uncut.
a. Jack evaded paying his taxes. Jack went to prison.
b. It stormed last night. The roof leaks.
c. Jenny whispered. She said, "Look at the ghost."
d. The people in the audience gasped. The magician set a small parrot on fire.
e. You are traveling to New York. You should be careful.

18.10 Common sentence patterns

The number of English sentences is limitless, but the number of patterns in which we use our language is quite limited. Grammarians debate over the exact number of English sentence patterns. Although patterns may be combined to form other more complicated patterns, the following are five *basic* patterns for English sentences.

a. Subject + verb

That boy runs in circles. [*That boy* is the subject. *Runs* is the verb. *Runs in circles* is a predicate made of the primary verb and the modifier, *in circles.*]

Those children have been swimming. [*Those children* is the subject. *Have been swimming* is the complete verb phrase. *Swimming* is the main verb and *have* and *been* are auxiliary verbs.]

b. Subject + verb + subject complement

The doughnuts are stale. [*The doughnuts* is the subject. *Are* is the verb. *Stale* is the subject complement that completes the meaning of the subject and the linking verb.]

That wound looks infected. [*That wound* is the subject. *Looks* is a linking verb. *Infected* is the subject complement that completes the meaning of the subject and the linking verb.]

My new car is an Oldsmobile. [*My new car* is the subject of the linking verb *is*. *Oldsmobile* is the subject complement. It completes the meaning of the subject and linking verb.]

c. Subject + verb + direct object

The cat carried five kittens into the garage. [*The cat* is the subject of the verb *carried. Five kittens* is the direct object of the verb *carried.*]

Carol slapped Bud. [*Bud* is the direct object of the verb *slapped. Carol* is the subject.]

d. Subject + verb + indirect object + direct object

The book gave Manuel a new idea. [*Gave* is the verb of the subject, *the book.* What the book gave was *a new idea*, which is the direct object. *Manuel* is the person to whom the idea was given and functions as the indirect object.]

e. Subject + verb + direct object + object complement

The movie made Ruby angry. [The adjective *angry* is the object complement of Ruby. (The object complement is always either a noun or adjective that describes or completes the meaning of the direct object.) The direct object of the verb is *Ruby.* The subject is *the movie.*]

The senior class elected Fran Ciardi prom queen. [*Prom queen* is a noun. It is the object complement of *Fran Ciardi*, the direct object of the verb *elected.* The subject is *The senior class.*]

Practice 14: Analyze and describe the sentence structures for the sentences in two paragraphs assigned by your instructor.

19 Revising Sentences

✍ **Student Comments on Writing**

I think the most important thing is to revise for content and organization, but the sentence revisions are important too. I've discovered in revising that I'll be doing two or even three things at about the same time.

Joan Woods

Learn to revise your sentences. One of the happiest moments for a writer is the completion of a first draft. Some writers are so happy to have their ideas down in black and white that they often think that once something is written, it cannot be changed. Revision can occur only after the writer or a reader discovers problems in the draft. Most often those perceptions of writing problems are vague. A writer will say, "This just doesn't sound right." A reader will say, "This paper needs something here." Writers trust those hunches that something is wrong and look carefully at the writing to see whether the paragraphs and sentences work as well as possible to develop the main idea. The goal of all revision is to make the writing more effective for the reader and more meaningful and clear in terms of purpose. There are many ways to talk about revision, but four strategies prove effective in revising sentences: addition, deletion, transposition, and substitution.

19.1 Addition

This is, quite simply, the adding of material to a sentence for specificity and clarification. It may help you to review the section on specific details in 3.1. The best reason for adding material is to support and develop the main idea. Often sentences need greater clarity and, almost without exception, most sentences would communicate more if they were more specific. Two common forms of sentence addition involve sentence expansion and subordination.

ORIGINAL   Mark, Mary, and I enjoyed ~~the~~ party. *Cyril's birthday*

ADDITION   *esp. the guitar music and Mexican food* Mark, Mary, and I enjoyed Cyril's birthday party., ∧

ADDITION   Mark, Mary, and I enjoyed Cyril's birthday party, especially the guitar music and the delicious Mexican food.

a. Sentence expansion

In sentence expansion, the author adds selected grammatical elements to a sentence to clarify and develop its meaning. Sentences can be expanded in many ways, and some of the most common expansions involve the addition of verbs, nouns, adjectives, adverbs, phrases, and clauses.

ORIGINAL The things moved.

VERBS The animals *woke up* and *began slithering.*

NOUNS The *black snakes* and the *garter snake* woke up and began slithering.

ADJECTIVES The *tiny* black snakes and the *old, spotted* garter snake woke up and began slithering.

ADVERBS The tiny black snakes and the old, spotted garter snake *quickly* woke up and began slithering *away.*

PHRASES The tiny black snakes *near the chicken coop* and the old, spotted garter snake *in the garden* woke up and began slithering away.

CLAUSE The tiny black snakes near the chicken coop and the old, spotted garter snake in the garden woke up and began slithering away *as soon as Mrs. Buda let her dog run out into the back yard.*

Practice 1: In light of the example, expand the following sentences by adding the elements indicated in parentheses.

ORIGINAL The book was on the table. [Adjectives]

EXPANSION The *child's* book was on the *dirty kitchen* table.

a. The car moved around the corner. [Verbs]
b. They screamed and shouted things at the opposing players. [Nouns]
c. The horse ate some hay. [Adjectives]
d. The boy walked across the street. [Adverb]
e. The sheriff saw the car crash. [Phrases]
f. The woman loved teaching. [Clauses]

b. Subordination

In terms of sentence addition, revising by subordination means restructuring the words, generally by adding one or more phrases (adjective, adverb) and/or one or more dependent clauses (noun, adjective, adverb, or absolute). This kind of revision can improve sentence structure and variety by eliminating short, choppy, simple sentences.

ORIGINAL ~Because~ I was feeling depressed, I listened to some music, ~and~ My spirits felt better.

REVISION Because I was feeling depressed, I listened to some music, and my spirits felt better.

Practice 2: Combine the following sentences into one single sentence by means of subordination. Keep your drafts to discuss revision in class.

ORIGINAL ✓James Whitehead ~~is a~~ *The* southern writer. ~~He~~ *wrote* ~~has written~~ a novel about professional

football. ~~It is titled~~ Joiner. ~~It was~~ his first novel.

COMBINATION The southern writer James Whitehead wrote his first novel, Joiner, about professional football.

a. Some people hate heavy metal music. They think it is a bad influence. They think it damages young people.
b. Janet wants to attend medical school. She hates some courses in the sciences. She especially hates biology and chemistry.
c. Those horses are lazy. They don't like to run. If you taken them for a ride, you find this out.
d. The boy was tired. He went in his room. He lay down on the bed. He fell asleep.
e. This is a hard problem. Some of the students want to smoke. Other students get sick when they are near cigarette smoke. This is one of the difficult things about living in a dorm.

Practice 3: Revise each of the following sentences by using effective subordination. Use some of the subordinating conjunctions listed in 18.7b.

ORIGINAL *Because* Jackie stayed home; she was tired.

REVISION Because Jackie was tired, she stayed home.

a. Mary Carter is still a close friend of mine, and she moved to Atlanta last Christmas.

b. The student did no work, and he slept in class, and he somehow passed the course.

c. My cat ran across the busy highway, and I saw it get hit and it was by a truck.

d. The student was unprepared for college, and he could not write very well.

e. One of my teachers taught me to love science, but that was in grade school.

Practice 4: Revise the following paragraph, adding material from your own experience, knowledge, or imagination to make the writing more lively and interesting.

> The room had about an average size. There were a lot of things in it. Some of the things were left over from his (or her) being a child. Many of the things were from high school. When the person wearing the old clothes turned around, all that could be seen outside was a coating of something on the window. The walls and floor were not too clean. There was a lot of stuff under the bed and the closet had a few things in it. The person went over to the mirror and wrote something on it.

19.2 Deletion

Many writers use more words than necessary. When writers delete, they erase material, particularly deadwood. A careful pruning during revision often clarifies the meaning, improves readability, and increases comprehension. Many writers claim that they can always remove 10 percent of the words from their final draft with very little trouble.

ORIGINAL ~~I think that the~~ people who ~~argue in favor of~~ [advocate changing]
~~reducing~~ the legal age for drinking, [alcohol] ~~the kid~~
~~drink advocates, from the present law of~~
~~being the age of 21 to 18 or 17~~ ignore ~~and do~~
~~not pay any attention at all to one very~~
~~important,~~ [the] fact ~~which is~~ that [in] most ~~of the~~ [teenage]
automobile accidents ~~which take place on~~
~~the highways involving teenage drivers~~
~~involve the consumption of beverages~~
~~containing~~ alcohol [is involved.] ~~in one form or another.~~

REVISION People who advocate changing the legal age
for drinking alcohol from twenty-one to
eighteen ignore the fact that in most teenage
automobile accidents alcohol is involved.

ORIGINAL Mike ~~was desirous of having~~ [wanted] an ice-cold ~~soda~~
~~such as a frosty~~ Pepsi or ~~chilled~~ Coke ⊙ ~~to~~
~~quench his thirst.~~

DELETION Mike wanted an ice-cold Pepsi or Coke.

Practice 5: Revise the following paragraph, deleting all
material that you find unimportant.

This Sunday morning, the first day of the week was exceptionally and beautifully mild and calm. This was true for both on land and on the water. I guess this meant that we would have a good and pleasant and safe trip across the river on the new raft which we had just finished building and putting together last week. We were afraid and scared that the weather would be stormy and rainy with a lot of frightening lightning and rain like it had been doing all last week and even this month. It almost reminded me of the year where it rained for 63 days in a row one summer like it was a replay of the Noah's Flood. On and on and on we dragged and hauled the large raft almost six foot square both across and sideways. The raft we had made out of old logs which we had pulled from the mighty river as they came floating along bobbing in the water during the spring flood. It must have taken about an hour to drag, pull, push, kick, and lug the raft down the river's edge.

19.3 Transposition

The prefix *trans-* indicates motion across. In speaking of sentences, *transposition* means the rearranging of the elements in a sentence for greater clarity and emphasis. In addition, a careful writer will often change the sentence structure in a paper to make sure that the reader has a sense of energy and variety instead of dullness and repetition. Occasionally, rearrangement is necessary because of logical or structural mistakes in composing.

ORIGINAL Professor Mann presented a discussion *verb* of his great invention as he first imagined it with a simple sketch on the blackboard for us.

REVISION   With a simple sketch on the blackboard for us,

Professor Mann presented a discussion *true verb?* of his

great invention as he first imagined *ing* it.

REVISION   With a simple blackboard sketch, Professor
Mann discussed the first imagining of his great
invention.

Practice 6: Revise the following sentences to improve clarity and effectiveness.

SAMPLE   Jeff felt the spider web as he walked across the

porch on his face.

REVISION   Jeff felt the spider web on his face as he walked
across the porch.

a. The bus stopped suddenly and an old woman hit her
head on the window in the middle of the road.
b. The doctor with the broken bone comforted the crying
child.
c. The last play was a penalty of the game between Central
and Boys Town.
d. The kite snapped loose and crashed from its string into
the lake in a high wind.
e. The gardener looked at the snake watering the roses.

19.4 Substitution

Substitution is the replacement of one word or phrase for
another. Most of the time, a substitution is made because
the writer senses that the substituted word or phrase has

greater clarity and a stronger effect than an earlier word or phrase. In addition, many substitutions are made to avoid confusion or ambiguity. The following examples show only a few of the countless ways a writer might substitute words and phrases to improve clarity and effectiveness.

ORIGINAL I ~~am wild about loud~~ clothes. *enjoy wearing bright* ~~Hawaiian shirts~~ (*sp.*)

REVISION I enjoy wearing flashy red and bright blue Hawaiian shirts. [Note how the concrete words substituted for the general phrase *loud clothes* make the sentence more vivid and informative.]

ORIGINAL Gretel ~~prevaricated diurnally~~. *lied daily*

REVISION Gretel lied every day. [*Prevaricate* and *diurnally* are ineffective, pretentious words for the simple and effective *lie* and *every day*.]

ORIGINAL That Lear ~~dude done took some grief from his bratty kids~~. *King* *suffered greatly because of his daughters.*

REVISION King Lear suffered greatly because of his daughters. [Slang words such as *dude* and *bratty* and the nongrammatical verb phrase *done took* weaken the powerful statement about King Lear.]

Practice 7: Revise the following sentences to make the meaning more accessible to your classmates.
a. About this essay I want to quibble with this scribbler in at least two parts.
b. "A poet has worked out a scheme for identifying his art with the ideal of a democratic 'empire' that he thinks

of as a matrix, an All-Mother, a principle of unity bestowing its sanctions upon a strong love of man for man, an 'adhesiveness' generally 'spiritual,' but also made concrete in imagery of athletic physical attachment." *Kenneth Burke*

c. "We can study language as a grammatical system (syntactics) or as a network of denotative or connotative meanings (semantics), but finally we must recognize that our actual *use* of language is always pragmatic: that is, we always speak and write in specific situations for immediate human reasons." *Robert Scholes*

d. Jane's of her brother's health analysis included a discussion of his drinking problem.

e. The professionalistic group inclines to hold in contempt the proletariat.

Practice 8: Combine the sentences under each letter into one clear, effective sentence.

a. He was often angry.
   He was angry with his children.
   He was angry with his wife.
   He was angry with his employees.

b. The congressman had a problem.
   The problem involved alcohol.
   The congressman was arrested for drunken driving.
   He was driving seventy miles an hour.
   He was driving in a residential area.

c. The fraternity wanted a party.
   They wanted a great band.
   They wanted a meal.
   They wanted to include steaks and baked potatoes.

d. Jane wanted something.
   She couldn't find it in a noisy dorm.
   She couldn't find it talking to her friend.
   It resembled silence.
   It resembled light.
   It resembled good music.

20 Sentence Problems

Any number of common sentence problems occur in writing. The problems might arise because the writer has heard since childhood nonstandard patterns of usage such as the following:

NONSTANDARD James *ain't* talking. He *think* his dog is lost.

STANDARD James *is not* talking. He *thinks* his dog is lost.

Or a problem of usage might arise from haste and carelessness, as in the sentence:

NONSTANDARD   The dogs in the laboratory *is* needed for an experiment.

STANDARD   The dogs in the laboratory *are* needed for an experiment.

It does not matter whether the errors arise from patterns of learning or patterns of carelessness. The result is the same: an error that annoys or distracts many readers and can even damage meaning. This chapter contains discussions of a number of serious sentence errors. Your instructor will assign material as the need arises, but you can teach yourself to avoid error by doing several things. First, acquire a clear understanding of the different kinds of serious errors. Second, practice writing sample sentences with the different kinds of error and then practice revising them for correctness. This two-sided approach, understanding the structure of error and learning strategies to correct error, will help improve your writing.

20.1 Sentence fragments

NOTE: A knowledge of the following grammatical terms may help you avoid and correct sentence fragments. You may need to study the definitions and examples of these terms in chapters 18 and 24:

Appositive	Gerund	Participle
Dependent clause	Independent clause	Phrase
Finite verb	Infinitive	Subject

a. A sentence fragment is not a complete sentence

Good writers learn to spot accidental sentence fragments. The conventions of standard written English require sentences with the first word capitalized and terminal punctuation at the end. When you use these conventions with a group of words that is not a sentence, you have a sentence fragment. Complete sentences are necessary and have the following elements: a subject, a finite verb, and the ability to stand alone with meaning.

Each sentence has a subject.

FRAGMENT Talking to all the players.

SENTENCE *Mary* was talking to all the players.

Each sentence has a complete, finite verb.

FRAGMENT The doctor smiling at the patient.

SENTENCE The doctor *was smiling* at the patient.

Each sentence is an independent clause.

FRAGMENT While the sheriff was looking in the trunk.

SENTENCE The sheriff was looking in the trunk.

SENTENCE While the sheriff was looking in the trunk, the Duke brothers escaped on foot.

b. Sentence fragments should be revised

Any writer can write a fragment in a draft; however, in revising or proofreading, such errors must be spotted and corrected. Certain constructions sometimes seem to be complete sentences but are not. These include verbal phrases, subjects with incomplete verbs, appositives, dependent clauses, and prepositional phrases.

Verbal phrases

A participle phrase, gerund phrase, infinitive phrase, or verb phrase is not a complete sentence.

FRAGMENT   *Seeing the big waves off Malibu.*

SENTENCE   Seeing the big waves off Malibu, Jack wanted to go surfing. [In the sentence, the participle phrase modifies the subject *Jack*.]

FRAGMENT   *Riding a horse at sunrise.*

SENTENCE   Riding a horse at sunrise can cure depression. [In the sentence, the gerund phrase functions as the subject of the verb *can cure*.]

FRAGMENT   *To drive her Corvette at high speeds.*

SENTENCE   Dr. Lannon likes to drive her Corvette at high speeds. [The infinitive phrase becomes the object of the verb *likes*.]

FRAGMENT   *Eventually arrived in Fresno.*

SENTENCE   The hitchhiker eventually arrived in Fresno. [A subject is added to the fragment to complete the verb phrase and create a complete sentence.]

Subject with incomplete verb

A subject and an incomplete verb phrase do not make a complete sentence. Make sure the sentence has, if required, both an auxiliary and a main verb.

FRAGMENT   *Mary swimming in her new pool.*

SENTENCE   Mary is swimming in her new pool. [The auxiliary verb *is* completes the sentence.]

Appositive

An appositive or an explanatory phrase is not a complete sentence. Connect the appositive to an adjacent sentence.

FRAGMENT   I love old movies. *Especially the comedies.*

SENTENCE   I love old movies, especially the comedies.

Dependent clause

A dependent clause is not a sentence. You can add or delete material to make a complete sentence.

FRAGMENT   *That help the students to improve their writing.*

SENTENCE   That teacher made several suggestions to help students improve their writing.

FRAGMENT   *The children who exhausted themselves swimming.*

SENTENCE   The children exhausted themselves swimming.

Prepositional phrase

A prepositional phrase is never a complete sentence. Connecting the phrase to an adjoining sentence generally solves the problem.

FRAGMENT   Marty drove a thousand miles. *In only twelve hours.*

SENTENCE   Marty drove a thousand miles in only twelve hours.

c. Different strategies can be used to correct fragments

You can correct a sentence fragment in different ways. First, determine an appropriate subject and verb that express your meaning. Then write a complete sentence, using them. The following examples give some of the ways to correct sentence fragments.

A fragment can be linked to an adjacent sentence.

FRAGMENT The pilot refused to fly. *Because of a tornado.*

SENTENCE Because of a tornado, the pilot refused to fly.

A word or words can be omitted.

FRAGMENT *Since Jackie had enjoyed cheerleading in high school.*

SENTENCE Jackie enjoyed cheerleading in high school.

A word or words can be added.

FRAGMENT *Because Jane loves astronomy.*

SENTENCE Because Jane loves astronomy, she is majoring in physics.

Word order can be changed.

FRAGMENT *While the doctor became ill in the hospital.*

SENTENCE While in the hospital, the doctor became ill.

d. Occasionally, a professional writer will use an intentional fragment

An unintentional sentence fragment strikes many readers as a serious error in writing. However, skillful writers occasionally compose intentional fragments. Many examples, both long and short, can no doubt be easily found. Beginning writers, though, should strive to write complete sentences with subjects, verbs, and modifiers.

TRANSITIONS   And now for the ghastly part. But first a word of caution.

ANSWERS TO   What is a marmoset? A small monkey.
QUESTIONS

LISTS   The high railings of Prospects rippled past their gaze. Dark poplars, rare white forms. Forms more frequent, white shapes thronged amid the trees, white forms and fragments streaming by mutely, sustaining vain gestures on the air. *James Joyce*

COMMENTARY   Somehow, I felt surprised that the room was still the same—except that Mary had changed the bed linen. Good old Mary. *Ralph Ellison*

NOTE: Your instructor may penalize you for the appearance of any sentence fragment. Ask if you can use fragments and whether you should signal such fragments.

Practice 1: Combine each of the following groups of words to make a single sentence. You may have to add, delete, or transpose material or combine sentences.

EXAMPLE   When you play on this field.
           You will try your hardest.

REVISION   When you play on this field, you will try your hardest.

a. Work very hard in practice.
   Football players all through the week.
   To win the game on Saturday.

b. To love the game.
   To hit hard.
   Football players.
c. It is human.
   It is part of our nature.
   That people want to feel good about themselves.
d. Some people will be unhappy, perhaps angry.
   Because the game is sold out.
e. Some people love sports.
   They love football games.
   Think what happens here is important.
f. Having the desire to win.
   The team was ready to play.

Practice 2: Revise each of the following sentence fragments.
a. When the snow had finally stopped and the little children were able to begin building a snowman.
b. Joan walking up the stairs to her room and thinking about the test she had just failed.
c. Surfing answer to anyone's desire to escape for a day and enjoy the beach.
d. You having known the answer to that tricky question all along.
e. Why any doctor would behave the way that Dr. Hill behaved in class?
f. And noticed that the leopard was climbing down from the tree.

20.2 Fused sentence and comma splice

A fused sentence is a serious error in writing. It occurs when a writer joins two independent clauses with no punctuation whatsoever.

FUSED SENTENCE   The book was poorly written the author praised it as a flawless masterpiece.

CORRECTION   The book was poorly written, but the author praised it as a flawless masterpiece. [The use of a comma with a coordinating conjunction is one of six common ways to correct a fused sentence.]

A comma splice is another serious error in a sentence. A writer can make a comma splice error in two different ways. One way is by joining two independent clauses with only a comma.

COMMA SPLICE   Some famous people have agoraphobia, they are afraid to go out in public.

CORRECTION   Some famous people have agoraphobia; they are afraid to go out in public. [The use of a semicolon to join two sentences is one of six common ways to remedy a comma splice.]

A second form of comma splice involves joining two independent clauses with a transitional device that requires more than a comma.

COMMA SPLICE   Mary is going to school, however Jose is at the library.

CORRECTION   Mary is going to school; however, Jose is at the library. [When the conjunctive adverb *however* connects two independent clauses and introduces the second one, it requires a semicolon before it and a comma after it.]

a. Six strategies can correct a comma splice or fused sentence

COMMA SPLICE   Mary is walking to school, Jose is already at the library.

FUSED SENTENCE Mary is walking to school Jose is already at the library.

1. Separate sentences can be used

PATTERN   _____Sentence_____.   _____Sentence_____.

CORRECT   Mary is walking to school.   Jose is already at the library.

2. Clauses can be joined with a comma and a coordinating conjunction: *and, but, or, nor, for, so, yet*

PATTERN   Independent   Coordinating   Independent
            ___clause___,   conjunction   ___clause___.

CORRECT   Mary is walking to school, but Jose is already at the library.

3. A semicolon can join the clauses

PATTERN   Independent clause; Independent clause.

CORRECT   Mary is walking to school; Jose is already at the library.

4. A semicolon and a conjunctive adverb can join the clauses

PATTERN   <u>Independent clause</u>; Conjunctive adverb, <u>Independent clause</u>.

CORRECT   Mary is walking to school; however, Jose is already at the library.

NOTE: See 18.7b for the list of connectives that can join clauses.

5. A dependent clause can be created and joined to the sentence

PATTERN   <u>Dependent clause</u>, <u>Independent clause</u>.

CORRECT   Even though Mary is walking to school, Jose is already at the library.

CORRECT   Because Jose is at the library, Mary is walking to school.

6. An introductory phrase can be created and joined to the sentence

PATTERN   <u>Introductory phrase</u>, <u>Independent clause</u>.

CORRECT   Walking to school, Mary saw Jose was in the library.

CORRECT   Studying at the library, Jose learned that Mary was walking to school.

b. Incorrect quotation can create a comma splice

To avoid a comma splice when quoting material, be careful in using the lead-in phrase. Notice in the following example how the lead-in phrase, *Manuel said*, is switched from the middle to the beginning of the quotation, thereby correcting the comma splice. (See also 22.6c and 22.6d.)

COMMA SPLICE   "I need to study French," Manuel said, "I plan to go to Paris next summer." [Notice that the comma follows the word *said*, which is the end of an independent clause.]

CORRECTED   Manuel said, "I need to study French. I plan to go to Paris next summer."

COMMA SPLICE   "Why did Marx prefer a dictatorship?" Dr. Jones asked, "why did Marx despise the idea of personal freedom?"

CORRECTED   Dr. Jones asked, "Why did Marx prefer a dictatorship? Why did Marx despise the idea of personal freedom?" [The lead-in phrase, *Dr. Jones asked*, has been moved to the beginning.]

c. Two exceptions can be found

Occasionally, professional writers use commas to join a series of short, parallel independent clauses. This is not an error, but beginning writers would do well to use semicolons.

POSSIBLE   The snake slithered, the duck quacked, the cow mooed, the dog barked.

TRADITIONAL   The snake slithered; the duck quacked; the cow mooed; the dog barked.

Writers will also occasionally use a comma to join a brief question and statement. This is not an error even though both the question and statement are independent clauses.

EXAMPLE   This food tastes funny, doesn't it?

EXAMPLE   You didn't know that, did you?

Practice 1: Revise each of the following in at least two ways: (1) by use of the semicolon; (2) by use of the comma and a coordinating conjunction.
  a. Some of these stories seem to be untrue, every single incident actually happened.
  b. Andrews had no intention of looking at reality, his theory needed to be guarded from the facts.
  c. A legal system can only be as good as the laws the people are ultimately the creators of the laws.
  d. Americans casually accept 500 deaths on the highways every week of every year they become alarmed when an airplane crashes every six months.
  e. "Some people have thought about suicide," Dr. Johns told us, "Some people keep thinking about it regularly, those people should talk to a medical doctor."

Practice 2: Rewrite the first four sentences in Practice 1 using the subordinating conjunctions *although*, *since*, *because*, and *even though*. Have each sentence contain one dependent clause and one independent clause.

Practice 3: Read the following sentences carefully. Mark *C* for a correct sentence. Correct any comma splices and fused sentences.

a. Certain people exploit for profit the bestiality of man, they deal in drugs, slavery, guns, prostitution, and stolen goods.
b. Some poets feel called upon to communicate a sense of mystery, they try to give their readers a sensation of awe and wonder.
c. When I am happy I will do almost anything I have been known to stay up all night painting or sculpting.
d. In Saudi Arabia, our tour saw a woman dressed completely in black, she carried a sewing machine on her head and in her right hand a sack with dates, figs, bananas, and grapes.
e. Walking along the highway, the old man picked up scraps of metal and empty cans he whistled as he tossed them into a shopping cart painted yellow, green, purple, and black.

20.3 Subject-verb agreement

NOTE: To understand how to create agreement between the subject and the verb, you may need to study the definitions and examples of these terms in chapters 18 and 24.

Collective noun	Noun	Pronoun	Singular
Number	Plural	Subject	Verb

If you don't know them already, you need to memorize the forms of the irregular verbs, *be*, *have*, and *do*, and the regular verb *like* to avoid errors in subject–verb agreement when you use them.

Present be	**Past** was	**Present** have	**Past** had
Singular			
I am	I was	I have	I had
you are	you were	you have	you had
he/she/it is	he/she/it was	he/she/it has	he/she/it had
Plural			
we are	we were	we have	we had
you are	you were	you have	you had
they are	they were	they have	they had

Present do	**Past** did	**Present** like	**Past** liked
Singular			
I do	I did	I like	I liked
you do	you did	you like	you liked
he/she/it does	he/she/it did	he/she/it likes	he/she/it liked
Plural			
we do	we did	we like	we liked
you do	you did	you like	you liked
they do	they did	they like	they liked

a. Subject and verb must agree in terms of number and person

The subject and verb must agree in number. Number is either singular (cat) or plural (cats).

SINGULAR The dog *likes* to bark.

PLURAL   The dogs *like* to bark.

The subject must agree in person with the verb. *Person* refers to the relationship between the speaker (I/we: first person), the person spoken to (you: second person), and the person or thing (he/she/it/they: third person) spoken about. In only the first and third person is there a difference between the singular and plural forms.

SINGULAR I *am* sad.

PLURAL   We *are* sad.

SINGULAR He *knows*. The door *is* broken.

PLURAL   They *know*. The doors *are* broken.

NOTE: In certain American regional dialects *be* is substituted for the helping verbs *am*, *is*, or *are*. Formal English requires the standard usage.

DIALECT   I *be* sad.

STANDARD I *am* sad.

b. Compound subjects joined by and or both . . . and take plural verbs

Compound subjects joined by *and* are plural and require a plural verb.

PLURAL Mary and May *are* prize violinists.

PLURAL The players and the coach *want* to win.

Compound subjects joined by *both . . . and* also require a plural verb.

PLURAL Both the dogs and the cat *have* gone to sleep.

PLURAL Both the teachers and the cook *want* better salaries.

c. Compound subjects joined by or, nor, or not only . . . but also vary in number

Compound subjects joined by these connectives take a singular or plural verb depending on the nearer subject.

CORRECT Neither he nor they *want* to join the army.

CORRECT   Neither they nor he *wants* to join the army.

CORRECT   Not only the pilots but also the navigator *was* wrong.

CORRECT   Not only the navigator but also the pilots *were* wrong.

d. Single-unit compounds take a singular verb

Some idiomatic compounds, such as *rod and reel*, function as a unit. When such a meaning is intended, a singular verb is appropriate.

SINGULAR Ham and eggs *is* my favorite breakfast.

PLURAL   Ham, eggs, and milk *are* good sources of protein.

SINGULAR The captain of the football team and president of the senior class *is* Mike Jones.

PLURAL   The captain and the president *are* at the ceremony.

e. Collective nouns are either singular or plural

A collective noun, such as *crowd, class, committee, couple, team, family*, or *jury*, may be either singular or plural, depending on intended meaning. The singular meaning takes a singular verb. The plural meaning takes a plural verb. If the noun signifies an *entire group* acting together as one unit at the same time, use a singular verb.

SINGULAR The crew of this ship *is* always asleep.

PLURAL   When it is time for supper, the crew *are* awake with knives and forks in their hands.

SINGULAR The band *was* too loud. [The band functions as a unit.]

PLURAL   The band of bikers *were* exceedingly vulgar in everything they did.

f. Some singular nouns have a plural appearance

Do not use a plural verb with any of the following singular subjects.

   ✎ Titles of books, albums, poems, movies, plays, magazines, newspapers, or organizations:

CORRECT The <u>New York Times</u> *is* a national newspaper. [Contrast: These times *are* hard.]

   ✎ Words used as words:

CORRECT <u>We</u> *is* a difficult word for a selfish person. [Contrast: We *are* lost.]

   ✎ Singular proper nouns:

CORRECT Elysian Fields *is* a suburb of Matawanee. [Contrast: The fields *are* dry.]

Do not use the following nouns as plural nouns. They are always singular.

aerobics	electronics	measles	physics
athletics	gallows	molasses	robotics
billiards	geriatrics	mumps	
economics	herpes	news	

CORRECT The gallows *is* for people who think physics *is* difficult.

g. Some foreign words have unique plural forms

With words from classical Latin and Greek, use the appropriate plural form. Consult a dictionary when in doubt.

PLURAL   The most influential media *are* newspapers and television.

SINGULAR The least expensive medium *is* radio.

Some common foreign words in their singular and plural forms are *bacterium/bacteria, criterion/criteria, datum/data, phenomenon/phenomena,* and *radius/radii.*

h. Singular pronouns require singular verbs

Do not use singular indefinite pronouns as plurals. Words such as *everybody* and *everyone* are common singular indefinite pronouns. Unless such words form part of a compound subject, they should always take a singular verb.

another	each	everything	somebody
anybody	each other	neither	someone
anything	either	nothing	whoever

SINGULAR Everybody *is* wearing a new hat.

SINGULAR Neither of the birds *is* injured.

i. Plural pronouns require plural verbs

The pronouns *both, few, many, others, several, these, those, they,* and *we* always take plural verbs.

PLURAL Several in the class always *leave* at the break.

PLURAL A few *try* to cheat on every test.

j. Pronouns variable in number take a singular or plural verb, depending on intended meaning

Several pronouns (*all, any, most, none, who, which, some, such, what,* and *that*) take a singular or plural verb depending on meaning and context.

SINGULAR All of this pie *is* moldy. [*All* refers to just one pie.]

PLURAL All of the pies *are* moldy. [*All* refers to more than one pie. Notice the word following the preposition *of* is a clue to singular or plural agreement.]

SINGULAR What *is* this food?

PLURAL What *are* his weaknesses?

k. Lengthy sentences create agreement problems

Lengthy, complex sentences can lead to agreement errors. Because the subject is removed from its verb in a lengthy sentence, writers must carefully check such constructions for the main verb of the main clause.

INCORRECT The problem caused by stray dogs or cats at the circuses and aggravated by the indifferent trainers *seem* to bother the city council a great deal.

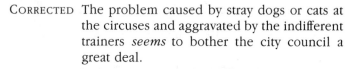

CORRECTED The problem caused by stray dogs or cats at the circuses and aggravated by the indifferent trainers *seems* to bother the city council a great deal.

IMPROVED The problem of stray animals at the circuses *bothers* the city council greatly.

l. Inverted sentences may create agreement problems

Occasionally an inverted sentence creates a rhythm so agreeable that the agreement error is masked.

INCORRECT With age *comes* pain and wisdom. [The sentence sounds correct because *age* and *comes* are both singular, but the subject is the compound, *pain and wisdom*.]

CORRECT With age *come* pain and wisdom.

INCORRECT *Does* the sergeant and the sheriff carry pistols?

CORRECT *Do* the sergeant and the sheriff carry pistols?

m. Intervening material can create agreement problems

Do not mistake an appositive or a parenthetical phrase for the subject. Check the subject-verb agreement in sentences that use a connective such as *rather than, along with, including, together with, but not, as much as, as well as, in addition to, also, more than.*

INCORRECT Steve, along with his brothers, love to fish.

CORRECT Steve, along with his brothers, *loves* to fish.

INCORRECT   Marie's favorite food, enchiladas, *were* not on the menu.

CORRECT   Marie's favorite food, enchiladas, *was* not on the menu.

Do not mistake intervening affirmative or negative expressions for the subject; make the verb agree with the true subject.

INCORRECT   The barn, not the stables, *were* destroyed.

CORRECT   The barn, not the stables, *was* destroyed.

n. The verb agrees with its subject, not with any other words

Make the verb agree with its true subject, not with any word or words after the verb.

INCORRECT   The funniest exhibit *were* the puppets.

CORRECT   The funniest exhibit *was* the puppets.

o. Expletive there is never the subject

Do not be confused by delayed subjects with the expletive *there*. Find the true subject introduced by the expletive *there*. The verb agrees with the subject, not with the expletive.

INCORRECT   There *is* only a few doctors in that clinic: Dr. Harpe, Dr. Foley, and Dr. Bass.

CORRECT   There *are* only a few doctors in that clinic: Dr. Harpe, Dr. Foley, and Dr. Bass.

INCORRECT   There *is* several phones in that room.

CORRECT   There *are* several phones in that room.

p. Use the correct verb when the subject is a clause, phrase, gerund, or infinitive

If the subject is singular, use a singular verb. If the subject is compound, use a plural verb.

CLAUSE   When they will leave *is* no mystery. [Singular]

CLAUSES   When they will leave and how they will travel *are* a mystery. [Plural]

INFINITIVE   To lie *is* wrong. [Singular]

INFINITIVES   To lie and to steal *are* wrong. [Plural]

GERUND   Worrying *makes* me tired. [Singular]

GERUNDS   Worrying and studying *make* me tired. [Plural]

q. The number *is generally singular;* a number *is generally plural*

The subject phrase *the number* is generally singular. The subject phrase *a number* is generally plural.

SINGULAR   *The number* of illiterates *is* quite large.

PLURAL   *A number* of illiterates *are* graduating from high school each year.

r. Numbered items are either singular or plural

If the items form a single unit, the subject is singular and requires the singular verb form.

MONEY   Fifteen dollars *is* too much to pay for a pencil.

Time   Two hours *seems* an eternity to a lover.

Distance   Twenty miles *was* an easy run for McFoote.

Measure   Three gallons of gasoline *takes* us sixty miles.

If each item in the subject can be considered separately, the subject is plural and takes a plural verb form.

Money   Ten dollars *were* placed in two rows on my desk.

Time   The doctor told me that twelve days *are* needed for complete recovery.

Distance   Twenty-six miles *make* up the marathon.

Measure   Thirty pieces of silver *were* scattered about the room.

s. In mathematics, number varies

In multiplication and addition, either singular or plural is acceptable.

Correct   Nine and six *is* fifteen.

Correct   Nine and six *are* fifteen.

In division and subtraction, the singular form of the verb is correct.

Correct   Ten divided by five *is* two.

Correct   Five into ten *goes* two times.

Fractions are singular or plural depending on intended meaning.

Singular   One half of the house *needs* paint. [The house is one unit, and one half of it is thought of as a single unit, too.]

PLURAL One half of the new houses *need* paint. [The houses are countable, hence plural.]

t. Some words have identical singular and plural forms

With words that have identical singular and plural forms, the form of the verb follows intended meaning. A unit requires the singular. Countable items require the plural.

CORRECT Tuna *is* valued for its delicious flavor. [A unit]

CORRECT The tuna *are* swimming upstream. [Many fish]

CORRECT The tuna *is* nibbling on the bait. [One fish]

Some words identical in singular and plural forms are *fish*, *deer*, *sheep*, and *moose*. When in doubt, consult a standard dictionary.

Practice 1: Revise the following sentences to correct any errors in subject-verb agreement.
a. In the new movie *Accident*, there is some amazing slow-motion studies of a female skateboarder.
b. It is true that I be sad many times during the day.
c. The grocery store with all its big officials have given our school one new computer.
d. Tony reads the London *Times* because it are interesting and well written.
e. Worlds of Fun are an amusement park in Kansas City.
f. The new phenomenon are appearing at the stadium tonight.
g. My sisters but not my brother is going to help us.
h. Everyone at Seraph Girls' School own a horse.
i. Most of the food were ready to be put on the tables.

j. Any time Mr. Smith need a loan, he just go into the bank and ask for Mr. Sledge.

Practice 2: Identify and correct any errors in subject-verb agreement in the following sentences.

a. The deer are hiding in its cage.
b. Rod told everyone that he don't know where Jeremy lost the money.
c. The book with the twenty missing pages are on the floor.
d. Most of the cake were eaten by those three children.
e. One half of the stores in this city is open until midnight.
f. A flock of birds are nesting in the oak tree.
g. There are a man with three dogs in the field.
h. How many players is there on the field right now?
i. The losers was the Virginia team.
j. A number of classes this semester was cancelled.

20.4 Verb problems

a. The verb tense signals time

Tense is indicated by inflected endings and auxiliaries, with different forms for the past, present, and future tenses. For regular verbs, past tense is indicated by the addition of the suffix *-d*, or *-ed* (*gaze/gazed*, *spell/spelled*). For irregular verbs, past tense is signaled by a change in spelling (e.g., *see/saw*). See 20.3 and study the term *conjugation* in chapter 24.

Simple	Regular verb	Irregular verb
Present	she touches	she sees
Past	she touched	she saw
Future	she will touch	she will see

Progressive		
Present	she is touching	she is seeing
Past	she was touching	she was seeing
Future	she will be touching	she will be seeing

Perfect		
Present	she has touched	she has seen
Past	she had touched	she had seen
Future	she will have touched	she will have seen

Present. Present tense indicates an action in the present.

> Now the hangover *begins*. [Verb in present tense]

Past. Past tense indicates an action that occurred in the past.

> Henry *wanted* to see the comet. [Past tense of verb]

Future. Future tense indicates action to occur in the future.

> I *will need* some aspirin. [Auxiliary *will* and base of verb *need*]

> I *shall need* some aspirin. [Formal usage]

Present perfect. The present perfect tense indicates an action begun in the past and completed or continuing in the present.

> Susan *has walked* to the park. [*has* + past participle]

> We *have finished* the experiment. [*have* + past participle]

Past perfect. The past perfect tense indicates an action that began and ended in the past.

Joseph *had finished* his homework. [*had* + past participle]

Future perfect. The future perfect tense indicates an action that will begin and be completed in the future.

Mark *will have painted* his room by next Monday. [*will* + *have* + past participle]

Present progressive. The present progressive tense indicates an ongoing present activity.

I *am dancing* on top of this table. [*am* + present participle]

Past progressive. The past progressive tense indicates an ongoing activity in the past.

I *was screaming* at the policeman. [*was* + present participle]

Future progressive. The future progressive tense indicates an ongoing activity in the future.

I *will be enjoying* my vacation in Jamaica. [*will* + *be* + present participle]

b. Present tense is used in special cases

Statements of universal truth

Compassion *makes* us human.

Water *boils* at 100 °C. [Contrast: Kevin boiled the water.]

Statements of habitual or expected action implying the future

The mail *arrives* at ten.

The bus *is departing* for Boston in twenty minutes.

Statements of the contents of literature, art, history

In 1492, Columbus *sets* foot on North America.

In Eliot's Poem, *The Wasteland*, the young man *weeps* after making love to his girlfriend.

c. Any sequence of tenses must be accurate, logical, and consistent

The following examples illustrate some common sequences involving verb tense. For those cases not presented, read the sentence carefully to check for logic and meaning, and adjust the sequences accordingly. The primary consideration is that the sentence expresses what you want it to mean.

✎ If the main clause contains a present-tense verb, the dependent clause generally contains a verb in the present tense.

PRESENT   While the teacher *speaks* the class *remains*
+ PRESENT silent.

✎ If the main clause contains a verb in the past tense, the dependent clause generally contains a verb in the past tense.

PAST   While the teacher *spoke* the class *remained* silent.
+ PAST

✎ If the main clause contains a verb in the past perfect or past tense, the dependent clause verb is generally past or past perfect.

PAST PERFECT   Indians *had lived* here long before the
+ PAST   settlers *arrived.*

PAST   The rose *died* of the pesticide after I *had*
+ PAST PERFECT   *sprayed* it.

✎ If the main clause contains a verb in the future perfect, the dependent clause verb is generally present tense.

FUTURE PERFECT This car *will have stopped* running long
+ PRESENT   before I *make* my final loan payment.

✎ If the main clause contains a verb in the past progressive tense, the dependent clause verb is generally in a past tense.

PAST PROGRESSIVE I *was listening* to the radio when I first
+ PAST   *smelled* the chemicals.

✎ Present infinitive signals action at the same time or later than the verb.

PRESENT INFINITIVE I want *to visit* Madrid.

PRESENT INFINITIVE Steve wanted *to meet* President Bush.

✎ Present perfect infinitive signals action earlier than the main verb.

PRESENT PERFECT I wanted *to have learned* Spanish before
INFINITIVE   my trip to Madrid.

PRESENT PERFECT   My employer wanted *to have been in-*
INFINITIVE   *formed* of my plans for vacation.

  ✎   Present participle signals action at the same time
      as the main verb.

PRESENT PARTICIPLE   *Listening* to the evening news, I will
                      fall asleep.

PRESENT PARTICIPLE   While *running* in the park, I saw a
                      hideous accident.

  ✎   Past or present perfect participle signals earlier
      action than the main verb.

PRESENT PERFECT   After *having seen* a film on Madrid, I
PARTICPLE   wrote a poem.

PAST PARTICIPLE   The cars *washed*, we opened a few
                  cans of cold soda.

  ✎   Compound verbs are in the same tense.

COMPOUND PRESENT   Hartwick *catches* the football and
                     races into the end zone.

COMPOUND PAST   Hartwick *caught* the football and
                  raced into the end zone.

Practice 1: Correct the sequence errors in the following
sentences.
a. While the dog barked, the class is silent.
b. When the wind blows, the flag made a loud, snapping
    sound.
c. When I lose my diamond ring, I was lying on the beach.
d. When I first heard Mahler's symphony, I will be in my
    backyard.

e. Jean picked up the tennis racquet and serves the ball to her opponent.

Practice 2: Explain the differences between the paired verbs in italics in the following sentences.
a. Clark Kent walked into the grocery just as the robber *pulled/was pulling* out a pistol.
b. The children *talked/have been talking* about airplanes.
c. Mary *had called* out/*was calling* out for help.
d. The room *does seem/seems* very bright and cheerful.
e. The teacher *spoke/should have spoken* to Bradley's parents.

d. Correct verb forms should be used

It is important for effective writing to avoid verb-form errors.

INCORRECT That boy has *broke* his ankle again.

CORRECT That boy has *broken* his ankle again.

INCORRECT The guard *seen* how the car *spinned* out of control.

CORRECT The guard *saw* how the car *spun* out of control.

The three principal parts of any verb are the present infinitive, the past tense, and the past participle. These vary slightly depending on whether the verb is a regular verb (e.g., *love, loved, loved*) or an irregular verb (e.g., *do, did, done*). Regular verbs form the past and the past participle by adding *-d, -ed,* or *-t*. A dictionary is the key to a verb's status.

Infinitive	Past	Past participle
attack	attacked	attacked
drag	dragged	dragged
drown	drowned	drowned
dwell	dwelt	dwelt

The dictionary lists the following forms of an irregular verb: present infinitive, past tense, past participle, and present participle. Occasionally past tense and past participle are identical. The following is a list of some common irregular verbs. For other verbs, consult the dictionary.

Present tense	Past tense	Past participle
am/is/are	was/were	been
arise	arose	arisen
beat	beat	beaten
become	became	become
begin	began	begun
blow	blew	blown
break	broke	broken
bring	brought	brought
choose	chose	chosen
come	came	come
do	did	done
draw	drew	drawn
drink	drank	drunk
drive	drove	driven
eat	ate	eaten
fall	fell	fallen
feed	fed	fed
feel	felt	felt
fly	flew	flown

Present tense	*Past tense*	*Past participle*
forgive	forgave	forgiven
freeze	froze	frozen
give	gave	given
go	went	gone
grow	grew	grown
know	knew	known
lay [place or put]	laid	laid
lead	led	led
leave	left	left
lend	lent	lent
lose	lost	lost
ride	rode	ridden
ring	rang	rung
run	ran	run
say	said	said
see	saw	seen
send	sent	sent
shake	shook	shaken
shrink	shrank	shrunk
sing	sang	sung
sink	sank	sunk
speak	spoke	spoken
spin	spun	spun
spring	sprang	sprung
steal	stole	stolen
stick	stuck	stuck
strike	struck	struck or stricken
swear	swore	sworn
swim	swam	swum
take	took	taken
tear	tore	torn
throw	threw	thrown
wake	waked or woke	waked or woken
wind	wound	wound
wring	wrung	wrung
write	wrote	written

e. *The verbs* lie, lay, raise, rise, sit, *and* set *need to be used correctly*

The following verbs are commonly misused. Learn their meanings and forms.

Present	Past	Past participle	Meaning
lie	lay	lain	to rest, to recline
lay	laid	laid	to place, to put
raise	raised	raised	to lift
rise	rose	risen	to move up
sit	sat	sat	to be seated
set	set	set	to place, to put

LAY   The workers are ready to *lay* the carpet.

LAID   Mike *laid* the roses at the girl's feet.

LIE   Mike *lies* down for a nap every afternoon at 5:00.

LAY   Yesterday Mike *lay* all day in bed.

RISE   Can you see the smoke *rise* from the chimney?

RAISE   Mike *raised* his hand.

SIT   The judge *sits* down to watch the late news.

SET   Mike *set* his drink down on the table.

Practice 3: Choose the correct verb form in each of the following sentences. Then write four sentences of your own using the verbs *lie*, *lay*, *sit*, and *set*.

a. If you (lie, lay) down your rifle, we can begin to talk about where your child will (sit, set) in class from now on.

b. If you (lie, lay) down on this featherbed, you will fall asleep in a few minutes and not be able to (rise, raise) until the morning.

c. If you (lay, laid) on the carpet, you probably saw some fleas (sitting, setting) on the windowsill.

d. If you want to (lie, lay) the carpet, you will need to get the tools that I (sat, set) on the back porch.

e. If you lie to me one more time, I will (raise, rise) my voice and say goodbye forever.

f. The subjunctive mood may be used when appropriate

The subjunctive mood is occasionally used in American English today to convey distinct shades of meaning. In formal writing, the subjunctive is used in a subordinate clause to express condition contrary to fact, command, necessity, wish, request, or the expression of a formal motion.

INDICATIVE   Bill Davis *buys* his new car today.

IMPERATIVE   *Buy* a new car today.

SUBJUNCTIVE If Bill *were* rich, he would buy a Rolls Royce. [Condition contrary to fact]

SUBJUNCTIVE His children demanded that Bill *buy* a new car. [Command]

SUBJUNCTIVE It is necessary that Bill *buy* a new car. [Necessity]

SUBJUNCTIVE Bill wishes that a new car *were* in the driveway. [Wish]

SUBJUNCTIVE Bill asked that they *be* patient. [Request]

SUBJUNCTIVE Bill made a motion that his club *buy* a new car. [Formal motion]

20.5 Pronoun problems

a. Agreement: A pronoun must agree in number with its antecedent

SINGULAR The *boy* wants a dog, and *he* wants a Doberman.

PLURAL The *parents* want a dog, but *they* do not want a poodle.

PLURAL The *cobra* and the *python* are asleep in *their* cages.

PLURAL The owner of the pet store would like to sell *them*.

A singular pronoun requires a singular antecedent

An antecedent is the word to which a pronoun refers. Some common singular pronouns are *he, she, it, one, each, anyone, anybody, everyone, everybody, either, no one, nobody, another, someone, somebody.*

INCORRECT When *anyone* in the boys' choir sang well, *they* received praise. [*Anyone* is singular. *They* is plural.]

CORRECT When *anyone* in the boys' choir sang well, *he* received praise. [*Anyone* and *he* are both singular.]

INCORRECT *Everyone* in the sorority has *their* own room.

CORRECT *Everyone* in the sorority has *her* own room.

A plural pronoun requires a plural antecedent

Plural pronouns such as *both*, *few*, *others*, *many*, *these*, *those*, and *several* always refer to plural antecedents.

INCORRECT The Dean *brothers* are reckless; *he* likes to drive drunk.

CORRECT The Dean *brothers* are reckless; *both* like to drive drunk.

INCORRECT Jane wrote *poems*; *many* had despair as *its* theme.

CORRECT Jane wrote *poems*; *many* had despair as *their* theme.

Pronouns with variable number are singular or plural depending on intended meaning

A few pronouns vary in number, depending on whether the reference is to a single unit or a group of items. Some common pronouns with variable number are *which*, *who*, *that* (relative), *all*, *any*, *most*, *some*, and *such*. Consider such pronouns singular or plural depending on their antecedents.

CORRECT We skated on the lake today. *Most* of it is frozen. [*Most* is singular because it refers to *lake*.]

CORRECT The girls were hungry. *Most* were ordering large sandwiches. [*Most* is plural because it refers to *girls*.]

A relative pronoun has the same number as its antecedent

Common relative pronouns are *which*, *what*, *that*, *whatever*, and the forms of *who* and *whoever*.

CORRECT   *Children who* live on candy may lose *their* teeth.

CORRECT   A *boy who* lives on candy may lose *his* teeth.

b. Reference: Pronoun reference must be clear

For clear understanding, a pronoun must have an obvious, logical antecedent and must clearly refer back to it. As a general principle, a pronoun usually refers to the closest preceding and most sensible antecedent.

> Jayne drives a new Porsche. *She* bought *that* for *herself.* As a medical doctor, Jayne commuted to a hospital *that* was fifty miles from *her* home. Last Tuesday, when *she* stopped for gas at Boomer, *she* noticed a bus. *It* was packed with Japanese tourists, *most* of *whom* stayed on board.

Avoid ambiguous pronoun reference

Ambiguity arises when the reader cannot tell what noun the pronoun refers to. Each pronoun needs a clear and obvious antecedent. In an ambiguous sentence, the pronoun might be moved closer to the clearly intended antecedent, or an intervening element can be moved out of the way to improve reference clarity.

AMBIGUOUS   When Jeff saw Larry, *he* waved. [Who waved? Jeff or Larry?]

REVISED   Larry waved when *he* saw Jeff.

AMBIGUOUS   Some children talk about their parents as if *they* were idiots. [Who are the idiots? Parents or children?]

REVISED   Some children talk like idiots about *their* parents.

Avoid hidden or imprecise reference

Each pronoun should have a clear reference. Avoid an implied antecedent contained in another noun, verb, adjective, or phrase.

HIDDEN   The tourist photographed the garden, but *it* was blurred. [To what does *it* refer?]

REVISED   The tourist photographed the garden, but the snapshot was blurred.

HIDDEN   The freshman enjoyed the rush party because *they* were friendly. [To what does *they* refer?]

REVISED   The freshman enjoyed the rush party because the fraternity members were friendly.

IMPRECISE Betty loved Italian wines. *It* was her favorite country. [The pronoun *it* seems to refer to a word inside the adjective *Italian*.]

REVISED   Since Betty's favorite country was Italy, she loved Italian wines.

Avoid general reference

Pronouns such as *it*, *such*, *this*, *that*, and *which* may refer not only to a single antecedent but to a preceding general idea. Unless the pronoun is used carefully, a reader may be confused.

SPECIFIC   Jean-Paul devoured the quiche; *it* contained
REFERENCE mushrooms and eggs. [*It* refers specifically to *quiche*.]

GENERAL   Jean-Paul loves fine foods, rare wines, exotic
REFERENCE delicacies, and rich pastries, but *it* shows in his waistline. [Here *it* does not have a specific antecedent, but instead refers to the general idea in the preceding clause.]

REVISED   Jean-Paul loves fine foods, rare wines, exotic
          delicacies, and rich pastries, but that love
          shows in his waistline.

Because general reference can easily create ambiguity in
meaning, some teachers require specific references for the
pronouns *it, such, this, that,* and *which.*

Practice 1: Revise the following sentences to eliminate
pronoun errors.

a. Mark begins working for Tom Upton next week, but
   they want him to wear a suit to work.
b. I wanted to work at the library, but they were closed.
c. The dog and the cat are playing in the yard. It is chasing
   a squirrel.
d. Everyone in the class failed their test.
e. All of our dogs takes good care of itself.
f. Each tree in the garden has their own brass name tag.
g. Maria wants to run in the Charleston marathon because
   they give a cash prize.
h. When Rodney looked at the birds, he saw that it had a
   broken wing.
i. The classroom is full of students. It is freshmen.
j. Lola wanted to see Landon's number and address in
   the directory but could not find it.

c. Pronoun case depends on function

Formal English uses *I, he, she,* and *who* for subjects and
me, him, her, and *whom* for objects. Pronoun case presents
problems in a number of special situations.

Case in compound constructions

Make sure the case of each personal pronoun reflects
its function in the sentence.

SUBJECT PRONOUN	Jim and *I* bought new bicycles.
OBJECT PRONOUN	My father gave Steve and *me* new bicycles.
INCORRECT	The road map puzzled Steve and *I*.
CORRECT	The road map puzzled Steve and *me*.
INCORRECT	*Hank* and *myself* bothered the teacher.
CORRECT	*Hank* and *I* bothered the teacher.
INCORRECT	*Her* and Gloria like to race motorcycles.
CORRECT	*She* and Gloria like to race motorcycles.

Case with appositives

Pronoun case in an appositive depends on the function of the noun it is in apposition to. If the pronoun is in apposition with a subject, use the subjective case. If the pronoun is in apposition with an object, use the objective case.

INCORRECT	*Us* cab drivers need protection against muggers.
CORRECT	*We* cab drivers need protection against muggers.
INCORRECT	Muggers seem to like *we* cab drivers. [*We* is a subject pronoun, but the object is *cab drivers*.]
CORRECT	Muggers seem to like *us* cab drivers.

Case with *as* and *than*

Choose the correct subject or object pronoun when using the conjunction *as* or *than*. The sentence, *Celia loves music as much as George*, has two possible meanings, depending on how the elliptical clause, *as much as George*, is interpreted.

MEANING A Celia loves music as much as George [loves music].

MEANING B Celia loves music as much as [Celia loves] George.

MEANING A Celia loves music as much as he.

MEANING B Celia loves music as much as him.

Be aware that such elliptical clauses create sentences with a double meaning. Decide which meaning you intend. Then use either the appropriate subject or the object pronoun.

Case of *who* and *whom*

In formal writing, use the correct form of *who* or *whom*. *Who* is always the form for subjects and *whom* is always the form for the object.

SUBJECT *Who* teaches at Miller School? [Compare: Mike teaches at Miller School.]

OBJECT *Whom* did the teacher praise? [The subject is *teacher*. Compare: *The teacher praised Bill.*]

OBJECT At *whom* did the teacher scream? [*Whom* is the object of the preposition *at*. Compare: *The teacher screamed at Bill.*]

SUBJECT The superintendent hired a person *who* teaches art. [*Who* functions as the subject of the verb *teaches* in the dependent adjective clause.]

OBJECT   The coach knew *whom* the teacher punished. [In the dependent clause, the subject is *teacher* and the object of the verb *punished* is *whom.* Compare: *The coach knew that the teacher punished Jim.*]

NOTE: Ignore intervening material when choosing between *who* or *whom.* Do not allow intervening material to influence your choice of pronoun case. Neither parenthetical phrases nor prepositions before noun clauses change the grammar of any noun clause with *who* or *whom* in it.

INCORRECT   Smith is the man whom, I believe, damaged my car.

CORRECT.   Smith is the man who, I believe, damaged my car. [*I* is the subject of the verb *believe,* but *who* is the subject of the verb *damaged.*]

INCORRECT   The judge was thinking about whom would catch the largest fish. [*Whom* is not an object in this sentence.]

CORRECT   The judge was thinking about who would catch the largest fish. [*Who* is the subject of the verb *would catch.*]

Possessive case before a gerund

INCORRECT   You dancing made the audience laugh.

CORRECT   Your dancing made the audience laugh.

CONFUSING   The father praised the child singing. [Does the father praise the child, or the singing, or both?]

CLEAR   The father praised the child's singing.

CORRECT   The father praised the singing child.

Object pronoun case with infinitives

For both the subject and the object of an infinitive, use a pronoun in the object case: *me, him, her, us, them,* or *whom.*

CORRECT The manager asked *me* to mop the floor.

CORRECT Jesse wanted to help *me.*

Practice 2: Revise the following sentences to clarify meaning and correct any pronoun errors.

a. My father and me painted the kitchen.
b. The exhausted horses fell asleep in its barn.
c. The players wanted the coach to let they choose the team's mascot.
d. A girl who eats five candy bars every day is going to give themselves a problem with tooth decay.
e. I read about Michael Jordan's game. It has to be a new record.
f. The nine inmates divided the food among theirselves.
g. When the bear played with the mountain lion, he was tired.
h. Mr. Jackson spoke to Randy and then to Bill. He told him that the track meet had been postponed.
i. During the game against Lincoln, the Fairbury players complained about his penalties.
j. Harry told Brad that he would have to go to the grocery store for milk.

Practice 3: Revise the following sentences to eliminate any problems with pronoun reference.

a. Henry searched Larry's dorm room for the album that his father had sent him.

b. Steve enjoyed fishing, but he had never been a good one.

c. Rebecca likes her Spanish class this semester. They are all very friendly.

d. Lord Byron loved Greece because they were great revolutionaries.

e. Patrick failed chemistry but received an *A* in both algebra and geography. It will disturb his parents.

f. Solano and Krebs wrote some reports on the bus schedules. They are very confusing.

g. Lana and Henry apologized for disturbing the neighbors. They were very embarrassed.

h. If you talk to a lawyer, they will generally say the same thing.

i. We are sending our daughter to Miller School. We are confident that when we meet the teachers we will like her.

j. Mary just had a new baby boy. It is healthy and very lively.

d. Personal pronouns

Certain problems constantly occur in writing that involve the use of the personal pronouns *I*, *you*, *he*, and *she*. Some people actually believe, for one reason or another, that the personal pronouns *I* and *me* must never be used. Because such a commandment would destroy the possibility of autobiography or personal essay writing, that warning must be carefully qualified. Although it is true that formal writing is impersonal and objective, some legitimate kinds of personal writing necessarily involve the use of first-person pronouns. The personal pronouns *I* and *me* generally have no place in research papers, technical reports, and proposals, but personal pronouns may properly be used in writing autobiography or first-person narrative. In all cases, the policy of the instructor or editor must be known and taken into account.

Similarly, a problem arises with the use of *you* in formal essays. The safest guideline to follow for using *you* is to avoid it unless you are actually addressing the reader in terms of directions or warnings. The following example, submitted to a male instructor, shows what problems might arise with the careless use of *you*:

> And then to the right is my grandmother's old cedar cabinet. Inside you can still see her wedding dress. When you put it on, you will see the beautiful white silk, the full bodice, and the rows of pearl buttons.

NOTE: When the possibility of misunderstanding is minimal, writers on occasion use the pronoun *you*, especially when providing directions, instructions, or a process analysis.

20.6 Adjective and adverb errors

An adjective modifies (tells something about) a person, place, or thing in a sentence. An adverb modifies (tells something about) a verb, adjective, or other adverbs in the sentence. Don't use one for the other.

ADJECTIVE The *happy* child gave his father a big kiss.

ADVERB The child danced *happily* across the wide lawn. [One would never say *A happily child danced.*]

a. Use the words good and well correctly. Understand their meanings

CORRECT A *good* teacher enjoys reading. [*Good* is an adjective modifying *teacher.*]

CORRECT This apple is *good*. [*Good* is an adjective following the linking verb *is.*]

CORRECT The president was *sick*, but now he is *well*. [Here the word *well* is an adjective that means *healthy.*]

CORRECT Despite the heat, Juan played *well* during the game. [In this instance, *well* is an adverb indicating how Juan played. He could have played badly, but he played well.]

b. The suffix -ly is a clear adverb signal in formal writing

Not all forms of the adverb end in *-ly.* Use the dictionary to determine whether a form is an adjective or an adverb. Readers appreciate the signal an *-ly* ending gives to an adverb. They can sense immediately the adverb *quickly* in the sentence *John quickly finished his homework.* When in doubt, use the *-ly* form for adverbs. Some adjectives and adverbs—such as *fast, straight, hard*—have the same form. Use your dictionary to discover these forms.

INFORMAL The car moved *slow* through thick traffic.

FORMAL The car *slowly* moved through thick traffic.

c. Use adjectives for subject complements after linking verbs

A verb, such as *feel*, *look*, *smell*, and *taste*, is a linking verb (see 18.2) if you can substitute a form of *to be* for it and not damage the meaning, as in the following sentences:

CORRECT Jane feels *sleepy*. [*Feels* is a linking verb. *Jane* is the subject. *Sleepy* is the subject complement. Compare: *Jane is sleepy*.]

CORRECT The strawberries taste *bitter*. [Compare: *The strawberries are bitter*. Contrast: *Lance complained bitterly about the strawberries*.]

CORRECT The rose smelled *sweet*. [You wouldn't write *The rose smelled sweetly* because that would give the rose a nose.]

CORRECT Mary looked *angry*. [The sentence explains what Mary looked like. Contrast: *Mary looked angrily at her mother*. *Angrily* explains how Mary looked at her parent. *Angry* is an adjective. *Angrily* is an adverb.]

d. Use comparative and superlative forms correctly

Many adjectives and adverbs regularly form the comparative and superlative by using *more/less*, *most/least*, or *-er/-est*. Several adverbs and adjectives have irregular forms.

Positive	Comparative	Superlative
bad	worse	worst
eagerly	less eagerly	least eagerly
eagerly	more eagerly	most eagerly
far	farther	farthest
good	better	best
greedy	less greedy	least greedy
happy	happier	happiest
unhappy	more unhappy	most unhappy
well	better	best

The comparative form is used for two items and the superlative for three or more

COMPARATIVE   English is *harder* to learn than French. [Two languages are compared.]

SUPERLATIVE   Some people say that English is the *hardest* language to learn. [More than two languages are referred to.]

Absolute adjectives should not be compared

Absolute adjectives (such as *perfect, unique, infinite, impossible, round, square, destroyed,* and *extinct*) do not have degree.

CURIOUS   The quarterback completed a *most perfect* pass.

IMPROVED   The quarterback completed a *perfect* pass.

A comparative form is not doubled

NONSTANDARD   This new album is *more better* than the last one.

STANDARD   This new album is *better* than the last one.

A superlative form is not doubled

NONSTANDARD Sarah had the *most happiest* birthday party ever.

STANDARD Sarah had the *happiest* birthday party ever.

Use *more* or *most* with trisyllabic adverbs or adjectives

CURIOUS She had the *wonderfulest* parents.

CORRECT She had the *most wonderful* parents.

CURIOUS Jake was *competenter* than Luke.

CORRECT Jake was *more competent* than Luke.

e. Use adjectives or possessives as modifiers instead of nouns

Avoid using nouns and strings of nouns as adjectives. If possible, use a one-word adjective, a participle, or a possessive form for modification.

WORDY The *college telephone address information directory* has a gold cover this year.

REVISED The *collegiate directory* has a gold color this year.

CONFUSING The child cried at the *doctor office*.

REVISED The child cried at the *doctor's office*. [A possessive form replaces a simple noun in the example.]

Practice 1: Choose verbs from the following list of linking verbs (*appear, become, remain, seem, feel, look, sound, smell*) and write six sentences imitating the following pattern:

Pattern	Subject	Linking verb	Subject complement
Sample	Her dress	looks	funny.

Practice 2.: Correct any mistakes in the following sentences.

a. The funniest of the two movies will receive an award.
b. Jane does her job good and will receive a large bonus.
c. I looked quickly at the picture and began to feel badly.
d. The Nikon X-825 is the most unique camera in the world.
e. Kevin seemed more friendlier than your brother.
f. *Last Tango in Paris* is one real sad movie, which proves that Marlon Brando is possible the greatest living actor.
g. The obnoxiously odors seeped into our house.
h. The experimentalist design for an automobile was done by an Italian student.
i. Jesse calm sat down in his seat.
j. The little kitten hid frightenedly in the garden.

20.7 Faulty parallelism

Parallelism can be an effective device to improve readability, increase comprehension, and add variety. Parallelism is the use of similar grammatical forms to express similar ideas. A disruption in similarity of meaning or similarity of grammatical structure creates faulty parallelism and weak writing.

NONPARALLEL   Ralph accused his father of acting like a *coward*, *being cheap*, *deceit*, and *thinking only of himself.*

PARALLEL   Ralph accused his father of *cowardice*, *cheapness*, *deceit*, and *selfishness.*

NONPARALLEL   Children here learn *to play*, *reading*, and *they write.*

PARALLEL   Children here learn *to play*, *to read*, and *to write.*

Use parallel structures in both drafting and revising. Practice the different forms of parallelism: words, phrases, dependent clauses, independent clauses, and sentences.

Parallel words

NOUNS   The *rats*, *parrots*, and *guinea pigs* are all on sale.

VERBS   All night the drummer was *banging*, *pounding*, and *thumping* on his new drum.

ADJECTIVES   The *wild*, *hypnotic*, *ecstatic* guitars faded out after the singer began his song.

Parallel phrases

NOUN   The *girls in their summer dresses* and the *boys in their tropical suits* walked along the beach.

PREPOSITIONAL   The boat glided *through the tangled vines, across the bayou, past the oil platforms* and docked at Sid's Marina and Bait Shop.

INFINITIVE   Some students come to college prepared *to attend every class, listen to every lecture, read all the books,* and *study for exams.*

Parallel dependent clauses

ADJECTIVE The cookie *that tastes like your grandmother made it, that has only twenty calories, that costs less than a nickel,* and *that is compatible with all diets*—this cookie, sad to say, does not exist.

ADVERB   *After he talked to his friends, after he read every issue of "Consumer Reports" for the past five years,* and *after he spent days talking to salesmen,* Keith went to the K-Mart and bought a cheap, but good, imitation Walkman manufactured in Milwaukee.

NOUN   *Whoever loves the sound of words, whoever has a vivid imagination, whoever values ideas and emotion,* and *whoever respects the truth*—such a person has the potential to be a poet.

Parallel independent clauses

CLAUSES I came; I saw; I conquered.

CLAUSES Candy is dandy, but liquor is quicker. *Dorothy Parker*

Parallel sentences

SENTENCES While my brother studied in college, I examined the flavors of rum. While he slaved in medical school, I studied the tan girls in Malibu. Now while he lives in comfort, style, and grace, I subsist on food stamps, TV dinners, and old *Lassie* reruns.

SENTENCES Mathematics will teach you the rules of logic. Lust will teach you that you have a body. Love will teach you that other people exist just like you.

Practice 1: Point out examples of parallelism in the following sentences. Then write sentences of your own imitating the parallel structures.

a. We wanted to go camping in the woods, sailing on the lake, and fishing in the bay.

b. If you think that English Composition is difficult, if you think that Chemistry 101 is impossible, if you have learned that Calculus 103 is unpassable, wait until you are the parent of a teenage child. Then you'll understand the meaning of failure.

c. "Tenderness . . . lives past words, opposes nothing, feeds all perception, cares for no concern past feeling." *Susan Griffin*

d. A picture is both silent and speaking, both light and dark, both colorful and colorless, both new and old— just like the world and just like our lives.

e. "Carnal and witty, chivalrous but not soft, these men do something in the world with pride and success and have graciously retained the wildness of adolescence." *David Denby*

f. Shelley wrote poems about the beauty of Greece, the glory of Rome, and the desolation of England.

a. *Various devices signal parallel structures*

Prepositions can show parallelism

NONPARALLEL Along the crowded highway, passed the deserted town, passing the dusty footpath, the old hospital, a group of weary men marched.

PARALLEL *Along* the crowded highway, *through* the deserted town, and *up* the dusty footpath *to* the old hospital, a group of weary men marched.

NONPARALLEL With love and having plenty of intelligence, energy, she was able to teach young people who had never before thought of learning.

PARALLEL *With* love, *with* intelligence, and *with* plenty of energy, she was able to teach young people who had never before thought of learning.

The definite article *the* or the indefinite articles *a* or *an* can emphasize parallelism

UNEMPHASIZED James spoke of way, truth, and light.

EMPHASIZED James spoke of *the* way, *the* truth, and *the* light.

UNEMPHASIZED Banana, peach, pear are what I want for lunch.

EMPHASIZED *A* banana, *a* peach, and *a* pear are what I want for lunch.

Infinitives can show parallelism

NONPARALLEL Kevin wants a major in astronomy, skiing each weekend, work on his car, and a date with Dolly Parton.

PARALLEL Kevin wants *to major* in astronomy, *to ski* each weekend, *to work* on his car, and *to date* Dolly Parton.

NONPARALLEL Our school motto should be "Building a strong body and to form a strong mind."

PARALLEL Our school motto should be "*To build* a strong body and *to form* a strong mind."

An initial word repeated can show parallelism

AWKWARD On the lake sunlight at dawn, the sun at noon bright on the highway, the last light on the river at sunset, at midnight the moonlight on the windows; all these are the memories of a single summer's day.

CLEARER *Remembering* the sunlight on the lake at dawn, *remembering* the bright glare on the highway at noon, *remembering* the faint light on the river at sunset, *remembering* the moonlight on the windows at midnight—all these are the memories of a single summer's day.

And who, and whom, or *and which* should parallel a *who, whom,* or *which* clause

NONPARALLEL John Carter is a coach with an interest in Little League and who wants to start a youth soccer league.

PARALLEL	John Carter is a coach *who* has an interest in Little League *and who* wants to start a youth soccer league.
NONPARALLEL	This ice cream will please people who are on a diet and which has plenty of cherries.
PARALLEL	This ice cream will please people *who* are on a diet *and who* like plenty of cherries.

Correlative conjunctions can emphasize parallel structures

BOTH . . . AND	Professor Glange explained *both* the causes of alcoholism *and* the effects of drug addiction.
NEITHER . . . NOR	*Neither* the music of Beethoven *nor* the poetry of Shakespeare can lift my spirits.
EITHER . . . OR	I have no way of knowing why *either* my father wants to go swimming in December *or* why my mother wants to go skiing in June.
NOT ONLY . . . BUT ALSO	*Not only* are high school teachers grossly underpaid *but* they *also* have to tolerate critical parents and deal with disrespectful students.
WHETHER . . . OR	Smithers cannot make up his mind *whether* to retire now *or* to wait until he is sixty-five.

Use parallel structures when creating comparisons with *than* or *as*

NONPARALLEL Smelling roses is less idiotic than to sniff cocaine.

PARALLEL *Smelling roses* is less idiotic than *sniffing cocaine.*

NONPARALLEL This test is difficult as the teacher gave earlier.

PARALLEL *This test* is as difficult as *the one* the teacher gave earlier.

Practice 2: Revise the following sentences in terms of parallel structure.

a. Was it your brother who talked about to ski and ice skating?

b. Kris had several alternatives; she could go to school, finding a job, or to join the army.

c. Either a lunch in the park or where Hank and Julie went to lunch at the mall would be a good idea.

d. The lecturer explained schizophrenia, which is a radical disturbance in thinking, and depression with a radical change in mood and emotion.

e. The losing team was silent when on the field and in an unhappy frame of mind in the locker room and tended to be noisy on the bus.

f. The joyful mother watched her child run on the sidewalk and playing in the sand.

g. My father was a man who once lost $50,000, with gambling in his blood, and who was fantastically lucky.

h. Playing football, working Sundays at his church, and five classes was hard for Owen.

i. Poetry is both exciting to my mind and it is emotionally satisfying.
j. The guests will arrive by boat, by driving a car, or some flying in.
k. Having vast sums of money is less meaningful than to be happy.
l. That man makes me want to debate and showing him the truth.

20.8 Dangling and misplaced modifiers

a. Avoid dangling modifiers

A dangling modifier is a word or word group that modifies an element that the sentence does not have. Common dangling constructions involve participles, prepositional phrases, infinitives, or clauses.

DANGLING   *Walking down the street*, the car had an accident. [The participle phrase *walking down the street* has no word to modify in the sentence.]

REVISED   Walking down the street, the old man was hit by a car.

A writer needs to connect the dangling modifier to an element within the sentence. Generally, the addition, deletion, or moving of a few words will clarify the meaning.

Dangling participles

DANGLING   *Hearing the weather report*, the snow began falling.

REVISED   After hearing the weather report, Kaye watched the snow begin to fall.

DANGLING   *Having burned out*, the janitor made the replacement.

REVISED   The janitor replaced the burned-out light bulb.

Dangling prepositional phrases

DANGLING   *Without leaving the house*, the water in the backyard can be turned on. [The sentence seems to have the water stay inside the house.]

REVISED   Without leaving the house, Henry can turn on the water in his backyard.

DANGLING   *After being kissed by her grandson*, a large stain appeared on Marie's new silk dress. [The sentence seems to suggest that the large stain was somehow kissed.]

REVISED   After Marie kissed her grandson, a large stain appeared on her new silk dress.

Dangling infinitives

DANGLING   *Unable to speak*, the teacher mentioned my grade of *A*.

REVISED   After the teacher told me I had earned an *A*, I was unable to speak.

DANGLING   *To learn about the stock market*, money is necessary. [The sentence lacks an actor and seems to suggest that the money will learn something.]

REVISED   To learn about the stock market, an investor needs money.

Dangling clauses

DANGLING   *When thrown from the saddle*, the horse might kick. [The sentence seems to suggest that the horse, not the rider, is thrown.]

REVISED   When thrown from the saddle, a rider might be kicked by the horse.

DANGLING   *Asked about the broken window*, silence filled the child's room.

REVISED   When the child was asked about the broken window, he was silent.

Practice 1: Revise each of the following sentences by clarifying all modifiers.

a. Mowing grass for four hours, a cold soda seemed a good reward.
b. Having just read the chapter on genetics, the filmstrip on the nucleus was requested for study.
c. By closing the refrigerator, the pizza was kept out of sight.
d. To be safe in the chemistry laboratory, the rules painted on the door must be followed exactly.
e. While walking down the highway, a police car sped by.
f. After studying biology, a bug becomes a very complex organism.
g. While repairing the damage, the window frames were destroyed.

h. To avoid failing this course, the teacher should give individual instruction.

i. When cooked on the grill, the kids love the flavor.

j. Instead of watering the garden, flight was taken from the snake.

k. To cook the steak, the skillet was greased.

b. Avoid misplaced modifiers

The placement of modifiers within a sentence can radically affect the meaning.

> Max, *who was looking for a ride*, talked to Sidney.

> Max talked to Sidney, *who was looking for a ride*.

Generally, modifiers limit the sentence element they are closest to.

MISPLACED The book fell on Homer's head *that was missing*.

REVISED The book that was missing fell on Homer's head.

Commonly, misplaced modifiers involve misplaced words, misplaced phrases, misplaced clauses, ambiguous or "squinting" modifiers, or awkward interruptions.

Misplaced words

MISPLACED *Hot and cheesy,* the cook removed the pizza from the oven.

REVISED The cook removed the hot, cheesy pizza from the oven.

Misplaced phrases

MISPLACED   Sally asked Bob to go to the dance *in a letter.*
[The sentence seems to suggest the dance is in a letter.]

REVISED   In a letter, Sally asked Bob to go to the dance.

Misplaced clauses

MISPLACED   We saw a computer at the K-Mart *that had two disk drives.*

REVISED   At the K-Mart, we saw a computer that had two disk drives.

Ambiguous modifiers: Squinters

These modifiers occur in the middle of two other constructions. They point two ways. Often the reader has difficulty with the meaning.

SQUINTER   The old chair I was painting *slowly* rocked. [Did the chair rock slowly? Or did the person paint slowly?]

REVISED   The old chair I was painting rocked slowly.

REVISED   The old chair I was slowly painting rocked.

Interrupting constructions

Occasionally a writer will place a group of words within a sentence so that meaning becomes confused. Sometimes these chunks of language resemble roadblocks that a reader must go around.

INTERRUPTION   My father did, taking pictures of everyone with his new camera, delay dinner for two hours.

REVISED   Taking pictures of everyone with his new camera, my father delayed dinner for two hours.

Split infinitives

The split infinitive has been a part of the English language since its earliest days. Many well-educated and well-meaning people believe that a split infinitive is best avoided. In our ordinary speech, a split infinitive is scarcely noticed, as in the sentence *Jesse wants us to quickly leave the party.* Occasionally, a split infinitive with only a single interrupting modifier creates a negative response in many readers. You are best advised, as a beginning writer, to avoid the construction in formal writing.

SPLIT INFINITIVE   The cook began to gently turn the omelet.

REVISED   The cook began to turn the omelet gently.

One kind of split infinitive, however, does create substantial problems in meaning and clarity. That is an interrupter with more than a few words. Almost always, such split infinitives need revision, generally the removal of interrupting material within the infinitive.

AWKWARD   The cab driver planned to, in order to buy his wife an expensive present for her birthday, work an extra hour each day for a year.

REVISED   To buy his wife an expensive present for her birthday, the cab driver planned to work an extra hour each day for a year.

Practice 2: Revise each of the following sentences to correct any errors in modification or interruption. Add, remove, or rearrange words if necessary. If the sentence is correct, mark *C* in the margin.

a. The coach asked us to immediately and completely clear everything out of the locker room.
b. The students have begun to for their writing classes use word processors.
c. After the accident, Jethro wrote a note on the windshield and left it on a piece of paper.
d. That man used mirrors on his bald head to tattoo the picture of an owl.
e. For a hundred years I have repaired this chair to last.
f. The new sports center will prove attractive to students with three basketball courts and a swimming pool.
g. My brother was attacked by a large cat reading a book.
h. I have many—in the dormitory—good friends.
i. The quarterback wore an old sweater with a large stain that had been crying.
j. Jay pointed to the photograph of the dog with his hand.

20.9 Lack of variety

Variety adds interest and emphasis to any writing. If a string of clauses or sentences becomes monotonous, the reader will become bored and lose interest. Sentence variety sustains interest and adds style and vitality to any writing. Consider the following writing samples in terms of variety in sentence structure.

PREDICTABLE STRUCTURE   I wanted to become a nurse for a long time. My parents encouraged me. I am now able to do this. I am proving something to myself. I like to work with people. Plus I need the opportunity to acquire an important job skill. I need to support myself. My dream is now coming true.

VARIED
STRUCTURE

Because I like to work with people, I have wanted to become a nurse for a long time. Now I am able, with my parents' encouragement, to begin nursing school and prove something to myself. My dream is now coming true, and I have the opportunity to acquire an important job skill.

The initial sample lacks sentence variety. It contains eight simple sentences; all of them begin with an identical subject-verb pattern. However, the other sample contains a variety of sentence structures: one complex, one simple, one compound. It also contains a variety of sentence beginnings. The first begins with a clause, the second with an adverb, the third with a subject and a verb. Experienced writers achieve sentence variety in a number of different ways. This section will focus on improving sentence variety in terms of structure, beginnings, coordination, subordination, and sentence types.

a. Sentence structure should vary

In addition to using a mix of simple, compound, and complex sentences, you can vary the patterns of your sentences by using the following: balanced sentences, cumulative sentences, periodic sentences, sentence interrupters, and rhythmic sentences.

Balanced sentences

A balanced sentence shows parallel structure. The parallelism comes from repetition of grammatical pattern and repetition of key words. (See 20.7.)

BALANCED We accept the dull, but we long for the mysterious.

BALANCED   Most of the students were cheering hard at the stadium, yet a few sturdy scholars were checking out books at the library.

BALANCED   The heavens declare the glory of God, and the firmament shows his handiwork.

Cumulative sentences

A cumulative sentence states the main idea at the very beginning of the sentence and then adds material so the reader can more fully understand the meaning. In this way, the sentence accumulates information as it goes on.

CUMULATIVE   You will fail the class unless you attend regularly, read the text, do the assignments, and pass the tests.

Periodic sentences

A periodic sentence presents the main idea toward the very end (near the period). When successful, a periodic sentence creates reader interest by withholding information until the end of the sentence.

PERIODIC   Unless you attend class regularly, read the text, do the assignments, and pass the tests, you will fail.

Sentence interrupters

Interrupters, such as phrases, clauses, or appositives, may provide information, emphasis, and variety when inserted within a sentence.

The three men together in one room—a mafia boss, a black ex-convict, and a Cuban pornographer—prove that America has become a melting pot.

The new football coach (his enemies refer to him as Bill Stalin) signed a three-year contract.

Rhythmic sentences

A rhythmic sentence is one with a definite pattern of stressed and unstressed syllables. The ear can hear such rhythms, and this rhythm can lend a pleasing quality to the sound. Most readers enjoy this kind of sentence. It is a good device for achieving variety and emphasis. A rhythmic sentence is especially effective as a conclusion.

RHYTHMIC He wrote unnecessary letters, free of sense and hard to read, which continually angered his superiors.

RHYTHMIC Let us all hope that the dark clouds of racial prejudice will soon pass away and the deep fog of misunderstanding will be lifted from our fear-drenched communities, and in some not too distant tomorrow the radiant stars of love and brotherhood will shine over our great nation with all their scintillating beauty. *M. L. King*

Practice 1: Revise each of the following strings of simple sentences two times: first into a cumulative sentence, then into a periodic sentence.

SAMPLE Jed embarrassed his fraternity brothers. He wore a pair of old jeans. He wore white golf shoes. He wore a ripped plaid shirt. He wore a tuxedo jacket.

CUMULATIVE   Jed embarrassed his fraternity brothers when he wore his golf shoes with a tuxedo jacket over a ripped plaid shirt and a pair of old jeans.

PERIODIC   Wearing his golf shoes and dressed in a pair of old jeans and a ripped plaid shirt with his tuxedo jacket, Jed embarrassed his fraternity brothers.

a. Mary had water and crackers for lunch. She had milk and toast for dinner. She had orange juice and a biscuit for breakfast. She was always hungry.

b. Larry signed up for math. He missed eleven classes. He failed every quiz. He failed every test. He received an *F* on his grade report.

c. My sister has a new cat. She loves it. It ruined her plants. It destroyed a rug. It broke a glass figurine.

d. Walking is good for you. It will relax you. It will help your heart. It will help your lungs.

e. The spider waits for dinner. It waits on its sturdy new web. It waits for a stray moth. It waits for a wandering fly.

Practice 2: Combine each of the following groups of sentences into a balanced sentence.

SAMPLE   Bob was running. He was racing down the road. He slowed down. He walked. He walked to the top of the hill.

BALANCED   Bob raced down the road, but he slowed down and walked to the top of the hill.

a. The sunlight was bright. It blinded Keith. It blinded him for a moment. He put his sunglasses on. He kept driving. He drove as if nothing had happened.

b. The man picked a worm. He slipped it on the hook. The worm squiggled away. It dropped into the water.
c. My father ordered lobster. It is his favorite seafood. The lobster arrived. It was cold. It was blue.
d. The storm arrived. It was a tornado with fierce winds. There was hail. Our family was safe. We were safe in the storm cellar.

b. Sentence beginnings should vary

By changing the beginnings of your sentences, you can avoid a string of three or more sentences all with the same opening pattern.

MONOTONOUS   This experiment lasted three days. It attempted to test two things. One was the humidity. The other was plant color. [Each sentence begins with a subject-verb pattern.]

REVISED   The experiment that lasted three days attempted to test the relationship between humidity and plant color.

Vary the sentence beginnings in different ways. The addition of an adverb, an adjective, a phrase, or a clause to the beginning will add variety to your sentences.

REPETITIVE   The kite floated above the trees. It snapped loose from the string. It plunged into the lake.

ADVERB   The kite floated above the trees. *Suddenly* it snapped loose and plunged into the lake.

ADJECTIVE   The *red* kite floated above the trees. Suddenly it snapped loose from the string and plunged into the lake.

PHRASE   The red kite floated above the trees. *With a jerk* it suddenly snapped loose and plunged into the lake.

CLAUSE   *While the red kite was floating above the trees,* it suddenly snapped loose and plunged into the lake.

Practice 3: Add material to or rearrange elements in each of the following sentences so that they do not begin with an initial subject-verb pattern.

a. Sam broke every piece of china in the kitchen.
b. The dog was outside sleeping.
c. The boys rested on the freshly mowed lawn.
d. Sarah was surprised to learn that she finished second.
e. The used car was a good buy for Vince.
f. The dog seemed to lose its sense of direction while walking in the park.
g. Gloria held onto the child's hand.
h. Jesse vowed to quit school after listening to the teacher's comments.

Practice 4: Read one of your early journal entries and list the kinds of sentences you used. Then read a recent entry and make a similar list. Revise one of the entries with the goal of improving sentence variety.

c. Excessive coordination should be avoided

Sentences with excessive coordination can be divided into two classes: (1) stringy sentences and (2) choppy sentences. A stringy sentence is sometimes called a run-on sentence because the words just continue to run on. A stringy sentence can be revised by careful subordination and the use of parallel structures.

STRINGY Some parents think their small children are already adults and they dress them in three-piece business suits and they listen to PBS radio with them and they buy them Berlitz language courses.

REVISED Because some parents think their small children are already adults, they dress them in three-piece business suits, listen to PBS radio with them, and buy them Berlitz language courses.

Choppy sentences are generally short, and they break thought into tiny, disconnected units. A choppy sentence can be improved by sentence combining and by effective subordination.

CHOPPY This novel by Norman Mailer confused me. Part of it takes place in Vietnam. But other sections occur in America. And it is full of sex and violence. And I did not enjoy reading it.

REVISED Even though Norman Mailer's new novel is full of sex and violence, I did not enjoy reading it. It confused me because parts take place in Vietnam and other parts occur in America.

Practice 5: Combine each of the following groups of short sentences into a single longer sentence.
a. The judge released a rapist today. He let a burglar out last week. Some people have written letters to the editor. The people are enraged at the judge.

b. Cigarette smoke gives me headaches. And it makes me cough. It makes my eyes swell up. I want smoking banned in public buildings.

c. The experiment lasted three weeks. It studied lack of sleep. It studied grades in a history class. I was a participant. I was exhausted.

d. The children saw the butterfly. It was motionless. It was orange and black. It was a monarch. It was beautiful. It was on a rose bush.

e. Augustine led a frenzied life. He confessed to worshiping sex. He confessed he loved evil for its own sake. He had a mistress. He had one illegitimate child. He became a Christian. He became a saint.

d. Subordination and coordination are effective strategies to create sentence variety

Notice the many different ways a writer might revise a stringy or choppy sentence.

STRINGY   Mr. Titus has a great sense of humor, and he asks the students to behave, and he assigns plenty of homework, and he expects it to be done.

CHOPPY   Mr. Titus has a great sense of humor. He asks the students to behave. He assigns plenty of homework. He expects it to be done.

Revision into a compound sentence

REVISED   Mr. Titus has a great sense of humor, but he expects the students to behave and do plenty of homework.

Revision using a compound predicate

REVISED Mr. Titus has a great sense of humor, asks the students to behave, assigns plenty of homework, and expects it to be done.

Revision using an appositive

REVISED Mr. Titus, *the humorist and the policeman*, assigns plenty of homework and expects it to be done.

Revision using a prepositional phrase

REVISED *Along with having a great sense of humor*, Mr. Titus expects his students to behave and do plenty of homework.

Revision using an adverb clause

REVISED *Even though Mr. Titus has a great sense of humor*, he still asks the students to behave and do plenty of assigned homework.

Revision using an adjective clause

REVISED Mr. Titus, *who has a great sense of humor*, still asks his students to behave and do plenty of homework.

Practice 6: Revise each of the following sentences in two different ways from among all the different revising strategies mentioned in 20.9.
  a. Mike's swimming pool is beautiful, and it is made entirely of glass, and it glows in the dark.
  b. Osell Blakely is a bank robber, and he robbed the savings and loan, and he fired several shots at the police officer chasing him.

c. The largest painting was by Hugh Apple, and it was a twelve-foot square, but it only had one color, black.

d. The Smiths were going to buy a new plane, and the Raneys were thinking of purchasing a new set of polo ponies.

e. This school has beautiful buildings, and the tuition is very inexpensive, but none of the teachers know anything.

f. Leslie wanted to study the effects of pornography, so he moved to Los Angeles, and he has begun writing a book on the subject.

g. The players went over to the gym, and they reported to practice, and the trainer talked to them, and the trainer told them that practice was cancelled.

Practice 7: Revise the following passages to improve readability, variety of sentence structure, clarity, and emphasis.

a. The tall woman sat on a little bench in the garden, and a gathering of birds began to gather about her feet because she would reach into a brown paper sack and she would take out a cracker and break it into four precise parts. She saw a small bird, and it could not get to the food or even the crumbs because it was too small, so she bent over and offered it a piece of cracker even though the little bird was a common sparrow, but it always ate the piece of cracker on her fingertip until a gray alley cat moved into the area.

b. Ray was sitting on the porch. The phone rang. He went inside to answer it. It was Spuds Grant. Spuds was a former friend from high school. Ray had not seen him for almost a year. Spuds asked Ray a question. He asked him, "How interesting does a kilo of grass sound to you?" Ray slammed down the receiver.

e. Excessive subordination should be avoided

Effective sentences have a clear and direct structure. Because meaning is blurred by the elaborate use of parentheses, qualifiers, or subordinate clauses, the removal of unnecessary material and the simplification of structure can help create effective sentences.

EXCESSIVE
SUBORDINATION

Because I am the sorority president, which is a new job for me, I will help Jane during rush, as she wants to join our sorority which she considers the best on campus for the coming year.

REVISED

Because I am the new sorority leader, I will help Jane during rush. She wants to join our sorority, which she considers the best on campus.

Practice 8: Revise the following sentences to eliminate unnecessary words and excessive subordination.

a. When the alarm clock that was broken went off, no one was in the house that was very old and the neighbors heard the sound and called the police.

b. Many people who came to see me in the hospital and after I had gone home to recuperate in my room surprised me by their kindness, as well as taking the time off to visit me.

c. In some cases, to an extent, what I wear is governed by other people's likes and dislikes, since I want other people that I know to like me and accept me.

d. Peter liked my car, which is similar to the one that his brother just bought, because it has a great style that reminds him of a Jaguar but is not one with an outrageous price tag coming in close to thirty thousand.

Practice 9: Make two different sentences from each of the following groups of words. Have one sentence show coordination. Have the other show subordination. Follow the example.

SAMPLE   The mayor lost the election. The mayor spent a million dollars.

COORDINATION The mayor spent a million dollars, but he lost the election.

SUBORDINATION Although he spent a million dollars, the mayor lost the election. [Or: Even though the mayor lost the election, he spent a million dollars.]

a. The boy is on trial for armed robbery. His father is in prison for manslaughter.
b. A thunderstorm is approaching. My sister is not frightened.
c. I have the boring job of a lifeguard. Many people think it is glamorous.
d. Henry drinks and smokes and gambles constantly. He is a bad example for his children.

f. Sentence types should be varied

Besides indicative sentences, experienced writers occasionally use different kinds of sentences for variety: rhetorical questions, imperatives, or exclamations.

RHETORICAL QUESTIONS   In some high schools, the average student cannot write an effective paragraph explaining the simplest facts about the Civil War. Why don't the students learn to write? Are they even asked to write?

IMPERATIVE   Students, take advantage of the cultural and intellectual life occurring on campus. Visit the art museum. Go listen to a debate on current events.

EXCLAMATION   Barry Hannah is somehow able to make violence funny. Yes, sadly, violence can be humorous!

Practice 10: Revise one entry in your journal with the goal of improving sentence variety. Turn in copies of both versions.

20.10 Emphasis problems

Emphasis occurs when certain elements have greater prominence than other elements. A sentence should always reflect the writer's actual intention and not an accidental pattern. Especially during the editing stage, a writer needs to read carefully each sentence and attentively revise, emphasizing intended meaning. Writers have a variety of different ways to emphasize material. Some common strategies involve placement of sentence elements, logical order, repetition, and verb choice. All of these strategies can be used for the sake of emphasis.

a. *An independent clause receives greater emphasis than a dependent clause*

> Even though the players were optimistic, *the team lost.* [The independent clause emphasizes the loss.]

> Even though the team lost, *the players were optimistic.* [The independent clause emphasizes the players' optimism.]

Practice 1: Explain the differences in emphasis in the independent clauses in the following pairs of sentences.
a. Although Smith did lose his job, he is not bitter.
   Although Smith is not bitter, he did lose his job.
b. When the whistle blows, the race will begin.
   When the race begins, the whistle will blow.
c. Even though Smith was a small lineman, he still had great power.
   Even though Smith had great power, he was still a small lineman.
d. If you like art, you will take that course.
   If you take that course, you will like art.

Practice 2: Combine each set of the following sentences into a single sentence using the indicated connector.

SAMPLE Jack lost something. He lost his shoes. He needed them to go camping. [which]

SAMPLE Jack lost his shoes, which he needed to go camping.

a. Miss Francke was the student teacher. Miss Francke was at Blevins Elementary. Miss Francke knew more than the regular teacher. [although]

b. Hodges had a dental appointment. Hodges had a painfully abscessed tooth. Hodges' dental appointment was set for 2:00. [because]

c. The new Woody Allen movie is coming. I plan to see it. It will be on campus next week. It is hilarious. [because]

d. The car can be driven again. It is a wreck. It is blue. [even though]

e. Our neighbor has a bulldog. It has rabies. It attacked our sleeping cat. [that]

b. Material can be emphasized at the beginning of the sentence

Jake asked for tutoring help after he had failed the first two quizzes. [Jake's asking is emphasized at the beginning.]

Jake had failed the first two quizzes before he asked for tutoring help. [Jake's failing is emphasized at the beginning.]

c. Material can be emphasized at the end of a sentence

Terrified, the young woman ran away from the mugger without giving up her purse. [Keeping the purse is emphasized at the end.]

Without giving the mugger her purse, the young woman ran away, terrified. [The terror is emphasized at the end.]

Without giving up her purse to the mugger, the terrified young woman ran away. [The running away is emphasized at the end.]

Practice 3: Combine each of the following pairs of sentences into a simple sentence by using the indicated subordinating conjunction.

SAMPLE Henry Ranker became rich. He ordered a new car with gold wheels. [when]

SAMPLE When Henry Ranker became rich, he ordered a new car with gold wheels.

a. The river flooded. Every square inch of the city was covered with water. [after]
b. We did not believe grandmother. Grandmother said that a flood in 1937 destroyed her father's factory. [when]
c. Gloria destroyed her tennis racquet. Gloria lost a tennis match to an old enemy. [because]
d. Wealth brings happiness. James is very happy. [if]
e. The team wants to win. The team will lose. [although]

d. A logical order of items in a series creates a pattern of emphasis

RANDOM ORDER There was a fight with a black eye and Mike landed on the floor after the bully insulted him. [The items are not arranged in logical sequence.]

CHRONOLOGICAL ORDER After the bully's insult, a fight began and Mike landed on the floor with a black eye. [The items are arranged in logical order.]

RANDOM ORDER Jeffrey's father searched the glove compartment and found one hundred grams of cocaine, a golf ball, and a plane ticket to Florida.

ORDER OF   Jeffrey's father searched the glove com-
IMPORTANCE   partment and found a golf ball, a plane
ticket to Florida, and one hundred grams
of cocaine. [The items are arranged in an
order of increasing importance.]

Practice 4: Revise each of the following sentences so that the most important elements, as you see it, come at the end.

a. Jason fell asleep after studying for twenty-four hours and taking a hot shower.
b. This book will show you how to pass your physics final, and it is easy to read and has a blue cover.
c. The boy was lying on the ground, and blood was streaming from a cut above his forehead, and his shirt was ripped.
d. Gloria confessed that she was afraid of loud sirens, robbers, rapists, and spiders.
e. We wanted to leave the city because of the murders, the dirtiness in the streets, the noise, and the smog.

e. Repetition can add emphasis

REPETITION   Max combed the stadium, the entire *stadium*, searching for his lost sunglasses.

REPETITION   I bought a parrot, a huge, red-and-green *parrot.*

NOTE: Frequent use of this type of repetition leads to a stilted, pretentious style.

Practice 5: Revise each of the following sentences by repeating a word or a phrase for emphasis.

a. The backyard was crawling with green lizards.
b. The artist used masking tape to cover up part of her painting.
c. These doughnuts taste like rubber food.
d. Carl Sagan knows everything about the universe.

20.11 Omissions

Writers commonly omit letters, words, and punctuation marks from their rough drafts. Careful editing can help catch errors of this kind. Many writers read their work out loud to hear the rhythms and catch any mistakes. Consider the following examples taken from different student papers.

OMISSION   The two teenagers were outside, throwing a ball to catch. [The sentence is a mystery. Only when the author was asked for the meaning was the mystery solved.]

REVISION   The two teenagers were outside, throwing a ball *for the dog* to catch.

OMISSION   Gregor claimed France's was the weakest in Europe.

REVISION   Gregor claimed that France's army was the weakest in Europe.

Some errors of omission arise from carelessness. Others arise from regional speech patterns. In certain parts of the country, people regularly say, "I done it" instead of saying, "I had done it." Whatever the cause, most readers react negatively when they discover such omissions. Many readers consider them a sure sign of low intelligence and a mark of illiteracy. You may not catch them as you write them, but you need to find and remove them in your revising and editing. Such errors generally involve incomplete verb forms; missing articles, conjunctions, prepositions, or relative pronouns; or incomplete comparisons.

a. All verbs need to be complete

Add the *-d* or *-ed* to the past tense of regular verbs; especially be alert when a word with a similar sound immediately follows the verb.

OMISSION   The survey *ask* ten questions about religion.

REVISION   The survey *asked* ten questions about religion.

Add both the auxiliary and the verb if you use two different tenses of the same verb.

OMISSION   Val has not and never will sing that song.

REVISION   Val has not *sung* and never will sing that song.

Include the auxiliary verb when needed.

OMISSION   The windows were broken and the door damaged.

REVISION   The windows were broken and the door *was* damaged.

Include the infinitive *to be* when needed.

OMISSION   This screen door needs fixed.

REVISION   This screen door needs *to be* fixed.

b. Necessary articles, relative adverbs, relative pronouns, or prepositions should be added

Some articles are often necessary for meaning and rhythm.

OMISSION Question on his test asked for discussion of rabies.

REVISION *A* question on his test asked for *a* discussion of rabies.

Some relative adverbs need to be added.

OMISSION We visited the cities T. S. Eliot lived.

REVISION We visited the cities *where* T. S. Eliot lived.

Some relative pronouns are essential to meaning.

OMISSION The book mentioned an experiment our teacher designed.

REVISION The book mentioned an experiment *that* our teacher designed.

A missing preposition can make a sentence incomplete.

OMISSION The astronauts went the moon.

REVISION The astronauts went *to* the moon.

c. An incomplete comparison can puzzle a reader

The connective *that of* is often needed in the second part of a comparison.

UNCLEAR Geri Smith's poem is longer than Mark Ward.

REVISED   Geri Smith's poem is longer *than that of* Mark Ward's. [Or: Geri Smith's poem is longer than Mark Ward's.]

A second possessive is sometimes essential.

UNCLEAR   Jerry Lewis's movies are funnier than Woody Allen.

REVISED   Jerry Lewis's movies are funnier than *Woody Allen's.*

The conjunction *as* emphasizes comparison.

UNCLEAR   The moon is old, but no older than, the earth.

REVISED   The moon is *as* old *as,* but no older than, the earth.

OMISSION The boy is tired as an old man.

REVISION The boy is *as* tired *as* an old man.

An incomplete comparison needs to be completed.

UNCLEAR   Patrick Rogan has scored more touchdowns.

REVISED   Patrick Rogan has scored more touchdowns *than any other quarterback at Becker High.*

Practice 1: Revise each of the following sentences after checking for omissions.
a. Mark is destine to be a doctor.
b. That grocery has not and never will make deliveries.
c. Jack so smart he can catch fish without using bait.
d. Nathan and Fritz need go see Dr. Solomon.
e. Jeffrey's new car needs repaired.
f. Museums have and always will excite me.

g. Jonas being watched because of trouble in the library.
h. Kyle played the music his sister composed.
i. The little boy repeated the father said.
j. I know Jane reading the book.

Practice 2: Revise each of the following sentences after checking for incomplete or imprecise comparisons.
a. The school piano has a softer tone than church.
b. This book contains more ignorance.
c. My French teacher is harder.
d. Cholesterol is more dangerous to your health.
e. I like Christmas vacation better than summer.
f. These spaniels are better trained than any other cats.
g. My paper is closer to completion than Henry.
h. Drax Bleach leaves your clothes whiter.
i. Michael is as fearful, if not more, than his sister.
j. Seven-Up and Sprite cost less and taste better.

20.12 Predication errors

The predicate is that part of the sentence that is not the subject and its modifiers.

> The boy *swam.* [*Swam* is the simple predicate.]

> The boy *dove in the river and swam to the other side.* [*Dove in the river and swam to the other side* is the complete predicate.]

Problems in predication occur when the subject and the predicate do not mesh smoothly together.

INCORRECT   If you have an hour at noon to see the new exhibit is a good time to visit the museum. [The predicate, *is a good time to visit the museum*, does not have an adequate subject.]

REVISED   The noon hour is a good time to visit the museum to see the new exhibit.

INCORRECT The biggest mistake in the game was the referee who ruled that Johnson was out of bounds.

REVISED   The biggest mistake in the game was the referee's ruling that Johnson was out of bounds.

Three common predication errors arise with the misuse of *when, where,* and *the reason is because.*

INCORRECT Religion is *when* you think about God and sacred things.

REVISED   Religion involves thinking about God and sacred things.

INCORRECT Hunger is *where* the smell of bacon and scrambled eggs can wake a person up in the morning.

REVISED   The smell of bacon and scrambled eggs in the morning can wake a hungry person up.

INCORRECT The *reason* the class failed the test *is because* no one studied.

REVISED   The class failed the test because no one studied.

Practice 1: Revise the following sentences to make the subjects and the predicates fit together logically.
a. The reason the computer no longer works is because an electrical storm damaged all the wiring.

b. Mystery, according to Eliade, is when the mind can understand something only incompletely.

c. Happiness is when it snows and a warm fire is blazing at home.

d. With a dull knife is how Jeffrey had to carve the turkey.

e. The problem of grade inflation is the answer to many students' prayers.

f. Paralysis is where you lose the ability to move.

g. Very often what students believe is how their parents taught them their beliefs.

h. The question of discrimination is still a problem for many black people in this country.

i. By taxing cigarettes at a high rate is a good way to cut down on smoking.

j. Due to the fact that Jeffrey ignored the stop sign caused the accident.

21 Using Words

If someone had told me I didn't know how to use a dictionary, I would have said that person was insane. The truth is, though, that my understanding of a dictionary was quite simple-minded and on a low level. I've come to see what a sophisticated tool the dictionary is and how it can help my revising by making my meaning deeper and more precise.

Gwen Markel

I like what John Dryden said: "The right words in the right places."

R. Y.

21.1 Vocabulary

Increase your supply of words whose various meanings you can recognize and use. Begin the habit now of looking up unfamiliar words in the dictionary. Don't be satisfied with the partial knowledge supplied by the context of a word. Make the dictionary your constant companion.

You can improve your vocabulary in a number of ways. One good way is reading. When you read, keep a good dictionary by your side and use it. Another way to improve your vocabulary is studying a foreign language, particularly Latin or Greek. Students have reported that their recognition vocabulary increased by thousands of words after learning several hundred Latin or Greek prefixes, suffixes, and roots.

Make a commitment right now to increase your supply of usable and useful words. Vocabulary improvement is not an overnight project, but its benefits are immense. A large vocabulary increases your reading skill and speed. It increases your knowledge of the world. It improves your writing style. It gives you more options in your choice of words. And it makes you more effective in conversation and discussion.

a. Prefixes, suffixes, and roots

Common prefixes

The prefix is a unit of one or more syllables placed before a word, such as *un-* before *knit* in *unknit*. A knowledge of prefix meaning can help you decipher the meaning of unfamiliar words and make learning new words easier.

Prefix	*Meaning*	*Example*
a-	without	amoral, atheist
ad-	to, toward	administer, admonition
anti-	against	antibody, antimatter
circum-	around	circumnavigate
com-, con-, co-	with	coauthor, concavity
counter-	against	counterplot
de-	down	defame, demerit
dis-	apart	discard, discourage
epi	on, beside	epiphenomenal

equi-	equal	equidistant, equivocal
ex-	out of	expatriate, express
homo-	same, equal	homosexual, homocyclic
hyper-	over, above	hyperactive
hypo-	under	hypomania
in-	no, not	indecent, incongruous
inter-	between	interstate, intersession
mal-	bad, badly	malpractice
mis-	wrong	mismatch, misconstrue
omni-	all	omnipotent
poly-	many	polyrhythm, polymath
pre-	before	pregame, preprandial
re-	again, back	reignite, resurge
semi-	half	semicircle, semiannual
sub-	under	submarine, submerge
sym-, syn-	with	symmetrical, synthesis
trans-	across	transmigration

Numerical prefixes

Prefix	*Meaning*	*Example*
uni-	one	unicycle, unilateral
mono-	one	monorail, monomania
bi-	two	bicycle, bilateral
di-	two	digraph, diphosphate
tri-	three	triangle, triacid
deca-	ten	decasyllabic, decapod
cent-	hundred	centimeter, centiliter
milli-	thousandth	millimeter, milliangstrom
kilo-	thousand	kilometer, kilogram
semi-	one half	semicircle, semiliterate

Common suffixes

A suffix is a recognizable group of syllables at the very end of a multisyllabic word. Learning a few common suffixes will improve your power of word recognition.

Suffix	Meaning	Example
-fy	make	purify, mollify
-ism	belief or practice in	Methodism, realism
-ist	one who believes in	communist, capitalist
-less	missing, without	loveless, hopeless
-logy	the study of	psychology, anthropology
-ous	full of	dangerous, bilious
-ship	ability or skill in	friendship, leadership
-tion	action or state	starvation, rejection
-tude	state of being	magnitude, longitude

Roots

The root of a word is the base it had in an earlier language. Roots may be either suffixes or prefixes. The most important non-Teutonic roots in English come from Latin and Greek. People claim that learning 500 word roots can increase one's vocabulary by 5,000 words. A great part of the vocabularies of medicine, biology, psychology, physics, and chemistry derives from a group of Greek and Latin roots.

Root	Meaning	Example
auto-	self	autograph, autism
biblio-	book	Bible, bibliography
dic-, -dict	say, speak	diction, predict
fac-, fact-, -fect	make, do	factory, perfect
-graph	write	photograph, hagiography
mega-, magna-	great	megaphone, magnify
-meter	measure	metric, kilometer
neo-	new	neoconservative, neologism
pan-	all	pantheism, pandemonium
-port	carry	transport, deport
pseudo-	false	pseudonym, pseudopodia
vis-	see, view	vision, visible

Practice 1: Read several pages from either *Huckleberry Finn* or *The Catcher in the Rye* and contrast the vocabulary in one of those books with the vocabulary found in either

an editorial in the *New York Times* or an essay in the *Atlantic Monthly*. How would you account for the differences?

Practice 2: Read an article in *Us* or *People* and another article in the *Nation*, the *New Republic*, or the *National Review.* How do the subjects dealt with in the magazines influence the vocabulary? Find examples for contrasting use of nouns, verbs, and adjectives. Make a list of some of the reasons for the contrasting vocabularies. Write a brief paper contrasting the two articles.

21.2 Dictionary

A good dictionary is indispensable for all your work in college. Three different kinds of dictionaries (unabridged, abridged, and special) are explained in the section on the library in chapter 15. The following pages contain numerous examples of these different kinds of dictionaries. A good dictionary can help you in your thinking, reading, and writing. Of the standard dictionaries, which are used in and out of class, the following are the most important:

- *The American Heritage Dictionary*
- *Funk and Wagnalls Standard College Dictionary*
- *The Random House College Dictionary*
- *Webster's New Collegiate Dictionary*
- *Webster's New World Dictionary*

The following section of a page from *Webster's Ninth New Collegiate Dictionary*, published by Merriam-Webster, Inc., contains markers that point to some of the more important features within that dictionary.

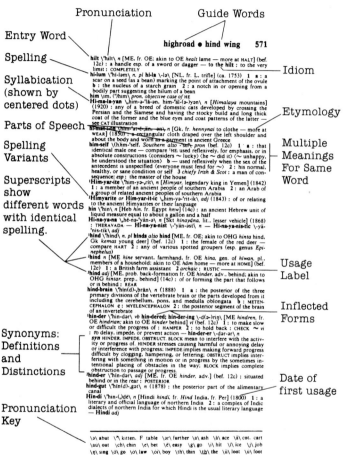

Pronunciation | Guide Words

Entry Word

Spelling

Syllabication (shown by centered dots)

Parts of Speech

Spelling Variants

Superscripts show different words with identical spelling.

Synonyms: Definitions and Distinctions

Pronunciation Key

Idiom

Etymology

Multiple Meanings For Same Word

Usage Label

Inflected Forms

Date of first usage

highroad ● hind wing   571

hilt \\'hilt\ n [ME. fr. OE *healt* lame — more at HALT] (bef. 12c.) : a handle esp. of a sword or dagger — to the **hilt** : to the very limit : COMPLETELY

hi-lum \\'hi-ləm\ n, pl hi-la \-lə\ [NL. fr. L. trifle] (ca. 1753) **1 a** : a scar on a seed (as a bean) marking the point of attachment of the ovule **b** : the nucleus of a starch grain **2** : a notch in or opening from a bodily part suggesting the hilum of a bean

him \im. (')him\ pron. objective case of HE

Hi-ma-la-yan \him-ə-'lā-ən. him-'äl-(ə-)yən\ n [*Himalaya* mountains] (1920) : any of a breed of domestic cats developed by crossing the Persian and the Siamese and having the stocky build and long thick coat of the former and the blue eyes and coat patterns of the latter — see CAT illustration

hi-ma-tion \him-'at-ē-ən. -ən.\ n [Gk. fr. *hennynai* to clothe — more at WEAR] (1850) : a rectangular cloth draped over the left shoulder and about the body and worn as a garment in ancient Greece

him-self \(h)im-'self\ pron (bef. 12c) **1** : that identical male one — compare [1]HE used reflexively, for emphasis, or in absolute constructions (considers ~ lucky) (he ~ did it) (~ unhappy, he understood the situation) **b** — used reflexively when the sex of the antecedent is unspecified (everyone must fend for ~) **2** : his normal, healthy, or sane condition or self **3** chiefly *Irish & Scot* : a man of consequence: *esp* : the master of the house

[1]Him-yar-ite \\'him-yə-,rīt\ n [*Himyar*, legendary king in Yemen] (1842) **1** : a member of an ancient people of southern Arabia **2** : an Arab of a group of related ancient peoples of southern Arabia

[2]Himyarite or Him-yar-it-ic \,him-yə-'rit-ik\ adj (1843) : of or relating to the ancient Himyarites or their language

hin \\'hin\ n [Heb *hin.* fr. Egypt *hnw*] (14c) : an ancient Hebrew unit of liquid measure equal to about a gallon and a half

Hi-na-ya-na \,hē-nə-'yän-ə\ n [Skt *hinayāna,* lit., lesser vehicle] (1868) : THERAVADA — Hi-na-ya-nist \-'yän-əst\ n — Hi-na-ya-nis-tic \-'yä-'nis-tik\ adj

[1]hind \\'hind\ n, pl hinds also hind [ME. fr. OE: akin to OHG *hinta* hind. Gk *kemas* young deer] (bef. 12c) **1** : the female of the red deer — compare HART **2** : any of various spotted groupers (esp. genus *Epinephelus*)

[2]hind n [ME *hine* servant, farmhand, fr. OE *hina,* gen. of *hiwan,* pl., members of a household; akin to OE *hām* home — more at HOME] (bef. 12c) **1** : a British farm assistant **2** *archaic* : RUSTIC

[3]hind adj [ME. prob. back-formation fr. OE *hinder,* adv.. behind: akin to OHG *hintar.* prep.. behind] (14c) : of or forming the part that follows or is behind : REAR

hind-brain \\'hin(d)-,brān\ n (1888) **1 a** : the posterior of the three primary divisions of the vertebrate brain or the parts developed from it including the cerebellum, pons, and medulla oblongata **b** : METENCEPHALON **c** : MYELENCEPHALON **2** : the posterior segment of the brain of an invertebrate

[1]hin-der \\'hin-dər\ vb hin-dered; hin-der-ing \-d(ə-)riŋ\ [ME *hindren,* fr. OE *hindrian;* akin to OE *hinder* behind] vt (bef. 12c) **1** : to make slow or difficult the progress of : HAMPER **2** : to hold back : CHECK ~ vi : to delay, impede, or prevent action — hin-der-er \-dər-ər\ n
syn HINDER. IMPEDE. OBSTRUCT. BLOCK mean to interfere with the activity or progress of. HINDER stresses causing harmful or annoying delay or interference with progress: IMPEDE implies making forward progress difficult by causing, hampering, or fettering; OBSTRUCT implies interfering with something in motion or in progress by the sometimes intentional placing of obstacles in the way; BLOCK implies complete obstruction to passage or progress.

[2]hind-er \\'hin-dər\ adj [ME. fr. OE *hinder,* adv.] (bef. 12c) : situated behind or in the rear : POSTERIOR

hind-gut \\'hin(d)-,gət\ n (1878) : the posterior part of the alimentary canal

Hin-di \\'hin-(,)dē\ n [Hindi *hindī,* fr. *Hind* India. fr. Per] (1800) **1** : a literary and official language of northern India **2** : a complex of Indic dialects of northern India for which Hindi is the usual literary language — Hindi adj

---

\ə\ abut \ᵊ\ kitten. F table \ər\ further \a\ ash \ā\ ace \ä\ cot. cart
\au̇\ out \ch\ chin \e\ bet \ē\ easy \g\ go \i\ hit \ī\ ice \j\ job
\ŋ\ sing \ō\ go \o̊\ law \o̊i\ boy \th\ thin \t͟h\ the \ü\ loot \u̇\ foot
\y\ yet \zh\ vision \ə. ḳ. ⁼. œ̅. œ̅. œ̅. ⁼\ see Guide to Pronunciation

---

Practice 1: For the following questions, refer to the reproduction of the preceding dictionary entry.

a. What are the plural forms of the noun *hind*, when the word refers to a deer?

b. How many syllables does *Himyarite* contain?

c. What are the primary stresses in the pronunciation of *himself* and *himation*? How are the words pronounced?

d. How many parts of speech can *hinder* function as?

e. What meaning does the word *hind* no longer have?

f. What are the etymologies of *Himyarite* and *hin*?

g. How many different meanings are given for *hinder*?

h. How do the synonyms of *hinder* differ?

i. How might someone in the South pronounce *himself*?

j. What does *Himyarite* mean? What does *Hinayana* mean? Are the words explained in the same way?

k. What does *to the hilt* mean?

Practice 2: What key differences do you find in the usage paragraphs for the verb *flaunt* taken from the following dictionaries: (a) *Webster's Ninth New Collegiate Dictionary*, (b) *The Random House College Dictionary*, and (c) *The American Heritage Dictionary*?

(a)

flaunt \'flȯnt, 'flänt\ *vb* [prob. of Scand origin; akin to ON *flana* to rush around — more at PLANET] *vi* (1566) **1** : to display or obtrude oneself to public notice **2** : to wave or flutter showily ⟨the flag ~s in the breeze⟩ ~ *vt* **1** : to display ostentatiously or impudently : PARADE ⟨~ing his superiority⟩ **2** : to treat contemptuously ⟨~ed the rules — Louis Untermeyer⟩ **syn** see SHOW — **flaunt** *n* — **flaunt·ing·ly** \-iŋ-lē\ *adv* — **flaunty** \-ē\ *adj*
 usage Although transitive sense 2 of *flaunt* undoubtedly arose from confusion with *flout*, the contexts in which it appears cannot be called substandard ⟨meting out punishment to the occasional mavericks who operate rigged games, tolerate rowdyism, or otherwise *flaunt* the law —Oscar Lewis⟩ ⟨observed with horror the *flaunting* of their authority in the suburbs, where men ... put up buildings that had no place at all in a Christian commonwealth —Marchette Chute⟩ ⟨in our profession we never excommunicate a colleague, never defrock or disbar ... ; very rarely do we publicly chastise a colleague who has *flaunted* our most basic principles —R. T. Blackburn, *AAUP Bull.*⟩ If you use it, however, you should be aware that many people will consider it a mistake. Use of *flout* in the sense of *flaunt* 1 is occas. found but is relatively infrequent.

(b)

flaunt (flônt) *v.* **flaunt-ed, flaunt-ing, flaunts.** —*tr.* **1.** To exhibit ostentatiously; show off: *flaunts his knowledge.* **2.** *Nonstandard.* To flout. —*intr.* **1.** To parade oneself ostentatiously; show oneself off. **2.** To wave grandly: *pennants flaunting in the wind.* [Orig. unknown.] —**flaunt** *n.* —**flaunt′er** *n.* —**flaunt′ing·ly** *adv.*

Usage: *Flaunt* and *flout* are often confused. *Flaunt* as a transitive verb means "to exhibit ostentatiously": *She flaunted her diamonds.* To *flout* is "to defy openly": *She flouted the proprieties.*

(c)

flaunt (flônt), *v.t.* **1.** to parade or display ostentatiously. **2.** *Nonstandard.* to treat with disdain; flout: *flaunting military regulations.* —*v.i.* **3.** to parade or display oneself ostentatiously. **4.** to wave conspicuously in the air. —*n.* **5.** the act of flaunting. **6.** *Obs.* something flaunted. [< Scand; cf. Norw *flanta* to gad about < *flana* to roam; akin to Gk *pládn̄* a roaming (see PLANET)] —**flaunt′er,** *n.* —**flaunt′ing·ly,** *adv.* —**Syn. 1.** flourish. —**Usage. 2.** This sense of FLAUNT stems from its confusion with FLOUT and, although this confusion is quite common, is regarded as nonstandard usage.

Practice 3: The following discussion of likely synonyms for the verb *flash* comes from *Webster's Ninth New Collegiate Dictionary*, published by Merriam-Webster, Inc. Write eight different sentences, using at least one of these words in each sentence. As you write your sentences, try to capture the differences in the meanings.

syn FLASH, GLEAM, GLANCE, GLINT, SPARKLE, GLITTER, GLISTEN, GLIMMER, SHIMMER mean to send forth light. FLASH implies a sudden and transient outburst of bright light; GLEAM suggests a steady light seen through an obscuring medium or against a dark background; GLANCE suggests a bright darting light reflected from a quickly moving surface; GLINT implies a cold glancing light; SPARKLE suggests innumerable moving points of bright light; GLITTER connotes a brilliant sparkling or gleaming; GLISTEN applies to the soft sparkle from a wet or oily surface; GLIMMER suggests a faint or wavering gleam; SHIMMER implies a soft tremulous gleaming or a blurred reflection.

Practice 4: What are the chief differences between the following entries taken from (a) *Webster's Ninth New Collegiate Dictionary,* published by Merriam-Webster, Inc., and from (b) the *Thesaurus of English Words and Phrases?*

(a)

¹dis•like \(')dis-'līk\ *n* (1577) **1** : a feeling of aversion or disapproval **2** *obs* : DISCORD
²dislike *vt* (1579) **1** *archaic* : DISPLEASE **2** : to regard with dislike : DISAPPROVE **3** *obs* : to show aversion to — **dis•lik•er** *n*

(b)

867. Dislike.—N. dis-like, -taste, -relish, -inclination, -placency.

reluctance; backwardness &c. (*unwillingness*) 603.

repugnance, disgust, queasiness, turn, nausea, loathing; avers-eness, -ation, -ion; abomination, antipathy, abhorrence, horror; mortal –, rooted- -antipathy, – horror; hatred, detestation; hate &c. 898; animosity &c. 900; hydrophobia.

sickener; gall and wormwood &c. (*unsavoury*) 395; shuddering, cold sweat.

V. dis-, mis-like, -relish; mind, object to; have rather not, not care for; have –, conceive –, entertain –, take- -a dislike, – an aversion- to; have no -taste, – stomach- for.

shun, avoid &c. 623; eschew; withdraw –, shrink –, recoil- from; not be able to -bear, – abide, – endure; shrug the shoulders at, shudder at, turn up the nose at, look askance at; make a -mouth, – wry face, – grimace; make faces.

loathe, nauseate, abominate, detest, abhor; hate &c. 898; take amiss &c. 900; have enough of &c. (*be satiated*) 869.

cause –, excite- dislike; disincline, repel, sicken; make –, render- sick; turn one's stomach, nauseate, wamble, disgust, shock, stink in the nostrils; go against the -grain, – stomach; stick in the throat; make one's blood run cold &c. (*give pain*) 830; pall.

Adj. disliking &c. *v.*; averse to, loth, adverse; shy of, sick of, out of conceit with; disinclined; heart-, dog-sick; queasy

disliked &c. *v.*; uncared for, unpopular; out of favour; repulsive, repugnant, repellent; abhorrent, insufferable, fulsome, nauseous; loath-some, -ful; offensive; disgusting &c. *v.*; disagreeable &c. (*painful*) 830; unsavoury &c. 395.

Adv. *usque ad nauseam.*

Int. faugh! foh! ugh!

Practice 5: Using your dictionary, identify the stress marks and pronounce the following words. Then write sentences using each of these words.

a. perfume (n) e. *aqua vitae* i. perfect (v)
b. perfume (v) f. metamorphosis j. incense (n)
c. incongruity g. Parousia k. incense (v)
d. tremulous h. perfect (adj)

Practice 6: Choose a word that you know to have two or more different meanings and write a brief passage explaining the meanings and the differences. Check your dictionary for etymology, parts of speech, definitions, synonyms, and usage. If possible, inspect the word in the *Oxford English Dictionary.*

Practice 7: Choose one of the following words that you would like to think about: *relaxation, vacation,* or *education.* Choose one of the words to write on and explain how two different social classes use, react to, or define the word.

Practice 8: How does a knowledge of the origin of the following words help you to understand their meaning: *pornography, vital,* and *holocaust?* Write brief definitions of these words that include the meaning of the words in the original Greek or Latin in such a way as to clarify and enrich the present meanings.

Practice 9: The following three entries for the word *altitude* come from two unabridged dictionaries and an abridged dictionary. An unabridged dictionary is a comprehensive dictionary not based on a larger one. An abridged dictionary is similar to your college dictionary and is based on a larger one. As you study the following entries, briefly list the content of each entry.

1. Oxford English Dictionary

Altitude (æ·ltitiud). Also altytude. [ad. L. *altitūdin-em* height, f. *alti-* (*altus*) high : see -TUDE. Cf. mod.Fr. *altitude*, not in Palsg. or Cotgr.]

1. *gen.* Vertical extent or distance ; the quality of being high or deep, as one of the dimensions of space ; height or depth.

c **1420** *Pallad. on Husb.* IV. 791 Her sydes longe, her altitude abounde [=abundant]. **1509** HAWES *Past. Pl.* I. viii, This goodly picture was in altitude Nyne fote and more. **1605** SHAKS. *Lear* IV. vi. 53 The altitude, Which thou hast perpendicularly fell. **1794** SULLIVAN *View Nat.* I, The gravity of the fluid .. will be always proportional to the altitude or depth. **1821** CRAIG *Drawing* ii. 63 It has neither form nor colour, nor altitude nor dimensions, and yet it is a flower.

2. *Geom.* The height of a triangle or other figure, measured by a perpendicular from the vertex to the base or base produced.

1570 BILLINGSLEY *Euclid* VI. def. 4. 154 Figures to have one altitude and to be contayned within two equidistant lines, is all one. **1751** CHAMBERS *Cycl.* s.v., Triangles of equal bases and altitudes are equal. **1810** HUTTON *Course Math.* I. 286 A triangle is equal to half a parallelogram of the same base and altitude.

3. Height of the mercurial column in a barometer. ? *Obs.*

1664 POWER *Exp. Philos.* II. 91 Its wonted pitch and altitude of 29 inches, or thereabouts. **1753** CHAMBERS *Cycl. Supp.* s.v., The different altitudes of the mercury may arise from the different states of the air.

2. Webster's Third New International Dictionary

al·ti·tude \'altə,tüd, -ə-,tyüd\ *n* -s [ME, fr. L *altitudo,* fr. *alti-* + *-tudo* -tude] **1 a :** the angular elevation of a celestial object above the horizon measured by the arc of a vertical circle intercepted between the object and the horizon   **b :** the vertical elevation of an object above a given level (as a foundation, the ground, or sea level) ⟨a city with an ∼ of 2547 feet⟩   **c :** the perpendicular distance from the base of a geometric figure to the vertex ⟨the ∼ of a triangle⟩ or to the side or face parallel to the base ⟨∼ of a parallelogram⟩   **2 :** the height or an extremity of some quality or degree of excellence ⟨the ∼ of human passion in Dante's poetry⟩ ⟨hopes raised to an ∼ of tension⟩ ⟨standards in the College have been rising, and ... despite their present ∼, they continue to rise —N.M.Pusey⟩   **3 a :** vertical distance or extent : height or depth ⟨greater than the neighboring hills in ∼⟩ ⟨∼ of the fluid in the tube⟩   **b** (1) : position at a height ⟨the plane lost ∼ rapidly⟩ (2) : exalted position (as in rank or power) ⟨a command issued from the ∼ of the general staff⟩   **c :** an elevated region : EMINENCE — usu. used in pl. ⟨mountain ∼s⟩   **4 altitudes** *pl, archaic* : haughty airs : POMPOSITY

3. Webster's Ninth New Collegiate Dictionary

al·ti·tude \'al-tə-,t(y)üd\ *n* [ME, fr. L *altitudo* height, depth, fr. *altus* high, deep — more at OLD] (14c)   **1   a :** the angular elevation of a celestial object above the horizon   **b :** the vertical elevation of an object above a surface (as sea level or land) of a planet or natural satellite   **c** (1) : a perpendicular line segment from a vertex of a geometric figure (as a triangle or a pyramid) to the opposite side or the opposite side extended or from a side or face to a parallel side or face or the side or face extended   **b** (2) : the length of an altitude   **2 :** the highest level of a quality or feeling ⟨the ∼ of passion⟩   **3   a :** vertical distance or extent   **b :** position at a height   **c :** an elevated region : EMINENCE — usu. used in pl.   *syn* see HEIGHT — **al·ti·tu·di·nal** \,al-tə-'t(y)üd-nəl, -ᵊn-əl\ *adj* — **al·ti·tu·di·nous** \-'t(y)üd-nəs, -ᵊn-əs\ *adj*

Practice 10: Make two lists. In one, list some differences between the entry for *altitude* in the *Oxford English Dictionary* and the entry for *altitude* in *Webster's Ninth New Collegiate Dictionary.* In the second, list some differences between the same entry in the *OED* and the entry in *Webster's Third New International Dictionary.* What are some reasons that a writer might use these different dictionaries in working on a paper?

Practice 11: Consult the table of contents at the beginning of your college dictionary to discover the location of the list of abbreviations and symbols used to indicate the etymology of words. When used in the etymology section of the dictionary entry for *altitude,* what does the symbol *L* indicate in terms of language origin? What do the following abbreviations mean in terms of etymology: *D, MD, ME, MF, MIr, NL, OE, OL, Pol,* and *Sp*? Besides etymological abbreviations, where does your dictionary list other abbreviations? Are they in a separate section, or are they included in the main part of the dictionary?

21.3 Spelling

Many students have problems with spelling. Some words are difficult for everyone; however, some people have problems with certain words. Most people are able to overcome spelling problems with the attentive use of a dictionary and careful reference to a corrected list of misspelled words. Keep and use a corrected list of words that you have misspelled. In addition to keeping a list, a weak speller can benefit from learning the following information:

- ✎ The meaning of *suffix* and *prefix* (See 21.1a.)
- ✎ The meaning of *vowel* (a, e, i, o, u, y); the long and short sounds
- ✎ The meaning of *consonant*: any letter not a vowel.
- ✎ The meaning of *syllable*: a short speech unit
- ✎ The meaning of *accent* or *stress*: the prominence of a syllable
- ✎ Accentuation of all one-syllable words: e.g., *shy, spit, dog*
- ✎ The accent or stress in words with more than one syllable.

a. Words with one syllable

Adding suffixes to one-syllable words follows a simple rule. If the one-syllable word has a short vowel just before the consonant at the end, the consonant is doubled. If the one-syllable word has a long vowel just before the concluding consonant, it remains single and is not doubled.

mate	mating (long)	mat	matting (short)
bead	beading (long)	bed	bedding (short)
spite	spiting (long)	spit	spitting (short)
mope	moping (long)	mop	mopping (short)
cute	cuter (long)	cut	cutter (short)

b. Words with i *before* e *or* e *before* i

Most words spelled with *ie* or *ei* follow a simple and predictable rule. To help understand the rules, memorize the following jingle: *I* before *E* except after *C* or when sounded like *A* as in *neighbor* and *weigh*.

- ✎ If the sound is *ee*, the *i* comes before *e*: *chief, believer, retrieve.*

✎ If a *c* comes before the *ee* sound, it is *ei*: *deceive, conceit, perceive.*

✎ If the combination has the *a* sound in *say* or *play*, it is spelled *ei*: *beige, freight, weight.*

✎ There are a few exceptions to these guidelines: *either, feisty, foreign, heifer, height, leisure, neither, seize, skein,* and *weird.*

c. Words that end with y

If the *y* is preceded by a consonant, change the *y* to *i* and add the suffix.

  try tried delivery deliveries wary wariest

If the *y* is preceded by a vowel, simply add the suffix.

  play player donkey donkeys essay essayist

d. Words that double the final consonant

When you add a suffix, double the final consonant in words with two or more syllables if the word has *all* the following:

 ✎ an accent on the last syllable
 ✎ a short vowel in the last syllable
 ✎ a vowel right before the final consonant

repel	repelled	repelling	repellent
occur	occurred	occurring	occurrence

Do not double the final consonant, when you add a suffix, if the word has *one* of the following:

 ✎ stress on any syllable but the last
 ✎ a long vowel in the last syllable
 ✎ the sound *x, ct, ph*—as in *relax, select, autograph*— in the last syllable

repeal	repealed	repealing	repealer
focus	focused	focusing	focuser
profit	profited	profiting	profiter
reject	rejected	rejecting	rejecter

Practice 1: Say the following words out loud. Listen for the short vowel sounds in each pair and then the long vowel sounds. Write eight different sentences. In each sentence use both words in the pair.

bate/bat	pet/peat	cut/cute	tap/tape
lit/light	tip/type	mitt/might	tot/tote

Practice 2: Say the following words out loud. Listen for the long vowel sound and the short vowel sound in each pair. Identify the long vowel and short vowel in each set. With which of the following words can you form additional words by adding the suffixes -*d* or -*ed* to the word? What spelling rule can you derive from the different sounds for these words? Write a sentence stating that rule.

pace/pan	type/tip	imbue/bud
appease/pen	mope/mop	

Practice 3: Correct all misspelled words in the following list. If the word is correct, place a *C* in front of it.

1. promission	11. portrail	21. grammer
2. humorus	12. murderous	22. calender
3. temperments	13. exaggerate	23. criticise
4. cannot	14. raduis	24. esential
5. reflexion	15. circumfrence	25. suspicius
6. rehersal	16. skedule	26. should of
7. my self	17. civilazation	27. receivable
8. Great Britian	18. carbahydrates	28. violance
9. accomplish	19. evapration	29. persevearance
10. intrest	20. could of	30. would of

e. List of commonly misspelled words

Many words commonly misspelled are listed in the Glossary of Usage in chapter 25. Consider that list an extension of the following collection.

absence	auxiliary	criticize
abundance	available	cruel
acceptable	average	curiosity
acceptance	bachelor	curious
accessible	basically	deceive
accidentally	believe	dependent
accommodate	beneficial	descend
accuracy	boundary	desirable
accustomed	brilliant	despair
achieve	Britain	difference
acquaintance	bureaucracy	dining
acquire	business	disappearance
actually	calculation	disappoint
adequately	calendar	disastrous
admittance	candidate	discipline
adolescence	cemetery	disease
a lot of	certain	dissatisfied
amateur	changeable	doubt
ambitious	characteristic	drawer
analysis	coarse	drunkenness
analyze	conceit	during
anxious	condemn	easily
apologized	conscientious	ecstasy
apparent	consciousness	efficiency
appreciate	consistent	eight
arctic	controversial	eighth
arguing	convenience	embarrass
arrangement	correspondence	emphasize
ascend	could have	entree
athlete	couldn't	environment
athletics	courageous	exaggerate
attach	criticism	excellence

excellent
exercise
exhaust
experience
familiar
fascinate
February
federal
foreign
forty
fourth
friend
fulfill
genius
government
governor
grief
guarantee
guard
guidance
harass
height
heroes
hideous
history
horrible
humorous
hypocrisy
hypocrite
imaginary
imagine
imitation
independence
industrial
inevitably
influence
ingenious
initial
inoculate
intelligence

interest
irresistible
island
it's
its
jealousy
jewelry
judgment
knowledge
laboratory
laid
language
lay
lead
led
leisure
length
library
license
lonely
losing
lying
magazine
maneuver
marriage
mathematics
miniature
minutes
mischief
misspell
monstrous
moral
morale
muscle
mysterious
naturally
necessary
neighbor
neither
nickel

niece
ninety
ninth
nuclear
occasional
occur
occurred
occurrence
occurring
omission
parallel
particular
peculiar
perform
permanence
permissible
pleasant
possess
possibly
practical
precede
prefer
prejudice
prepare
prevalent
primarily
principal
principle
privilege
probably
proceed
psychology
publicly
quantity
realize
receive
recommend
referred
rehearsal
relief

relieve
religious
repetition
responsible
restaurant
rhythm
ridicule
roommate
sacrifice
safety
satisfied
schedule
science
secretary
seize
selected
separate
sergeant
several
shining
should have
significant
similarity

sincerely
sincerity
sit
ski, skiing
sophomore
succeed
success
summarized
surprise
suspicious
technique
temperament
temperature
tendency
thorough
though
thought
through
together
tragedy
twelfth
unnecessary
until

using
usually
vacuum
valuable
varies
various
vegetable
vengeance
veteran
vicious
view
villain
weather
Wednesday
weird
whether
wholly
woman
women
would have
writing

21.4 Abstract words

An abstract word expresses generality (e.g., *phenomenon*) instead of concreteness (e.g., *sun*). Abstract words are valuable, but at times, some writers use so many abstract words that reading and comprehension become difficult. This was the point Orwell made when he wrote an abstract translation of a passage from the Book of Ecclesiastes. Contrast this translation to the original passage.

ABSTRACT Objective consideration of contemporary phenomena compels the conclusion that success or
failure in competitive activities exhibits no tendency to be commensurate with innate capacity,
but that a considerable element of the unpre-
dictable must invariably be taken into account.

SPECIFIC I returned and saw under the sun, that the race
is not to the swift, nor the battle to the strong,
neither yet bread to the wise, nor yet riches to
men of understanding, nor yet favor to men of
skill. But time and chance happen to them all.

Writers will use abstract words when necessary. Experienced writers avoid relying entirely on abstraction and
abstract passages. As a beginning writer, you should constantly attempt to move your writing away from abstraction
to concrete and specific language.

ABSTRACT My emotions for Susan tend toward adoration of
her music.

SPECIFIC I like the way Susan can play jazz tunes on the
piano.

ABSTRACT Casual wearing apparel for students should indicate a reflection of casualness for the picnic
and lack excessive formality.

SPECIFIC Students should dress casually and informally
for the picnic.

Practice 1: Rewrite the following sentences so that they
supply specific information.
a. Jake enjoys participation in dining activities involving
desserts.

b. The dormitory population has reached overcrowding conditions.

c. The class appreciates with passion the public orations Dr. Bryan delivers on the survivability of religious belief.

d. Jane shows great freedom in her wearing apparel.

e. People's basic humanity will never allow complete self-centeredness and general unresponsiveness to the needs of others.

f. The reasoning behind this strongly defined rule of my not wearing T-shirts is that my aesthetic values find T-shirts a bad usage of design qualities.

g. With an aim to reaching her goals, this person works very hard to get to them through her dedication to her responsibilities in light of obstacles.

h. The museum has largeness.

i. Some graduates display incredible generosity to that institution.

j. The students displayed great charity.

21.5 Active voice and passive voice

a. Active voice of verb focuses on the agent and the action

ACTIVE VOICE   The dog *bit* the boy. [Active voice emphasizes the agent and the action.]

PASSIVE VOICE   The boy *was bitten* by the dog. [The agent of the action is at the very end of the sentence.]

Practice 1: Rewrite the following sentences, changing verbs from passive to active voice.

a. The boys were attacked by a tiny white poodle.
b. The parrots had been brought from Africa by Reverend Frank.
c. This pure gold key should be worn by you at all times so it is shown that Sigma Pi is considered important by you.
d. The party was ruined by an idiot with cocaine.
e. The lawn was mowed by my father.
f. The diamond was hoped for by Heidi for her birthday.
g. It is not known by anyone why the prisoner was given a small package by the guard.
h. Your friend can be helped by you with a little kindness.

b. Passive voice of verb focuses on elements other than the agent

Normal English word order places the subject at the beginning of the sentence. The subject is often the agent. The passive voice inverts the normal order and pushes the agent to the end of a prepositional phrase and in some cases omits the actor entirely.

ACTIVE VOICE   Smith *wrote* a letter to the mayor.

PASSIVE VOICE   The mayor *was written* a letter by Smith.

The persistent use of the passive voice deemphasizes human activity and hides the agent. If the agent is unimportant or if the writer wishes to emphasize the verb or the object of the action, then passive voice may be effective.

PASSIVE VOICE   The street *was covered* with garbage.

ACTIVE VOICE   Garbage *covered* the street.

PASSIVE VOICE Johnson's finger *was smashed* by the defective drill press. [Here the passive voice emphasizes the smashed finger.]

ACTIVE VOICE A defective drill press *smashed* Johnson's finger. [The active voice here emphasizes the defective drill press.]

Avoid using the passive voice with impersonal abstractions and vague language.

WEAK A statistical analysis of the game *was studied* by the coach.

IMPROVED The coach *studied* the game's statistics.

Practice 2: Rewrite the following sentences, changing the passive constructions to active voice.
a. The books were not read by the boys.
b. The papers have been graded by the teacher.
c. These gold plates were created by Spanish workers.
d. The room was made hot by a broken radiator.
e. The plan was devised for emergencies by a student committee.
f. It has been stated by the newspaper that Henry Smith will run for governor.
g. These instruments are to be considered dangerous.
h. Your calculations have been shown by Hooper to be accurate.
i. A few discussions on the nature of morality have been carried on between the Atheist Club and the Newman Association.
j. The rules regarding alcoholic drinks have been regularly ignored by students.

21.6 Clichés

A cliché is a word or phrase spoken or written many times. When a writer describes someone as "brown as a berry" or speaks of the weather as "cold as ice," that person is relying on clichés to express thought and feeling. Clichés dull the reader's mind and should be avoided. When the phrase "blind as a bat" was first used, it interested the readers. After countless repetitions, the phrase loses much of its effectiveness. A cliché resembles a boring song heard hundreds of times. The unthinking, repetitive quality of clichés makes them ineffective in good writing.

CLICHÉ-RIDDEN   *With fear and trembling*, the young speller *came across* with the right spelling *in the nick of time*.

REVISED   The nervous youngster spelled the word correctly just as the buzzer rang.

Practice 1: Rewrite the following sentences to avoid clichés. Identify the clichés and replace them with specific and detailed language that is fresh and original.

a. Temple played their hearts out beyond anyone's wildest dreams and sent Rutgers to the showers while they chalked up their sixth victory in a row.
b. An unidentified young man wearing a regulation army ROTC uniform as quick as a wink knocked a would-be rapist to the ground a short while before midnight.
c. This unfortunate incident occurred outside of a local eating establishment.
d. The anonymous rescuer of the fair maiden held the vicious criminal pinned to the ground by brute force while a crowd of interested onlookers gathered and

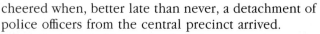
cheered when, better late than never, a detachment of
police officers from the central precinct arrived.

e. When the boys in blue arrived on the scene, the youthful and dashing young hero departed for parts unknown, leaving behind him a cloud of mystery and a
whole cartload of unanswered questions.

f. Sad to say, but my brother should burn a little bit of
midnight oil in the book department.

21.7 Connotation and denotation

The denotation of a word remains fixed in a dictionary (a
dog is a domesticated carnivore); however, the connotation or emotional associations or overtones vary from reader to reader. A word in general has a positive or negative
connotation for most people. For example, for many people the word *religion* may have positive associations. However, for some it may have superlative ones, but for others
it may have negative ones. Because it is impossible to escape the emotional shadings that words cast, effective writers use the emotional power inherent in words to help
them accomplish their purposes in writing. Consider the
meaning in the following sentence:

> Joseph's lust for antique cars took him to a different
> city and a different auto show every weekend. [Most
> connotations associated with lust are unfavorable.
> The sentence would have a different, possibly better,
> meaning if the word *love* or *liking* were substituted
> for *lust*.]

Your principles in word choice should be guided by
the following questions: Does the word express a precise

and intended meaning? Might a reader respond to the emotion in the word but be confused by the intended meaning?

Practice 1: Discuss the differences between the following words. For each pair, decide which has the greater emotional connotation for you. What are those emotional meanings? Select five of the following word pairs and write sentences using those words to illustrate the differences in connotation.

a. boss/employer
b. cancer/illness
c. cuisine/food
d. demand/request
e. procrastinate/delay
f. stench/aroma
g. cruel/brutal
h. thrifty/frugal
i. scab/nonunion worker
j. shark/fish

Practice 2: Explain the differences in connotation and denotation in the following sentences.

a. My grandmother lives in a small (shack, hovel, house, rat trap) on Lovell Avenue.
b. Matthew bought Jenny some (expensive, fashionable, antique, platinum, gold) jewelry.
c. Mary's (female parent, mom, mother, old lady) paid her a surprise visit.
d. Jed is (skinny, slim, slender, twiggy, thin, wispy).
e. The food was (tasty, delicious, refined, excellent, superior, delightful, good, tops).
f. The room (smelled of, reeked with, filled with, stank of) her perfume.

Practice 3: Say the word *dog* out loud and let your imagination develop the first image and idea that comes into your mind. Write nonstop on that idea for five to ten minutes, using as many specific details as you can. Then use a standard college dictionary to write out the denotative meaning of the word *dog*. Then freewrite for another five to ten minutes on a dog from a movie, TV show, book, song, poster, or comic strip. Read your first freewriting in a group and discuss the differences between these three different approaches to the word *dog*. What implications do differences in connotation have for a writer?

21.8 Euphemism

Euphemism (from a Greek word that means "sounding good") is a roundabout way of saying something. By employing euphemisms, a writer attempts to use language to improve reality and to make things seem better than they are. Such a goal may be noble. Occasionally, a writer may want to spare the reader embarrassment or pain. We say we are "going to use the rest room" or that someone "has found eternal rest." In neither case today does the word *rest* have any literal meaning. The phrases are used for the sake of politeness or to spare a person's feelings. Used very often, however, euphemisms mask reality and make a reader question the writer's skill and honesty.

POLITE   John Jones *passed away* yesterday after a *long illness*

STARK   John Jones *died* yesterday of *cancer*.

EVASIVE   The funeral director sought help after problems led to a health decline and straitened financial conditions.

REVISED   The undertaker joined AA after drinking destroyed his health and ruined his business.

Certain parts of reality make many people squeamish. Writers often have good reasons to be polite in writing. Use euphemisms to be polite or to avoid hurt or embarrassment. Do not use euphemisms to conceal or distort reality. Here are some examples of evasive expressions:

Evasive Euphemism	*Direct*
counterfactual propositions	lies
criminal assault	rape
deteriorating housing area	slum
laid to rest	buried
passed away	died
perspiration	sweat
previously owned vehicle	used car
revenue enhancement	tax
sanitary engineer	garbage collector
stretches the truth	exaggerates or lies

Practice 1: Rewrite the following sentences to make them more effective.

a. The head of the tenants' association blamed the foul odors on parental oversight and inattentiveness to rancidity attendant upon disposable refuse.

b. The flight plan of the Korean airplane was interrupted because of a provocative encroachment on the integrity of the Russian people.

c. Jeter Thorpe, Imperial Grand Dragon of the Harper Klan, will be laid to eternal rest at the Golden Thrones Garden of Perpetual Rest Public Cemetery Sunday morning at 6:00 in a simple nondenominational service after a lifetime of staunch defense of the principles of separate development and democratic freedoms.

d. The new leader has begun a process of elimination of undesirable elements.

Practice 2: What might the following expressions mean and how could you translate them into plain English?

a. adult entertainment
b. foot-in-mouth disease
c. financial enticement
d. lacking in delicacy
e. place in custody
f. wayward youth
g. pecuniary difficulties
h. amorous dalliance
i. Indian resettlement policy
j. underprivileged student
k. pre-owned vehicle
l. overzealous disciplinarian

21.9 Expletives

An expletive is a filler word in a sentence, most commonly *it* or *there*. The constant use of expletives with forms of *to be* creates weak, wordy, and ineffective writing. Omission and revision of expletives will help improve most sentences containing them. Consider the following sentences:

EXPLETIVE   *There is* excitement in the crowd each time Jean dives from the high tower.

REVISED   The crowd grows excited each time Jean dives from the tower.

EXPLETIVE   *It is obvious* that I will have to work hard to pass Physics 201.

REVISED   Obviously, I will have to work hard to pass Physics 201.

Unless you have a precise meaning intended, avoid phrases such as *It can be assumed . . . , It might be objected . . . ,* and *It is* the occasion of. . . .

EXPLETIVE   *It is* the occasion for a rise in paper costs next month.

REVISED   The cost of paper will rise next month.

Practice 1: Remove expletives and revise each of the following sentences to make them more concise and effective.

a. There is a problem in that there are not enough coaches for Little League baseball.
b. It is safe to say that the tuition costs will increase fifty dollars next year.
c. Evolution, some Christians believe, shows that there is a divine force controlling the origin and development of all living things.
d. There are some drafty windows in this building that Mr. Meadows needs to repair.
e. It is a matter of fact that there are now 2,000 cocaine addicts living (if you can call it that) in this city.

21.10 Figurative language

A figure of speech is an expression that uses language in a nonliteral manner to emphasize meaning, heighten effect, and convey emotion. Experienced writers use figures of speech to improve their writing by making it more vivid.

21.10
wds

LITERAL	The boy was very thin.
METAPHOR	The boy is a stick. [A metaphor is an implied comparison between two unlike things that omits *like* or *as*.]
SIMILE	The boy is as thin as a stick. [A simile is a comparison between two unlike things using *like* or *as*]
HYPERBOLE	That boy is so thin that his shadow disappears into a crack in the sidewalk. [Hyperbole is exaggeration to add interest.]
IRONY	That boy had better watch out. He is likely to be drafted by the Washington Redskins. [Irony is a statement contrary to fact—not to lie or distort but to emphasize, instruct, or amuse.]
METONYMY	That shinbone came in here and asked for a quart of Pepsi. [Metonymy is the substitution of a part of something for the whole. A common example is the *White House*, which means the executive branch of the Federal government, as in *The White House said. . . .*]
ONOMATOPOEIA	The thin boy laughed at the long word *onomatopoeia* in class and kept whispering, "Bees buzz. Bees buzz. Bees buzz." [In onomatopoeia the sound of a word, such as *buzz*, mimics its meaning.]

OXYMORON   At the end of the day, the boy always felt a sad joy when his father would call him to come home. [*Sad joy* here is an oxymoron, which is a linking of opposites. Some further examples would be *calm rage* and *brutal love.*]

PERSONIFICATION The night covered the thin boy with a dark and silent blanket. [Personification credits nonhuman things and creatures with human characteristics. Here night is personified as a person covering the boy with a blanket.]

Practice 1: Rewrite one of your journal entries by using several figures of speech to make your reader see your examples and details more clearly.

21.11 Formal and informal English

Both standard formal English and standard informal English are correct. Like patterns of dress and behavior, patterns of language (whether formal or informal) depend generally on the audience and social circumstances. For example, a tuxedo is appropriate when worn to a formal dinner, but it is ludicrous when worn by a player on a tennis court. Similarly, informal language is acceptable when you speak to your friends at lunch, but it is completely inappropriate when you write a letter of application for a job at a law firm. Formal English is expected by readers in many situations: in professional publication and correspondence, in business publication and correspondence, and especially in academic discourse. Informal

English is commonly used at home, at play, and at work when we are among friends and not with our superiors. The formality or informality of a writing sample may depend on word choice, word order, use of contractions, and use of shortened forms. A standard dictionary is a valuable guide to formal and informal usage.

Word Choice

INFORMAL   The *kids* have been *bugging* the teacher again.

FORMAL   The *children* have been *bothering* the teacher again.

INFORMAL   *Who* did the President *put up for* chief justice?

FORMAL   *Whom* did the President *nominate as* chief justice?

Word Order

INFORMAL   *What* tool did Smith repair that machine *with?*

FORMAL   *With what* tool did Smith repair that machine?

INFORMAL   The boats began to *slowly* turn toward shore.

FORMAL   *Slowly*, the boats began to turn toward shore.

Contractions and shortened forms

INFORMAL   The patient *hasn't* responded to *chemo.*

FORMAL   The patient *has not* responded to *chemotherapy.*

INFORMAL   The *phone's down* and the *power's off.*

FORMAL   The *telephone is not working* and the *electricity has been disconnected.*

Practice 1: What are some formal and informal (colloquial) meanings for the following words: *rat, deal, hang out*, and *crab*? Write sentences using each formally and informally.

FORMAL   Jane's *dog* won a blue ribbon.

INFORMAL My brother is the *dog* who won the lottery.

21.12 General words and specific words

General words, such as *shoe, vehicle*, or *game*, indicate the members of a general class. Specific words indicate individual things such as *tennis shoe, bus*, or *football*. General words are necessary in all kinds of writing, but they become a problem when the writer relies solely on them, as in the following example:

GENERAL A person said, "Go to that building and get something for my pain."

SPECIFIC The mother whispered to her son, "Run over to the drugstore and buy some aspirin for my headache."

a. Specific nouns contain more specific information than general nouns

The generality or specificity of nouns varies and moves along a continuum from the general to the specific:

General			*Specific*
Writing	Literature	Poem	Keats's "Lamia"
Food	Junk food	Candy	Snickers

Depending on audience and purpose, a writer will decide whether to use a general or specific word. Sometimes the general word is appropriate, but experienced writers generally strive to use specific language in place of vague, general words.

As an example, consider some of the many words that could specify the general words *man* or *woman*: *saint, pilot, thief, lawyer, surgeon, parent, nun, coach, coward*, and *cook*.

b. Specific verbs emphasize action more than general verbs

Some verbs are more specific than other verbs. Verbs such as *have, get, go, walk, talk, move*, and *do* are more general than other verbs. At times a writer wants to use a general verb; at other times a writer might want the precise meaning that a specific verb can communicate.

GENERAL My printer *has* the ability to type 250 words a minute.

SPECIFIC My printer *can type* 250 words a minute.

GENERAL Fran *got* up and *talked* about the traffic.

SPECIFIC Fran *jumped up* and *complained* about the traffic.

GENERAL The runner *moved* across the field.

SPECIFIC The runner *sprinted* across the field.

GENERAL Music *does* something to me.

SPECIFIC Music *excites* me and *makes me want to dance.*

Practice 1: Revise the following sentences by substituting more effective active verbs. Add, delete, or transpose material if necessary.

a. Our school library has more than a million books.
b. Children get happy when a parent has tiny toys for them.
c. The leaf moved across the empty parking lot.
d. If you have a problem, get in touch with the counselor.
e. When I am not doing composition, I am doing artwork.
f. The children had fearful emotions related to the dark.
g. My mother goes on a shopping trip every Saturday.
h. The babysitter was aware that Hank had a high fever.
i. This coupon will get you admission to the concert.
j. Parents make their children safe from harm.

Some specific words that might replace a vague word such as *move* include the following: *bounce, bound, hurry, leap, limp, saunter, shuffle, sprint,* and *strut.* Use your dictionary or a dictionary of synonyms to discover specific words.

c. Specific adjectives provide more precise information than general adjectives

Adjectives, too, may be either general or specific. Consider the specific adjectives that could be used in place of the general adjective *bad*:

bad book	boring, obscene, stupid, difficult
bad weather	snowy, windy, rainy, scorching
bad hamburger	rotten, uncooked, burnt, greasy

Practice 2: Revise the following sentences. Make them more specific, particular, informative, and effective by adding specific details, giving the words a concrete context, or developing meaning with figures of speech.

a. Jack knows a lot about that subject.
b. I am interested in a difficult job.
c. We learned some strange things about that person.
d. Jane works there.
e. Children want to do something to help needy people.
f. Those people are not friendly.
g. The food was wonderful.
h. He was dressed strangely.
i. There were posters all over that place.
j. What happened was funny.

21.13 Idiomatic expressions

An idiom is a unique, nonliteral expression in a particular language. People who experience problems with idiom should listen as often as possible to intelligent programs on American television and radio. The only way to learn the idioms of a language is by hearing the peculiar way unique expressions convey meaning through context. In France, someone who wants to say "I am hungry" says "J'ai faim." If those words are translated literally, the meaning is "I have hunger."

IDIOMATIC When my mother cried, she *gave herself away.* [The idiom *gave herself away* means "revealed herself."]

LITERAL My mother *gave away* her diamonds.

IDIOMATIC Students *have* to learn the spelling rules. [The idiom *have* means "must."]

LITERAL Students *have* stereos in their rooms.

A word may have multiple meanings, but the multiple meanings do not form an idiom. An idiom involves a unique phrasing to create a certain meaning. This use of language by native speakers in a nonliteral sense, yet with a clear meaning, is called idiom. Consider the idiomatic meanings of the following expressions, all of which involve the word *pass*:

pass on	to die
pass out	to become unconscious
pass up	to go without
pass a football	to throw a football
pass over	to ignore
make a pass	flirt

Many idioms arise from the use of prepositions. Different prepositions used with the same word often lead to completely different meanings. Students who have problems with correctness in idiom should pay particular attention to each use of a preposition and consult either a standard dictionary for correct usage or one of the following special dictionaries:

- *A Dictionary of Contemporary American Usage*
- *Handbook of American Idioms and Idiomatic Usage*
- *The Harper Dictionary of Contemporary Usage*
- *Modern American Usage*
- *Webster's Dictionary of English Usage*

Practice 1: Revise each of the following sentences to improve the idiom.

a. Amy is independent from her parents.
b. I took away the subway to 42nd Street.
c. The manager for the store told me not to worry.
d. Her thoughts were centered around Jesus.
e. I want some mash potatoes in gravy, coffee in cream, hot fudge this Sunday with whip cream.
f. College is different than high school.
g. Mary wanted to sleep at outside under the pup tent.
h. The students had to wait on teacher who was late forever.
i. The steam engine proved being a great invention.
j. Black Larsen died December 1890, and it happened on accident.

21.14 Jargon

A polite description of jargon would be "specialized language for a particular profession or activity." Within those specialized journals and magazines, technical jargon is acceptable—even preferred. As always, the audience plays an important role in word choice. Jargon within technical publications is perfectly acceptable; however, outside of special publications, jargon should be avoided rigorously.

JARGON   Young subadults manifest conformability patterns in peer groups. They experience moderate enjoyment in the presence of others approximating the same age level. Clothing-wise and action-wise, they exert high levels of attention and energy to be in resemblance to those about them.

REVISED   Teenagers are conformists. They enjoy the company of people their own age. They prefer to dress and act like those teenagers around them.

One common form of jargon is the invention and use of new words ending in *-wise, -type,* or *-ize.* Avoid inventing and using words such as *telephone-wise, library-type,* and *tacoize.* Find common words to replace jargon. If there is no common word or phrase, then the technical word or phrase is acceptable.

Jargon words   *Common words*
ingress and egress   entrance and exit
strategize   plan a strategy
separate entity   individual
convallaria majalis   lily of the valley

Practice 1: Revise each of the following to eliminate jargon.

a. *Moby Dick* is a text that exemplifies the nature of Melville's obsessiveness with the contrarieties of voluntarism and determinism.

b. This policy gives exclusion in terms of coverage of all personal property while the insured is engaged in travel outside the continental United States.

c. Garvey slammed a three-bagger off the center wall, and Smith sailed him home with a sacrificial offering to the shortstop's stomping grounds.

d. The level of environmental cognitive awareness augments appreciably when the subject attains a level of consciousness following a deep sleeping pattern.

e. The participants denied their corporeal beings any semblance of solid nutritiveness or liquid replenishment for a period of 72 hours.

f. Clark rapped about his copout in school and said his bad grades were a horse of a different color.
g. The mother had made her little three-year-old daughter telephone-wise.
h. Telephone-wise, the accountant recommends that we shift our business back to AT&T.

Practice 2: From your college textbooks, find five sentences with jargon and revise them.

21.15 Mixed diction

In most academic assignments, the instructor asks for writing in formal English. Mixed diction is a lapse from formal diction. This lapse occurs when two styles or levels of language clash with each other. Writing should be consistently formal or informal. It should not mix different levels of diction.

MIXED DICTION   Humphrey Bogart plays a stoic character in the movie *Casablanca* who's able to really take it on the chin.

REVISED   In the movie *Casablanca*, Humphrey Bogart plays a stoic character who is able to endure great hardship.

MIXED DICTION   After studying hard for one semester, John zonked out with the druggies and bagged school.

REVISED   After studying hard for one semester, John began using drugs and quit school.

Practice 1: Revise the following sentences to eliminate mixed diction.

a. Professor Cory explained that the Greek gods had human characteristics and really got it on with the earthly chicks.
b. Older people require less sleep than young people, and their bodies cry out in need of an augmentation of ingestion of calcium.
c. Isn't it a crying shame that Sarah Ann will be splitting Thursday to begin college in Boston?
d. Runners shouldn't purchase a pair of el-cheapo shoes.
e. Gloria is planning *haute cuisine* for Friday's bash.

21.16 Mixed metaphor

In a mixed metaphor, the comparison includes an element that does not belong. Mixed metaphors often imply conditions contrary to fact and, as such, violate logic.

MIXED METAPHOR   When our principal patrolled the lunchroom, the students became a flock of small fish flying away from him. [Fish do not fly in flocks. They swim in schools.]

METAPHOR   When our principal patrolled the lunchroom, the students became a school of small fish and swam away from him.

In an awkward metaphor, a comparison is made that strains the meaning or weakens the purpose.

AWKWARD METAPHOR   Michael Jordan is the Beethoven of basketball. [Because their skills have nothing in common, it is completely inappropriate to compare a composer and a professional athlete.]

METAPHOR

Michael Jordan is the Willie Mays of basketball.

NOTE: To analyze a metaphor or a simile, divide the comparison into two parts: the tenor and the vehicle. In the sentence *Mary is an angel*, *Mary* is the tenor and *angel* is the vehicle. The tenor is the base of the comparison. The vehicle is the person, place, or thing to which the tenor is compared.

Practice 1: Analyze the following comparisons and identify the tenor and vehicle in each.

a. Marge likes to smoke. I call her Smokestack. Her children nicknamed her Forest-Fire.
b. Jed turned the herb garden into a low-class slum.
c. Mark wasn't a listener to the news. He was an addict.
d. College is the key to success.
e. Mandy's mother is a barracuda in tennis shoes.

Practice 2: Write five sentences of your own, writing comparisons on the topics of smoking, gardening, news, college, and parents.

Practice 3: Revise the following sentences to correct the confused metaphors.

a. College is no bed of roses for a student to stay awake all night partying.
b. Jim had an ace in the hole to use in his tennis match with Keith.
c. The commander of the ship had to change horses in midstream.
d. This chapel is a peaceful refuge for spiritual warfare against the forces of evil in the world.

e. Fight to extinguish the lamp of slavery in South Africa with a loud voice of protest.

21.17 Negative words

Direct and positive language has great power. Unless you intend to show a sharp contrast or to make a clear contradiction or denial, avoid negatives such as *not*, *no*, or *never*. Most of these can be revised to avoid the negative.

Adjectives		*Prepositions*	
not careful	careless	not inside	outside
not sober	drunk	not for	against

Adverbs		*Verbs*	
not clearly	unclearly	not remain	leave
not properly	improperly	not remember	forget

Nouns	
not the truth	a lie
not a possibility	an impossibility

Practice 1: Find synonyms for the following: not hungry, not eat, not young, not able to read, not able to hope, never smiling, never working, not experienced, not orderly. Write a series of sentences using each of the synonyms.

21.18 Nominalization

Nominalization refers to the process of making an abstract word out of a simpler and less abstract word, either a noun, a verb, or an adjective. Although nominalization is occasionally a valuable tool, it is best avoided.

DIRECT   The farmers had some *hope* of rain.

NOMINALIZED   The farmers had some *hopefulness* for rain. [An abstract noun is transformed into a more abstract noun.]

DIRECT   The quarterback was *aware* of his error.

NOMINALIZED   The quarterback had an *awareness* of his error. [An adjective is transformed into an abstract noun.]

DIRECT   The experiment *failed*.

NOMINALIZED   The experiment resulted in *failure*. [A verb is transformed into an abstraction.]

Practice 1: Identify any nominalizations in the following sentences and revise them accordingly, removing all nominalization.

   a. The intentionality of the teacher was that he wanted to make the students think for themselves.

   b. The mechanic offered an explanation of why the carburetor malfunctioned.

   c. Representative Rope made a presentation explaining his views on terrorism.

   d. A team of agents from the FBI made a thorough examination of the apartment.

e. There were complaints in the office when the managers encountered the discovery of mice in the cabinets.

f. A reevaluation of the client's status will be conducted by Mr. Dinger next week.

g. There has been a petitional request by the students for a wider range of recreational possibilities over the weekends in the Sports Complex.

h. Participation in the Special Olympics was done by Phi Mu and Delta Zeta sororities despite the fact there was an occurrence of a rainfall event over the weekend.

21.19 Noun-noun-noun constructions

One of the great resources of the English language is its remarkable ability to create compound nouns such as *football* or *houseboat*. Note, however, that those compounds are formed from specific words, such as *foot* and *ball*. Such words are easily understandable and present no problem. In contrast to the specificity of the previous words, some writers today like to join nouns together to form abstract compounds, such as *vehicle identification* or *alcoholism analysis*. Many readers have difficulty understanding the meaning of such terms. Even more difficult, some writers string together a series of nouns, inventing expressions such as *atmosphere rainfall event*, when all that is meant is rain or rainstorm. As a rule, writing is more effective if the writer avoids a string of three or more nouns, especially abstractions.

Avoid	*Prefer*
credit verification check	credit check
linguistic analysis theory	linguistics
sanitary landfill center employees	garbage workers

Practice 1: Revise the following sentences, eliminating triple-noun constructions.

a. The heart attack prevention center entrance needs a new electronically adjusted, color-coded vehicle-flow control mechanism to prevent automobile accident occurrences.

b. The corporation board chair ordered a divestiture action plan to be formulated for strategy planning seminars by next Tuesday.

c. The childhood fright treatment center at the university wants to inaugurate a person contact coordination reference bureau to aid in policy decision formulation.

d. The astrology dream interpretation discussion group will have cognition exercises and rap sequence interaction sessions on Friday night.

e. That company manufactures individual hand-held, manual-operation, metallic composition combat emplacement evacuators.

21.20 Pretentious words

Some writers have curious ideas of grace and elegance. Through haste, carelessness, or lack of knowledge, they write sentences like the following:

PRETENTIOUS Helen *transpired to modify* three words in her paper.

REVISED Helen *changed* three words in her paper.

PRETENTIOUS   My partner for the tennis match has indicated that we *are deficient in our supply of yellow-colored spherical projectiles.*

REVISED   My partner just told me we *need some tennis balls.*

a. Pretentious verbs should be revised

Use verbs for their precise meaning, not for their length or their intellectual sound. Large verbs do not communicate more than small verbs. When possible, use a plain English verb in place of a longer Latinate verb if the meanings are the same.

Avoid	*Prefer*	*Avoid*	*Prefer*
anticipate	expect	interface	talk or meet
endeavor	try	facilitate	help
envisage	see	terminate	end

b. Pretentious nouns should be revised

Words should contain precise meaning and nuance. Quite often, a short word can have more effect than a lengthy word. The following list contains some lengthy words and reasonable translations into plain English.

Avoid	*Prefer*
chronometer	wristwatch
fiscal improprieties	theft
illumination device	candle

Practice 1: Revise the following sentences, eliminating pretentious words and phrases.

a. After reception of a response from his spouse in the affirmative, Bob proceeded to complete his application for postal employment.

b. Information regarding a special personalized regimen effecting weight reduction can be obtained by interview with a sales information area representative customer consultant.

c. Mark investigated the optimum price for new individual aerial deceleration mechanisms for the skydiving club.

d. The well-known regrettable eventuality of a failure of the deterrence policy began in the Pacific Theater at Pearl Harbor in 1941.

e. Verbal contact between neighboring residents living in proximity should precede a manifestation of hostility concerning the incineration of the arboreal refuse.

21.21 Unnecessary repetition

A redundancy is a word or phrase that can be removed with no damage to meaning in a sentence. Effective writers strive to identify and remove all repetitive and pointless material from their writing.

a. Redundant prepositions and prepositional phrases should be removed

Many prepositional phrases are unnecessary or meaningless. If they add nothing to the meaning, remove expressions such as the following: *in appearance, in character, in religion, in price, in color, in number, now in this day and age, in size, in shape, in weight,* or *in texture.*

REDUNDANT Smitty is small *in size* for a lineman.

REVISED Smitty is small for a lineman.

Some expressions using a preposition seem so inevitable that it might come as a surprise to learn they are redundant and, except for minor emphasis, contribute no meaning to any sentence.

PRECISE The boy ran up the road.

REDUNDANT The blue bird was *up* above the boy's head.

REVISED The blue bird was above the boy's head.

b. Redundant qualifiers should be removed

Unless you want to emphasize that a statement is opinion and not fact, remove qualifiers such as *I believe, I feel, I think, in my opinion,* or *it seems.*

WORDY The president, I believe, won forty-nine states.

REVISED The president won forty-nine states.

Practice 1: Eliminate all redundant material from the following sentences.
a. Young Fenton, I think it is perfectly clear, is too bright in terms of intelligence to go into accounting.
b. He should, I have been thinking, have a chance to meet a great accountant in person.
c. The coat is the right size, it seems, but I feel that the color is too bright.
d. I wanted to stop for dinner—for some food, for a drink, for some good talk, and for a good meal.

e. One of the silliest things going on all the time in the movie was the movie repeating over and over again the theme song from the beginning of the film to the very end.

c. Redundant conjunctions should be avoided

The English language has acquired an enormous stockpile of wordy substitutes for basic, simple words. To some, these phrases may sound intelligent and even important, but they are wordy and tedious. Find simpler, clearer words.

Avoid	*Use*
because of the fact that	because
by virtue of the fact that	because
despite the fact that	although
for the purpose of	for
for the reason that	because
the question as to whether	whether
due to the fact that	because
in the event that	if

d. Redundant nouns should be deleted

The following nouns should be used with care: *action, angle, area, aspect, case, character, circumstances, element, facet, factor, field, kind, nature, problem, process, regard, respect, situation, sort,* and *type.* Sometimes they have a precise meaning: "a *case* in court," "the different *types* in a newspaper," or "the *facet* of a diamond." Generally, you can simply delete such words from most sentences with no loss of meaning.

UNNECESSARY Bill's *field* of teaching is history. [Contrast with *The field is muddy.*]

REVISED   Bill teaches history.

UNNECESSARY   The *character* of Hamlet seems to dislike
women. [Contrast with the sentence, *Pin-
ter's play has five characters.*]

REVISED   Hamlet seems to dislike women.

Practice 2: Identify any redundant words or phrases in the
following sentences. Revise the sentences accordingly, removing or rearranging words as necessary.

EXAMPLE   One important factor is that Hank is in a desperate situation.

REVISION Hank is desperate.

a. We read our history books for examination purposes in
this history course.
b. In the case of George Dow, are you aware of the fact
that he is in a bad health situation?
c. The aspect that interests me must be that the roses are
all of the red type.
d. Backgammon is a sort of game that has elements of
chance.
e. The nature of this medical, surgical operation is dangerous, but we cannot ignore the severe pain problem
and the suffering it would alleviate.
f. At all times, Harold is in a position to be a volunteer
fireman on account of the fact that at present he is
unemployed.

e. Redundant adverbs can be removed

Many adverbs can be removed in many cases with no loss
of meaning. Think twice before using any of the following

words: *absolutely, actually, basically, certainly, completely, definitely, extremely, incredibly, intensely, just, literally, perfectly, positively, quite, rather, really, simply, so, somewhat,* and *very.*

DESCRIPTIVE The child *slowly* ate the ice cream.

REDUNDANT The child *really* ate that ice cream.

Unnecessary adverbs are often attached to verbs.

Avoid	*Use*	*Avoid*	*Use*
completely end	end	continue on	continue
enter into	enter	look visually	look
join together	join	repeat again	repeat
retreat back	retreat	share in common	share

f. Redundant adjectives can be removed

Adjectives are best when lively, exact, and informative.

EFFECTIVE The *tiny* sports car was covered with *wet* leaves.

EFFECTIVE His *chalk-white* face had *five red* pimples.

EFFECTIVE Mary was *silly, sexy,* and *loud.*

Be sparing in your use of vague, meaningless adjectives, such as *actual, awesome, awful, certain, cute, dreadful, fabulous, fantastic, fierce, fine, funny, gorgeous, grand, great, horrible, horrid, keen, lovely, marvelous, nice, pretty, real, sensational, smooth, splendid, stunning, sure, sweet, swell, terrible, terrific, true,* and *wonderful.* Unless you use such words with their precise dictionary meanings, it is best to avoid them. Find the precise word to indicate your meaning.

UNNECESSARY   Illegitimate births for teenage girls create a *real* problem. [What would an *unreal* problem be?]

REVISED   Illegitimate births create devastating problems for teenage girls.

In some situations, the noun implies the meaning of the adjective. If that is so, then simply omit the adjective. In the following examples, the adjectives are unnecessary:

angry rage	free gift	new innovation
dead corpse	hot fire	personal opinion
dull boredom	new beginner	true fact

Practice 3: Rewrite the following sentences to eliminate redundant adverbs and adjectives.

a. The black crow flew in a round circle over the roof above our heads.

b. Basically the pure and spotless heroine seemed to have sporadic episodes of real amnesia.

c. A dangerous and deadly poison is really there and present in the children's grade school classrooms.

d. Why are you desirous and eager for me to truly express to you my personal opinion about our own private relationship?

e. Premedical students who go to college and plan to apply to medical school must be positively smart and also fantastically dedicated and disciplined.

f. Certainly the company needs to advance forward into new markets instead of just going in a circle around where it has always been.

g. *Redundant clauses beginning with* who, which, *and* that *can often be revised*

Many adjective clauses can be turned into a one-word adjective or adjective phrase with no loss of meaning. Careful revision can lead to shorter sentences and clearer meaning.

REDUNDANT The truck driver *who was confused* stared at the road map.

REVISED The *confused* truck driver stared at the road map.

Practice 4: Simplify each of the following sentences by revising each adjective clause.
  a. The spider that is blue that Dr. Frumbee trapped is exceedingly rare.
  b. The five bananas that Isidora bought are covered with green mold.
  c. The pitcher who was in a game made a wild pitch that lost the game.
  d. The man who is an ex-marine applied for a job as a night watchman.
  e. The critic saw some paintings that the painter Mark Rothko painted.

Practice 5: Underline the key words in the following sentences and revise each sentence accordingly.
  a. I find it very boring and usually find other things to do such as sports or any other outdoor activities rather than sit down and read a novel or a magazine.
  b. Homer is describing driving a stake into the eye of the evil Cyclops just like killing a vampire or when you go to a horror movie and see something really gory.

c. My problem is getting the books I need for this paper and that my roommate has begun acting like he has found a year's free supply of the stupidest possible dope imaginable.

21.22 Sexist language

The personal pronoun *he* can occasionally present a problem as the following sentences, adapted from a TV commercial, illustrate:

PROBLEMATIC   If these symptoms appear when brushing your teeth, you should visit your dentist. *He* will examine your teeth and set you on a program of careful dental hygiene.

If the reader is male, he may not be bothered by the *he* in the sample sentence. However, many readers might rightly ask, "Why *he*? Why not *he* or *she*? Are all dentists men?" The use of male pronouns to refer to all people can lead in some cases to intense negative reactions. Care must be taken in using the pronoun *he* to refer to both men and women. To avoid problems, observe the following guidelines: If you know your audience is entirely female, use *she*. If you know your audience is entirely male, use *he*. If you know your audience involves both men and women, you might use *he or she*. In most cases, a writer can revise a problematic sentence in one of three ways: (1) by using plurals, (2) by using the phrase *she or he*, or (3) by using common gender.

PROBLEMATIC   By the time a child is six, *he* has acquired a complete system of grammar.

PLURALS	By the time children are six, *they* have acquired complete systems of grammar.
HE OR SHE	By the time a child is six, *he or she* has acquired a complete system of grammar.
COMMON GENDER	A *child* of six has acquired a complete system of grammar.

See also *he/she, him/her, his/her* in the Glossary of Usage.

Practice 1: Revise each of the following sentences in at least two different ways.

a. When learning to play chess, a young man needs intense concentration.

b. If you ask the manager of any important company how he rose to the top, you will hear a story of hard work and dedication.

c. In college, a dean is the person to ask because he knows everything.

d. A police officer will always tell you his biggest problem is lack of citizen support.

e. An elementary school teacher is very influential because she is often a role model for the children.

In addition to the preceding principles for care in selecting pronouns, writers should use the following guidelines to avoid false impressions and negative reactions.

✎   Use neutral words in common gender when speaking of people in general.

Avoid	Use
man	the human race
mankind	people
manpower	workers, personnel

✎ Use gender-free titles and nouns.

Avoid	Use
chairman	chair
policeman	police officer
poetess	poet

✎ Use *Miss* or *Mrs.* only when you know that the person desires that form of address. In all other cases, use *Ms.*

Mrs. Phyllis Schaffly
Miss Katie McKernan
Ms. Daniela Pozo

21.23 Slang

Slang is any of the various informal words and phrases invented by particular groups: teenagers, athletes, and so forth. Like fads in fashion, slang words and phrases are interesting for a while. Although slang may sound new and fresh, it presents problems in communication. One, it is hard to understand the specific meaning of slang because the meaning of such words shifts from day to day and from city to city. Two, slang words reinforce cliquishness and make it difficult for an "outsider" to understand the meaning. For these reasons, slang can be a good emotional release but a disaster in terms of communication. Phrases such as *That's bad* or *That's cool* are as purely expressive as jazz, but words are not music. They have meaning. *Cool* means something. *Bad* means something else. Slang works to blur meaning by substituting feeling for precise definition. In some cases, however, when the writer knows that the audience would respond enthusiastically to a few well-placed, judicious slang phrases, using them can be an effective rhetorical device. If a composition teacher asks for formal prose, the writing should be free of slang phrases, and slang should be carefully avoided in the papers for other college courses.

SLANG   The death of John Kennedy was *a real nerve frazzler.*

REVISED The death of John Kennedy was *a great tragedy.*

SLANG   In *Moby Dick* the loony captain *goes bananas* over a whale that *gave him a gimp leg.*

REVISED In *Moby Dick* Captain Ahab *becomes enraged at the whale that* destroyed his leg.

Practice 1: Write twelve sentences, each of which uses one word from the following pairs.

a. narc/inform   d. scab/nonunion miner
b. pad/room   e. nuts/insane
c. mug/visage   f. cool/excellent

Which sentences that you have written here contain slang? What response do you have when you hear people use slang?

Practice 2: Revise the following sentences, making each appropriate for an academic audience.
a. President Truman was the dude who nuked the Japanese.
b. King Lear had a Mickey Mouse attitude toward life.

c. Those fat cat athletes got more money than brains.
d. That flash from Nebraska got stopped cold by the Oklahoma linebackers.

Practice 3: Identify each of the following words as either slang, formal diction, or more formal diction. Create sentences to illustrate the differences between the words.

a. talk/discourse/rap   d. duds/clothing/apparel
b. suds/malt beverage/beer   e. leave/depart/buzz off
c. enjoyment/kicks/gratification   f. taciturn/tight-lipped/silent

21.24 Ineffective forms of *to be*

A writer can generally improve the effectiveness of a sentence by substituting active verbs for ineffective forms of the verb *to be*. Such a revision usually reduces the number of words in the sentence at the same time that it allows an active verb to express with emphasis the writer's intended meaning.

LINKING VERB   Dr. Bolcar *is* on a continual search for new ways to treat acne.

ACTIVE VERB   Dr. Bolcar continually *searches* for new ways to treat acne.

An excessive reliance on linking verbs, especially forms of *to be*, leads to weak and ineffective writing. Sentences with linking verbs can often be improved if you replace *to be* forms with verbs indicating action.

LINKING VERB   The children *are* hopeful for large presents.

ACTIVE VERB   The children *hope* for large presents.

21.24
wds

LINKING VERB This *is* a school with a stress on academics.

ACTIVE VERB This school *stresses* academics.

Practice 1: Revise the following sentences by removing or replacing all forms of the verb *to be*. You might underline the key word that signals action in each sentence and then revise, using that key word as an active verb that replaces the *to be* form.

a. It is obvious that Mary is in love with Juan.
b. My shoes are in need of repair.
c. Our team was the only one to defeat Ironton.
d. I am desirous that there be plenty of cake and ice cream at your birthday party.
e. There is going to be a meeting today of the town council.
f. This is the chair that Mike painted.
g. It was a surprise to the teacher that Robert was on good behavior.
h. I am eager to know more about a summer job in New York City.
i. The child will be sad at the knowledge of the dead pet.

It takes time and patience to learn helpful revising strategies. The following questions might help a writer who wants to improve variety and effectiveness in verb choice.

✎ Can two shorter sentences be combined into a longer sentence?

SHORT SENTENCES Friday *will be* a day for celebration for Henry. Now Henry *is* without crutches on his walks.

COMBINATION   Because Henry can now *walk* without crutches, he will *celebrate* this Friday.

✎   *What* happens in the sentence?

LINKING VERB   It *is* the duty of the sheriff *to be* the collector of the property tax.

ACTIVE VERB   As his duty, the sheriff *collects* property taxes.

ACTIVE VERB   The sheriff *must collect* the property taxes.

✎   *Who* does the action in the sentence?

LINKING VERB   Trout *was* Ed's suggestion for dinner.

ACTIVE VERB   Ed *suggested* trout for dinner.

✎   *What adjective* might yield an idea for a verb?

LINKING VERB   The child *is* controllable by the baby sitter, but not by the parents.

ACTIVE VERB   The baby sitter, but not the parents, *can control* the child.

✎   If you remove *it is*, what is left?

LINKING VERB   *It is* the time now for an oil change by Mike in his car.

ACTIVE VERB   Mike *needs* to change the oil in his car now.

✎   If you remove *there is* or *there are*, what is left?

LINKING VERB   *There is* no time for me to read this novel.

ACTIVE VERB   I *have* no time to read this novel.

LINKING VERB   *There are* crowds of people all over the city who screamed "Death to dictators!"

ACTIVE VERB   All over the city crowds of people screamed, "Death to dictators!"

✎   Can a lengthy sentence be divided into shorter sentences?

LINKING VERBS   What the map *is* not an indicator of *is* that a small creek *is* the divider between the old graveyard and the new golf course and it *is* ignorant of the fact that a huge oak tree *is* the marker for the site of the first grave.

ACTIVE VERBS   The map *fails to indicate* that a small creek *divides* the old graveyard from the new golf course. It also *ignores* the fact that a huge oak tree *marks* the site of the first grave.

Undesirable revision of *to be* *forms*

Sometimes a writer makes a mistake when trying to revise a sentence with a form of *to be.* Often, a writer's best choice involves a form of *to be,* especially when the writer wants to express an identification, a definition, or an identity, or wants to use a progressive verb tense.

IDENTIFICATION   That child with the blue hat *is* the thief.

DEFINITION   A sentence fragment *is* a group of words that form an incomplete sentence.

IDENTITY   Nine times six *is* fifty-four.

PROGRESSIVE   You *are blaming* me for the mistake you made!

PROGRESSIVE   Bacteria *are destroying* the experiment.

Practice 2: Revise each of the following sentences by substituting more active and more lively verbs for the *to be* forms.

a. My uncle plans to be on a fishing trip in the Bahamas in January.
b. It is my belief that the traffic commissioner is in total ignorance of anything related to traffic safety.
c. Our plan is to visit New York and then be in Boston in time for Kevin's graduation.
d. There are some good reasons presented in this essay why children should be learners of a foreign language.
e. I am desirous for you to tell me where there is a shoe repair shop that is nearby.
f. It is a recent discovery by Godfrey that the river is contaminated by mercury.
g. There should be no obstacles in relation to your studying hard.
h. *The Catcher in the Rye* is a novel that is a pleasure to many young readers.

Practice 3: Revise the following paragraph by substituting active verbs for *to be* forms whenever possible.

> Migraine headaches are painful and incapacitating. Once an attack begins, no drug is able to stop it. Some people are in the habit of taking sedatives, narcotics, sleeping pills, or tranquilizers, but none of them is good at stopping a migraine. Often the drugs are a worse thing for the sufferer. While migraine is a source of hallucinations or blindness in some, it may be the creator of intense bodily pain for others. Most sufferers are possessed by a need to lie down. They

are in that state of feeling too weak to breathe, too tired to move, and too confused to think. Some migraine sufferers are known to report that the faintest light or the tiniest sound is an experience which feels like a molten metal being poured into their eyes or ears. Before the migraine, many afflicted people are in a mysterious "aura" of curious effects. During the "aura" they are without the power of language, without a sense of time, without consciousness while remaining awake. Some even are known to not have the ability to perform routine tasks such as opening a door or drinking a glass of water. A headache is the signal of the final stage of a migraine. Accompanying that may be some or all of the following: fever, chills, sweat, nausea, and absolute weakness.

J. Grant

PART 7

Writing
Conventions

22 Punctuation

Punctuation marks are invented symbols, signals for the reader. They provide information and direction. One might compare them to highway signs. Some signs are essential, others less so. Knowing the various punctuation marks and their traditional rules can help most writers, especially in the final editing stages of writing.

22.1 Terminal punctuation

The period, the exclamation point, and the question mark signal to a reader the end of a sentence. In addition to indicating finality, terminal punctuation can also signal exclamations and questions.

a. Periods end declarative sentences, imperative sentences, and polite requests

DECLARATIVE   My brother forgot to return the book.

IMPERATIVE   Edward, give me the book.

REQUEST   Will you please return the overdue library book. [Note that this question has no answer. It is a polite request.]

NOTE: Do not add another period to an abbreviation at the end of a sentence.

CORRECT   The invasion occurred in 66 BC.

b. A question mark signals the end of a question or indicates uncertainty or approximation

QUESTION   Who has stolen that library book?

UNCERTAINTY   Weldon Kees died (?) in 1954. [The poet Weldon Kees vanished in 1954. The date of his death is unknown.]

NOTE: Do not use a question mark after an indirect question (see chapter 24). Not all sentences with the words *ask, why, how,* or *whether* are questions.

INCORRECT We asked the boy whether he knew the answer?

CORRECT We asked the boy whether he knew the answer.

CORRECT We asked the boy, "Do you know the answer?"

NOTE: Do not use punctuation, such as a question mark, to attempt irony, humor, or sarcasm. Revise the sentence to convey your tone.

WEAK She gave me a meal (?) of bread and onion.

REVISED She gave me a sumptuous meal consisting of a piece of dry white bread and a thick slice of raw onion.

c. An exclamation point is used to express strong feeling

EXCLAMATORY The new student is going to eat a worm!

EXCLAMATORY Ha! What an idiot Garza is!

Practice 1: Correct the following sentences by putting in terminal punctuation and capital letters where needed.

  a. When I saw Mary, she asked about the trip we are planning to take she had heard that we might go on a field trip to the marshes last semester in introductory biology, the teacher had asked the class whether anyone had ever eaten a mushroom
  b. When I raised my hand, Mary asked me, "why did you eat such a form of plant life"
  c. Mary thought mushrooms were disgusting

d. "Oh no," she said "why would Mr. Rabb have to talk about slimy mushrooms"

22.2 Comma

The comma is a punctuation mark used most often to separate elements in a sentence. Commas carry meaning and should be used with care and precision. Sentences without needed commas often cause confusion and slow down comprehension.

PUZZLING The child was tired afraid wet and hungry.

REVISED The child was tired, afraid, wet, and hungry.

The comma is the most widely used mark of punctuation. It should be used carefully in the following cases.

a. *Before the coordinating conjunctions* and, but, or, nor, for, so, *and* yet, *a comma is used to join independent clauses*

Wally washed the windows, and Joe mopped the floors.

PATTERN

Independent clause ,	Coordinating conjunction	Independent clause

Mary danced in the street, but Mo moped in the hallway. [Note that the comma goes *before* the coordinating conjunction in each of these sentences.]

Amos will direct the play, or I will leave town. [Some writers omit the comma in short sentences: *Mike fished and Bill hunted.*]

b. To separate items in a series, a comma is used

Sluggo ordered *radishes, carrots, garlic*, and *coffee* for breakfast. [series of nouns]

The team swam *past the dock, around the lake*, and *up the creek*. [series of prepositional phrases]

The officer asked Eliott *where he lived, what he did for a living, why he was out so late*, and *how he had managed to fall asleep in a tree*. [series of noun clauses]

The carrots were *old, brown, warm, spotted*. [Series of adjectives. Occasionally, the *and* is omitted for rhythm and emphasis or to indicate the series is not exhaustive. Compare: *The garlic had a faint, rancid, metallic aroma.*]

c. To set off introductory elements, a comma is used

ADVERB CLAUSE
Whenever James Simon Jones visits Russia, he dreams of Lenin.

PREPOSITIONAL PHRASE
Even with a seriously sprained ankle and a broken hand, the girl was still able to swim across the lake.

SENTENCE MODIFIER
Yes, Sean was taken to the emergency room at the hospital last night.

CONJUNCTIVE ADVERB
Mark is planning to spend the weekend studying; *however*, Mario is ready to go gambling in Atlantic City.

PARTICIPLE   *Exhausted*, Todd fell asleep on the porch.

PARTICIPLE PHRASE   *Playing middle linebacker for the Bulldogs*, Kirk made nine unassisted tackles in the game.

ABSOLUTE PHRASE   *The whale having been washed up on the beach*, a team from the aquarium flew to the scene immediately.

INTERJECTION   *Well*, it looks like Nebraska will go to the Orange Bowl again.

APPOSITIVE   *A poet of great lyrical intensity*, Richard Wilbur has just finished translating a book of French poetry.

d. To mark off parenthetical elements, a comma is used

Although a parenthetical element supplies information, it is not essential to the meaning in a sentence.

PARENTHETICAL The driver, *according to the police*, sped through the red light.

Parenthetical expressions, such as *according to the critics, it seems, I believe, it is reported*, and *I understand*, are generally set off by a comma or a pair of commas.

PARENTHETICAL His plan, *for a change*, makes sense. [Contrast: His plan for a change makes sense.]

PARENTHETICAL This car, *I think*, is three years old. [Contrast: I think this car is three years old.]

e. Certain large numbers, addresses, dates, places, and degrees or titles after a name require a comma

NUMBER We caught 1,209,453 mosquitoes at the lake last summer. [Note that the comma is used to separate hundreds, thousands, millions, billions in large numbers: 1,076,323; 1,076,321,606.]

ADDRESS Our new address is 45 Stanley Lane, Driscoll, WV 25468. [Note: No comma appears after the postal abbreviation.]

DATE Sidney had a mystical experience on January 1, 1980. [Note: On 1 January 1985, I was fired. October 12, 1972, is the date Katie was born.]

PLACE Beatrice, Nebraska, is the birthplace of Weldon Kees.

DEGREE The girl made a fancy name tag for Joe Smith, M.D.

TITLE Jo-Bob Rearer changed his name to J.W. Reardon, III.

f. Nonrestrictive elements are set off by commas

A nonrestrictive modifier provides information but it does not identify or limit a noun or pronoun. If the nonrestrictive element is removed, the sentence suffers some loss of information, but little loss in meaning.

ADJECTIVE The small child, *terrified*, began to cry.

APPOSITIVE   Dr. Rink, *a heart surgeon*, fainted last Tuesday.

APPOSITIVE   I like Pink Floyd's The Wall, *their best album*.

ADJECTIVE PHRASE Jan's oldest daughter, *afraid of no one*, walked out into the backyard when she heard a noise.

ADJECTIVE CLAUSE Melanie, *who is a bigot*, began talking.

The following examples show some of the differences between restrictive and nonrestrictive sentence elements. Generally, nonrestrictive elements are set off by commas.

Adjectives

RESTRICTIVE   The silly clown made everyone laugh.

NONRESTRICTIVE   The clown, *silly and old*, made everyone laugh.

Noun

RESTRICTIVE   Inspector W. G. Webster will visit the scene of the crime.

NONRESTRICTIVE   W. G. Webster, *the Inspector*, will visit the scene of the crime.

Phrase

RESTRICTIVE   Students *inspired by Professor Myles* solved the problem.

NONRESTRICTIVE   The new students, *inspired by Professor Myles*, solved the problem.

Clause

RESTRICTIVE   Students *who never went to class* failed physics.

NONRESTRICTIVE Ten students, *who never went to class*, failed physics.

NOTE: The subordinating conjunction *that* always introduces a restrictive clause.

CORRECT The paper *that I bought* cost a quarter.

The relative pronoun *which* introduces both restrictive and nonrestrictive clauses. However, some writers prefer to use *which* only with nonrestrictive clauses.

CORRECT My pencil, *which happens to be yellow*, has no eraser.

Practice 1: Discuss the differences between the italicized elements in the following pairs of sentences.
a-1. Smith's *last* pass amazed the spectators.
a-2. Smith's pass, *the last in the game*, amazed the spectators.
b-1. Sweet blackberries, *which I love*, grow wild in Lincoln County.
b-2. The place *that I love the most* is Lincoln County.
c-1. My *neighbor's* duck is named Bozo.
c-2. My neighbor's duck, *which is coal black*, is named Bozo.
d-1. The *mayor* is on vacation.
d-2. The mayor, *Cedric Quimby*, is on vacation.
e-1. This spider, *I believe*, is harmless.
e-2. *I believe* that this spider is harmless.

f-1. Martin Hanna, *who teaches in the local high school*, won $10,000 in the lottery.

f-2. I know *who teaches in the local high school.*

g. In direct address and direct quotation, commas are used

DIRECT ADDRESS Melanie, did Professor Green discuss protein metabolism in class yesterday?

QUOTATION Joe whispered, "I believe the war will soon be over."

QUOTATION "That dancer," Joe said, "moves like water."

QUOTATION "I dislike hamburgers," Joe told the waiter.

h. To set off contrasting elements, commas are used

CONTRAST The bold, but amazingly lazy, captain scolded Sam.

CONTRAST Power, not money, intrigued Lord Byron.

i. To prevent a misreading, a comma may be used

CLEAR As Dr. Parr ate, the kitten began climbing the drapes. [If the comma were missing, a reader might at first think that the sentence was about Dr. Parr's food.]

CLEAR Above, the children were asleep. [Contrast: Above the children was a large mobile.]

Practice 2: Insert commas where needed in the following sentences.

a. The new book which Jack read last month has changed his life.
b. The bicycle has twelve speeds new tires new brakes and red paint.
c. The teacher said "Yes I like to teach."
d. When students refuse to complete their homework what is a teacher to do?
e. The janitors had to shovel snow and the school was closed on January 10 1983.
f. Dr. Macke has a new office in Ripley West Virginia.
g. General MacArthur the Commander of the Pacific Forces alienated President Truman.
h. In a second room will be available.

22.3 Unnecessary comma

Remove all unnecessary commas in your writing. The idea of placing a comma at every pause in a sentence is not correct. It leads to overuse of the comma. Unless there is intervening material, a comma is not used in the following cases.

a. A subject and its verb are not separated by a comma

INCORRECT   We watched Keith, sneak into the theater.

CORRECT   We watched Keith sneak into the theater.

b. A verb and its object are not separated by a comma

INCORRECT   Karen showed us, her motorcycle.

CORRECT   Karen showed us her motorcycle.

c. Noncoordinate adjectives are not separated by a comma

INCORRECT   Karen bought an antique, jade, letter opener.

CORRECT   Karen bought an antique jade letter opener. [Contrast: Karen wrote a long, angry, serious letter.]

NOTE: If you can substitute *and* for the comma and the meaning is not damaged, use the comma.

SUBSTITUTION   Karen wrote a long and angry and serious
TEST   letter. [*And* is substituted for the comma.]

NOTE: If you can rearrange the adjectives and the meaning is not damaged, use the comma.

REARRANGEMENT   Karen wrote an angry, serious, long let-
TEST   ter. [The adjectives are rearranged.]

d. Before or after a period, exclamation point, dash, or a question mark in a quotation, a comma is not used

INCORRECT "What is the boiling point of water?," Greg asked.

CORRECT Greg asked, "What is the boiling point of water?"

e. With restrictive *that* clauses, a comma is not used

INCORRECT The wine, that my grandfather makes, tastes delicious.

CORRECT The wine that my grandfather makes tastes delicious.

f. After *such as* or before *like*, a comma is not used

INCORRECT These theories such as, creationism and evolutionism, create enormous emotional turmoil.

CORRECT These theories, such as creationism and evolutionism, create enormous emotional turmoil.

INCORRECT Gloria enjoys outdoor activities, like hiking, camping, and boating.

CORRECT   Gloria enjoys outdoor activities like hiking, camping, and boating.

Practice 1: Remove any unnecessary commas from the following sentences.

a. Max will graduate, in June, 1994.

b. He lives at 4155 Cass in Omaha, Nebraska, 68131.

c. Molly is studying, for her biology test, but Mary is, out dancing.

d. The teacher needed, paper, pencils, chalk, erasers, scissors, and a raise.

e. If you have a chance, to read *Gulag Archipelago*, read it by all means.

f. On February, 2, 1992, the factory will increase its production from 5,00 to 5,000 new chairs a week.

g. Richard, Lamb, PhD, will lecture on "The Nature of Faith" at the temple at 4567 Brass Lane, Cleveland, Ohio, at eight o'clock.

h. Professor Grant, a world-famous astronomer, teaches a popular course, on the origin, of planets, galaxies, and stars.

i. Henry whispered, "Amy, I want to know, where my automobile has gone."

j. A, hungry, yet puzzled, dog stared at a large plate, of peas.

22.4 Semicolon

a. A semicolon links main clauses without a coordinating conjunction

The semicolon connects closely related main clauses or sentences into a compound sentence.

CORRECT At dawn, the herons swooped down upon the ocean's surface; they feasted on the school of mackerel.

CORRECT When she was a child, Alice loved playing doctor with dolls; today she graduated from medical school.

CORRECT The hamburger was old; the catsup was runny; the lettuce was wilted; the bun tasted like paper.

b. A semicolon with a conjunctive adverb can link main clauses

CORRECT My friends warned me about that movie; however, I went anyway and wasted my money.

CORRECT That building is unsafe; therefore, it should be condemned.

A question arises concerning the use of punctuation with these connecting words and phrases. A semicolon without the comma is used with one-syllable words such as *too, then*, and *thus.* A semicolon and a comma are always used with *however* and usually used with long words or phrases, such as *as a result, consequently, in addition*, and *for example* when they join independent clauses.

CORRECT My old car was dangerous to drive in the winter; consequently, I bought a newer model.

When conjunctive adverbs are used to join independent clauses, the following pattern often occurs:

Independent clause ;	Conjunctive adverb ,	Independent clause

Generally, the semicolon is not used with the coordinating conjunctions *and, but, or, nor, for, so,* and *yet.* See the list of conjunctive adverbs and transitional phrases in 18.7b.

c. Items in lists with internal punctuation can be separated with a semicolon

CORRECT She did not want much for Christmas: just a new bicycle; a dozen books, preferably by Zane Grey; a tiny, white, cuddly kitten with blue eyes; four or five winter and summer dresses; and a pass to the ice skating rink.

CORRECT Last year, Professor Glynn lectured in Aurora, Illinois; Marlinton, West Virginia; and Cooperstown, New York.

Avoid unnecessary or incorrect use of the semicolon

Do not use a semicolon to link a phrase to a clause.

INCORRECT Walking to school; the child spotted a large bear.

CORRECT Walking to school, the child spotted a large bear.

Do not use a semicolon to link a dependent clause to a main clause.

INCORRECT When my parents heard the story; they cried.

CORRECT When my parents heard the story, they cried.

Do not use a semicolon to link a sentence fragment to a main clause.

INCORRECT Chemistry 201 is a difficult course; even for people who know mathematics. [*Even for people who know mathematics* is a dependent phrase. Dependent phrases set off by semicolons create sentence fragments.]

CORRECT Even for people who know mathematics, Chemistry 201 is a difficult course.

Do not use a semicolon to introduce a list or set off a terminal appositive. Use a colon.

INCORRECT This is what you will find in Faulkner's story; Mississippi, black people with dignity, poor white people, rich planters, small children, and beautiful prose.

CORRECT This is what you will find in Faulkner's story: Mississippi, black people with dignity, poor white people, rich planters, small children, and beautiful prose.

Practice 1: Use semicolons to correct the errors in the following sentences.

a. The rafting trip has been cancelled the guide told us there would be no refunds.
b. The lecture was short, brilliant, and relevant, however, the discussion was an exercise in boredom.
c. The experiment failed the next one may succeed.
d. The sentences in that textbook have a curious structure, in fact, they resemble matted noodles.
e. On the trip, our class visited Oxford, Mississippi, where William Faulkner was born, Jackson, Mississippi, where James Whitehead lived, and Natchez, Mississippi, where Richard Wright was born.

22.5 Colon

The colon is a formal introductory signal that something important is to follow. Like the semicolon, it is medial punctuation and never appears at the end of a sentence.

a. *A colon introduces a list, a series, or a quotation*

CORRECT She had good reasons to become a novelist: an exciting life, an interest in people, and a love of language.

CORRECT Sue's safe contained a treasure: namely, a dozen gold coins, ten large diamond rings, and a string of pearls.

Use the colon for formal introductions using *as follows, in part, the following, these words,* or *this.*

> Sally Fitzgerald described O'Connor's arrival in Iowa as follows:

Flannery O'Connor had appeared in Iowa City
in September of 1945, fresh from Milledgeville,
Georgia, bearing a fifteen-pound muskrat coat and
a talent of proportionate weight, balanced by
a steely will. . . .

b. Do not use the colon with lists after a linking verb or a preposition

INCORRECT Some of the things on the playground are: a jungle gym, a slicky slide, and a sand pile.

CORRECT Some of the things on the playground are a jungle gym, a slicky slide, and a sand pile.

INCORRECT The prosecutor accused Michaels of: gun running, embezzlement, tax evasion, and armed robbery.

CORRECT The prosecutor accused Michaels of gun running, embezzlement, tax evasion, and armed robbery.

c. A colon introduces an emphatic appositive

CORRECT This desert needs something: water.

CORRECT One word describes her cooking: sick.

d. A colon introduces a second clause of amplification or explanation

CORRECT The coach made an announcement: from now on, everyone would run ten laps before breakfast.

CORRECT Some tobacco products cause cancer: they are cigarettes, cigars, and chewing tobacco.

e. The colon is used for subtitles, Bible reference, time, bibliography, and formal salutation

Subtitle	*Jojo: The Saga of a Hermit Mouse*
Biblical reference	John 3:16
Time	7:20 A.M. 22:30
Publication information	Lincoln: U of Nebraska P, 1971
Bibliographical citation	(2: 121–129) (See chapter 17.)
Formal salutation	Dear Dr. Yu:
	Dear Ms. Nunn:

Practice 1: Add or remove punctuation as needed in the following sentences.

a. The most important minerals needed for human nutrition are the following sodium calcium magnesium and potassium

b. Here is a list: of some novels you should read this summer, *Animal Farm, 1984, Gulliver's Travels,* and *Doctor Zhivago*

c. At the beach: at dinner: around the pool: and at the theater, everyone was talking about one thing. Henry's discovery of a million gold coins

d. Every morning at exactly 9:30 Professor Tasito would quote his favorite line of poetry "A cloud has only one disguise"
e. Because Wes had lost his baseball glove: his father screamed at him: and sent him to his room without supper.

22.6 Dash, parentheses, brackets, slash

a. Dash

In handwriting, a dash is a line a bit longer than a hyphen. In typing, a dash is two hyphens without any space before or after. Avoid overusing the dash. When relied on too heavily, it becomes a tedious stylistic gimmick. However, it can be used legitimately in the following situations.

The dash signifies variation or abrupt change
Use the dash to signal an interruption or abrupt change in thought. Occasionally, the dash is used to signify a change in intonation or pitch of the speaker's voice.

CORRECT The accident happened—I'm not too sure about this—right next to that tree.

CORRECT The patient said, "I want to go—oh, where can I go?"

The dash sets off nonessential elements
A dash may be used to set off parenthetical elements, such as appositives with internal commas, asides used for emphasis, and nonessential commentary.

CORRECT   The small red lights in the display room—about a dozen of them—are burned out.

CORRECT   These tiny insects—they are no larger than a grain of sand or salt—can destroy a field of wheat or soybeans in less than two weeks.

The dash can emphasize elements at the beginning or end of a sentence

CORRECT   That playboy writes about philosophy, but he is only interested in one thing—sex.

CORRECT   Crumpled Frito snacks, broken Coke bottles, moldy Big Mac wrappers, and a nest of catsupy napkins—all cover the back seat of my Cadillac.

The dash signals a summary or appositive at the end of a sentence

CORRECT   Weldon said he was tired of school—tired of the endless papers and meaningless learning.

CORRECT   She gave away to charities for the poor all her wealth—diamonds, homes, stocks, and oil wells.

b. Parentheses

Parentheses are used to signal a word, word group, or sentence used for commentary, explanation, definition, or translation. Parentheses should replace commas or dashes when the material is to be deemphasized or when the parenthetical element contains internal comma punctuation.

Use parentheses for commentary within the sentence

CORRECT The coach (an oak in a field of thistles and crabgrass) actually forces the student athlete to go to class.

Use parentheses for explanations

CORRECT The stadium (that is the large building shaped like a beanie) is five miles west of the lake.

Use parentheses for definitions

CORRECT Julio studied ichthyology (the science of fishes) while a student in Finland.

CORRECT The lecturer claimed that *agape* (spiritual love) is as necessary to human life as water.

Use parentheses to number items in lists

CORRECT The book gave analyses of (1) movies, (2) silent films, (3) cartoons, and (4) TV shows.

Use parentheses for documentation

CORRECT Quince argues that meaning is separate from truth (Gargi 27). [This follows MLA style. See chapter 17.]

Use the correct punctuation for parenthetical elements. Within a sentence, omit the initial capital letter (except for *I*) and omit terminal punctuation. Between sentences, include capitals and terminal punctuation.

WITHIN SENTENCE   The small lizard (it was a yellow spider lizard) crawled into the children's pool.

BETWEEN SENTENCES The boy devoured the ice cream. (It was a huge chocolate cone.) His smile was as wide as an ice cream scoop.

c. Brackets

Brackets signal material added to a quotation for attention to error, for additional information, explanation, clarification, or identification. See also 22.7l.

ERROR   The mayor said today, "Crime in the city is favorable [sic]." [The *sic* in brackets calls attention to the mayor's curious comment.]

ADDITION   Here are Professor Harper's actual words: "He [T. S. Eliot] wrote the poem [*The Wasteland*] while he was severely depressed." [The bracketed material is not a part of the original quotation. The writer adds this material for clarification.]

INFORMATION   Dram's essay stated: "Children who suffer the loss of a parent during critical periods in their lives [between the ages of eleven to fifteen] display the greatest amount of damage." [The person quoting Dram has supplied information for the reader.]

Although parentheses within parentheses are indicated by brackets, this form of punctuation should be avoided.

d. Slash

The slash with no space shows options

CORRECT   Students like to sign up for pass/fail courses.

CORRECT   This ticket is good for the winter/spring quarters.

The slash with spaces is used to separate lines of poetry

CORRECT   This element of stark contrast appears often as, for example, in the lines: "Mother is strange to-day / With ashes on her white forehead."

The slash is used in writing out phonemes or word sounds

CORRECT   Milton dropped the /v/ in <u>heaven</u>. Today such a pronunciation would almost rhyme with <u>hen</u>.

Practice 1: Add or remove punctuation marks when necessary in the following sentences. Revise if necessary.
a. Allow the dough to rise usually about 30 minutes and then shape into small rolls.
b. Some new ideas in poetry / the use of unknown languages, the lack of a clear narrative, the abandonment of meter and rhyme / appear in Ezra Pound's poems.
c. Mary keeps putting off studying for her tests one of the most dangerous things for any student
d. My mother praised Gloria it's about time somebody did for helping with the Easter Seals campaign.
e. Football the science of violence does strange things to grown men.

22.7 Quotations, quotation marks, ellipsis marks

a. Avoid free-floating or stand-alone quotations

UNCLEAR   Some interesting ideas appeared. "The proper study of mankind is man." Writers in the Neo-Classical period showed a serious interest in man as a social being. [Quotation marks surround some words, but the writer gives no clues to the author.]

CLEAR   During the Neo-Classical Period, many interesting ideas appeared. Most writers showed a lively interest in man as a social being. Alexander Pope seems to sum up this emphasis with the words, "The proper study of mankind is man." [Quotations need introductions. The introductory tag, *Alexander Pope seems to sum up this emphasis with the words*, introduces the quotation that follows.]

UNCLEAR   When we were walking, Steve screamed. "Watch out for the snakes." Mike screamed. [Who gives the warning?]

CLEAR   When we were walking, Steve screamed, "Watch out for the snakes." [The two words *Steve screamed* introduce the quotation.]

b. Quoted material may be shifted within a sentence for rhythm, emphasis, style

CORRECT   Pope wrote, "The proper study of mankind is man."

CORRECT   Pope believed that man is "the proper study of mankind."

CORRECT   "The proper study of mankind," according to Pope, "is man."

Note that each quotation has an introductory or medial tag: *Pope wrote, Pope believed,* or *according to Pope.*

c. Quotations need introductions

A comma or commas separate the introduction from the quotation.

CORRECT   Greg asked Horace, "Where will you live in New York?" [The words *Greg asked Horace* form the introduction. Some people refer to the introduction of a quotation as an explanatory tag.]

CORRECT   "Where," Greg asked Horace, "will you live in New York?"

In formal writing a colon may separate the introduction or explanatory tag from the quotation.

CORRECT The report had this to say: "We have studied the incidence of drug abuse in Bradley Hall and sadly must conclude that a disastrous situation has been allowed to develop."

CORRECT The message was clear: "Wait."

d. Quotations should not create comma splices

Do not create a comma splice by joining two quoted sentences together with a comma. (See also 20.2b.)

COMMA SPLICE "The microscope gave us new eyes," Dr. Lane told me, "It also helped give us a new way of thinking about life."

CORRECTED Dr. Lane told me, "The microscope gave us new eyes. It also helped give us a new way of thinking about life."

e. Punctuate the end and the middle of a quotation correctly

Commas and periods go inside the quotation marks

CORRECT "The lemons," the grocer told us, "are rotten."

Colons and semicolons go outside the quotation marks

CORRECT Dr. Smith ridiculed Yeats as a "Southern Californian ESP type"; however, he spoke kindly of Robinson Jeffers, whom he called a "poet of grace, delicacy, and beauty."

CORRECT   The article called the following the "most comic social problems": "blue jean color," "shade of summer tan," and "loss of red meat in the diet."

Question marks and exclamation points go inside the quotation marks if they are a part of the original

ORIGINAL   Try finding that kind of bargain in Detroit!

QUOTATION The magazine mentioned the city in one sarcastic sentence: "Try finding that kind of bargain in Detroit!"

ORIGINAL   What would you do with a million dollars?

QUOTATION The comedian asked, "What would you do with a million dollars?" [The quotation is a question; the introduction is a statement.]

Question marks and exclamation points go outside the quotation marks if they are not part of the original

ORIGINAL   Poetry tells us we are alive.

QUOTATION Did Richard Hugo say, "Poetry tells us we are alive"?

NOTE: If *both* the original and your sentence are questions or exclamations, then the question mark or exclamation point goes inside the quotation marks.

f. The presentation of research requires the appropriate form

This handbook basically follows the MLA Guidelines for parenthetical documentation. There are, however, a number of other acceptable formats for documenting research. When in doubt, ask your instructor for the correct form. The examples below follow MLA form. (See 17.1–17.6.)

CORRECT   Theodora is described as "a theatrical prostitute" (Gibbon 652).

CORRECT   Gibbon writes: "Theodora . . . assumed, like a skillful actress, a more decent character . . ." (649).

CORRECT   Gibbon admits "the beauty of Theodora" (648) while at the same undercutting her personality with the simple truth.

g. Ellipsis marks signal omissions

Do not begin any quotation with three spaced periods to signal an omission

ORIGINAL   Yet, in the meanwhile, Atilla relieved his tender anxiety, by adding a beautiful maid, whose name was Ildico, to the list of his innumerable wives.

INCORRECT Gibbon mentions the following: ". . . Atilla relieved his tender anxiety, by adding a beautiful maid . . . to the list of his innumerable wives" (584).

CORRECT   Gibbon mentions the following: "Atilla relieved his tender anxiety, by adding a beautiful maid . . . to the list of his innumerable wives" (584).

Three spaced periods (. . .) signal an omission in the middle of a quoted passage

ORIGINAL   The main character, Parker, marries a strange woman. She is silent, ugly, thin, and pregnant.

QUOTATION   One critic refers to Parker's wife as "strange . . . silent, ugly, thin, and pregnant."

Three spaced periods (. . .) signal an omission at the end of a quoted passage

ORIGINAL   Most readers, in spite of the violence and unhappy ending, find the story hilarious and powerfully moving.

QUOTATION   One critic claims, "Most readers . . . find the story hilarious . . ." (Smithers 19). [The three dots indicate an omission.]

A line of spaced periods signals the omission of a line or more of poetry

CORRECT Nerval writes:

> Go on. Stare at the sun for a minute.
> You'll think you see floating before your eyes,
> All around you, on the air, a colored spot
>
> . . . .
> Now, on everything like a widow's veil,
> Everywhere, at each point my eye stops
> I see and re-see the black mark.

h. Quote poetry correctly

Poetry is quoted by the phrase or up to three lines surrounded by quotation marks. Four or more lines of poetry appear as a block. The block is indented ten spaces and printed exactly as it appears on the page from which it is quoted. Because the visual effect of a poem is important, do not change or reposition anything in the poem.

ONE LINE   Jim Henson mentioned Ted Weems, "whose whistling eclipsed even the birds."

TWO LINES   The poet describes the sight of the chickens and "their shiny feathers as they rise / to the rafters like powder puffs." [Note that the lines of poetry are treated as individual units and are divided by a slash.]

STANZA   McPherson presents a satirical portrait in the lines:

> A funny-looking microphone
> In front of the poet's teeth
> Droops like a bright silver
> Tongue down to his feet.

NOTE: Do not revise anything that a poet writes. Do not change capital letters or spellings even if you think they are wrong.

i. Block quotation is used for more than four lines

Prose quotations of more than four typed lines are set off in blocks, indenting from the left-hand margin ten spaces. Double-space all indented block quotations unless your instructor tells you differently. Quotation marks are omitted.

Arnold Bennett gives a fairly good description of London in one section of the novel <u>These Twain</u>:

> It was six-thirty. The autumn dusk had already begun to fade; and in the damp air, cold, grimy, and vaporous, men with scarves round their necks and girls with shawls over their heads, or hatted and even gloved, were going home from work past the petty shops where sweets, tobacco, fried fish, chitterlings, groceries, and novelties were sold. . . . (79)

Guidelines for block quotation

- ✎ Introduction with a colon
- ✎ Ten-space indentation
- ✎ Double-spaced
- ✎ No quotation marks before or after
- ✎ All words and all punctuation marks copied accurately
- ✎ Indentation of three spaces for all paragraphs after the first

j. Quote dialogue correctly

Two things are immediately noticeable about the quotation of dialogue. One, each quotation, no matter how long or short, is a unit to itself with beginning and ending marks. Two, a new paragraph, which is always indented three spaces, indicates a different speaker. The following passage illustrates the quotation of dialogue:

> We were walking down the road leading to the old abandoned coal mine, the one where my brother had

found the gold coins. It was late August. A few scrawny sparrows were piping.

"What day do you plan to leave?" I asked after a while.

"What?"

"When are you leaving for school?"

"I don't know," she said, being as honest as she could.

"Huh?"

"Next week sometime. I don't know exactly."

"Will you miss me? Will you try to think of me at least once a day while you are in class?"

"Of course. I'm thinking of you right now and how hard it is going to be to leave next week."

k. Single quotation marks are used for a quotation or a title within a quotation

QUOTATION   Our teacher read to us from her journal: "I am pleased that some students make comments such as 'This book is great,' for it shows me their interest."

TITLE   Mary asked, "Was I supposed to read 'Barn Burning' today?"

NOTE: It is best to avoid using a sentence that has a quotation within a quotation within a quotation.

l. Any change in quoted material, no matter how minor, must be indicated

Acknowledge within parentheses any emphasis added to the original

If you underline something in a quotation for emphasis, indicate that within parentheses.

Professor Gagne was unfair when he called Robinson Jeffers "a tame <u>hyena</u> from California" (emphasis added). [Notice that the author's comment is *outside* the quotation.]

An error or omission in the original can be indicated by using [sic]

ORIGINAL   The Vietnam War was a vast exercise in loveliness, terror, death, cowardice, and destruction.

QUOTATION A student described the war as "a vast exercise in loveliness [sic], terror, death, cowardice, and destruction."

Note that in this passage from a paper, the author—presumably—meant *loneliness,* but a reader has no way of knowing. Brackets are used with *sic* inside a quotation, but parentheses are used with *sic* after a quotation.

QUOTATION The letter writer referred to "Joan Fitzgerald Kennedy" (sic) as a "great martyr for the cause of freedom."

Brackets indicate added material

QUOTATION General Thomas said, "Mr. Hardy [his high school math teacher] was the greatest influence on my entire life."

QUOTATION James Joyce ends his story, "The Dead," with these words: "[Gabriel Conroy] heard the snow falling faintly through the universe and faintly falling, like the descent of their last end, upon all the living and the dead."

Only periods or commas may be changed when you quote

ORIGINAL   The experiment was a disaster.

QUOTATION   "The experiment was a disaster," one scientist complained.

m. Some words are capitalized when quoted

The first letter of the first word of a quotation is capitalized if it begins a sentence.

ORIGINAL   I hurl a skull-size stone at him. *John Gardner*

QUOTATION   "A skull-size stone" is only one of the many clear, interesting images in John Gardner's *Grendel*.

ORIGINAL   The green toads of desire multiply. *Hoto Tanka*

QUOTATION   Tanka is capable of incredibly bad poetry as in the line, "The green toads of desire multiply."

The first word in a quotation after a colon is capitalized

QUOTATION   Mark screamed: "Holy cow!"

QUOTATION   I stopped reading when I came to the line: "The moon was once a large lump of molten rock."

Do not capitalize the first word in the second part of a sentence divided in a quotation unless that word is *I*, a proper noun, or a proper adjective

QUOTATION   "The wolf and lamb shall," as Isaiah says, "feed together."

n. Quotation marks indicate some titles

Quotation marks are used for the titles or names of shorter creative works: stories, essays, articles, songs, works within larger works, parts of books (except for the Bible), short poems, lectures, speeches, and episodes of television or radio programs.

STORY   O'Connor's "A Good Man Is Hard to Find"

ARTICLE   Bill Smith's "New Guide to the Nautilus"

SONG   "Heloise" by the Sneetches

PREFACE   Harry Levin's "Introduction" to <u>James Joyce</u>

POEM   Llewellyn McKernan's "Mother Milking"

LECTURE   Professor Fromm's "Lecture on Freud"

TV EPISODE   "Amazon: The Flooded Ecosystem"

o. Quotation marks signal distinctive word use

Invented words or words used in a special sense

CORRECT How can an athlete "shave" points?

CORRECT I wish I could "disinvite" the latest arrivals.

Slang words in formal prose

CORRECT   Our history teacher really "socked it" to us in the last test. [Compare: *Our history teacher really challenged us in the last test.* Slang is generally avoided in formal English.]

Curious names

CORRECT   John talked to "Aqualung" about Ruth and Steve, who were the other homeless alcoholics on the block.

Intentional bad grammar

CORRECT   I am happy to learn that you "done" it perfectly. [The marks tell the reader that the writer is aware of the mistake.]

Translations of foreign words and special terms

CORRECT   The kick on the first play is called the "kickoff," but just kicking the ball is called a "punt."

CORRECT   Henry's motto, *noli tangere*, means "Do not touch."

CORRECT   *Cave canem,* 'Beware of the dog,' was a common sign on Roman homes. [Use single quotation marks for definitions or translations that appear without intervening material.]

Practice 1: Insert the correct punctuation in the following sentences.
a. What are the lyrics to the song, Walk Like an Egyptian?
b. Milly asked where are you going

c. The formation of stars our professor said takes millions of years

d. The substitute teacher told us You will have a test next Tuesday

e. The pause in the middle of a line of poetry is called a caesura

f. After running nineteen miles Andy said I feel torqued.

g. Tell that child to come here she screamed

h. John read the poem Mosquito by Rodney Jones in the *Atlantic Monthly*

Practice 2: Rewrite the following conversation with the proper punctuation, proper indentation, and proper capitalization. (See 22.7j.)

> Jack asked Mary Where are you going She whispered I don't know Looking away Jack said Stay here No I must go she said Jack then began to speak louder as he said Today I saw my grandfather he was thin and pale as a sheet of paper his eyes glowed like blue jewels in his face I was afraid as I have never been before. Why didn't you tell me she asked.

22.8 Apostrophe

a. An apostrophe can indicate possessive case

Singular nouns and indefinite pronouns: add apostrophe + s

Jake's garbage   someone's dog

Singular nouns ending in s: add the apostrophe + s

gas's odor   the waitress's tiny shoes

Singular proper nouns, the names for persons and places ending in s: add the apostrophe + s

Socrates   Socrates's death

Avoid distracting sound effects

CURIOUS   the whistle's ceaseless noise

REVISED   the ceaseless noise of the whistle

Regular plural nouns ending in s: add only the apostrophe

the poets' jobs   the athletes' laughter
the Joneses' money   twelve monkeys' weight

Irregular plural nouns not ending in s: add apostrophe + s

the mice's nests   the children's toys
his teeth's dull color   the alumni's gift

Compound words or groups of words: add apostrophe + s to the final word

Sonny and Cher's song   my father-in-law's anger

Individual ownership:
add apostrophe + *s* to all nouns

Joe's and Ann's gardens   the dog's, cat's, and gerbil's fleas

Joint ownership:
add apostrophe + *s* to the last noun

Iran and Iraq's war   Mary and Jon's new car

b. The apostrophe is used for contractions, omissions, and certain unique plural forms

Use apostrophes for contractions and omissions

| it is | it's | would not | wouldn't |
| 1956 election | '56 election | she will | she'll |

NOTE: **Avoid contractions in research and formal writing.**

Use the apostrophe + *s* to form unique plurals

WORDS USED   Mike loved the word <u>nice</u>, and Miss Gue
AS WORDS   circled ninety <u>nice's</u> in Mike's paper.

LETTERS   Miss Jacks never gives <u>A's</u>.

LETTERS   Her <u>p's</u> look just like <u>g's</u>.

NOTE: **Apostrophes are not used to form the plurals of abbreviations (BAs, CDs), numbers (30s, 300s), or decades or centuries (1950s, 1800s).**

c. Avoid misusing the apostrophe

Apostrophes do not form regular plurals

INCORRECT   The *paper's* were beautiful and exciting.

CORRECT   The papers were beautiful and exciting.

The pronouns *his, hers, its, ours, yours, theirs,* and *whose* never have apostrophes

INCORRECT His' dogs liked to bark at her's.

CORRECT His dogs liked to bark at hers.

Practice 1: Change the prepositional phrases or adjective clauses into a possessive noun form. Conform to the pattern of the example.

EXAMPLE   a house for the young couple
           the young couple's house

a. the car belonging to Mike and Sally
b. the phone of my mother-in-law
c. some music for Elvis
d. a beard on the man
e. the cars owned by Mike and Sally
f. the journey Moses took
g. a piano in the church
h. shoes that Barb lost
i. the silly sounds of Mo

Practice 2: Read through the following sentences, checking for apostrophes. If the sentence is correct, place a *C* before it. Add any needed apostrophes. Remove all unnecessary apostrophes.

a. The dog kept scratching it's fleas.
b. Reading his' paper was difficult. The as looked just like os and the ps resembled qs.
c. He'll forget if you don't remind him.
d. Alice and Jeffrey cars are both in Smiths Garage.
e. He bought two dollar's worth of candy.
f. Josephs mother recited five of Yeats poems.
g. The manager liked his employees. He raised each's salary.
h. Is this pencil yours, mine, or Sidneys?

23 Mechanics

23.1 Capital letters

a. The first letter in the first word in each sentence is capitalized

CORRECT James dyed some spiders green. He did it today.

b. The words in lines of poetry and in prose are capitalized exactly as the author wrote them

CORRECT She dwells with Beauty—Beauty that must die.
John Keats

c. The first word in a parenthetical expression between sentences is capitalized

CORRECT   This book treats rock music seriously. (Some consider this an impossible task.) It gives an excellent analysis of rock and roll's beginning.

d. Proper nouns and adjectives are capitalized Follow the usage in standard dictionaries

PROPER NOUNS   Jesus Christ, T. S. Eliot

PROPER ADJECTIVES   Christian, Eliotic

AWARDS, PRIZES   a Pulitzer Prize, an Oscar

BRAND NAMES   Wheaties, Keds, Chevrolet

BUILDINGS   Smith Hall, Drake Hotel, the White House

BUSINESSES   White Way Laundry, General Motors

DAYS, MONTHS   Monday, April, Christmas, Yom Kippur

DOCUMENTS   the Bill of Rights, Magna Carta

DOGMAS   Nicene Creed, Communist Manifesto

ETHNIC GROUPS   Iroquois, Eskimo, Slav, Quechuan [Special note: The words *Negro/Negroes* are capitalized. The words *black/blacks* and *white/whites* are generally not capitalized when referring to races of people.]

FAMILY NAMES	Mike, Mr. Harper, Uncle Otis [For a specific family member, many writers use a capital: *I wanted to leave a note for Mother.* Do not use a capital in a common noun following a personal pronoun: *My mother left.*]
FORMS OF ADDRESS	Judge Bean, Dean Hoope, Chief Justice Burger
GEOGRAPHY	the South, Southern, Southerner, the West, the Midwest, the Middle East, the Orient, South America [Not compass directions—north of here, south side of the street]
GOVERNMENT	the Army of the Potomac, Marine Corps, West Virginia Legislature [Not common nouns such as *army, agency, navy*]
HEAVENLY BODIES	Mercury, Milky Way, the Big Dipper
HISTORY	the New Deal, the Roaring Twenties, the Middle Ages, the Treaty of Versailles, the Stone Age, World War I, the Russian Revolution, the Battle of Bull Run, the Last Supper [Not common nouns such as *period, age, war*]
IDEAS, MOVEMENTS	Communism, the Reformation, Romanticism, the Agrarians, the Renaissance [Opinions vary. Check a dictionary.]
LANGUAGES	COBOL, Greek, English, American Sign Language, Braille

NATIONALITIES	Ethiopian, Finns, Irishman, German, Arab
ORGANIZATIONS	Alpha Xi Delta, Oberlin College, the American Red Cross, the University of Nebraska
PEOPLE'S NAMES	Eudora Welty, Miles Davis, Jackie, Babs
PLACE NAMES	France, U.S.A., Hawaii, Elk River, Paris, Mount Rainier, South Oyster Bay, Horseshoe Bend, Middle East, the Equator, Northern Hemisphere, Strait of Dover, the Windy City, Motown, the Bible Belt, the Big Apple, the North Shore, the Combat Zone
POLITICAL TITLES	the President of the United States, the Queen of Siam
POLITICAL UNITS	Ontario Province, the Roman Empire, Cook County, Union Parish, Area G, New York State, New York City [Note: When a noun comes before the place name, the noun is not capitalized; the province of Ontario, the empire of Rome, the county seat, the state of New York, the city of New York.]
PRONOUN	Capitalize first-person singular *I*.
RELIGION	Judaism, Protestantism, Greek Orthodox Church, Jewish, Mormon, Catholic

SACRED BOOKS	the Bible, New Testament, Koran, Gospel of Matthew, Talmud, Penta-teuch, Revised Standard Version [Note: Do not capitalize the word *biblical*.]
SACRED NAMES	God, the Lord, Jehovah, Holy Spirit, Brahma, Allah [Note: Many writers capitalize pronouns, except *who* and *whom*, that refer to the Deity.]
TITLES	West Side Story, Guernica, New York Review
TRADEMARKS	Jell-O, Valium, Xerox, Jeep
VEHICLES WITH NAMES	Apollo 7, Air Force One, Delta Queen, Greased Lightning, Lindbergh's Spirit of St. Louis

e. Abbreviations are capitalized according to a standard dictionary

AR Ar   PhD   LED   SAT

f. Course titles, department names, names of schools are capitalized

Psychology 203 [Not *psychology*]

Chemistry Department [Not *department*]

College of Science [Not *college*]

Cathedral High School [Not *school* or *high school*]

g. Titles and subtitles have special rules

Capitalize the first and last words of the title as it appears on the title page and all other principal words except for articles (*a, an, the*), coordinating conjunctions (*and, but, or, nor, for, so, yet*), subordinating conjunctions (*when, if, since*, and so forth), prepositions, and the *to* in an infinitive.

Book   The Years of Lyndon Johnson: The Path to Power

Paper   "A Study of my Grandfather's Heroism in the Flood"

Thesis   "An Analysis of Meter in the Poems of James Whitehead"

Story   "A Clean, Well-Lighted Place"

Practice 1: Insert capitals where needed in the following sentences.

a. wanting to impress mary, i took a course in computers where i learned fortran, and i wrote her a poem, imitating eliot's *the wasteland.*

b. the south may not rise again, but one high school in texas had more merit scholarship finalists than any school in the entire usa.

c. my dear sister said to us at mcdonalds, "don't you think it is time for christians and jews to take their faiths seriously and see what is happening?"

d. the freshman honors course is marxism and contempt of freedom, which is taught by professor r t s haldane, the author of *marx's two theories of dictatorship.*

e. elinor bail walked to chicago to buy a carton of camels, which she threw in lake michigan in a demonstration sponsored by the american cancer society.

Practice 2: Remove unnecessary capitals from the following sentences.

a. The California Coast is beautiful, especially North of Santa Barbara.
b. I went hunting with my Dad in Southern West Virginia.
c. Mary is writing an article on the Senator from Iowa.
d. In the Summer, Ice Cream tastes best.
e. In my Psychology Class, the Professor constantly complains about the Federal Government.
f. La Ronda and Lamont were married yesterday in the County Court House and left for their Honeymoon in Colorado.
g. Whenever I go to a Rock Concert, I always bring a Picnic Basket with some Good Food.

23.2 Underlining: Italics

a. Titles of individual works are underlined

BOOK	The Scarlet Letter
COMPUTER PROGRAM	WordStar
LONG POEM	The Rape of the Lock
MAGAZINE	Redbook
MOVIE	Casablanca
MUSICAL COMPOSITION	Appalachian Spring
NEWSPAPER	New York Times
PAINTING	People at Night
PLAY	King Lear

23.2 mech

RECORD ALBUM	<u>White Album</u>
RADIO SHOW	<u>Mike's Midget Puppets</u>
TELEVISION SHOW	<u>NBC Nightly News</u>

Do not underline the following items:

ARTICLES	"The Dangers of Children's Toys"
THE BIBLE	The entire book and any translation
BOOKS IN THE BIBLE	Acts, Revelations, Amos
NAMES IN BOOKS	Gatsby, Huck Finn
CONSTITUTIONAL DOCUMENTS	Bill of Rights, First Amendment
LEGAL DOCUMENTS	Hawley-Smoot Tariff
SHORT STORIES	"A Clean, Well-Lighted Place"
SONGS	"Blue Bayou"
TITLES OF YOUR PAPERS	The Vacation of Death
PARTS OF BOOKS	"Preface to . . ." or "Introduction"

b. Foreign words and phrases are underlined

SPANISH We visited the Prado, a great <u>museo</u>, in Madrid.

FRENCH Brendan Galvin's new book of poems is a <u>tour de force</u>.

c. The names of vehicles are underlined

AUTOMOBILE   The Green Hornet

BOAT OR SHIP   The Jane Aire, U.S.S. Iowa

PLANE   Air Force One

TRAIN   City of New Orleans

SPACECRAFT   Apollo 7

d. Numbers, words, and letters used as referents are underlined

WORD   The word library comes from Latin.

NUMBER   He painted a large 8 on the side of his car.

LETTERS   I don't know whether this mark is a 1 or an l.

e. Scientific names for living things are underlined

CORRECT   The gibbon belongs to genus Hylobates.

f. For emphasis or stress, underlining is used

EMPHASIS   What is a reasonable level of corruption?

STRESS   My father asked me, "What are you doing?"

Use this device only rarely when the emphasis or stress is intended and cannot be achieved by other means. Excessive underlining is adolescent and ineffective.

NOTE: **If the printer to your computer is able to print an italic font, you may want to use italics instead of underlining.**

Practice 1: Underline where needed in the following passage.

> Last week, Cedric Hopewell finished Moby Dick and began reading the Bible. The week before he had been expressing an interest in a new album, Spun from a Web, by the Four Pits. People who read about him in the New York Times might think he is a pure phony. I have known him for three years (I met him at the Indianapolis 500 where he was driving Ray Tipp's new Ford, the Will to Live) and think he is a bit strange but a decent fellow. It is just that a person never knows what to expect. One minute Cedric might be listening to Ray Charles's album Georgia on my Mind. The next minute he will be planning a coup d'état in Nigeria.

23.3 Abbreviations

Formal writing requires as few abbreviations as possible, all of which must follow standard usage. When in doubt, consult a standard dictionary.

a. Titles when used before full names are abbreviated

In formal writing, use titles before names: *Dr., Fr., Messrs., Mlle., Mme., Mr., Ms., Rep.*, and so forth. Do not use abbreviations before last names alone.

Dr. William J. Smith	Doctor Smith
Capt. W. G. Webster, III	Captain Webster
Prof. John Merck	Professor Merck

b. Follow standard usage

Use only abbreviations found in a standard dictionary. Do not invent your own abbreviations.

CORRECT Nurse Yuan will start work in the clinic today.
[Not: Nr. Yuan will start work in the clin. today.]

c. Titles after names are abbreviated

In formal writing, use the following abbreviated titles after names: *CPA, DD, DDS, Esq., Jr., LLD, MA, MD, PhD, Sr.,* and others.

Lance P. Homerton, Jr. [Not: Jr. Homerton]

Becky Underhill, CPA

CORRECT We addressed the letter to Diane Feinman, CPA.

d. Certain words used with times, numbers, amounts, and dates are abbreviated

Use the abbreviations *$, A.M., P.M., AD, BC, mph, rpm.* Use them only with numbers. Never use ¢ in formal writing.

6:00 A.M. or 6:00 a.m.	AD 274
332 BC	127 mph
9500 rpm	$25.94

e. Standard abbreviations should be used

PLACE NAMES	D.C. or DC, U.S.A. or USA, U.S.S.R. or USSR
TECHNICAL TERMS	CB radio, FM, ICBM, i.v., MIRV, TV
COMPANIES	AT&T, NCR, TWA
SCHOOLS	UCLA, MU, SUNY, CUNY, MHA
GROUPS	PTA, AFL-CIO, ROTC
AGENCIES	CIA or C.I.A., FBI, NATO
GOVERNMENTS	US or U.S. Government
PEOPLE	JFK or J.F.K., FDR or F.D.R.

Unless you are following MLA or APA format, avoid abbreviations in formal writing for the following: days and months, geographical areas, academic subjects, first names, and the word *and*.

INCORRECT Last Mon. Jos. wrote to a school in New Engl. asking whether they offered programs in psych. & Eur. His.

CORRECT Last Monday, Joseph wrote to a school in New England, asking whether they offered programs in psychology and European history.

f. Plurals of abbreviations are formed with s

The *MLA Handbook* recommends the plural form without an apostrophe: MFAs, MDs, SATs.

Practice 1: Correct any errors in the following sentences.

a. Doctor William Smith will visit Hond., Alas., and Gr. Br. on his trip.
b. The Lat. teacher asks for more writing than the Eng. teacher.
c. The Parent–Teacher Association is planning to meet on Fri. Mar. 12 in the H.S. Aud.
d. Greg spends all his time talking about cars that travel at 140 miles per hour at 3,000 revolutions per minute.
e. Ursula is a Jr. executive with a NY company that gives full MD and DDS insurance.
f. Send these documents to CPA Becky Underhill.

23.4 Numbers

The following rules for numbers generally apply to formal expository writing where numbers are used infrequently. Some kinds of scientific and technical writing require other formats. Consult the appropriate style manual when necessary.

a. Numbers that begin sentences are spelled out

INCORRECT 37 dogs invaded our backyard.

CORRECT Thirty-seven dogs invaded our backyard.

b. Numbers with one or two words are spelled out

Spell out one- or two-word numbers such as *ten* or *two hundred*. Use figures for numbers with three or more words such as *101,* or *2,097.* Also spell out *first, second, third,* and so forth. In formal writing avoid abbreviations such as *1st, 2nd,* and so forth.

CORRECT Ben bought nine snakes. [Not: Ben bought 9 snakes.]

CORRECT Janet caught 733 butterflies. [Not: Janet caught seven hundred and thirty-three butterflies.]

Hyphenate the spellings of numbers from twenty-one to ninety-nine and fraction adverbs (one-ninth finished).

c. Use figures for addresses, highways, days and years, decimals, fractions, percentages, measurements, money, Roman numerals, scores, statistics, temperatures, time of day, and literary reference

ADDRESSES	437 Madison Avenue
HIGHWAYS	Interstate 40, State Road 356
DATES	May 11, 1942 [Not May 11th, 1942]; 1970s; from 1970 to 1981; AD 321
PARTS	1.25; 99⅓; 12% or 12 percent; 3.5 yards; 3″ × 5″ notecards
MONEY	$9.75 million or $9,750,000; $6398
ROMAN NUMERALS	I, II, III, and so forth. Use in outlining.
SCORES	an SAT of 380; 9 to 3
STATISTICS	a mean of 38; ratio of 20 to 1

TEMPERATURES	98.6; 300 degrees below zero; 12°C, or 12 degrees Celsius
TIME OF DAY	4:15 A.M.; 3:00 P.M.; 24:00
LITERARY REFERENCE	Act 3; chapter 2; line 43; page 12; Scene 7

d. Be consistent in each paper
Do not mix forms

Follow the pattern you began with

If you use either cardinal numerals (one, two, three) or ordinal numerals (first, second, third) in a sentence or a string of related sentences, be consistent. If you begin with *first*, continue with *second* and so forth. If you begin with (1), continue with (2) and so forth. Do not write "*first . . . two . . . thirdly.*"

Do not mix words with figures in pairs or series

INCORRECT	Ben bought nine snakes and 33 parrots.
CORRECT	Ben bought nine snakes and thirty-three parrots.
INCORRECT	Seth bought his sweater for $75.00, but I bought mine for nine dollars.
CORRECT	Seth bought his sweater for seventy-five dollars, but I bought mine for nine dollars.
CORRECT	Seth bought his sweater for $75, but I bought mine for $9.

Spell plurals correctly without apostrophes

CORRECT The students in our class had ACT scores in the 20s.

Practice 1: Revise the following sentences for any mistakes in the use of numbers.
a. 89 percent of those eligible voted in the nineteen eighty-five election.
b. We counted forty cows, 66 sheep, 301 pigs, and nine horses.
c. Helen worked on that novel from 1978 to eighty-four.
d. At 3 o'clock P.M. in the afternoon, 9 police cars arrived at the jail.
e. 33 and one-third percent of the students failed Spanish.

23.5 Hyphen

The hyphen is, perhaps, the most confusing unit of punctuation, and usage varies among writers. When in doubt, consult a standard dictionary.

a. The hyphen is used to divide a word at the end of a line

CORRECT

Al was walking down the street when a huge ornament crashed to the ground in front of him.

INCORRECT

The small boy had been sitting on the sidewalk near our house.
[Do not divide one-syllable words.]

CORRECT   The small boy had been sitting on the sidewalk near our house.

INCORRECT While Jeffrey walked to the playground, A-mos was in the library reading a book.
[Do not divide a word and leave one letter at the end of a line.]

CORRECT   While Jeffrey walked to the playground, Amos was in the library reading a book.

NOTE: The following rules apply when a hyphen is used at the end of a line: the dictionary's division of the syllables is the guide; a one-syllable word is never divided; a single syllable is not placed on a separate line; a hyphen should not appear at the very end of a page; a hyphenated word is divided only at a hyphen.

b. Hyphens are used to spell out compound numbers from twenty-one to ninety-nine

CORRECT He ate twenty-three doughnuts.

CORRECT The forty-ninth customer won a large prize.

Hyphenate compound adjectives formed from numbers such as *fifty-yard run* or *ninety-pound weakling.*

c. A standard dictionary contains the guidelines for the hyphen

Compound words present many problems, even for good spellers. Here are some different spellings for a few closely related words.

washbasin	wash down	washed-out	wash-and-wear
firearm	fire fight	fire-eating	fire-and-brimstone

Because no rule can explain correct spelling in all cases and because no one has a perfect memory, a careful writer must use a standard dictionary.

d. Identical words can be distinguished by the use of hyphens

CORRECT Jed will recover that couch.
[It was lost or stolen.]

CORRECT Jed will re-cover that couch.
[He will reupholster it.]

e. Compound adjectives, used before nouns, are formed with hyphens

CORRECT The out-of-work janitor swept his own porch.
[Contrast: The busy janitor was out of work.]

CORRECT He is a world-famous, eighty-year-old neurosurgeon.

f. Omit the hyphen when placing an -ly adverb beside an adjective

CORRECT Jane swam in the quickly flowing stream.

g. The hyphen is used in certain unique cases

WITH INVENTED WORDS	Pat showed us some filthier-than-anyone-could-have-believed photographs. He called his degrading work "art-outside-the-camera."
WITH SUSPENDED COMPOUNDS	We want a one- or two-year warranty on this dryer. Pat showed his evil- but brilliant-minded skill.
WITH FRACTIONS	Frank was two-thirds jealous of Hiram. [adverb] Peter has finished painting two-thirds of the barn. [noun]
WITH SERIES	files 111–27, pages 89–101, 875–1011
WITH DATES	1920–30, June-September, 1820–1930
WITH EX- AND SELF-	ex-husband, self-denial
WITH PREFIXED IDENTICAL VOWELS	re-entry, co-opted

Practice 1: Supply needed hyphens or remove unnecessary hyphens from the following sentences. Use a dictionary and the preceding guidelines.

a. This is a well built house, but the price is out-of-my-salary-range.

b. The foot-ball is described on pages 3–7 in this new novel.

c. My brother-Bill has just been elected secretary-treasurer of the school board, and he wants to purchase new play-ground things for the children's re-creation.
d. Where is that fair weather friend sister-of-mine?
e. His recipes are good for nothing except maybe to-feed-the-pigeons.

PART 8

Glossaries

Glossary of Grammatical and Rhetorical Terms

Absolute Phrase: A participial phrase, generally with a noun or pronoun as the subject of a participle. An absolute phrase lacks a conjunction, relative pronoun, or preposition connecting it to a clause or sentence. It modifies the rest of a sentence or clause.

> The lifeguard having waved his hand, the swimmers entered the water. [The absolute phrase, *the lifeguard having waved his hand*, does not modify any word in the sentence. It also lacks a connector. Contrast this with the adverb clause in the sentence *After the lifeguard waved his hand, the swimmers entered the water.*]

Abstract Noun: A noun that expresses a general concept (*freedom, love, beauty*) rather than a physical object grasped by the senses in the form of a concrete noun (*jail, kiss, rose*). See *Concrete Noun.* See also 21.4.

Abstraction: A word, phrase, or sentence that is based on, but separated from, sensory reality. The word *slavery* is an abstraction. The phrase *the young man in chains* is not an abstraction.

Academic Discourse: The different kinds of writing that are required for different college courses such as anthropology, history, nursing, and so forth.

Acronym: A shortened, capitalized form of a meaningful series of words. SAC is the acronym for Strategic Air Command.

Active Voice: See *Voice.* See also 21.5.

Adjectives: Modifiers of nouns and pronouns with three classes: descriptive, limiting, and proper. Descriptive adjectives are words such as *green, sad*, and *high*. Limiting adjectives are words such as *many, the, our, this*, and *three*. Proper adjectives—such as *Freudian, Christian*, and *Russian*—are derived from proper nouns. See 18.4 and 20.6.

Adjective Clause: See *Clause*. See 18.9.

Adverb: A part of speech that generally modifies a verb (walked *quickly*), verbal (playing *hard*), adjective (*very* ugly), or adverb (*too* quickly). See 18.5.

Adverb Clause: See *Clause*. See also 18.9.

Agreement: The logical relationship between word forms of number, gender, and person. See subject-verb agreement in 20.3 and pronoun reference agreement in 20.5a.

> I know that the boy is laughing, but his parents are angry. [The noun *boy* and the verb *is* agree in number because both are singular. The noun *boy* and the pronoun *his* agree in gender because both are masculine and singular. The pronoun *I* and the verb *know* agree because both are first-person forms. The noun *parents* and the verb *are* agree because both are plural.]

Alliteration: The repetition of initial consonantal sounds. *Redd Ryder ridiculed the rodeo in his review.*

Allusion: An indirect, intended, and meaningful reference to a person or event in literature or history.

Ambiguity: A condition, a common occurrence, in which a word, phrase, clause, or sentence yields two or more possible meanings. The sentence *He was lying there* is ambiguous because it may refer to a lie or a nap.

Analogy: An extended comparison between things that are not similar. See 3.7 and 5.7i.

Analysis: The division of a whole into its parts and the examination of those relationships. See *Synthesis*.

Anecdote: A very brief story with an emotional or humorous point. See 3.2 and 3.4.

Antecedent: The word or word group a pronoun refers to. See 20.5a and 20.5b.

The girl looked at *her* new fishing rod. *It* was silver and glowed in the sunlight. [The personal pronoun *it* has the antecedent *fishing rod*. The possessive pronoun *her* refers back to its antecedent, *the girl*. Pronouns and antecedents agree in gender and number.]

Antonym: Synonyms are words with similar meanings (*cold, chilly*), but antonyms are words with opposite meanings (*hot, cold*).

Appositive: A word or group of words beside and equivalent to a noun or a noun unit. Appositives identify the preceding or following word or words. Nonrestrictive appositives preceding or following the noun are set off by commas.

My uncle *Harry, a confirmed bachelor*, worked in the C.I.A. for twenty years and never talked about his job. [The noun *Harry* is a restrictive appositive that identifies a single person. *A confirmed bachelor* is a nonrestrictive appositive presenting information about *My uncle Harry*.]

Archaism: A word or phrase once widely used but seldom used today or used only in special contexts. The preposition *forth of* is archaic.

Article: The indefinite article *a/an* precedes a singular noun with *a* before consonants (*a tiger*) and *an* before vowels (*an apple*). The definite article *the* precedes both singular nouns (*the spider*) and plural nouns (*the eggs*).

Audience: In writing, the intended reader or readers. See 1.5, 7.2, 8.2, 10.2, and 14.2.

Auxiliary Verb: Also called *helping verb*. With the main verb, an auxiliary verb forms the verb phrase by indicating tense, voice, person, number, or mood. Common auxiliaries are forms of *be, do*, and *have*. Common modal auxiliaries include *can/could, may/might, shall/should, will/would, must*, and *ought*. See 18.2a.

Balanced Sentence: A sentence whose two parts form careful parallel structures. *The snow rose higher, and the icicles grew longer*. See 20.9a.

Case: The location or form of a noun or pronoun that reveals its function in a sentence. Grammarians identify three cases: subjective case, possessive case, and objective case. Subjective case is the case of subjects. Possessive case is very often the case of ownership. Objective case is the case of objects. For nouns, subjective case and objective case are identical, whereas possessive case has *'s* or *s'*. For the personal pronouns, subjective, objective, and possessive cases are distinctive: *he, him*, and *his*.

Clause: A group of words (independent or subordinate) containing a subject and a predicate. A clause functions as a sentence, a main clause, or a subordinate clause (adverb, adjective, or noun). See 18.9.

> **Sentences** The pool was freezing. No one went swimming. [Each sentence is an independent clause containing at least one subject and one verb.]

> **Main Clause** Because the pool was freezing, *no one went swimming.* [The main clause is *no one went swimming,* and the dependent or subordinate clause is *Because the pool was freezing.*]

> **Subordinate Clause** Because the pool was freezing, no one went swimming. [*Because the pool was freezing* is a subordinate clause functioning as an adverb.]

> **Subordinate Clause** No one went swimming in the pool that was freezing. [*That was freezing* is a subordinate clause, functioning as an adjective modifying *pool.*]

> **Subordinate Clause** The hostess knew that the pool was freezing. [*That the pool was freezing* is a noun clause, which functions as the object of the verb *knew.*]

Collective Noun: A noun that refers to collections of people or things, such as *class, crowd, herd*, or *committee.* Collective nouns take singular or plural verbs, depending on their meaning.

> **Singular** That *team is* looking for a new coach. [If a collective noun refers to a unit, it takes a singular verb.]

> **Plural** The *team are* involved in a scavenger hunt. [If a collective noun refers to the members of a group, that collective noun takes a plural verb.]

Colloquialism: The language of everyday speech in informal situations. See 21.11.

Comma Splice: A serious error of joining two sentences or independent clauses together with only a comma. See 20.2.

Common Gender: Gender that refers to either masculine or feminine such as *student, child, teacher.*

Common Noun: See 18.1b.

Comparison: In grammar, the change in form for adjectives or adverbs to show differences in degree, manner, quality, and quantity. See 18.4b, 18.5c, and 20.6d.

Complement: A word or word group that completes the meaning of a subject, verb, or object. See *Predicate Adjective, Predicate Nominative, Object,* and 18.1a.

> Maria was *happy.* She was now a *citizen.* [*Happy* is a subject complement, also called a predicate adjective. *Citizen* is a subject complement, also called a predicate nominative.]

> We gave the *teacher* a *green apple.* [*Teacher* is a complement of the verb and is also referred to as the indirect object. *Green apple* is the other complement of the verb and is referred to as the direct object.]

> If you call Smith a *coward,* he will make your life *miserable.* [*Coward* is an object complement, a noun that completes the meaning of the object *Smith. Miserable* is an object complement, an adjective that completes the meaning of the object *life.*]

Complete Predicate: The complete predicate is the complete verb with any complements, objects, and adverbial modifiers. See *Complete Subject* and *Predicate.* See 20.12.

> Maria *planned her vacation carefully.* [*Planned* is the verb, but *planned her vacation carefully* is the complete predicate.]

Complete Subject: The subject and all its modifiers. In the sentence immediately preceding, the complete subject is *Maria.* See *Complete Predicate.*

> *The letters on the board* were erased. [*Letters* is the subject, but *The letters on the board* is the complete subject.]

that, which with things
who, whom with people

Complex Sentence: See *Sentence.*

Compound Complex Sentence: See *Sentence.*

Compound Elements: In a sentence, a group of words, such as a compound subject or compound verb, with two or more parts functioning as a unit.

> At midnight *the dogs and the cats howled and ran* through *the yard and garden.* [*The dogs and the cats* is a compound subject. *Howled and ran* is a compound verb. *The yard and garden* is the compound object of the preposition *through.*]

Compound Sentence: See *Sentence.*

Compound Subject: See *Compound Elements.*

Compound Verb: See *Compound Elements.*

Compound Words: A word made out of two or more words, such as *football, foot soldier,* or *foot-pound.*

Concrete Nouns: Words (*butter, thorn, sand*) whose meaning can be grasped by the physical senses. See 21.12.

Conjugation: The forms of a verb. The complete conjugation contains all forms of the verb for all the personal pronouns (*I, you, he, she, it, we, you, they*), for all the tenses (present, past, future, present perfect, past perfect, future perfect), for both voices (active and passive), for all forms (simple and progressive), and for all moods (indicative, subjunctive, imperative). See 20.4a.

Indicative Mood

Active voice		**Passive voice**	
Singular	*Plural*	*Singular*	*Plural*
	Present tense		
1. I love	We love	I am loved	We are loved
2. You love	You love	You are loved	You are loved
3. He/she/it loves	They love	He/she/it is loved	They are loved

	Active voice		*Passive voice*	
Singular		*Plural*	*Singular*	*Plural*

Past tense

Singular	Plural	Singular	Plural
1. I loved	We loved	I was loved	We were loved
2. You loved	You loved	You were loved	You were loved
3. He/she/it loved	They loved	He/she/it was loved	They were loved

Future tense

Singular	Plural	Singular	Plural
1. I shall love	We shall love	I shall be loved	We shall be loved
2. You will love	You will love	You will be loved	You will be loved
3. He/she/it will love	They will love	He/she/it will be loved	They will be loved

Present perfect tense

Singular	Plural	Singular	Plural
1. I have loved	We have loved	I have been loved	We have been loved
2. You have loved	You have loved	You have been loved	You have been loved
3. He/she/it has loved	They have loved	He/she/it has been loved	They have been loved

Past perfect tense

Singular	Plural	Singular	Plural
1. I had loved	We had loved	I had been loved	We had been loved
2. You had loved	You had loved	You had been loved	You had been loved
3. He/she/it had loved	They had loved	He/she/it had been loved	They had been loved

Future perfect tense

1. I shall have loved	We shall have loved	I shall have been loved	We shall have been loved
2. You will have loved	You will have loved	You will have been loved	You will have been loved
3. He/she/it will have loved	They will have loved	He/she/it will have been loved	They will have been loved

Subjunctive mood

Active voice		*Passive voice*	
Singular	*Plural*	*Singular*	*Plural*

Present tense

If I, you, he, she, it love	If we, you, they love	If I, you, he, she, it be loved	If we, you, they be loved

Past tense

If I, you, he, she, it loved	If we, you, they loved	If I, you, he, she, it were loved	If we, you, they were loved

Present perfect tense

If I, you, he, she, it have loved	If we, you, they have loved	If I, you, he, she, it have been loved	If we, you, they have been loved

Past perfect tense

If I, you, he, she, it had loved	If we, you, they had loved	If I, you, he, she, it had been loved	If we, you, they had been loved

Imperative mood

Present active:	Love	Present passive:	Be loved

Conjunction: Connective word used to join other words and units together: either coordinating (*and, but, or, nor, for, so,* and *yet*), correlative (*both . . . and, either . . . or, neither . . . nor, not only . . . but also,* and *whether . . . or*), or subordinating (such as *because, if, when*). See 18.7.

Coordinating Spiders *and* ants disgust *but* intrigue me.

Correlative *Not only* am I hungry, *but* I am *also* sick.

Subordinating *While* the cat is away, the mice will play.

Conjunctive Adverb: A connector and sentence modifier (such as *thus, however,* or *indeed*) that links together main clauses in a sentence. See 18.7b.

Bill failed the test; *therefore,* he will drop that class. [*Therefore* is a conjunctive adverb joining the two main clauses together.]

Connective or Connector: Conjunctions and prepositions that link main clauses or parts of sentences together. See 18.6 and 18.7.

Connotation: The suggestions that a word carries. A poet defined connotation as "the emotional shadow a word or a phrase casts." For example, the word *Nazi* denotes a member of a German political party in the 1930s and 1940s. The word *Nazi* connotes or suggests powerful evil and inhumanity. See *Denotation.* See also 21.7.

Consonant: Any letter of the alphabet except the vowels *a, e, i, o, u,* and *y* as in *cry*.

Construction: A group of related words (phrase, clause, or sentence) acting as a unit.

Context: The background in terms of the audience, occasion, and significance of a discussion of a subject. The material surrounding a word, phrase, sentence, or paragraph that helps give that element its meaning. Words mean different things in different contexts. The word *star* means something different to an astronomer than to a Hollywood gossip columnist.

Contraction: The shortened form of a word (*I'm* for *I am*) in which an apostrophe takes the place of the omitted letter.

Coordinating Conjunctions: *And, but, or, nor, for, so, yet.* See *Conjunction.* See 18.7b.

Coordination: Joining elements of equal rank in a compound subject, verb, phrase, or clause, usually with a coordinating conjunction. Contrast with *Subordination*. See 20.7, 20.9c, and 20.9d.

The dog and the spider disappeared, but the fox and the weasel remained. [The compound subjects, *The dog and the spider* and *the fox and the weasel*, are coordinate. The two main clauses joined by *but* are coordinate.]

Correlative Conjunctions: See *Conjunction*. See 18.7 and 20.7a.

Dangling Modifier: A word, phrase, or clause with no logical link to the sentence within which it appears. See 20.8a.

Dangling *Looking out the window*, the snow began to fall.

Revised While I was looking out the window, the snow began to fall.

Revised I was looking out the window, and the snow began to fall.

Declension: The change in the inflected forms of nouns and pronouns to show case (subject, object, possessive), number (singular, plural), and person (first, second, third). See *Inflection*.

Deduction: A logical process used to arrive at true statements. See 6.2.

Degree: The extent of an adjective or adverb: positive (*happy*), comparative (*happier*), or superlative (*happiest*). See *Comparison*. See 18.4b, 18.5c, and 20.6d.

Demonstrative Adjectives: *This, that, these,* or *those* used to modify nouns. *This* green chair is older than *that* blue sofa.

Demonstrative Pronouns: *This, that, these,* or *those* used in place of a noun. *That* stinks. Throw *this* out with it, too.

Denotation: The literal or explicit meaning of a word found in the dictionary. See *Connotation*. See also 21.7.

Dependent Clause: Another term for subordinate clause. See *Clause*. See also 18.9.

Descriptive Adjective: An adjective that evokes a sensory impression of reality (*circular, spicy, feverish*). See 18.4a.

Determiner: A signal that a noun or noun construction will appear soon. The articles (*a/an, the*) and possessive pronouns (such as *my, your, his*) are clear determiners.

Dialect: Language from a particular geographical area. Dialects are characterized by unique vocabulary, distinctive grammatical structures, and obvious pronunciation of vowels and consonants.

Dialectic: An intellectual style that emphasizes thought as a two-sided dialogue or conversation between opposing points of view.

Direct Address: In a sentence, the parenthetical element indicating to whom someone speaks: *John, the toast is burning.*

Direct Object: See *Object*. See also 18.1a.

Direct Quotation: The exact word or words (spoken, written, thought) from any source. See *Quotation*. See also 22.7.

Direct Mike said, "I need to go downtown."

Indirect Mike said that he needed to go downtown.

Double Comparative: The unnecessary and ungrammatical use of an *-er* suffix or *more* with the comparative form of an adjective or adverb: *more better, more happier.*

Double Negative: The nonstandard use of two negative words.

Nonstandard Mike don't have no money.

Correction Mike has no money.

Nonstandard I don't have hardly a chance in this course.

Correction I don't have a chance in this course.

Double Superlative: The unnecessary and ungrammatical use of an *-est* suffix or *most* with the superlative form of an adjective or adverb: *most happiest, most best.*

Ellipsis: In a quotation, an omission indicated by three spaced dots: Dean Jacks said, "The swimmers . . . are in deep water." See 22.7g.

Elliptical Construction: A phrase, clause, or sentence that omits a word or words without any loss of clarity or meaning. See 20.5c, 20.11c, and 22.7g.

Elliptical When waiting for the bus, I noticed a large rip in my coat. [The sentence is clear even though it omits *I was* before *waiting.*]

Incomplete Mary disliked Yuma more than Robert. [What did Mary dislike more? Yuma or Robert?]

Equivocation: The deliberate use of words, phrases, clauses, or sentences with multiple meanings to mislead or confuse a reader or listener. See 6.3l.

Essay: The word has multiple meanings. Outside of college, the word generally refers to an article that one might find in a magazine such as the *Atlantic Monthly* or the *New Yorker*. In college, teachers often assign essay examinations, which are short or long answers to questions designed to test a student's knowledge and thinking about a subject. See chapter 13. Also in college, teachers use the term to refer to a genre of writing with a thesis statement and full development that generally focuses on one of the following: personal narrative, argumentation, description, or exposition.

Expletives: *There* or *it* with no grammatical function in a sentence. See 21.9.

Adverb We walked *there* last night. [Omitting *there* changes the meaning of the sentence.]

Expletive *There* are three dimes on the table. [Omitting *there* does not change the meaning of the sentence. *Three dimes are on the table.*]

Expository Writing: Writing that deals with ideas (as opposed to personal experience or narrative) and generally follows a format with a thesis statement and extended development of the thesis.

Expressive Writing: Self-expression in the form of a writer's emotional and intellectual response to a subject. See 1.1a.

Finite Verb Form: A verb form with inflection (person, tense, number) that functions by itself as the main verb in a sentence. In the sentence *Bill finished his homework before watching the movie*, the finite verb form is *finished*. The nonfinite verb forms are the participle, gerund, and infinitive. See *Nonfinite Verb, Participle, Gerund,* and *Infinitive*. See 18.2.

Fragment: A serious sentence error in most cases. An incomplete sentence such as *Bill doing his homework* or *Because Mary is going to a party*. See 20.1.

Function Word: A word (article, connective, preposition, auxiliary) in a sentence that indicates relationships of meaning and grammar among vocabulary words. See *Vocabulary Word*.

> When the teacher turned and wrote on the board, the students in the room laughed. [The function words in this sentence are *when, the, and, in*, and *on*. The vocabulary words are *teacher, turned, laughed, students, room, wrote*, and *board*.]

Fused Sentence: An error in joining two independent clauses together with no punctuation and no connecting words, such as *She went her desk was empty*. See 20.2.

Future Perfect Tense: Tense to express action completed in the future. See 20.4a.

Future Tense: Tense to express action in the future. See 20.4a.

Gender: Identification of nouns and pronouns as masculine (*Mike, he*), feminine (*Mary, she*), neuter (*badge, it*), or common (*teacher, worker*).

Gerund: A nonfinite verb form whose present active form ends in *-ing* and functions as a noun. See 18.1c.

> *Walking* to class wakes me up. [*Walking* is a gerund. *Walking to class* is a gerund phrase functioning as the subject of *wakes*.]

> Seth surprised us by *being prepared* for the test. [*Being prepared* is a gerund. *The test* is the object of *being prepared for*, and together they make up the gerund phrase, *being prepared for the test*, which is the object of the preposition *by*.]

Helping Verb: See *Auxiliary Verb*. See 18.2a.

Homonym: One of two words spelled and pronounced alike but with different meanings. The adjective *rank* and the noun *rank* are homonyms.

Idiom: An expression whose meaning is completely different from the literal meaning of the words, as in the following sentence: *We polished off the cake in two minutes*. See 21.13.

Illustration: An example with narrative and descriptive elements that clarify, develop, or explain a writer's point. See 3.2–3.4.

Image: A word, phrase, clause, or sentence with evocative sensory details used to create a picture in the reader's mind.

Imperative: A command such as *Run!* or *Go home*.

Incomplete Comparison: A construction that omits part of the comparison, such as *My car is faster*. See 20.11c.

Indefinite Adjectives: Adjectives that do not set precise limits, such as *any, much*, or *some*.

Indefinite   *Some* books are missing.

Definite   *Five large* books are missing.

Indefinite Articles: *A, an*. See *Article*.

Indefinite Pronouns: Pronouns, such as *anyone, everyone, someone*, that do not refer to a specific person. See 18.3b.

Indefinite   *Anyone* can ride a horse.

Definite   Sarah claims that *she* can ski.

Independent Clause: A group of words with a subject and verb, which can function as a sentence. See *Clause* and *Sentence*. See also 18.9.

Indicative Mood: The verb form that indicates statements or questions. See *Mood*.

Indirect Object: See *Object*. See also 18.1a.

Indirect Question: A reported question within a sentence that does not require a question mark or an answer.

Direct Question   Sandy yelled, "Where is the car?"

Indirect Question   Sandy asked me where the car was.

Indirect Quotation: The meaning, not the exact words, from a source. See *Direct Quotation*. See also chapters 10 and 11.

Induction: Logical process of beginning with specific facts to support a generalization. See 6.1.

Infinitive: A nonfinite form of the verb with *to* stated or implied. An infinitive may function as an adjective, adverb, or noun. See 18.1c.

The girl wanted *to sleep.* [The infinitive *to sleep* functions as a noun, which is the object of *wanted.* Compare with *The girl wanted a nice room.*]

Infinitive Phrase: An infinitive with its modifiers and/or complements, functioning as an adverb, adjective, or noun. See also 18.8b.

Inflection: A change in the sound or spelling of a word to signal a change in meaning. See *Conjugation* and *Declension.*

Nouns boy, boys, boy's, boys', man, men, man's, men's

Verbs be, am, is, are, was, swim, swims, swam, swum

Pronouns I, me, my, mine, we, us, our, ours

Adjectives near, nearer, nearest

Adverbs sadly, less sadly, least sadly

Intensifier: A modifier, such as *very* in *very sad,* that attempts to create emphasis.

Intensive Pronoun: A pronoun ending in *-self* or *-selves* that intensifies or emphasizes a word in a sentence. In the sentence *The owner himself told us the apartment was unsafe,* the word *himself* is the intensive pronoun.

Interjections: Connected or unconnected exclamations, such as *my, wow,* or *oh.* In sentences, connected interjections are set off with commas: *My, cats are noisy!* Contrast with: *My cats and my dogs are noisy.* Unconnected interjections are set off by exclamation points: *Dogs! I despise dogs.*

Interrogatives: Words used to ask a question: *which, what, who, whom, where, when, how, why, whose.*

Adjective *Which* novel did you read?

Adverb *Where* are you going?

Pronoun *Who* is going to the game?

Intransitive Verb: A verb that does not take a direct object. See *Verb* and *Transitive Verb.* See also 18.2a.

Inversion: A change of word pattern in a sentence when the verb precedes the subject, as in the sentence *Out of the cabinet slithered a large green snake.*

Irony: A figure of speech. See 21.10.

Irregular Verb: A verb whose past tense forms end in something other than *-d* or *-ed*: *wear/wore/worn*. See *Regular Verb*. See 20.4d.

Kinetic Details: Sensory details in writing that suggest motion, change, or process. *The dry, brown leaf spun like a corkscrew as it bounced and skidded across the frozen pond*. The adjectives *dry, brown*, and *frozen* are static details. The phrases *spun like a corkscrew* and *bounced and skidded* are kinetic details. See 3.3b.

Linking Verb: See *Verb*. See also 18.2.

Main Clause: See *Clause*. See also 18.9.

Mapping: The visual devices used by writers to generate or represent ideas. See *Clustering* in 1.3b. See *Listing* in 1.6b. See *Outlining* in 1.7b.

Mass Noun: See 18.1b.

Misplaced Modifier: A word, phrase, or clause placed too far from the element it modifies. See 20.8b.

Misplaced   I put the book next to the TV *on birds*.

Revised   I put the book *on birds* next to the TV.

Modal Auxiliary: In a sentence, a part of the verb signaling possibility, probability, necessity, or tense: *may/might, can/could, must, shall/should, will/would*.

Modifier: In a sentence, a word or word group (adverbial or adjectival) qualifying, limiting, describing another word or word group. See *Adjective* and *Adverb*.

Mood: The form of the verb expressing statement or question (indicative), command (imperative), desire, condition, hypothesis, or recommendation (subjunctive).

Indicative   Mike bakes me a pie on my birthday.

Subjunctive   It is important that Mike bake me a pie.

Imperative   Please bake me a cherry pie.

Nominal: A word, phrase, or clause that functions as a noun.

The students thought *that the assignment was simple*.
[The noun clause, *that the assignment was simple*, is a

nominal. It functions as the noun object of the verb *thought*.]

Nominative Case: Alternate name for subjective case. See *Case*.

Nonfinite Verb: A verb form (infinitive, participle, or gerund) that does not function—by itself—as the main verb of a clause. See *Infinitive, Participle,* and *Gerund.*

Infinitive Here is the book *to read* this summer.

Participle The child *reading* the book looks puzzled.

Gerund *Reading* this book was a challenge.

Nonrestrictive and Restrictive: Terms used to describe the inessential or essential nature of a modifying word, phrase, or clause in a sentence. An essential modifier is restrictive because it limits the meaning of its antecedent. See 22.2f.

Restrictive The man who gave me a ride this morning has just moved into the neighborhood. [The adjective clause, *who gave me a ride this morning,* is essential to the meaning of the sentence.]

An inessential modifier is nonrestrictive because it does not limit meaning.

Nonrestrictive John Harper, who gave me a ride this morning, plans to open a new bookstore. [The adjective clause, *who gave me a ride this morning,* is not essential to the meaning of the sentence. It provides information, but it does not define, limit, or identify *John Harper,* the proper noun it modifies. Note that the nonrestrictive clause is marked off by commas.]

Noun: A part of speech that names a person, place, thing concept, quality, or activity: *Mary, Nevada, spoon, gravity, softness, bowling.* Nouns change in inflection to indicate number (*hut/huts*) and case (*hut/hut's/huts'*). See 18.1.

Noun Clause: See *Clause.* See also 18.9.

Noun Phrase: In a sentence, a noun or a pronoun and its modifiers. See *Phrase.* See also 18.8.

Number: The aspect of a word that indicates singular or plural: *that/those, cot/cots, man/men, He does/They do.*

Object: A noun or noun substitute controlled by, completing, and usually following a transitive verb, preposition, gerund, participle, or infinitive. See 18.1a.

Direct Object The boy bought a *bicycle*. [*Bicycle* is the direct object of the verb *bought*. A direct object answers the question *what* or *whom* after an active transitive verb.]

Indirect Object Kim handed *me* a fifty-dollar bill. [*Me* is the indirect object of the verb *handed*. An indirect object identifies who or what receives the direct object and is placed before the direct object.]

Nonfinite Verb Object Fixing the *bicycle* was a chore. [*Bicycle* is the object of the gerund *fixing*. The object of a nonfinite verb follows and completes the meaning of an infinitive, gerund, or participle.]

Object of Preposition The flowers were on the *table*. [*Table* is the object of the preposition *on*. The object of a preposition follows the preposition, and together they make up a prepositional phrase.]

Object Complement: See *Complement*. See also 18.1
Object of Preposition: See *Object*. See also 18.6.
Objective Case: The case of objects. Only a few pronouns show a difference in the nominative and objective cases: *I/me, he/him, she/her, we/us, they/them, who/whom*. See *Case*.
Obsolete Word: A word no longer in use.
Paradox: A seeming contradiction. Light is both a particle and a wave. Hamlet, at certain times, is both happy and sad.
Parallelism: Condition of having similar grammatical and syntactical structures. The prepositional phrases in the following sentence exhibit parallelism: *The old fisherman cursed at the boat, at the weather, and at his tangled line*. See 20.7.
Parenthetical Element: An inessential, interrupting word, phrase, or clause within a sentence that is set off by commas, parentheses, or dashes.

Parenthetical All the students, *if the teacher is correct*, cheated on the final examination.

Parenthetical Weldon Kees (*1914–1955*) was an American writer who (*this may be hard to believe*) excelled in both poetry and painting.

Participle: A past or present verb form used as an adjective (the *running* water, the *wounded* deer) or as part of a verb phrase (The boy is *running* down the street. The hunter had only *wounded* the deer). See *Nonfinite Verb*.

Participle Phrase: A group of words containing a participle and its modifiers and/or complements. In the sentence *The boy running down the street was laughing*, *running down the street* is a participle phrase. See *Phrase*. See also 18.8.

Parts of Speech: The words used in sentences divided by function and meaning into eight separate classes: adjectives, adverbs, conjunctions, interjections, nouns, pronouns, prepositions, and verbs. See each of these terms discussed in this Glossary. See also chapter 18.

Passive Voice: See *Voice*. See also 21.5.

Past Participle: One of the three principal parts of the verb formed by adding *-d* or *-ed*. *Tired* and *bought* are the past participles of *tire* and *buy*. See 20.4.

Past Perfect Tense: Verb tense using *had* and past participle (*had lost, had been lost*) to signal action that began and ended in the past. See 20.4.

Past Tense: Verb tense that signals past action. See 20.4.

Person: In grammar, point of view of subject in a sentence. *First person* indicates writer or speaker: *I, we*. *Second person* indicates the person addressed: *you*. *Third person* indicates the person or thing spoken about: *he, she, it, they*.

Personal Pronouns: The subject pronouns—*I, you, he, she, it, we, you, they*—and all the object and possessive forms of them used to replace nouns in sentences. See 18.3.

Phrasal Preposition: A preposition composed of two or more words: *out of, in spite of, with the exception of*. See 18.6.

Phrasal Verb: An idiomatic verb-adverb combination functioning as a unit. Consider the sentence *Pat ran down the highway*. If *ran down* means criticized, it is a phrasal verb. If *ran down* signifies speedy motion, it is not a phrasal verb.

Phrase: A group of connected words functioning in a sentence as a noun, verb, adjective, or adverb. See 18.8.

Plot: The ordered series of events that flow together to create a narrative or a story.

Plural: More than one. The plural of *dog* is *dogs*. In the sentence *I am happy, but they are sad*, the verb form *are* is plural.

Point of View: The position that a writer takes toward a subject. In descriptive writing, the phrase indicates the actual perspective from which the observing writer views the materials. In argumentative and persuasive writing, the phrase indicates which side of the argument the writer will be arguing for or against. The phrase also indicates the author's relationship to the written materials. A first-person point of view (*I, my*) deals with personal writing. A second-person point of view (*you, your*) usually deals with instructional or directive writing. A third-person point of view (*he/she, his/her*) generally deals with objective or impersonal writing.

Positive Degree: A term to describe a positive quality of an adjective or adverb. The words *sad* and *sadly* are in positive degree. The words *sadder* and *more sadly* are in comparative degree. The words *saddest* and *most sadly* are in superlative degree. See *Comparison*.

Possessive Adjective: See 18.4a.

Possessive Case: See *Case*.

Possessive Pronouns: See *Pronoun*. See also 18.3.

Predicate: In a sentence, the finite verb and all its modifiers and complements, excluding the complete subject. See *Complete Predicate*. See also 20.12. In the sentence *The boy shouted*, *boy* is the subject. *Shouted* is the predicate. In the sentence *The boy shouted at his teacher in the classroom*, the complete predicate is *shouted at his teacher in the classroom*.

Predicate Adjective: An adjective functioning as a subject complement. In the sentence *Andy's car is old*, *old* is the predicate adjective. See *Complement*.

Predicate Nominative: A noun functioning as a subject complement. In the sentence *Andy's car is a Studebaker*, *Studebaker* is the predicate nominative. See *Complement*.

Prefix: A letter or group of letters attached to the front of a word that changes its meaning (*wise, unwise*). See 21.1a.

Premise: In logic, an assumption in the form of a statement or proposition on which an argument is based. See the discussion of major premise and minor premise in *Deduction*, 6.2.

Preposition: A part of speech (such as *in, with, around*) that links a noun or a noun substitute to another word or words in a sentence. See 18.6.

Prepositional Phrase: A group of words (such as *at home, in the old car, across the streets and highways*) consisting of a preposition and its object and any modifiers. Prepositional phrases generally function as adjectives or adverbs within a sentence. See 18.8.

Principal Parts: The three forms of a verb: present (*go, buzz*), past (*went, buzzed*), and past participle (*gone, buzzed*). See 20.4d.

Process Analysis: The dividing of a simple or complex process into a series of steps. Examples would be a paragraph explaining how to tie a knot or an essay explaining the mechanism of photosynthesis.

Progressive Tense: Verb tense that indicates ongoing activity. See 20.4a.

Pronoun: A word used in place of a noun. See 18.3.

Personal I, you, he/she/it, we, you, they

Demonstrative this, that, these, those

Indefinite any, each, few, many, some

Intensive myself, yourself, himself/herself/itself, ourselves, yourselves, themselves

Interrogative who, whom, which, what

Reciprocal each other, one another

Reflexive identical to intensives

Relative who, whom, whose, that, which

Proper Adjective: An adjective, always capitalized, derived from a proper noun: *American* from *America*, *Freudian* from *Freud*.

Proper Noun: A specific name of a person, place, or thing, which is always capitalized. *Lora, Boston, Challenger*.

Quotation: The words of another, whether in thought, speech, or writing, that must be put in quotation marks and whose source must be acknowledged. See 22.7.

Reciprocal Pronouns: *Each other* and *one another.* Pronouns used to express reciprocal relationships or mutual activities. *Love one another. Be kind to each other. Each other* is used for two; *one another* for more than two.

Reflexive Pronoun: A personal pronoun with the suffix *-self* or *-selves* referring back to the subject. In the sentence *Gina kissed herself in the mirror, herself* is a reflexive pronoun.

Regionalism: Language, pronunciation, or grammatical structure unique to a certain area. See *Dialect.*

Regular Verb: A verb that forms its past tense by adding *-d* (*moved*) or *-ed* (*wanted*). See 20.4.

Relative Pronouns: The pronouns *that, what, which, who, whom, whose, whoever, whomever, whatever,* and *whichever* used to introduce subordinate clauses (noun, adjective, adverb). Jane knows *who* started the fire. See 18.3b.

Restrictive Modifier: An essential modifier in a sentence. See *Nonrestrictive.* See also 22.2f.

Rhetoric: A system of strategies of thought for communicating ideas and persuading a reader or listener.

Sentence: A group of related words that contain a subject and a verb and that can stand alone. See *Clause.* Sentences can be classified in terms of structure as simple, compound, complex, or compound complex. See also 18.10.

Simple The spider trapped the fly. [Subject + Predicate]

Compound The wind blew, and the windows rattled. [Main clause + Main clause]

Complex When the door opened, a black cat ran in. [Subordinate clause + Main clause]

Compound Complex After the class ended, the teacher went home, and the student went to the library. [Subordinate clause + Main clause + Main clause]

Sentence Fragment: An incomplete sentence. Generally considered a serious sentence error. See 20.1.

Sentence Modifier: An adverbial modifier of the rest of the sentence: *No*, you may not leave the yard. *Generally speaking,* TV game shows are boring.

Singular: One. In the sentence *The spider ate three flies*, the noun *spider* is singular.

Subject: A basic unit (noun or nominal) of the sentence. The subject is the agent or topic developed by the predicate. In the sentence *The students in the library always complain about the heat, students* is the simple subject. *The students in the library* is the complete subject.

Subject Complement: See *Predicate Adjective* and *Predicate Nominative*. See also 18.1a.

Subjective Case: See *Case*.

Subjunctive Mood: See *Mood*. See also 20.4f.

Subordinate Clause: See *Clause*. See also 18.9.

Subordinating Conjunction: A word or word group that signals a subordinate clause. See 18.7b.

Subordination: The joining of dependent elements (clauses, phrases) to independent clauses (main clauses, sentences). See 19.1b, 20.8, and 20.9d–e.

Suffix: An addition to the end of a word to change a meaning, create a new word, or show grammatical function. See 21.1a.

Superlative Degree: The form of an adjective (*greatest*) or adverb (*most greatly*) that expresses an extreme level or extent.

Syllable: A unit of spoken or written language consisting of at least one vowel or a vowel and a consonant. The word *door* has one syllable. The word *doorbell* has two syllables.

Syllogism: A process of deductive reasoning generally involving three stages. See 6.2.

Syntax: The structure of a sentence. The grammatical relationships among the elements in a sentence.

Synthesis: The putting together of different ideas, generally the positive and negative points of a subject, and arriving at a conclusion.

Tautology: Circular reasoning or circular definition. To define an air pump as "a machine to pump air" is to create a tautology. See 6.3d.

Technical Writing: Writing by scientists, engineers, and technicians to publicize their work and to explain scientific and technical material.

Tense: Verb forms using inflections or auxiliaries to show time distinctions in a sentence. The five tenses are present (*dream*), progressive (*am dreaming*), past (*dreamed*), perfect (*have dreamed*), and future (*will dream*) Two or more of these may be combined, as in future perfect (*will have dreamed*). See 20.4a.

Thesis Statement: A brief statement containing the main idea of an essay. See 1.4 and 5.2.

Tone: In a narrative or a story, tone is the narrator's attitude toward the characters and events in the story and, perhaps even, the attitude toward the reader. In an argumentative, expository, or personal essay, tone is the author's emotional and intellectual attitude toward the subject and toward the materials used to develop that subject. There are hundreds of possible tones; the following is a list of some of them: bitter, informative, sympathetic, distant, hostile, and curt.

Transitive Verb: When in the active voice, a verb that takes a direct object. See *Verb*. See also 18.2a.

Verb: A word or group of words used in a sentence to express activity, occurrence, or being on the part of the subject. In terms of sentence meaning, verbs are divided into three classes: transitive, intransitive, or linking. See 18.2 and 20.4.

Transitive The cook *tasted* the apples. [Transitive verbs take objects.]

Intransitive The apples *rotted*. [Intransitive verbs do not take objects.]

Linking The apples *were* red. [Linking verbs are followed by complements.]

Verbals: A general term for nonfinite verb forms. See *Infinitive*, *Participle*, and *Gerund*.

Verb Phrase: The main verb of a sentence or clause and any auxiliary verbs. The trailer *was sliding* down the side of the hill.

Vocabulary Word: In a sentence, a word with reference to "things in the world," in contrast to function words that show the relationship between the elements in a sentence. See *Function Word*.

Voice: The verb form (active or passive) that expresses the relationship between the subject and the verb in a clause. In the active voice, the subject performs the action of the verb. In the passive voice, the subject is the recipient of the action, or the agent of the action may be missing.

Active voice The girl slapped the boy.

Passive Voice The boy was slapped by the girl.

Active Voice Someone stole Glenn's wallet.

Passive Voice Glenn's wallet was stolen.

Word Order: The arrangement of words in a sentence. Word order determines meaning in an English sentence as in the following sentences: *The man bit the dog. The dog bit the man. Sign the check. Check the sign.*

25 Glossary of Usage

a / an: Indefinite articles. Use *a* before consonant sounds: *a box, a union*; use *an* before vowel sounds: *an apple, an honor.*

accent / ascent / assent: *Accent* means "the sound or the stress of words." *Ascent* means "a going up" or "a climbing." *Assent* means "an agreement."

accept / except: *Accept* means "to take or receive." *Except* as a verb means "to leave out." *Except* as a preposition means "omitting or leaving out." *The school accepted everyone except me.*

access / excess: *Access* means "an entry or approach." *Excess* means "an abundance" or "too much." *Mike left the excess baggage on the access ramp.*

adapt / adept / adopt: *Adapt* means "to adjust to." *Adept* is an adjective meaning "skillful." *Adopt* means "to take as one's own."

addition / edition: *Addition* means "an adding on." *Edition* means "a published book or object."

advice / advise: *Advice* is a noun: "direction or guidance." *Advise* is a verb: "to counsel, direct, or guide."

affect / effect: The verb *affect* means "to influence." The noun *effect* means "result." *Elvis Presley affected people strongly. One effect of his death was that his home was turned into a national shrine.*

afraid of / frightened at / frightened by: Use these words with the correct prepositions. *My cat is afraid of the dark. Jane was frightened at the sound of gunfire. Jane was frightened by the sound of the wind.*

aggravate / irritate: *Aggravate* means "to make worse." *Irritate* means "to annoy."

agree to / agree with: Distinguish between the two. *You will agree to a thing, but you will agree with a person.*

aid / aide: *Aid* as both noun and verb means "help" and "to help." *Aide* means "helper, assistant."

ain't: Nonstandard. A contraction avoided by writers except for satiric emphasis or humor.

aisle / isle: Both words rhyme with *I'll*. *Aisle* is "a space between rows." *Isle* is "an island."

alley / ally: *Alley* is a "narrow street or walk." *Ally* is a "friend."

a lot / a lot of: These words create spelling and usage problems. In spelling, remember that *a lot* is two words and *a lot of* is three words. In usage, *a lot of* is a synonym for "many." Use the phrase sparingly. Once in a paper is enough. Some good substitutes are *many, more, some*, and *a number of*. Use figures of speech to convey a sense of size. Use approximate figures to show number.

allude / elude: *Allude* means "to refer to." *Elude* means "to avoid or escape."

allusion / illusion: *Allusion* is "an indirect reference." *Illusion* is "a mistaken belief or perception." *Professor Vendler made an allusion to Wordsworth's fascination with illusion.*

almost / most: *Almost* is an adverb: "nearly or very nearly." *Most* is an adjective or pronoun: "greatest number, amount, degree." *Most* is not a contracted form of *almost*.

already / all ready: *Already* is a time adverb: "earlier or previously." *All ready* is an adjective: "completely prepared."

all right: The expression is two words. Most readers will consider *alright* a misspelled word.

altar / alter: *Altar* is a noun: "religious table" or "place of religious sacrifice." *Alter* is a verb: "to change."

altogether / all together: *Altogether* means "wholly or thoroughly." *That speech was altogether brilliant. All together* means "in a group." *We listened to the senator's speech all together.*

A.M. / P.M. or a.m. / p.m.: Generally used with figures: *I wake at 5:00 a.m. every day.* Do not write the following: *I wake at five o'clock a.m. every day.*

among / between: *Among* indicates three or more: *The five thieves divided the jewels among themselves. Between* generally refers to two: *He planted grass between the house and the garage. Between* is always used in comparing and contrasting: *They had to decide between ice cream and cookies.*

amount of / number of: *Amount of* indicates a singular unit and is followed by singular nouns. *The manager has only a small amount of work to do. Number of* signals the plural and is followed by plural nouns. *The manager fired a number of workers just yesterday.*

an / and: *An* is an indefinite article used before vowels or a voiceless *h. And* is a conjunction. It means "in addition to."

and / but: These present no problem in grammar. They do have an effect rhythmically and rhetorically in developing your ideas. Use them rarely at the beginning of a sentence, and avoid a long succession of such usages.

and / or: This usage is grammatical, but it is often confusing. Avoid or revise. Confusing: *Wendy will take Latin and / or Greek.* Revised: *Wendy will take Latin or Greek, or both.*

angel / angle: *Angel* means "messenger from another world." *Angle* means "figure formed by two lines."

angle / point of view: *Angle* is best reserved for literal angles. *Point of view* is best reserved for "way of looking at something." See *Point of View* in chapter 24.

anti- / ante-: Both are prefixes. *Anti-* means "against." *Ante-* means "before."

angry at / angry with: *You are angry with a person, but you are angry at a thing.*

anxious / eager: *Anxious* means "nervous" or "worried." It is usually followed by *because* or *about. Eager* means "excited" or "looking forward to." It is usually followed by *for* or *to.* Psychologists and medical doctors use the word *anxiety* to mean "an overwhelming sense of apprehension." To confuse the two adjectives is to confuse two very different emotional states. Correct: *Jane was eager to go to the dance, but she was anxious about meeting Roger.*

anybody / any body: *Anybody* is a one-word indefinite pronoun. It is interchangeable with *anyone: Anybody can read this. Any body* is two words—an adjective modifying a noun. *Any body* *of fresh water will have plant life in it.* These same distinctions are also true for *everybody, nobody, somebody.*

anymore / any more: These words are not the same. *Anymore* is an adverb meaning "now": *Jane does not work here anymore. Any more* is two words and is often used with a negative: *I have eaten too much food. I do not want any more.*

anyone / any one: These are not the same words. *Anyone* is a one-word indefinite pronoun: *Anyone can sing this tune. Any one* is two words—an adjective modifying a pronoun. *Read these poison labels. Any one of them will frighten you.* These same distinctions are also true for *everyone* and *someone.* A problem arises with the use of pronouns to refer to *anyone, everyone,* and other singular pronouns. It does not occur with *one,* which is never used in a plural sense. In a curious way, some writers believe that *everyone* means *all,* as in the sentence *Everyone in the room took their seat.* It may be best to write the following: *All the people in the room took their seats* or *Everyone sat down.* Many readers are offended by seeing a plural pronoun refer to a singular antecedent. Avoid pronoun agreement errors in formal writing.

anywheres: Nonstandard. A regional pronunciation for *anywhere.*

appraise / apprise: *Appraise* means "to judge worth or value." *Apprise* means "to tell or inform."

apt to / liable to / likely to: *Apt to* means "having a tendency to." *Likely* means "probably going to." *Liable* means "in danger of" or "responsible for." *I am apt to fail this test. Seth is likely to do the same thing. If I drive Seth's car, I am liable for any damages.*

arc / ark: *Arc* is "a curve" and *ark* means "a boat."

as: Avoid using this word as an all-purpose connective. Try to use it in one of the following senses.

1. As a conjunction: *Kirk did as he was told.* [The conjunction *as* indicates a sameness of degree, manner, or quantity.]
2. As a preposition: *Kirk is happy as a lark.* [The preposition *as* indicates an equivalence. The preposition *like* indicates a similarity as in the following sentence: *Kirk is singing like a lark.*]

NOTE 1: Avoid the imprecise use of *as* as a synonym for *if, that,* or *whether.* Imprecise: *Kirk did not know as the coach*

was angry. **Precise:** *Kirk did not know if the coach was angry.* **Precise:** *Kirk did not know that the coach was angry.* **Precise:** *Kirk did not know whether the coach was angry or not.*

NOTE 2: **Avoid the imprecise use of** *as* **as a synonym for** *because, since,* **or** *while.* **Imprecise:** *As it started raining, Kirk stayed in the library working on his research paper.* **Precise:** *Because it started raining, Kirk stayed in the library working on his research paper.* **Precise:** *Since it has started raining, Kirk has stayed in the library working on his research paper.* **Precise:** *While it was raining, Kirk stayed in the library working on his research paper.*

as . . . as: The double use of *as* emphasizes and clarifies the comparison: *Organic Chemistry 102 is as difficult as Physics 102.*

as good or better than: Avoid this wordy phrasing. Choose one: *good* or *better.* Write "as good as." Or write "better than."

as / as if / like: *As* and *as if* introduce adverb clauses such as the following: *As I walked, I dreamed* and *My book looks as if a bear had chewed it. As* and *like* are prepositions that can introduce nouns, as in the sentences *This spider looks like an ant* and *Hector joined the army as a paramedic.*

as regards: See *in regard to.* See *regarding.*

assistance / assistants: *Assistance* means "help." *Assistants* is the plural of *assistant:* "helper."

assure / ensure / insure: All are verbs. *Assure* means "to promise or guarantee." *Ensure* means "to make certain." *Insure* means "to grant an insurance policy." *I can assure you of one thing, Mrs. Smith. Our company can insure your poodle for a million dollars. What will it take to ensure that you believe me?*

as / than: See 20.5c and 20.11c.

as to: Avoid when you mean the preposition *about* or *concerning.*

at: The word *at* after *where* is redundant. Example: *Where is Joe at?* should be *Where is Joe?*

at this point in time: Avoid. Substitute *now* or *at this time.*

awful / awfully: Avoid unless used in their literal sense: "filling with awe." Especially avoid using them as synonyms for the following intensives: *very, strongly,* or *extremely.*

bad / badly: *Bad* is an adjective. *Badly* is an adverb. *This is a bad road. Mo drives badly.* After linking verbs that refer to any of the five senses and after any other linking verb, use the adjective *bad. That was a bad meal. It looked bad. It smelled bad. It tasted bad.*

bare / bear / bear: *Bare* is an adjective meaning "naked." *Bear* is "a wild animal." *Bear* is also a verb meaning "to carry."

basis / bases: *Basis* is a noun meaning "fundamental or basic principle." *Bases* is a plural noun meaning "corners of a baseball diamond." *Bases* is also the plural of "basis."

bazaar / bizarre: A *bazaar* is "an open marketplace" or "a fair." *Bizarre* is an adjective meaning "strange or outrageous."

being as / being that: Nonstandard idioms for *because* or *since.*

belief / believe: *Belief* is a noun meaning "a conviction." *Believe* is a verb meaning "to be convinced."

beside / besides: The words should be kept distinct. The preposition *beside* often indicates "next to." *Kirk sat beside Jennifer.* The preposition *besides* often indicates "except for." *Besides study and painting, Jennifer has no other human interests.* The adverb *besides* often means "in addition to" or "also." *My father prepared a ham, a turkey, a stuffed goose, and a dozen pies besides.*

be sure and: If you mean *be sure to*, you should write that: *Be sure to study his notes.*

better: This is not a synonym for "ought to." Use *should. Lee should pay attention in class.*

between / among: See *among.*

birth / berth: *Birth* means "being born." *Berth* means "a place to rest or sleep."

board / bored: *Board* means "a piece of wood" or "food" in the idiom "room and board." *Bored* means "uninterested" or "apathetic."

born / borne: *Born* means "having been delivered as a baby." *Borne* means "carried" or "transported."

borrow / lend / loan: *Borrow* means "to have temporary use." *Lend* means "to give temporary use." Example: *I wanted to borrow a hammer, but Harry would only lend me a wrench. Loan* generally refers to money that will be repaid. Example: *My brother loaned me five hundred dollars.*

bottom line: Use this cliché only to indicate in a literal sense the last line on a page. Find acceptable substitutes such as *conclusion, decision, situation*, and so forth.

break / brake: Both these words are pronounced the same. *Break* means "to crack or shatter." *Brake* means "to slow down."

breath / breathe: *Breath* rhymes with *death*. *Breath* is a noun, and it means "air taken in or exhaled." *Breathe* is a verb, and it means "to inhale and exhale."

bring / take: *Bring* suggests movement toward; *take* suggests motion away. Example: *Each time Henry brings us a new bucket, a thief takes it.*

burst: *Burst* is the same in its present, past, and past participle forms. *Burst* means "to break open because of pressure." Do not use the archaic and comic *bursted*. Do not confuse *burst* with the slang word *bust.*

bust / busted: As a verb, it means "to hit" or "to smash." As a slang verb, it means *to arrest.*

but however / but yet: Avoid. Remove the unnecessary *but.*

but that / but what: Avoid. Remove the *but*. Revise to a positive *that* construction. Wrong: *I don't know but that I will fail.* Correct: *I believe that I will fail.*

Calvary / cavalry: *Calvary* means "a hill near Jerusalem where Jesus was crucified." *Cavalry* means "a group of soldiers—originally on horseback."

can / may: The distinction is important. *Can* refers to ability. *May* refers to permission. Example: *I can do that. May I?*

can't hardly: This is a double negative. Revise to *can hardly.*

can't help but: Informal. Remove the *but*. Informal: *A dog can't help but bite people.* Revised: *A dog can't help biting people.*

canvas / canvass: *Canvas* is "a heavy cloth." *Canvass* is a verb meaning "to poll."

capital / capitol: As an adjective, *capital* means "large" or "major." As a noun, it means, "wealth", or "supply of money," or "the governmental center of a state or country." The noun *capitol* refers to "a building or group of buildings where a state or national government meets."

case: Often, this is a mere wordy sentence filler. Unless you refer to a *case of beer*, a *case in court*, a *case of polio*, or other actual *cases*, remove the word. Wordy: *In the case of John, he was unhappy.* Improved: *John was unhappy.*

censor / censure: *Censor* means "a person who will not allow something." *Censure* means "a public condemnation."

center around: The phrase is illogical and wrong. You walk around something, but you center on something.

century / centuries: Use lowercase letters to spell centuries (*the twentieth century*). Use hyphens when forming adjectives (*nineteenth- and twentieth-century poetry, thirteenth-century art forms*).

choose / chose / choice: *Choose* is a verb meaning "to pick or to select." *Chose* is the past tense and means "picked or selected." *Choice* is a noun meaning "selection."

cite / site / sight: *Cite* is a verb meaning "to refer to" or "to acknowledge." *Site* is a noun meaning "a place." *Sight* is a noun meaning "seeing" or "thing seen."

climactic / climatic: *Climactic* is an adjective from *climax* that means "most intense experience." *Climatic* comes from *climate* and means "concerning the weather."

close / clothes / cloths: *Close* as a verb means "to shut" or "to end." *Clothes* as a noun means "things worn." *Cloths* is the plural of *cloth*, a word that rhymes with *moth*.

coarse / course: The adjective *coarse* means "rough" or "not fine." The noun *course* means "a class in school" or "a path."

compare / contrast: When used precisely, *compare* points to similarities and *contrast* points to differences.

compare to / compare with: In informal usage, the expressions are used interchangeably, but in formal writing, a distinction should be observed. Use *compare to* when classifying or showing only similarity, and use *compare with* when showing similarity and dissimilarity of two things side by side. Example: *The child compared the planet to a baseball. How does last week's paper compare with this week's?*

complement / compliment: As a noun, *complement* means "something added for balance or form" or "a counterpart." As a verb, *complement* means "to add balance or harmony." *Compliment* refers to speech or writing. As a verb, *compliment* means "to praise" or "to flatter." As a noun, it means "praise" or "flattery." Example: *The color green complements the color red. Mary complimented Jean.*

conscious / conscience: *Conscious* is an adjective meaning "awake" or "aware." *Conscience* is a noun meaning "interior sense of right or wrong."

considerable: The word is an adjective. Any other usage is confusing or nonstandard. Avoid using it as a noun or an adverb.

contact: This is an overused word. Essentially, it means *touch*. Avoid repeating the word and use other, more precise words: *ask, consult, find, inform, meet, meet with, question, reach, talk with, telephone, write to.*

continual / continuous: *Continual* means "repeated or very frequent, with interruptions." Example: *The month of May was memorable because of the continual snow. Continuous* means "uninterrupted or unceasing." Example: *The snow was continuous for thirty-six hours.*

contractions: Avoid using them in formal writing: *doesn't, don't,* and all others.

core / corps / corpse: *Core* means "the center or innermost part." *Corps* rhymes with *door* and refers to "a military group." *Corpse* refers to "a dead body."

could of / would of / should of: Nonstandard. These words sound the same as the contractions *could've, would've,* and *should've.* Revise to *could have, would have,* or *should have.*

couldn't care less: Because this is a cliché, you might find some other way to express your lack of interest in the matter.

council / counsel: *Council* means "a group that decides or legislates." *Counsel* as a verb means "to advise" and as a noun means "an adviser."

criterion / criteria: *Criterion* means "a standard for judgment." The plural is *criteria.*

cute: Use this word precisely or find a substitute.

dairy / diary: *Dairy* rhymes with *berry* and is "a place for the making and selling of milk and milk products." *Diary* rhymes with *fiery.* It is "a journal for a person to write in."

dam / damn: *Dam* is "a structure to hold back water." The verb *damn* means "to condemn" or "to send to hell."

data: The word *data* is a collective noun. It takes either a singular or plural verb. The plural is preferred by many people.

deal: This is an overworked noun. Unless you are referring to cards, you might choose a more precise word: *agreement, bargain, contract, pact, plan, secret arrangement,* or *transaction.*

decent / descent / dissent: *Decent* is an adjective meaning "fitting" or "respectable." *Descent* is a noun meaning "a going down" or "the way down." *Dissent* means "disagreement" as a noun and "disagree" as a verb.

defer / differ: *Defer* means "to postpone or put off." *Differ* means "to show lack of resemblance" (*differ from*) or "to disagree" (*differ with*).

deference / difference / diffidence: *Deference* means "respect" or "acknowledging and yielding." *Difference* means "a lack of similarity." *Diffidence* means "hesitancy caused by lack of self-confidence."

desert / desert / dessert: The noun *desert* means "dry land" and has an accent on the first syllable. The verb *desert* means "to leave or abandon." *Dessert* means "a sweet thing at the end of a meal."

device / devise: *Device* rhymes with *ice* and means "a machine or tool for doing work." *Devise* rhymes with *eyes* and means "to imagine or think up."

differ from / differ with: *Differ from* shows essential contrast: *New Orleans jazz differs from New York jazz. Differ with* indicates disagreement: *Smith differs with Russell on the value of music.*

different from / different than: *Different from* is traditionally preferred for formal writing. Many authorities on usage accept either form in informal usage.

discreet / discrete: *Discreet* means "prudent, careful, circumspect." *Discrete* means "individual, separate, distinct."

disinterested / uninterested: *Disinterested* means "clear-sighted, unbiased, objective, fair-minded." *Uninterested* means "bored, apathetic, not caring."

dominate / dominant: The verb *dominate* rhymes with *ate* and means "to control." The adjective *dominant* rhymes with *runt* and means "ruling or controlling."

done: The past participle of *do*. Example: *Joe had done my job.* Or it is an adjective meaning *finished*. Example: *The work is done*. Often, it is used incorrectly as a wordy sentence filler for emphasis. Wrong: *He done went and bought a new car.* Correct: *he went and bought a new car.*

don't: A contraction of *do not*. Make sure that the subject and the verb agree. Wrong: *The broom don't work.* Correct: *The broom does not work.*

dual / duel: *Dual* with *a* means "double" or "two." *Duel* with *e* means "a rivalry or contest between two people."

due to: *Because of* or *on account of* are preferred in sentences such as the following: *On account of the snowstorm, the final examination was cancelled.*

due to the fact that: This wordy expression can be easily revised to *because.* Wordy: *Due to the fact that the coal strike lasted two years, my father lost his job and moved to North Carolina.* Revised: *Because the coal strike lasted two years, my father lost his job and moved to North Carolina.*

dyeing / dying: *Dyeing* (from *dye*) with an *e* means "changing color." *Dying* (from *die*) means "losing life."

each and every: Wordy phrase. Remove one of the words.

each other / one another: In formal usage, use *each other* with two items: *The couple gave each other presents.* Use *one another* with more than two: *The members of the sorority gave one another Christmas presents.*

either / neither: These pronouns are singular. They signify "one of two / none of two."

elicit / illicit: *Elicit* is a verb meaning "to draw out" or "to bring forth." *Illicit* is an adjective meaning "illegal or unlawful."

emigrate from / immigrate to: *Emigrate* means "to leave one country for permanent residence elsewhere." *Immigrate* means "to move to one country from another in order to live there." The noun forms are *emigrant* and *immigrant.*

enthuse / enthused / enthusiastic: The verb *enthuse* is acceptable, but some writers feel it suggests ignorance, artificiality, and insincerity. Many writers suggest finding a substitute for *enthused. Enthusiastic* is an adjective meaning "eager or passionate."

envelop / envelope: *Envelop* rhymes with *up* and means "to surround and enclose." *Envelope* rhymes with *rope* and means a "container for a letter."

etc. / et cetera: Latin for "and the other things." Many writers use *and so forth* or *and the others.* Avoid *and et cetera.* The *and* is redundant.

expect: *Expect* does not mean "suppose" or "think." It means "to wait for" or "to anticipate." Use it precisely.

explicit / implicit: *Explicit* means "directly stated or presented." *Implicit* means "implied or indirectly stated."

fabulous / fantastic: Use the words with their precise meanings. *Fabulous* means "resembling a fable." *Fantastic* means "based on fantasy."

facet / feature: Use precisely. *Facet* means "the surface of a cut stone." *Feature* means "the structure, form, appearance of some thing or a leading article in a publication." Weak: *One feature of college is that students have enormous freedom.* Improved: *In college, students have enormous freedom.*

the fact that: Avoid. This is a wordy expression. Revise for precision. Weak: *The fact that John failed Physics 212 made him sad.* Improved: *John's failure in Physics 212 made him sad.* Especially avoid when used with *due to.*

factor: Avoid. In general use, it is a vague, imprecise word meaning "thing" or "part." Use only in one of the precise meanings found in a dictionary. Avoid in most cases, or find specific substitutes. Weak: *Study is a great factor which leads to success in college.* Improved: *Study leads to success in college.*

fair / fair / fare: *Fair* is a noun meaning "a celebration, exhibition, or gathering." *Fair* is an adjective meaning "pleasing, pale, or impartial." *Fare* as a noun means "the expense" or "the food." As a verb, it means "to travel."

farther / further: In conversation, the words are often interchangeable. *Farther* signifies measurable distance. Example: *Hoxie is ten miles farther. Further* indicates conceptual distance. Example: *Henry could go no further in his studies.*

fewer / less: The words are often used similarly. In writing, a distinction exists. *Fewer* indicates the countable, actual numbers. Example: *Greg sold fewer tickets last week than the week before. Less* indicates amount, value, or degree. Example: *Jane had less money than I.* Contrast: *Jane had fewer dollars than I.* Use *fewer*, not *less*, when speaking of calories.

field: Use with a precise meaning. This word (like *case, instance, line*) is often redundant. Weak: *Sid is going into the field of medicine.* Improved: *Sid is going into medicine.*

figuratively / literally: *Figuratively* means "as a figure of speech" or "not literally." *Literally* means "specifically following the letter" or "in a prescribed manner."

figure: This is an imprecise and informal word occasionally used for more precise words such as *believe, conclude, predict,* or *conclude.*

finalize: Avoid. Use *finish, complete, conclude,* or *end.*

fine: An imprecise adjective indicating approval. Use it with a precise meaning: "free from impurity, very thin, very small, very delicate."

firstly: Omit the *-ly*. Write *first, second*, and so forth.

flaunt / flout: *Flaunt* means "to display boldly or impudently." *Flout* means "to scorn" or "to treat with contempt."

for: The preposition *for* is used in sentences such as *For the love of money, that man would sell himself into slavery.* The coordinating conjunction *for* is used to join sentences together as in the following: *My parents are planning a trip to the airport, for grandmother arrives today.*

former / latter: Use only with two previously mentioned items, as in the following sentence: *Krebs and Dose both went on to graduate school: the former to Marshall, the latter to Yale.* For more than two items, use *first* and *last*.

formerly / formally: *Formerly* is an adverb of time meaning "before." *Formally* is an adverb of manner meaning "in a formal style."

forth / fourth: *forth* is an adverb meaning "in front or ahead." *Fourth* is an adjective made from *four*.

freshman / freshmen: The first noun is singular, the second plural. The adjective form is *freshman* as in *freshman dormitory*.

frightened at / frightened by: See *afraid of*.

geld / gild / guild / guilt: *Geld* means "to castrate." *Gild* means "to cover with gold." *Guild* means "a labor organization." *Guilt* means "a negative emotion acknowledging wrongdoing or sorrow."

get: by itself, this is one of the most overused words in the entire English language. You can improve your style immediately by using other and more precise words to indicate your exact meaning. In a precise sense, the word *get* means "obtain" or "receive." In all cases, avoid using a string of *get* forms in your writing. Avoid in formal writing informal uses of *get*: *get going, get with it, get off it, get cracking, get one's goat.*

good / well: The word *good* is an adjective. The adverb form of *good* is *well*. Use *good* when you want to explain what something is. Example: *The food is good*. Use *well* when you want to explain how something occurs. Example: *Jeanie plays golf well*. See 20.6a.

good and: Revise when used in sentences such as the following: *J. Alfred Prufrock is good and tired, always thinking of sleep*. Revised: *J. Alfred Prufrock is exceedingly tired, always thinking of sleep*.

gorilla / guerrilla: *Gorilla* means "a jungle animal." *Guerrilla* means "a soldier who uses unconventional strategies, especially surprise.'"

got: Avoid using *got* as a synonym for *have*. Wrong: *I got a new desk in my room.* Correct: *I have a new desk in my room.*

got to: Avoid using this term as a substitute for *has to, have to , must,* or *ought.* Wrong: *He gots to catch the bus.* Correct: *He has to catch the bus.*

guy: The word means "a kind of wire or rope," "a kind of large doll," "a man," "a boy or a girl," or "a person." Use the word precisely or avoid it.

had drank / had drunk: The correct form is *had drunk.*

had of: Wordy and nonstandard for *had.*

had ought: Wordy and nonstandard for *ought.*

half / a half / half a: Formal writing avoids using *a half a, a half of,* or *half of.* Correct: *Half my homework is lost.* Correct: *I took a half-hour nap.* Correct: *The poodle was sick half a day.*

hanged / hung: *Hang / hanged* refers to death by hanging. *Hang / hung* refers to suspending objects. *The hanged the rapist, but they hung the drapes.*

hard / difficult: *Hard* means "not soft" or "solid." *Difficult* means "requiring great labor or skill to accomplish." Informally, the words are synonymous. In formal writing, use them precisely or find synonyms.

hardly / scarcely: Negative adverbs. Do not use with *no, none, not,* or *never.* Wrong: *I can't hardly stop laughing.* Correct: *I can hardly stop laughing.*

have / of: Do not spell *have* as *of.* Even though some people may hear or pronounce these words the same, they are quite different. Try to hear the difference between the two words spoken out loud. Pronounce the *h* sound and the *a* sound in *have.* Wrong: *Joe could of gone to the church.* Correct: *Joe could have gone to the church.* Check constructions such as *would have, must have,* and *ought to have.*

he / she, him / her, his / her: You might avoid such awkward constructions in one of three different ways: (1) substitute *he or she*; (2) delete the pronouns entirely; (3) change the singular to the plural.

> **Negative** Dr. Glumm will test each student for his ability in art.

Awkward Dr. Glumm will test each student for his / her ability in art.

Substitution Dr. Glumm will test each student for his or her ability in art.

Deletion Dr. Glumm will test each student's ability in art.

Plural Dr. Glumm will test the students' abilities in art.

hear / here: *Hear* is a verb meaning "to be aware of sound" or "to listen." *Here* is an adverb meaning "in this place."

heard / herd: *Heard* is the past tense of the verb *hear. Herd* is a noun meaning "a gathering or group of similar animals."

hisself: Incorrect form of *himself.*

historic / historical: *Historic* means "of great importance in human history." *The tearing down of the Berlin Wall is one of the most historic events in recent times. Historical* means "having happened in history" or "related to history."

hole / whole: *hole* means "an opening" or "a gap." *Whole* means "complete, entire, unhurt, or unbroken."

holy / holey / wholly: *Holy* means "sacred." *Holey* means "full of holes." *Wholly* means "completely."

hopefully: *Hopefully* may be effective on occasion. Many writers consider the word misused in the sense of *I hope.* Replace with constructions that use *hope* as a verb rather than part of an adverb. Weak: *Hopefully the plane will land on time.* Improved: *I hope the plane will land on time.*

human / humane: *Human* is a noun or adjective referring to the species "Homo sapiens." *Humane* is an adjective meaning "sympathetic, kind, or considerate."

if / whether: Use these words precisely to indicate conditional statements or alternative possibilities. Use *if* for conditional clauses. *If I fail this course, my parents will be angry.* You would not say, *Whether I fail this course, my parents will be angry.* Use *whether* to indicate alternatives. *I do not know whether I will go to Notre Dame or Creighton.*

impact: Use as a noun. Avoid especially as a verb meaning "to have an effect." Use it in its strict technical sense of "a pushing against." Noun as verb: *The fire will impact negatively on* *the company's profit.* Revised: *The fire's impact will decrease the company's profits.*

imply / infer: *Imply* means "to hint" or "to suggest." *Infer* means "to reach a conclusion." Example: *Professor Fromm implied that Marx had no respect for historical truth, and the students inferred that Dr. Fromm was not a Marxist historian.*

in / into: The two words are often used interchangeably. The word *in* seems to signify *fixed location: The car was in the square. Into* seems to imply *motion into: The man drove his car into the grocery store.*

incidence / incident / incidents: *Incidence* is a singular noun meaning "rate or frequency of some occurrence." *Incident* is a singular noun meaning "an event." *Incidents* is the plural of *incident.*

incite / insight: *Incite* is a verb meaning "to arouse or provoke." *Insight* is a noun meaning "perception" or "understanding."

in fact: This phrase can generally be deleted.

inferior than: Confusing idiom. Use *worse off than* or *inferior to.*

ingenious / ingenuous: *Ingenious* means "clever" or "resourceful." *Ingenuous* means "innocent" or "naive."

input: The word is often used imprecisely and excessively. It has various meanings in different trades and occupations. Use precisely or replace with synonyms such as *advice, comment, opinion, role,* or *voice.*

in regard to / as regards / with regard to: These are the correct forms. The incorrect forms are *in regards to* and *with regards to.* See *regarding.*

inside of / outside of: The *of* is wordy and unnecessary. If you mean *inside* or *outside,* use the word. Drop the *of.*

instant / instants / instance: *Instant* is singular and it means "a moment." *Instants* is plural and it means "moments." *Instance* is singular and means "an example."

in the worst way: Avoid. A meaningless cliché and exaggeration. Use another expression to indicate strong desire.

invaluable / valuable: *Invaluable* means "priceless" or "irreplaceable." *Valuable* means "important," "precious," or "worthwhile."

irregardless: Remove the unnecessary *ir-* prefix. The correct spelling is *regardless*.

irrelevant / irreverent: *Irrelevant* means "not pertinent" or "inapplicable." *Irreverent* means "disrespectful," "pert," or "saucy."

is when / is where: Words cannot be accurately defined by telling the reader *when* they are or *where* they are. Revise the sentence accordingly. Weak: *A desert is where you find barrenness and no water.* Revised: *A desert is a barren area lacking water.* Weak: *An election is when the people go to vote.* Revised: *An election is an opportunity to vote for candidates or issues.* See 20.12.

it: Avoid *it* without a specific reference except in idiomatic expressions such as *It is raining*. If possible, avoid using *it* as an expletive. See *Expletive* in chapter 21. Wordy: *It is a fact that Joan gave $500 to charity last week*. Improved: *Joan gave $500 to charity last week*.

its / it's: *Its* is a possessive personal pronoun. *My dog eats its fleas. It's* is a contraction for *it is. It's hot outside.*

-ize: Avoid inventing words that end in *-ize*, such as *tacoize* or *nerdize*. Do not add this suffix to a noun or an adjective to invent a new word. Beware of nominalized words, such as *prioritize* or *prioritization*. Use English words such as *rank* or *ranking*. See 21.18.

kind / sort: *Kind* and *sort* are singular nouns. Do not use plural adjectives to modify them. *These kind* is an error: make it *this kind*.

kind of / sort of: Avoid using these as synonyms for *rather, almost,* or *somewhat.* Revise *John is kind of stupid* to *John is rather stupid* or *John is stupid*.

kind of a: When this appears in a sentence, decide whether the entire phrase is wordy. Wordy: *That student is kind of a cheater.* Revised: *That student is a cheater* or *That student cheats*.

know / no: *No* is a negative adverb or adjective meaning "none" or "not." *Know* is a verb meaning "to understand."

latter / later: *Latter* means "the last thing mentioned previously." *Latter* is often a part of the expression *the former . . . the latter. Later* is the comparative form of *late.* It means "after some time."

lay / laid / laid: This verb means "to place" or "to put." *I lay the book down on the bench. You laid the steak on the grill. We had laid the cloth over the picnic table.*

lead / lead / led: *Lead* rhymes with *dead* and is a noun meaning "a heavy metal." *Lead* rhymes with *deed* and is a verb meaning "to guide" or "to direct." *Led* rhymes with *bed* and is the past tense of the verb *lead.*

learn / teach: *Learn* means "to acquire knowledge." *Teach* means "to instruct." Example: *I hate to learn what Dr. Gun teaches.*

leave / let: The words have great differences. *Leave* means "depart" or "abandon." *Let* means "allow" or "permit." Wrong: *The guard would not leave us laugh.* Correct: *The guard would not let us laugh.*

less: See *fewer.*

lessen / lesson: *Lessen* is a verb meaning "to lighten" or "to reduce." *Lesson* is a noun and means "something to be studied in a book or a class."

let's us: Redundant. Remove the *'s. Let's* is the contraction for *let us.*

liable: See *apt to.*

libel / liable: *Libel* is a noun and means "the crime of publishing damaging misrepresentation." *Liable* is an adjective and means "legally responsible" or "inclined, disposed."

lie / lay / lain: Do not confuse with *lay / laid / laid. Lie* means "to rest" or "to recline." Example: *I need to lie down. You lay down last night on the sofa. He has lain on that bed for three hours.* See 20.4e.

lie / lied / lied: This verb means "to tell a falsehood."

lightening / lightning: *Lightening* with an *e* means "becoming lighter." *Lightning* without the *e* means "electricity created during a storm."

like / as / as if: Formal writing preserves the distinctions between *like* and *as.* Some writers and readers display informal attitudes toward the use of *like* and *as.* Other writers and readers, however, have a firm formal attitude toward these two words and prefer them to be used in one of the following ways. Formal: *Jane acts as if* (not *like*) *the end of the world were near. My new word processor performs as* (not *like*) *the salesman promised. Mavis sings like* (preposition) *an angel.* Careful writers know that misuse of *like* and *as* can distort intended meaning. The safest rule is always to consider *like* as a preposition.

line: An overused, generally imprecise word. Use in its original meaning of *thread, string, cord, rope.* Avoid using the word to mean *area* or *field.* It is also a wordy sentence filler. Wordy: *Seth is interested in something in the line of a part-time job.* Revised: *Seth is interested in a part-time job.*

lose / loose / loose: The verb *lose* rhymes with *dues* and means "to suffer defeat," "to misplace," "to experience destruction," and so forth. *Loose* as a verb rhymes with *goose* and means "to release" or "to untie." *Loose* as an adjective rhymes with *goose* and means "not tight" or "not securely fastened."

mad / angry: The words are often carelessly used as synonyms, but they signify different meanings and different intensities of meaning. *Mad* has a double meaning in that it refers to (1) a state of rage or (2) a state of mental illness. Thus *mad* may indicate (1) "beside oneself with rage" or (2) "disconnected from reality." *Angry* indicates a negative emotional reaction, but it does not signify the intensity of the reaction. Some adjectives with gradations of precise meaning are *irate, raging, furious, indignant,* and *wrathful.*

man: Use this word in a specific sense. Some readers have strong negative responses when the word is used as a synonym for "humanity, the human race, or human beings."

marshal / martial / marital: *Marshal* as a noun means "an officer of the law." As a verb, *marshal* means "to arrange clearly." *Martial* comes from the Latin *Mars,* the god of war. It means "warlike" or "brave." *Marital* means "concerning marriage."

may be / maybe: *May be* is two words: the verb *be* and the helping verb *may. Scott may be lying. Maybe* is a one-word adverb meaning "perhaps." *Maybe Scott is lying.*

me and . . . : Nonstandard usage when appearing in a sentence such as the following: *Me and Chad plan to visit Paris in the spring.* Revised: *Chad and I plan to visit Paris in the spring.*

medium / media: *Medium* is singular. *Media* is plural: *The news media include television, radio, and newspapers.*

might of: Nonstandard spelling for *might have.*

mighty: *Mighty* is an adjective meaning "powerful or strong." It is not an adverb meaning "truly," "very," or "exceedingly."

Avoid such usage. Incorrect: *My roommate is a mighty kind friend.* Correct: *My roommate is a very kind friend.*

miner / minor: *Miner* means "a worker in a mine." As an adjective, *minor* means "unimportant" or "small." As a noun, *minor* means "a person under legal age."

moral / morale: As an adjective, *moral* means "good." As a noun, it means "point" or "meaning." *Morale* is a noun meaning "attitude or state of mind."

Ms. / Mrs. / Miss: Use these words carefully. Consider your audience. Observe the wishes of the person addressed. When in doubt, use *Ms.*

myself / himself / herself: Do not use these reflexive or intensive pronouns as replacements for *I, me, he, him, she,* or *her.* Wrong: *Myself and my good friends enjoyed the movie.* Correct: *I and my good friends enjoyed the movie.*

new / knew: *New* means "recently made." *Knew* is the past tense of *know.*

nice: Avoid if possible. Use other words with a specific sense, such as *precise, delicate,* or *careful.*

no ... or: This is the correct usage: *There was no gas or electricity in the apartment.* Do not use *no . . . nor.*

nocount / nohow / nowheres: Avoid. Nonstandard for *of no account, in no way* or *not at all,* and *nowhere.*

not .. no: A double negative construction. Nonstandard when used in the same sentence or clause. Wrong: *That bird didn't build no nest in my backyard.* Correct: *That bird did not build a nest in my backyard.*

number: When a subject, *a number* is usually plural, and *the number* is singular. See *amount of.*

number of: See *amount of.*

off of: Wordy. Remove the *of* when redundant.

OK / O.K. / okay: These are imprecise words of approval used most often in speech. In writing, make your meaning formal and precise. Use words such as *acceptable, passing, flawless, perfect, average.*

on the one hand / on the other hand: Use these connectives together. Use them rarely. Substitute other contrasting connectives: *but, however, yet,* or *in contrast.*

ought: Never use *oughta.* Do not use auxiliary verbs with *ought.* Wrong: *Mike had ought to learn to write.* Correct: *Mike ought to learn to write.*

parameter / perimeter: *Parameter* means "a constant," or "a fixed element." *Perimeter* means "the distance around or about something."

passed / past: *Passed* is the past tense of *pass*. Example: *He passed the course. Past* is an adjective meaning "previous" or "earlier." As a preposition, *past* means "beyond" or "after." As a noun, *past* means "time gone by."

patient / patients / patience: *Patient* as an adjective means "careful" or "noncomplaining." *Patient* as a noun means "a person being treated for a medical or dental problem." *Patients* is the plural of the noun *patient*. *Patience* is a noun meaning "the condition of being patient."

peace / piece: *Peace* means "the absence of war." *Piece* means "a part."

pedal / peddle: As a verb, *pedal* means "to use a pedal." As a noun, it means "a foot-operated part of a machine." *Peddle* is a verb and means "to carry things from place to place for sale."

people / persons: *People* is preferable to *persons* in formal contexts: *The people in this community* (not *the persons*) *are proud of its history.*

per: *Per* is commonly used to mean *a* or *every* in a sentence such as the following: *The interest on this mortgage has been lowered to 8.5% per year.* When used as a preposition, *per* should be revised to *according to, by, in,* or *through.* Problematic: *Per your letter of last week, you refer to the theft of a shipment of 10,000 dirt bikes.* Revised: *In your memo of last week, you refer to the theft of a shipment of 10,000 dirt bikes.*

percent / per cent / % / percentage: Correct: *63 percent, 63 per cent,* or *63%.* Wrong: *A large percent of the students own computers.* Correct: *A large percentage of the students own computers.*

persecute / prosecute: *Persecute* means "to bother—often cruelly or brutally." *Prosecute* means "to charge with a crime."

personal / personnel: The adjective *personal* means "private" or "intimate." The noun *personnel* is plural and means "employees." It takes a plural verb: *The personnel are happy.*

perspective / prospective / perceptive: *Perspective* is a noun meaning "a view." *Prospective* is an adjective meaning "likely," "potential," or "expected." *Perceptive* is an adjective and means "intelligent" or "observant."

phenomenon / phenomena: *Phenomenon* is singular. *Phenomena* is plural. A *phenomenon* is something seen or visible.

plain / plane: As an adjective, *plain* means "ordinary" or "undecorated." As a noun, *plain* means "a level field." As a verb, *plane* means "to make smooth or level." As a noun, *plane* means "a surface" or "an aircraft."

plenty: Avoid overuse of this word as a general magnifier. Find a more precise term, or omit. Some substitutes are *abundantly, exceedingly, overwhelmingly, widely, loudly.*

plus: Avoid in formal prose. Substitute *and, in addition,* or *also.*

poor / pour / pore: *Poor* means "destitute" or "lacking." *Pour* is a verb meaning "to come out in volume" or "to rain heavily." As a noun, *pore* means "a tiny opening in the skin." As a verb, *pore* means "to read or study intently."

precede / proceed: *Precede* means "to go before." *Proceed* means "to carry on or to continue."

prescribe / proscribe / subscribe: *Prescribe* means "to indicate a medical remedy." *Proscribe* means "to banish, outlaw, or forbid." *Subscribe* means "to place an order for something over a period of time."

presence / presents: *Presence* means "physical being in a certain place." *Presents* is the plural form of *present*, meaning "a gift."

previous to / prior to: Avoid these inflated expressions in favor of the clearer *before.*

principle / principal: *Principle* means "a rule" or "a guideline." As a noun, *principal* means "a primary administrator at a grade or high school." As an adjective, *principal* means "major" or "most important."

prophecy / prophesy: The noun *prophecy* rhymes with *see* and means "a prediction." The verb *prophesy* rhymes with *sigh* and means "to make a prediction."

purpose / propose: The noun *purpose* means "aim" or "goal." The verb *propose* means "to present" or "to suggest."

quick / quickly: *Quick* is generally an adjective: There goes the *quick* red fox. *Quickly* is always an adverb: The red fox ran *quickly* across the open field.

quiet / quit / quite: *Quiet* rhymes with *buy it*. As an adjective and a noun, *quiet* means "silent" and "silence." *Quit* rhymes with *bit* and means "to stop." *Quite* rhymes with *bite* and means "very."

raise / rise: *Raise* means "to lift." *Rise* means "to move upward" or "to stand." See 20.4e.

rap: *Rap* means "to hit or to knock." As a slang word, it has many meanings including "talk," "blame," or "punishment."

real: The word *real* is generally weaker than any of its synonyms: *genuine, fixed, actual, fundamental, essential, complete, utter.* Avoid the word when possible. Always avoid using the word when you mean *very* or *extremely.* Find precise substitutes.

really: Avoid if possible. A wordy and generally meaningless sentence filler.

rear / raise: The verb *rear* refers to children. The verb *raise* refers to crops and livestock.

reason because / reason why: Avoid. Revise. Use the phrase, "the reason that. . . ." See 20.12.

reckon: Unless used in an appropriate context, avoid in formal writing. Substitute *think, guess, imagine*, or *suppose.*

regarding / in regard to / with regard to / as regards: All are acceptable—even if wordy. All mean "concerning" or "about." Do not use "in regards to."

rep: Avoid in formal writing. It is an abbreviated slang term for "reputation," "representative," and "repertory."

respectfully / respectively: *Respectfully* means "with respect." *Respectively* means "separately" or "in the order just given."

right / rite / write / wright: *Right* as a noun means "a claim" and as an adjective means "correct." *Rite* is a noun and means "a ritual." *Write* is a verb and means "to express in writing." A wright is a worker as in the compound word *shipwright.*

ring / wring: *Ring* as a noun means "a circle." *Ring* as a verb means "to make a clear sound." *Wring* as a verb means "to twist with force."

rise / raise: See *raise / rise.*

rise / rose / risen: *Rise* is an intransitive verb meaning "to move upward." It does not take an object. Do not confuse with "raise." *Smoke rises. Kirk raised the window.*

says / said: *Says* is present. *Said* is past. In narration or exposition, do not confuse tenses. Confusing: *Alberto ran into the hotel and says, "The great bullfighter killed seven bulls."* Clear:

Alberto ran into the hotel and said, "The great bullfighter killed seven bulls." See 20.4c.

sense / since: *Sense* means "intelligence" or "any of the five senses." *Since* as an adverb means "from then till now." *Since* as a conjunction means "because" or "from a past time."

set / sat: *Set* is the present and past tense of a verb that means "to place or put." *Sat* is the past tense of *sit* and means "occupied a seat." Correct: *Joe sat down.* Incorrect: *Joe sat the dog in the chair.* Correct: *Joe set the dog in the chair.* See 20.4e.

set / sit: *Set* means "to put or to place." *Sit* means "to occupy a seat" See 20.4e.

shall / will: In highly formal English, *shall* indicates the future for first person: *I shall die, but we shall meet in the sky. Will* is used in all other persons. Most American writers avoid using *shall* to express the future. Most writers and readers in America accept *will* for the future tense in all persons.

shined / shone: Make a distinction between the words. *Shined* means "polished." *Shone* means "glowed." *Bill shined my shoes while the sun shone on the water.*

shone / shown: See *shine* immediately above. *Shone* is the past tense of *shine. Shown* is one form of the past participle of *show.*

sit / sat / sat: *Sit* means "to be seated." Do not confuse *sit* with *set,* meaning "to place or put." Example: *Randy sat down on the bench. Randy set his bat on the ground.*

so: Avoid when used to mean "very," "truly," or vague intensives. Weak: *James was so happy.* Improved: *James was wildly happy.* Correct: *James was so happy that he screamed.*

sometime / sometimes / some time: *Sometime* means "at some point in the future." *Sometimes* means "occasionally." *Some time* means "a set period of time."

some / somewhat: Do not use these words interchangeably. *Some* is an adjective: *Kit ate some stale cookies. Somewhat* is an adverb meaning "slightly": *The cookies were somewhat stale.*

somewheres: Avoid. A misspelling and mispronunciation for *somewhere.*

sort of a: Wordy. Remove in revision. Wordy: *Jake is sort of a bum.* Improved: *Jake is a bum.*

stationary / stationery: *Stationary* means "unmoving." *Stationery* means "sheets of paper for writing."

statue / stature / statute: *Statue* means "sculpted art work." *Stature* means "height" or "importance." *Statute* means "a law."

strait / straight: As an adjective, *straight* means "going in a line." *Strait* as a noun means "a narrow passageway joining two large bodies of water."

suit / suite: *Suit* always rhymes with *shoot*. *Suit* means "clothing." *Suite* often rhymes with *sweet*. *Suite* means "a set of connected rooms" or "a set."

supposed to / used to: The words, *supposed* and *used*, are sometimes misspelled when used with *to*. Make sure you put a *d* at the end of each.

sure: Do not use as an adverb. Use a correct and more precise term. Wrong: *The rain was sure cold.* Correct: *The rain was surprisingly cold.*

taut / taught / taunt: *Taut* is an adjective meaning "tight." *Taught* is the past tense of the verb *teach*. *Taunt* is a verb meaning "to provoke" or "to tease."

teach: See *learn*.

than / then: *Than* is a connective used to show comparison: *Jess is quicker than Joe. Then* is an adverb meaning "in time past": *Then I was a drunkard.* Pronounce the *a* in *than* and the *e* in *then*.

that / which: *Which* is never used to refer to a specific human. Always use *that* or *who*. Some writers prefer to use *which* with commas for any nonrestrictive clause and to use *that* (never with commas!) for any restrictive clause. Nonrestrictive clause: *These shoes, which I bought at a discount store, disintegrated after I had walked two miles.* Restrictive clause: *I returned the shoes that I had bought at a discount store.* See 22.2f.

themself / theirself / theirselves: Nonstandard usage for *themselves*.

there / their / they're: *There* means "in that place": *There is my car. Their* is a plural possessive pronoun: *The kids broke their toys. They're* is a contraction for "they are." *The Smiths don't know which day they're leaving.*

this here / that there / these here / those there / them there: Wordy, nonstandard expressions. Drop the *here's* and *there's*. Rewrite as *this, that, these, those, them.*

threw / through: The verb *threw* is the past tense of *throw*. *Through* is generally used as a preposition: *through the door.*

through / thorough: *Through* as a preposition means "passing in and out." As an adjective, *through* means "direct" or "finished." *Thorough* is an adjective meaning "complete."

thusly: Prefer the simpler *thus.*

till / until / 'til: *'Til* is archaic. *Till* and *until* both function as prepositions and conjunctions and are completely interchangeable. The noun *till* means "a container for valuables. The verb *till* means "to plow."

to: Redundant when used in a sentence such as the following: *Where did Jed go to?* Revision: *Where did Jed go?*

to—adverb—infinitive: This is one form of a split infinitive. The English language has always had acceptable examples of the split infinitive. The question does not involve grammar or correctness. A split infinitive can be both grammatical and correct. Many split infinitives dilute the force of the verb and may emphasize the adverb. With one-word adverbials, this may present no problems. With longer and bulkier adverbials, the verb is de-emphasized. See 20.8b.

to / too / two: *To* is a preposition or an infinitive signal: *To the pure, all things are pure. Hamlet wanted to kiss Ophelia. Too* as an adverb often means "also": *That new book is stupid too. Two* is a number: *Give me two hot dogs with mustard, please.*

toward / towards: *Toward* is commonly used in the United States. *Towards* is common in Great Britain.

track / tract: As a verb *track* means "to hunt." As a noun, *track* means "a path" or "a road." *Tract* means "a small booklet or pamphlet."

try and / try to: Avoid *try and.* Use *try to* to emphasize the verb: *Bill will try to climb the mountain.*

-type: Avoid this suffix if at all possible. Tortured: *He wanted a good singing-type performer.* Improved: *He wanted a good singer.*

unique / perfect / flawless: Grammarians label such adjectives absolute terms. According to logic, they cannot be compared. Many writers avoid the use of *more* or *most* with such words. Avoid using *quite, rather, somewhat, very* with "absolute" words. If you need to modify an absolute adjective, use a term such as *almost* or *nearly.*

usage / use: *Usage* means "the way a word or phrase is customarily written or spoken." *Use* as a verb means "to make use of."

use / utilize: Avoid *utilize*. Use the simpler *use*.

use to: Nonstandard usage in a sentence such as the following: *The snack bar use to sell huge bags of popcorn for a quarter.* [The *t* sound after the word *use* makes the ear hear the word as if it were spelled *used.* Revised: *The snack bar used to sell huge bags of popcorn for a quarter.*

used to could: Avoid. A quaint, nonstandard, often humorous version of *once could* or *used to be able to.*

vain / vane / vein: All three words rhyme with *rain*. The adjective *vain* means "conceited." The noun *vane* means "a device to point into the wind." The noun *vein* means "a blood vessel."

varies / various: *Varies* is a form of the verb *to vary*: *The weather varies from day to day. Various* is an adjective meaning "different or numerous in kinds or sorts."

vice / vise: *Vice* means "crime" or "a bad habit." *Vise* means "a tool for holding or clamping objects."

wait on: A regional idiom meaning "to wait for." However, in most parts of the country the words mean *attend, take care of,* or *serve.*

ways: Ineffective substitute for *way*. Do not use as a singular word. It is plural. Example: *You have three ways to drive to Hebron, but it is a long way from here.*

weak / week: The adjective *weak* means "lacking in strength." *Week* means "seven days."

wear / where: The word *wear* is commonly used as a verb: *I like to wear old clothes.* The word *where* is commonly used as an adverb to ask questions: *Where are my old shoes?*

were / we're: *Were* is the plural past tense form of *be: There were nine fish in the bottom of the boat. We're* is a contraction for the words *we* and *are.*

weather / whether: *Weather* is a noun meaning "changes in climate." *Whether* is a connective indicating condition or alternatives.

where: Do not use as a synonym for *that*. Wrong: *I read where the price of oil is going to rise again.* Revised: *I read that the price of oil is going to rise again.* See 20.12.

which / who / that: Use *who* or *that* to refer to humans. Do not use *which. Which* never refers to human beings. *The car which Mack bought was green. Jezebel, who just broke her leg,* *bought a new car. The woman that bought the ugly yellow car has a broken leg.*

who / whom: Formal writing observes the distinction. *Who* is for subjects. *Whom* is for objects. Example: *I want to know who gave me this present.* [*Who* is the subject of the verb *gave*.] *I want to know to whom you gave my orange cookie.* [*Whom* is the object of the preposition *to*.] To discover whether *who* or *whom* is formally correct, substitute a third-person singular masculine or feminine pronoun. If it is *he* or *she*, use *who.* If it is *him* or *her*, use *whom.*

who's / whose: *Who's* is the contraction for *who is*: *Who's going to eat all this food? Whose* is the possessive form of *who*: *Whose food is this? Jim's or Mike's?*

-wise: Avoid inventing words ending in *-wise*, such as *car-wise*, which would mean "relating to cars" or "knowledgeable about cars." Use words ending in *-wise* precisely as they are defined in the dictionary.

would of: Nonstandard for *would have* or *would've.*

you and I: Use *I* only as a subject. Avoid using *I* as an object. Wrong: *Just between you and I, this car is a piece of junk.* Correct: *Just between you and me, this car is a piece of junk.*

You was: An agreement error for *you were.*

your / you're: *Your* is a possessive pronoun: *Watch your step. You're* is a contraction of *you are.*

APPENDIX A

Writing With Computers

Appendix A
Writing With
Computers

A

✍ Student Comments on Writing

Last summer I worked in an office where
everything from ordering supplies to writing letters
was done on a computer. If I had not learned word
processing in my composition course, I would not
have gotten the job.

P. Gallagher

I do not know if using a computer makes me
smarter, but I do know that using a computer
makes writing a paper less of a chore. I used to
hate all the retyping, but now I can have a new
printed copy in four minutes!

Jamie Erwin

Helpful Terms to Learn

COMMAND
A command is an instruction to the computer. A command is the code letters
typed into the computer keyboard. Some
common commands are ED or D to open
a document file and begin writing or PR
or P to print a document file. Commands
are listed on the screen of the Help
Menu.

CURSOR	The cursor is the blinking mark on the display screen. The cursor marks the spot where words can be typed onto the screen. The cursor can be moved up and down and sideways when you move a "mouse" or press certain keys.
DIRECTORY	A directory is a list of document files on a disk.
DISK	Sometimes called a "floppy disk," disks store software programs, files for further revision, or backup copies of files. A disk must be inserted into the computer's disk drive to enable the writer to begin working.
DOCUMENT FILE	A document file is a paper, story, essay, letter, or research paper entered into the computer. When naming documents, use names that are easy to remember, such as "journal," "Paper1," or "Notes."
FORMATTING A DISK	The preparation of a disk for use in word processing is called formatting a disk. All disks must be formatted before they are used. Formatting a disk erases all files and operating information from it. Only new disks or disks containing unnecessary files should be formatted.
FORMATTING A DOCUMENT	These are the instructions after a document is ready to print regarding margins, indenting, spacing, pagination, type size, italics, and so forth.

HELP MENU — A help menu is a set of directions (commands) that appear on the computer screen. The directions explain the operation of the word processing program.

HARD COPY — A printed copy of a document is referred to as a hard copy. It is wise to print a hard copy of your latest draft. Many writers like to edit and revise from a double-spaced hard copy.

HARD DISK — Some computers have a hard disk located inside the computer. The hard disk contains the operating system, software programs such as word processors, and files that have been written.

KEYBOARD — The keyboard is the part of the computer with typewriter-style keys. Commands and data are entered through the keyboard.

MONITOR — The monitor is the display screen. Most monitors can display up to twenty-one lines of text.

SAVE — The SAVE command stores new or revised documents in the computer memory.

SEARCH OR FIND — The SEARCH and FIND commands can be used to locate overused words (for example, *is, are, was, were*); spelling errors (*its, it's; too, to*); weak adjectives or adverbs (*nice, very, awesome*); and grammar errors (*their, there*).

Some Advantages of Writing with Computers

1. A writer can easily correct, rearrange, or reorganize documents without retyping an entire paragraph or page.

2. Revision is easier and more efficient. A writer can discover new ways to revise a paper.

3. Papers produced on a word processor are generally easier to read than handwritten papers.

4. Ideas for topics and content material can be easily stored in the word processing file and used at a later time.

5. Word processing features such as spelling check, punctuation check, grammar check, and style check help writers avoid common errors.

General Suggestions

1. Do not try to learn everything about word processing at once. A reasonable scenario would be the following:

> a. Learn to start up the program, enter some information, and save it as a file.
> b. Learn to print a hard copy of the file.
> c. Learn to insert new or revised material and delete material in the file.
> d. Learn how to move words, sentences, and paragraphs from one place to another in your papers.
> e. Begin learning how to use the other functions on the help menu.

2. Ask a friend who is familiar with word processing to show you the basic steps such as formatting a disk, and starting (booting up) the word processing program.

3. Locate the computer lab at your school. Ask the lab instructor if you will need to purchase a disk, and if so, the correct size and type (5 1/4″ or 3 1/2″, formatted or unformatted, double- or single-sided).

4. When you use the word processor, save your document approximately every ten minutes. Frequent saving helps prevent loss of a document due to a power surge or computer failure.

5. Always make a backup copy of your document. Documents can be lost, erased, or damaged as a result of your error or a computer malfunction.

6. Print a hard copy and make a backup copy of your document each time you revise it. If you lose your disk or it is damaged, you will still have a record of your work.

Computer Tutorial

1. Become familiar with the basics of operation by reading the directions for word processing. Make reference notes on how to turn on the computer, insert disks in the disk drive, boot up the word processor, and create a document. List the steps on a note card for future reference.

2. Observe a friend from the moment that person sits down in front of a computer to do some word processing until a few minutes after he or she has begun entering material onto the screen. Take notes. List the steps the person takes.

3. Start the word processing program. Open a file and write for at least ten minutes on anything at all about a person in your family whom you consider notable or heroic. Do not use the return key when you come to the end of a line. Name the file "Hero." Save and close the file.

(Note: This also may be the first assignment your instructor will give for the writing task in chapter 1.)

4.   Print a hard copy of the "Hero" file.

5.   Open the "Hero" file and move the cursor to the end of the file. Using photographs, your memories, or other information, create a list of concrete and specific words, phrases, and sentences that supply detailed information about the person in that file. Write for at least ten minutes. Save and close the file.

6.   Print a double-spaced copy of the "Hero" file. Insert by hand any additional sensory details you can think of. After you have finished, open the "Hero" file and insert this new material in the appropriate places.

7.   Use the computer to play around with ideas. Create a file called "Freedom" and use it to write anything you want to. Freewrite on any topic without worrying about grammar and punctuation rules, meaning, correctness, or a reader. Write for therapy: reduce anger, sadness, worry, turmoil, or confusion by expressing these emotions and their causes in the "Freedom" file.

8.   Use the computer to develop a keener sense of language and writing as a form of mental play. Create a file called "Private" and write the most outrageous or wonderful sentences you can imagine. If you are brave enough, save them; if you are not, delete them.

9.   Open a file called "Other" and write for twenty minutes on the person you focused on in the "Hero" file. Try to write from the perspective of another person such as a family member or close friend. Add information.

10.   Study the word processing manual or the help menu and learn how to merge the "Other" and "Hero" files you have created.

Revision Tutorial on a Computer

    1.   Add material to clarify or strengthen the organization of your document. Refer to the examples of revision by addition in 4.3 and 19.1.

        a. Add a thesis statement that clearly states the main point of the paper. (Refer to 1.4.)

        b. Add a topic sentence to a paragraph, if it will help develop and organize the paper. (Refer to 2.3.)

        c. Illustrate the main point of your paper by adding at least one good example. (Refer to 3.2.)

        d. Add specific details, figures of speech, and concrete language, if they will help a reader see the main point clearly. (Refer to 3.1, 21.10, and 21.12.)

    2.   Delete unnecessary material. Study the examples of deletion in 4.4, 19.2, and 21.21. Delete sentences or paragraphs that digress from the main point of the paper as well as any unnecessary words and phrases.

    3.   Arrange material to present your main points more effectively.

        a. Move related sentences closer together. (Refer to 2.5 through 2.7.)

        b. Rearrange paragraphs after studying an outline of your paper. Create a clear pattern of organization. (Refer to 1.7, 6.1, and 6.2.)

    4.   Substitute effective language for ineffective language. Study the examples of substitution in sections 4.5 and 19.4.

        a. Substitute effective verbs for ineffective *to be* verbs. (Refer to 21.24.) Substitute active voice for ineffective passive voice. (Refer to 21.5.)

b. Substitute specific, concrete language for vague, general language. (Refer to 21.12.)

INDEX

Symbols Used in Marking and Revising

ED!	excellent detail	**formal**	Use formal English. 21.10
EW!	effective word choice	**frag**	sentence fragment 20.1
FI!	fine sense of humor	**fus**	fused sentence 20.2
GI!	good idea	**id**	error in idiom 21.13
GIN!	good introduction	**inc**	incomplete construction 20.11c
GO!	good organization		
GT!	good tone	**intro**	weak introduction 5.1–5.3
LS!	lively style	**ital**	Underline. Italicize. 23.2
SW!	strong writing	**jarg**	jargon 20.13
TF!	thoughtful, thought provoking	**lc**	lower case letter needed
		limit	Limit your discussion to the main point. 1.4
ab	Spell out abbreviation. 23.3		
ad	adverb/adjective error 20.6	**log**	error in logic 6.3
agr	error in subject-verb agreement 20.3	**MI?**	What is the main point of the paper? 1.1, 1.4, 5.2
av	Avoid such language.	**mm**	misplaced modifier 20.8b
awk	awkward	**ms**	manuscript form 1.11
back	Add more background information. 1.6	**nnn**	noun-noun-noun construction 21.19
cap	capital letter needed 23.1	**num**	numbers 23.4
case	error in pronoun case 20.5c	**o**	omission 20.11
cli	cliché 21.6	**org**	problems in organization 1.7, 2.5
coh	lack of coherence 1.7, 2.7		
conc	weak conclusion 5.4–5.6	**P**	error in punctuation 22
confused	meaning unclear	**par**	error in parallel structures 20.7
conj	error in use of conjunction 18.7	**pass**	excessive use of passive voice 21.5
coor	confused or excessive coordination 20.7, 20.9c	**pl**	plural needed
		pm	punctuation missing 22
cs	comma splice 20.2	**pred**	error in predication 20.12
dang	dangling modifier 20.8a	**quo**	error in quotation or quotation form 22.7
def	definition needed 9.1, 21.2		
det	specific details needed 21.4, 21.12, 3.1	**ref**	problem with pronoun reference 20.5b
dic	mixed diction 21.15	**rep**	unnecessary repetition, redundancy 21.21
dig	digression 2.3–2.6		
divide	Divide into separate paragraphs. 2.6	**shift**	confusing shift 4.6
		sing	singular needed
doc	documentation needed 17	**sp**	spelling error 21.3
emph	What do you want to emphasize? 20.10, 21.5	**sub**	Use some subordination. 20.9d–e
eu	euphemism 21.8	**subex**	excessive subordination 20.9d
ex	example or support needed 2.4, 3.2		
		tense	error in verb tense 20.4a–c
find	Find better material. 1.6, 6.3a	**timp**	Improve thesis or topic sentence. 1.4, 2.3, 5.2
focus	Focus on your main point more. 1.4, 2.3		